"If you want to understand how a tru
our strategy and tactics for the coming
insurgencies, and terrorism, read this   ...arted
book for a host of ideas and wisdom."

—THOMAS R. PICKERING, former under secretary of state for
political affairs and ambassador to Russia, India, the
United Nations, Israel, El Salvador, Nigeria, and Jordan

"Mines speaks from almost unparalleled experience. . . . The result is a
book that nation-building aficionado and nation-building doubter will
find equally rewarding, in the lessons it provides, the questions it leaves
unanswered, the real-life stories he tells so well."

—ROBERT MALLEY, president and CEO of International Crisis Group

"For on-the-ground experience in activist diplomacy in what he terms
the post-Westphalian world, few can outdo foreign service officer Keith
Mines. In accounts ranging from El Salvador, Colombia, and Haiti
during the late Cold War to Iraq, Afghanistan, Somalia, and Darfur in
the post-9/11 era, Mines presents a vivid narrative of personal involvement in the successes and failures of our helping fragile states defeat
insurgencies and stabilize. . . . This is a riveting account by an exceptional, expeditionary American—an outstanding read understandable
both to the public and to those who share similar experiences."

—RUFUS PHILLIPS, author of *Why Vietnam Matters:
An Eyewitness Account of Lessons Not Learned*

"Keith Mines's major premise is that many of America's security challenges abroad will not be manageable unless we address root causes—
weak governance and institutions, political-criminal collaboration,
organized violence and corruption, and abysmal educational efforts.
Having viewed these problems as a soldier, foreign service officer, and
expeditionary diplomat, Mines candidly assesses past successes and failures to distill how the United States can tackle similar problems we
will face well into the future. Scholars and practitioners alike will find
this book invaluable and very readable."

—ROY GODSON, professor emeritus of government,
Georgetown University

WHY NATION-BUILDING MATTERS

ADST-DACOR Diplomats and Diplomacy Series

SERIES EDITOR

Margery Boichel Thompson

Since 1776, extraordinary men and women have represented the United States abroad under widely varying circumstances. What they did and how and why they did it remain little known to their compatriots. In 1995, the Association for Diplomatic Studies and Training (ADST) and DACOR, an organization of foreign affairs professionals, created the Diplomats and Diplomacy book series to increase public knowledge and appreciation of the professionalism of American diplomats and their involvement in world history. In *Why Nation-Building Matters*, Keith Mines explores the need to integrate elements of our soft power—diplomacy, economic development, and political consolidation in failed and fragile states—with our war-fighting hard power into a full package that can be deployed effectively against threats in an increasingly fragmented world.

WHY NATION-BUILDING MATTERS

Political Consolidation, Building Security Forces, and Economic Development in Failed and Fragile States

KEITH W. MINES

Potomac Books

An ADST-DACOR Diplomats and Diplomacy Book

AN IMPRINT OF THE UNIVERSITY OF NEBRASKA PRESS

Library of Congress Cataloging-in-Publication Data
Names: Mines, Keith W., author.
Title: Why nation-building matters: political consolidation,
building security forces, and economic development in failed
and fragile states / Keith W. Mines.
Description: Lincoln: Potomac Books, an imprint of University
of Nebraska Press, 2020. | Series: Diplomats and diplomacy
series | Includes bibliographical references and index.
Identifiers: LCCN 2019054497
ISBN 9781640122826 (paperback)
ISBN 9781640123373 (epub)
ISBN 9781640123380 (mobi)
ISBN 9781640123397 (pdf)
Subjects: LCSH: Nation building—Case studies. | Humanitarian
intervention—Case studies. | Economic development
projects—Case studies. | Failed states—Case studies. | Postwar
reconstruction—Government policy—United States—Case
studies.
Classification: LCC JZ6300 .M56 2020 | DDC 327.1—dc23
LC record available at https://lccn.loc.gov/2019054497

Set in Sabon Next LT by Laura Buis.

For my parents, Herman and Maxine, whose decency
and humanity guided me in tough places.

For Cecile, who inspired my better ideas
and redirected the bad ones.

For Jonathan, Joshua, Rachel, and Daniel, who
never let me take myself too seriously.

And for Dinesh, whose sacrifice helped secure
the freedom of a grateful people.

CONTENTS

ILLUSTRATIONS

Following page 176

PREFACE

It is a long way from the Westphalian town halls of 1648 to the San Salvador Zoo of 1995. But it is a journey worth making.

The bloodletting of the Thirty Years' War from 1618 to 1648 was on a scale that might seem familiar to us today after the Somme, Auschwitz, and Rwanda. But at the time it was unlike anything Europe had experienced, including under the sword of the Huns and Mongols. As many as eight million Germans died in the long struggle, 40 percent of the population, compared to 12 percent in the Second World War.

An interim agreement to bring the conflict to a conclusion, the Treaty of Lübeck, was signed in 1629. Lübeck is a few kilometers from Grinau, the region my German ancestors inhabited for centuries. The treaty removed Denmark from the conflict, but Sweden quickly took its place, and the war dragged on, bringing religious and political experiments and leaving behind marauding mercenaries and devastation. Our family history affirms that the people of Grinau, lying directly in the path from Scandinavia to Central Europe, suffered tremendously during the period.

The Peace of Westphalia that finally ended the conflict took over four years to negotiate. The signing ceremony on October 24, 1648, itself took three weeks to prepare and reflected the harsh divisions of the signatories to the end. My ancestors were not plugged in to the larger geopolitical issues at play and probably would not have been impressed if they were. But the structure of the world was changing, for them and everyone else.

The Peace of Westphalia was about more than just ending the immediate conflict. It was the first step in the reorganization of the world away from the identification of people with their prince and his statelet, or worse, with a mercenary leader and his marauding band, and toward their identification with a nation-state. Over time this identification, coupled with advances in warfare and economics, led to the consolidation of power, with a loose compact by governments to provide services and protection to citizens in return for their loyalty to the state. This nation-state system also required governments to impose a monopoly on the use of force among their respective citizens. Out of it gradually emerged a "Westphalian order," in which nation-states would respect each other's internal sovereignty and coexist, with a rough balance of power. Deterrence and alliances emerged as key principles of statecraft and led to long periods of relative peace between 1648 and 1914.

It was a decidedly imperfect system, and when it broke down, as it did between 1914 and 1945, the results could be catastrophic. They were not, however, as catastrophic as what came before 1648. And built into the system were the means of recovery. But it was all notably dependent on the existence of viable and capable nation-states.

The height of the Westphalian order came during the Cold War, when the struggle for ideological supremacy and territory led the two superpowers to collect previously ungoverned or poorly governed territories and ensure they were friendly and well-administered. The end of the Cold War, however, led to a collapse of the system in many artificially constructed states such as Yugoslavia, Somalia, and Afghanistan, which broke apart or broke down. Declining interest in territory by the lavish superpowers was then followed by their own diversion from good governance. The Soviets lost their ability to fully govern their own territory for a decade, and the United States dabbled with fantasies of the liberation that would come from their country not being well governed at all, a fantasy that has since accelerated. It led the political theorist Francis Fukuyama to remark in 2004, "For well over a generation, the trend in world politics has been to weaken stateness."[1]

The Westphalian order was fraying at the seams. Governance in many parts of the world broke down, and there was no one to help get it back. Meanwhile the world saw the rise of "post-Westphalian" actors—criminal gangs who could threaten states and corporations that were richer than states—against a backdrop of weapons that could destroy cities from within and pandemics that could cross multiple borders in days. We were edging ever closer to a post-Westphalian era.

By 2003 the commentator and analyst Michael Ignatieff talked of a "band of failed states, running from Somalia on the east coast of Africa through Congo to Liberia on the west," and a second band on the "southern edge of the former Soviet empire."[2] It has accelerated since then; Ignatieff mentioned Libya as a "cohesive state with control throughout its territory" and did not mention Iraq, Syria, or Yemen at all.[3]

Which brings us circuitously to the San Salvador Zoo.

Of all the peoples I have lived among, the Salvadorans have the most pronounced sense of humor. They are full of riddles and brainteasers and amusing verbal images. On a Saturday afternoon in 1995 I accompanied ten of the young men I mentored in a local church group to the zoo. They had all been there before but post–civil war San Salvador had precious little public space that did not require armaments to enjoy, so they indulged my curiosity.

As we strolled along looking at the various animals a certain theme emerged. The animals all looked hungry, eager for hand-outs. One of our youth had a wicked sense of humor that around campfires evoked his long renditions of what "Jaaaaason," of *Nightmare on Elm Street* fame, was going to do to us that night. When we got to a pathetically skinny brown bear with a pitiful look on his face, the youth stared in disgust. He suddenly blurted out four simple words that I have never forgotten: *Este país no sirve* (This country [just] doesn't work). He walked away questioning whether a government that could not even feed the animals in the zoo would be able to manage the more complex human eco-system of El Salvador.

In fairness, his country was just coming out of a horrific civil war, and I thought he could have given the regime more credit. It had infrastructure to repair, kids to educate, security forces to train and equip, and diplomatic relations to expand. The animals in the zoo were legitimately not the highest priority. But as it turned out, most of those other things did not really get done either. The economy never took off, education improved only on the margins, and gangs replaced insurgents such that criminal violence led to higher casualties in some years than during the civil war. Twenty years later a 2017 survey showed that 40 percent of the country's citizens aspired to leave the country.[4]

The Failed State Circuit

This book recounts my experiences in shoring up the Westphalian order in eight failed or fragile states in various conditions of pre-conflict, conflict, and postconflict. I served in these countries as a missionary, soldier, diplomat, United Nations official, and occupation administrator, and worked on our policies from Washington. In all cases I could travel widely and meet with warlords and governors, peasants and factory workers, sheikhs and imams, human rights defenders and police chiefs, ministers and presidents, educators and midwives. I was face to face with thousands of Iraqis, Afghans, Salvadorans, Colombians, Somalis, Darfuris, and Haitians, in small meetings, conventions, lunches, dinners, and rant sessions.

I worked with some of the heroes of our contemporary foreign affairs landscape: Army Civil Affairs officers, diplomats, aid workers, UN officials, soldiers, and contractors. They were the ones who went to many places no one else would.

In my travels I found an imam who sought desperately to achieve a "world without terror" and paid for that desire with his life; a clever governor and his staff who believed there was an "Iraqi solution" to most problems; business communities finding their footing in the ramshackle transition from a kleptocratic command economy to a free market; innumerable citizens who sought a voice in their country's affairs; and young people, thousands of them, who are clever, energetic, and smart and want desperately to be connected to the wider world.

They were very different countries with wildly diverse problem sets. The one condition they had in common was that the

United States considered how they were governed to be important to the U.S. national interest and sent people and resources to try to improve it. Though it sounds bluntly arrogant when one puts it that way, communism, terrorism, militarism, genocide, and human-induced famine are undeniably part of a mash of conditions that create a more threatening world, or in some cases are simply offensive to American sensibilities.

In all cases that I observed the United States achieved its initial objective through purely military means. In Grenada it retrieved a country hijacked by Cuban-backed hardliners; in El Salvador it staved off a communist insurgency; in Somalia it stopped a famine; in Haiti it restored a democracy; in Afghanistan it expunged a terrorist-supporting regime; and in Iraq it overthrew a menacing dictator. Other interventions in this period took place in Panama, where the United States expelled a dictator, and in the Balkans, where it helped pacify a fractious corner of Europe. There was a nonmilitary intervention in Darfur, where through sanctions and international pressure the international community stopped a genocide, and the assistance mission in Colombia, where America helped a country recover ungoverned territory.

These initial objectives were no small matter and should be appreciated. In many cases the initial gains were consolidated into long-term stability and have evolved into thriving societies. But in many others they did not coalesce; in some cases early gains were swept away by larger threats than the one we went in to expunge. Ultimately, only leaving behind a functional state will secure the objectives America wages war to achieve. As Nadia Schadlow, author of one of the defining works on nation-building after war, puts it, "Success in war ultimately depends on the consolidation of political order, which requires control over territory and the hard work of building local government institutions. . . . Leaders have grappled with how to link effectively the destruction and violence that is war to the reconstitution of new forms of order."[5] And notably the consolidation of political order in fragile states will often preclude the need to go to war in the first place.

This book is a collection of the hard lessons I learned in thirty-five years of observing and participating in the consolidation of political order during and after war. The lessons also apply to most peacetime challenges of institution building. Much of what I learned runs counter to conventional wisdom. But rather than leaving me depressed, it has left me seized with how we can do better, to which this work is dedicated

INTRODUCTION

Boots on the Ground, Wingtips in the Palace

This is fundamentally and unabashedly a book about nation-building. I was told that I needed to rebrand it for the current political environment but see no realistic way to do so. There is simply no other phrase that captures the essence of what I am advocating. And I am finding the concept has increasing relevance to our own national project, not just that of the failed states abroad that we have sought to assist.

WHAT IS NATION-BUILDING? Nation-states consist of two distinct components, both political in nature. At a higher level, the "nation" is the result of a political compact that unites a people of a certain territory under a single identity. In a few cases, notably Canada, the United Kingdom, Switzerland, and Belgium, the entity is multinational in character. The "nation" is more emotional, a sense or feeling, "blood and belonging," as Michael Ignatieff puts it.[1] The "state," on the other hand, consists of the institutions that can manage the business of governing within that nation. It is more bureaucratic: Do I have running water, and security? Can I open a small business? Is there an electoral process that takes account of my aspirations? Put another way, J. Kael Weston suggests "there's a difference when a country, but not a nation, goes to war."[2] In some recent conflicts we mobilized the instruments of the state, but we did not successfully mobilize our nation.

When one side of the equation is weak, the nation-state can break. In 1991 Yugoslavia had good state institutions but no shared sense of nation, while the Somalis were a nation with no state. The near breakup of Iraq after 2003 led to strong state institutions in Kurdistan, but the Kurds are now struggling with whether to be an independent Kurdish nation or stay a part of the Iraqi nation.

In Afghanistan both the nation and the state were frayed. And El Salvador, through the negotiated end of the civil war, recovered a sense of nation, but the state institutions have yet to fully cohere.

A successful nation has both a sense of nationhood and the institutions of a state; the process of nation-building has to do with developing and then blending the two components into a functional whole.

WHY BOTHER? Assisting countries to be able to fully control what transpires on their territory and form a viable social compact among citizens, while minimizing the violent reaction to that control, is vitally important to the security of the United States and the well-being of the American people. Several recent examples make the case, but there are dozens more.

In 2001 a global terrorist network carved out a protected sanctuary from ungoverned space in Afghanistan, which the international community had abandoned after violently competing over it during the Cold War. In 2004 Thailand was required to kill forty million chickens to get ahead of a global pandemic that could have killed thousands of people, something only a functioning nation-state could do. And in 2014 a "global caliphate" that attracted tens of thousands of militants and inspired and directed attacks across the globe came from a continued failure to address political grievances by the Sunni minority in Iraq.

From pandemics and terrorism to unprecedented migration, the quality of the nation-state remains the core of international order. As Clare Lockhart, CEO and cofounder of the Institute for State Effectiveness, and the researcher Michael Miklaucic put it, "If the 20th century was consumed by the global struggle between incompatible ideologies—fascism, communism, and democratic capitalism—the 21st century will be consumed by the epic challenge of creating and sustaining viable, effective states.... A rule-based system of sovereign states ... is the best remedy against the destructive effects of illicit actors and networks."[3] It is difficult to see how the United States can stay ahead of key challenges absent a world of strong and capable states that can control what transpires on their territory and apply local solutions to global problems.

CAN OUTSIDERS DO NATION-BUILDING? Citizens must build their own nations. The international community can be helpful, even decisive, however, in both nation- and state-building, generally from a respectful distance. In 2002 the international community directly influenced the course of the Afghan nation by its support for the Bonn process and the resultant Loya Jirga, an event that brought the Afghan people together for the first time in decades in a forum that all Afghans understood and accepted. It bought the country a measure of stability and set the course, however imperfectly, for Afghanistan to continue the struggle to fully functional nationhood.[4] It would not have happened without Germany's logistics, UN facilitators, international peacekeepers providing security, and U.S. back-channel negotiators.

Follow-on assistance helped in the development of state institutions. As one example among hundreds I have been involved with, in 2013 I presided over the graduation in Jawzjhan province of twenty midwives who had been trained by the international community. These midwives were part of a growing public health system in Afghanistan, developed over the preceding fifteen years, which had led to some of the most dramatic gains in physical health of any people in history. Notably, the maternal mortality rate had been cut by 50 percent and the infant mortality rate by 60 percent.

The track record of the international community in all this is not as bad as many believe. Ambassador James F. Dobbins describes a memo circulated by a prominent official in the National Security Council in 2002 asserting that "peacekeeping was . . . a failed concept, one that had been tried and found wanting throughout the 1990s." The memo was simply wrong. "By 2002," Dobbins points out, "tens of millions of people in such places as Namibia, Cambodia, Mozambique, El Salvador, East Timor, Sierra Leone, Albania, Bosnia, Kosovo, and Macedonia were living at peace—and for the most part under freely elected governments—because UN, NATO, American, or European troops had come in, separated combatants, disarmed contending factions, rebuilt the country, held elections, installed new governments, and stayed around long enough to watch them take root. Such was the prevalent prejudice against nation building within the Bush administration, however, that this ludicrously misleading paper went unchallenged."[5]

Nation-building can work. It is not automatic, and outsiders operating clumsily can collapse states that otherwise would have been marginally functional or can create additional fissures that lead to new conflicts. And the branding of this highly contested concept obviously matters, but outsiders can play a positive role in the development of nation-states.

WHAT IS THE CONTEXT? We do have to be realistic, though, about the context and setting. We are dealing not with a small "cuts and bruises" clinic but with the emergency room. And it is usually the emergency room for patients who have been serially abused. The societies in question, especially those in the Middle East and North Africa, are undergoing multiple transitions, any one of which would be brutally difficult. From command economies to globalized free markets, from narrow dictatorships to inclusive democracies, from tribally organized entities to civil societies, from isolation to global connectivity, from secular regimes to newly discovered religiosity, all against a demographic picture that would make Malthus cringe.

None of these societies will have the luxury of managing these transitions in an orderly way; history and geography have thrown everything at them at once. But it should not be surprising when they break down and should not discourage us from taking stock of what it will take to bring them back to a healthy place. As a World Bank official who covers the Middle East and North Africa recently said, "Every country I deal with is in either pre-conflict, conflict, or post conflict." It is daunting. But it will not make it any easier to ignore these factors or wish them away. Nor will it do any good to just say, "They aren't like us."

Hard Lessons Learned, and Unlearned

The cases in this book elucidate many of these points. All were harder than they needed to be, but all were destined by circumstance to be hard. What follows is a quick preview of what the reader will encounter.

For fifty years *Colombia* experienced a highly complex and evolutionary economic and ideologically driven civil war, initiated by traditional violent political divisions but perpetuated by Cold War support from the communist bloc. It evolved into a battle between a flawed democracy and insurgents who grew rich from drug money and kidnapping. The United States, never disinterested, became seized with the challenge of a failing state in its hemisphere after 9/11 and surged training, equipment, and advisors for nearly a decade as the Colombian government recovered guerrilla-controlled territory and ultimately drove the insurgents to sue for peace. By staying in a supporting role to a Colombia that was well led and intent on winning, the U.S.-Colombian partnership yielded a successful end-state. It was a classic case where patience, a blend of soft and hard power, and national determination on both sides combined to get the country to a place of relative stability, ending one of the modern age's longest conflicts.

Grenada was a rare case of black and white in a haze of gray. The U.S. "rescue" of this small country, which had been kidnapped by communist hardliners with support from Cuba, showed that there is a time and place for straightforward military intervention supported by the tools to do so surgically. It also demonstrated the value of having a good neighborhood to land in when the fighting stops—with trade and supportive relations buttressing and even insisting on human rights and democracy. The expulsion of Manuel Noriega from Panama and restoration of democracy there in 1989 largely fits the same model. Both were rare enough to be deceiving.

El Salvador was the most dramatic of the Central American countries (including Guatemala, Nicaragua, and Honduras) left behind by modernization and evolved into ticking socioeconomic and political time bombs. Their explosion took a more violent turn when drawn into the Cold War struggle over territory and economic models. The course El Salvador would take was highly susceptible to American influence, and the United States supported the country massively, albeit from a respectful distance that allowed the country's leaders to match their opponent's nationalist credentials. It was one of the most comprehensive integrations of political, economic, and military tools and a case where the United States stayed the course, at least to the end of the civil war and just into the postconflict period. It is now clear that the United States lost interest before the postwar gains were consolidated, however, a long process in a country with such a weak socioeconomic foundation. With good leadership and a surge of resources (theirs and ours) things could yet come together.

The post–Cold War 1990s gave the United States the luxury of taking on hard cases for purely humanitarian reasons. *Somalia* was the first truly failed state in recent history, where all elements of government collapsed and defied reconstruction. It is perhaps the best example of how intractable social, cultural, and religious factors can conspire to foil well-meaning efforts to raise a people up from a destructive path. Our impatient, overbearing, and technically incompetent efforts to stop a famine and build a nation succeeded at first but were stopped cold in the second stage. With brutal effectiveness Somali fighters in the fall of 1993 delivered the lesson of what happens when we do not have the right leadership or the political and cultural understanding of the landscape. In the end it might not have mattered. The Somalis were simply resistant to nationhood, something that should have been identified up front before lunging in. After the drama of our sixteen-month intervention, international assistance landed in a more sustainable place for the next two decades, albeit with various surges and withdrawals still to come. A facilitated Somali solution to governance and a slightly improving economy, with some international assistance, are now giving the country a third or fourth chance. Apparently it was always a question of acceptance of internal reality, a sustainable level of effort, and patience.

Like Somalia, *Haiti* was a difficult country historically, culturally, and politically. Like Central America it suffered from isolation, broad-based lack of development, and a predatory ruling class. American efforts to help build a functional state amid the wreckage of the François Duvalier dictatorship were honest, important, and reasonably well managed, although the economic component could have been more patient, the building of government institutions more directed, and the training and equipping of security forces more comprehensive. None in the end, though, could have compensated for a political process that simply never came together. Unfortunately that was the piece the United States had the least control over. The Haitian people simply needed several decades to learn democratic principles and to finally disgorge from the country their beloved but destructive leader, Jean-Bertrand Aristide. Like Somalia, the lesson was pacing, with enough inputs to the economy to avert collapse and enough improvements in governance and security to keep the country on a modestly improving trajectory until the overall political picture improved. And it is yet another country that may still come together, something that will not likely happen without our involvement.

While I was only on the margins of the *Balkans*, not mentioning it would leave a large gap in this account, as it was one of the most successful cases of the period. Full international support, lavish resources, skilled negotiators with their governments' complete backing, and one of the more complete blends of military force and diplomacy brought a seemingly intractable conflict to an end. It has yielded a jagged but functional peace that has held, allowing these societies to rebuild and integrate into the wider world, surrounded by a high-functioning neighborhood that supported the process fully. It is one of the clearer examples of what is possible with skill, leadership, and resources.

An anomaly among the cases in not including direct military intervention was *Darfur*, like Somalia purely humanitarian in nature. The province's African citizens were being systematically killed and their villages destroyed by local Arab tribes who had been empowered by a government of Sudan that feared a breakaway province. Darfur presented a compelling case of using tools short of intervention—primarily sanctions and international isolation—to persuade a government to follow the international community's insistence that nations have a "responsibility to protect" their own citizens. That pressure led to an opening that the international community exploited to install an African-led security force, funded and supported by Europe and the United States and later evolving into an African Union–European Union hybrid force. It was the clearest case of achieving initial objectives, in this case the not insignificant ending of genocide, without achieving longer-term consolidation. But it was an odd situation, where the victims we were helping were at times just as difficult to work with as the government we were protecting them from. It demonstrated the imperative of good political action and of tools and capacity to forge political solutions. And it was yet another example of how these political solutions can take several decades to play out, often landing as they do in a "gray zone."

The United States entered *Afghanistan* armed with several decades of lessons from other interventions and a robust understanding of Afghanistan itself, based on earlier decades working there. For reasons that even now are opaque, policymakers ignored all this and imagined an Afghanistan that would simply change course and become functional on its own. Surges and withdrawals followed an initial period of willful neglect, and progress was marked, if uneven, in most institutions and regions. Institution-building was always made less effective by our lack of a standing capacity to manage it. In the end, if the core political contest between the traditionalist Pashtuns and everyone else had been settled satisfactorily, then all the missteps could be forgiven. But until that contest is settled, everything will remain at risk under a resurgent Taliban. The struggle will not be won quickly, but it can be won slowly, by continuing to support the moderate central government and its security forces until a political settlement is found. It was always going to be a long, difficult path. But given the centrality of Afghanistan to the post-9/11 world, it is difficult to see a better path.

The operation in *Iraq* began before the dysfunction of our Afghan policy was fully manifest, so we were able to repeat many of the same mistakes while adding others. Unlike Afghanistan, where we quickly set up an Afghan government, in Iraq we endeavored to govern the country ourselves. As in Afghanistan, our many missteps in reconstruction and local governance would have been forgiven if the political formula had been right, primarily a question of finding a place for the Sunnis in the new Iraq. But it is not clear in retrospect whether there was a way to do this that did not involve a long period of violent adjustment as the sides established the new political reality. And it may still be the case that the country cannot survive as it is constituted. But as the rise of ISIS shows, there is always something worse on the horizon, hence staying the course in support of a reasonably well-governed, pluralistic, democratic Iraq remains the best option. Meanwhile one hopes we will absorb the lessons of the primacy of a solid political baseline, buttressed by full-spectrum security forces and a functional economy, all sustained from a respectful distance over a long period of time. The lessons were most decidedly not absorbed in Libya in 2011 and are constantly under assault in charting a way forward in Iraq and Afghanistan today. I suppose they are, as the special inspector for Iraqi reconstruction titled his report, simply hard lessons.

WHY NATION-BUILDING MATTERS

PART ONE

Cold War Low-Intensity Conflict

ONE

Colombia, 1978

A Battered State and a Dramatic Comeback

The Scrappy State Circuit

I have long been attracted to dysfunctional states. It is hard to explain really. I grew up in the calmest part of the most successful country in history. Between my birth in Denver and formative years in Kansas City we were never more than a few hours from the geographic epicenter of the lower forty-eight states and firmly in the middle of the American middle class. But a call at age nineteen by the Church of Jesus Christ of Latter-Day Saints to spend two years in Colombia opened up a new world for me and upended my plans for a career in the criminal justice system.

Colombia in the late 1970s was largely peaceful, and LDS missionaries could travel widely there and did so. My own service took me to the coastal metropolis of Barranquilla, the capital of Bogotá, and the small town of Garzón in the south. Other duties allowed me to travel along the Caribbean coast, into the northern mountains, down to the eastern plains, and through the southern jungle, stopping at small towns along the way to hunt for food and lodging while engaging with our congregations.

I recall driving from the airport in Barranquilla on my first night in country as I sat atop a truck on my luggage while we passed concrete-block row houses. The adults were sitting on the stoop watching television or talking until the power went off, which it did every night, while kids played soccer in the street. When darkness descended, candles and flashlights came out, and life went on. Perhaps it was the openness of the culture, the resilience of the people, or the fact that otherwise simple tasks—ordering a meal, reading a newspaper, driving across town—were an adven ture. Or perhaps it was the constant surprise that comes with dysfunction. I was hooked on overseas life, but more, hooked on the countries that had not yet arrived.

Colombia was, of all my future endeavors, the closest I would get to a foreign culture, living as I did very directly on the economy. Within three months of arriving in Barranquilla I was working with a Colombian companion who didn't speak English, and for weeks on end I did not see another American. We had no small amount of hardship and deprivation: the seeming near-death experience of dengue fever, constant stomach maladies, scorching heat that was only reprieved by stops to the air-conditioned post office. But I don't remember ever wanting to be anywhere else (except perhaps during dengue fever week).

I later came to realize we had an incredible window on a scrappy country that was about to go through a horrific decades-long struggle, a bookend with the hell it had just come out of a few years before I arrived. Colombia in the 1940s and 1950s was wracked by socioeconomic strife that translated into political meltdown and large-scale violence. "La Violencia" was an apt name for a period that took as many as 300,000 lives and led to a general breakdown of social order and governance and the establishment of violence as a tool of politics. The Liberal and Conservative parties whose power struggles were at the heart of the violence eventually made a deal in which the two sides would alternate power in a "national front" from 1958 to 1974.

The plan was effective in reestablishing peace among the institutional parties, but the violence had by then pushed many Colombians to the fringes of the country, where they lived without government contact or services and, more important, without land. In 1964 the Revolutionary Armed Forces of Colombia (FARC) was founded as an active Marxist-Leninist armed movement, ostensibly to protect peasants from army attacks and to wrest agrarian reforms from the state. That same year the National Liberation

Army (ELN) was founded, with a focus on socioeconomic inequality. Both were rabidly anti-imperialist and anti-American, with the ELN bringing its craft more to bear against international interests through pipeline bombings and the FARC focused on attacks on security forces and government installations. Both were aligned with and supported by Cuba and the Soviets. A decade later an additional insurgent group, the M-19, emerged as an intellectual movement capable of dramatic urban attacks.

Other than the M-19, whose attacks were sporadic, none of the groups bumped up against the areas where we worked, and the drug business was not yet developed. But in retrospect we were first-hand observers of what would drive the conflict in later decades. Much of what I would later apply to my work came out of this formative period.

First, we experienced the truly truncated nature of the Colombian state. We had missionaries in the frontier town of Villavicencio in the east, the first city before emerging onto the vast eastern *llanos* (plains), and in Florencia in the south, the last city before reaching the Amazonian jungle. I visited both cities several times, on one occasion getting stuck on a bus from Pitalito to Florencia for nine hours while we waited for bulldozers to clear a succession of seventeen landslides that had blocked the road. The one-and-a-half-lane dirt road was the only way in and out of not only Florencia but the entire southeastern sector of Colombia. Cutting it would not have taken more than a handful of determined insurgents. And independent of cutting the road, the government did not have much of a presence in these remote areas to begin with.

Additionally we were on a budget of just over $100 a month for room and board and so lived with low-end middle-class families who needed a bit of extra cash. In one house the only furniture was a small table and two chairs for eating, the family taking turns standing when they gathered for dinner in an otherwise empty living room. We often took trips to the smaller villages around Bogotá—Sesquilé, Cajicá, Zipaquirá—and saw the struggles of the countryside, where cardboard nailed to a simple wooden frame was the norm for housing, water was from wells or ditches, and sanitation was nonexistent. I came to associate a certain smell with poverty in Colombia that stays with me even now, a swirl of burning wood and unwashed woolen clothing. Aspirations were dashed early in that environment. Resentments stewed. As one observer would later put it, "Colombia is often described as a country bifurcated between metropolitan areas with a developed, middle-income economy, and some rural areas that are poor, conflict-ridden, and weakly governed. The fruits of the growing economy have not been equally shared with this ungoverned, largely rural periphery."[1]

Our Colombian missionary companions were an interesting light on all this as well. One told us we would never fully understand their reality and should leave well enough alone when we encountered things that challenged our North American assumptions. There is more behind the antigovernment demonstrations, patience with socialism, or even a direct sympathy for the "armed struggle," he said, than you will understand.

We did come to understand how some could fight against whatever model of capitalism was being practiced, but we could also see that what was being practiced wasn't true capitalism. Rather it was a form of mercantilism in which a small elite controlled land and capital and had developed an administrative state that shut out small businessmen and women from access to capital or markets. During a visit by one of our regional leaders, the international banker Robert Wells, I sat in on discussions he held with our mission president, Kirt Olson, who had dedicated his life to seeking ways to improve the conditions of peasants in Mexico and Native Americans in the American Southwest. "It is all about access to capital," Wells said. "They have ideas and energy and family organizations that can be mobilized. They just don't have capital." His experience was urban and he was a banker, but if applied to the countryside, capital equaled land.

Finally, I spent four months with a *paisa* from Medellín. His energy was unstoppable, demonstrating the incredible entrepreneurial spirit and drive of this region and its people, which was similar in Cali and Bogotá. That energy, when it was misdirected into the drug trade a decade later, would hijack the entire country as it generated wealth on such a scale that it could actively threaten the institutions of the state. It was the same energy that, redirected, led the country into one of the most dramatic national recoveries in modern times. Sometimes it is all about who captures a nation's energy.

I returned to work on Colombia as an intelligence analyst in 1991. By then, in addition to drug traffickers and burgeoning guerrilla movements, there were paramilitaries who were the enforcers for the wealthy landowners. Their bloody tactics depopulated whole villages and made regions uninhabitable. Colombia was well on the way to having the largest number of internally displaced persons in the world as the army, guerrillas, and paramilitaries fought for control of the country's truncated and complex terrain, with the peasants always caught in the middle. It was not a failed state but a highly dysfunctional state that was exerting control over less and less of its territory.

Guerrillas, Paramilitaries, and Drug Traffickers

Several events and trends in 1991 were instructive of the future. The M-19 had recently demobilized after it had been thoroughly penetrated by Colombian intelligence. When it faced the proposition of being wiped out or making peace and taking its movement in a political direction it chose the latter, and while it was a somewhat bloody entry into politics, and many of its candidates were assassinated, it would not return to the battlefield. The FARC was also alternating between fighting and politicking, suffering the assassinations of hundreds of its candidates in the lead-up to the Constituent Assembly elections of 1990. The Colombian government hoped in the new constitution to knock down some of the support for the insurgency by bringing up to date many of the socioeconomic issues that garnered sympathy for their cause and calculated its case would be bolstered by the ideological collapse of communism. Peace seemed a possibility.

But unlike in Central America, where the end of external funding fundamentally shifted the balance of power, in Colombia external financing from the Soviets was replaced by internal funding as guerrilla groups turned to kidnapping and drug trafficking, by one estimate later coming to yield $2.4 billion to $3.5 billion a year.[7] They were quickly becoming criminal gangs hiding behind a tired ideological façade.

Frustrated over continued incursions during a period when the government believed the FARC should be standing down in the interest of peace, the army attacked and leveled the insurgent's headquarters, the Casa Verde. For twenty years this had been a safe zone in an "independent republic" in Uribe province. The FARC reacted with such ferocity that it caused the government to back off, allowing the restoration of a certain amount of independence. And the insurgents weren't the only players. Pablo Escobar, in custody when I started the account, would escape and continue his rampage against the state until his eventual demise two years later. The other cartels would pick up whatever space Escobar left, and the transshipment of narcotics would continue to grow, with drug trafficking contributing to a general sense of lawlessness in much of the country.

The government went through several phases in dealing with the challenges to its authority and sovereignty. For years, given the firm territorial entrenchment of the guerrillas and the coercive ability of drug traffickers, Colombian leaders worked to varying degrees in a spirit of accommodation. They allowed the independent republics to operate, constantly repaired the pipeline, endured the kidnappings, and let drugs flow north. Successive Colombian governments simply did not possess the confidence, resources, or manpower to bring the country fully under the control of the state.

This reached its height under Andrés Pastrana, elected in 1998 with the mandate to end the conflict definitively. Pastrana offered the FARC a demilitarized zone of forty-two thousand square kilometers to entice them to negotiate, an effective state the size of Switzerland. The guerrillas used the breathing space to regroup, and then the violence continued, albeit much of it now from paramilitaries ostensibly defending landowners from the guerrillas and from drug traffickers. The homicide rate went from 59 per 100,000 in 1998 to nearly 70 per 100,000 in 2002, with 390 attacks on settlements and three thousand kidnappings a year. Paramilitary violence also spiked, with nine hundred massacres in the same period.

Peasants and often whole villages fled the violence in what came to be an incredibly complex phenomenon that involved the nexus of persistent rural conflict, weak state institutions, inequal land distribution, and the land requirements of the illicit drug and mining trades. One analysis notes that displacement was "a weapon of war used by all parties of the conflict."[3] By the time the country made peace seventeen years later Colombia would have the largest number of internally displaced people in the world, seven million, or 15 percent of the population. Because of the violence the economy was at a breaking point, with the unemployment rate in 1999 at a staggering 18.2 percent and GDP retreating by 4.2 percent, the worst figures since the Great Depression.

By the late 1990s the state was simply failing, as one observer describes it: "Under the combination of a weak central government, an army incapable of standing up to insurgents, a police force unable to effectively maintain order, even in many urban environments, and the ability of the insurgents and paramilitaries to access supplies and weapons from abroad, legitimate state authority imploded."[4]

The United States saw real threats from the increasing trafficking of narcotics but also from fear of a more opaque danger from ungoverned territory. One State Department official, Stuart Lippe, who worked on Colombia for thirteen years, wrote, "The prospect of a major Latin American country falling to a narcotics-fed insurgency/terrorist group sent geopolitical chills up the spines of the foreign policy establishment in Washington."[5]

Presidents Clinton and Pastrana agreed in 1999 to a closer partnership and increased U.S. funding, although they saw the issue differently. Pastrana wanted to revive his country and save the drug issue for later, while the U.S. Congress sought a pure antinarcotics initiative.[6] The proposal submitted to Congress in January 2000 was a compromise that would assist Colombia to "combat drug production and trafficking, foster peace, increase the rule of law, improve human rights, expand economic development, and institute justice reform."[7] It was the beginning of what would become a remarkable partnership that both parties knew as Plan Colombia.

The ups and downs of peace efforts continued and finally culminated in the FARC's hijacking of a commercial airliner to extract additional leverage. Taking that as the final indication he had been played, Pastrana finally pulled the plug in February 2002 and began bombing the FARC's territory. But it was late in the game. By the time he left office "some observers estimated that as much as 40% of Colombian territory was controlled by the FARC and the state had no presence in 16% of Colombia's 1,099 municipalities." According to a 1999 poll, a majority of Colombians thought the FARC and its sixteen thousand to twenty thousand fighters might someday take power by force.[8]

The Colombian people were by now fed up with the whole thing and sought answers outside the conventional parties in the independent and harder line Álvaro Uribe, elected president in 2002 under the banner of "Democratic Security"—no dialogue with the FARC without a cessation of hostilities. The FARC returned the favor by greeting his inauguration with mortar fire.

Plan Colombia

The United States now had a partner with whom it could work and from 2000 to 2017 poured nearly $11 billion into Colombia, slowly and methodically strengthening the security forces, judiciary, and society itself to help the country regain control of territory and reduce the levels of violence. It helped immensely that the program received consistent support from both sides of the aisle in the U.S. Congress and was effectively never politicized.

But the program would always be in support of the Colombian government's efforts, with the question of Colombian "ownership" never in question. "Even with a large U.S. personnel footprint [a cap of eight hundred military and six hundred contractors]," Lippe notes, "the Colombians considered the U.S. a partner in its efforts," and it never became a "U.S. war."[9] The nature of the partnership was also reinforced in the structure of funding, which was 90 percent Colombian and only 10 percent U.S., as Colombia increased its spending from 2 to 4 percent of GDP between 2000 and 2009.

The program was also balanced between so-called hard and soft programs. Over the course of the first decade the emphasis shifted from 75:25 hard:soft mix to 50:50 as the initial large expenditures on helicopters and other expensive hardware gave way to rural development, rule of law, and improving the judiciary.

And on both sides a "whole of government" approach to the problem was set. U.S. programs guided by an array of government agencies provided training, equipment, and funding to the government of Colombia, civil society, local governments, and nongovernmental organizations (NGOs). They included programs devoted to counternarcotics and counterterrorism, alternative development, law enforcement, institutional strengthening, judicial reform, human and labor rights, humanitarian assistance for the displaced and victims, conflict management and peace promotion, reintegration of ex-combatants, humanitarian demining, and environmental preservation. "U.S. civilian and military cooperation and interagency unity," Lippe notes, "provided an object lesson in how to bring all elements of power—diplomatic, military, public relations, economic, and intelligence—to bear to help resolve the Colombian crisis."[10]

Under Uribe's leadership Colombia confronted the roots of the problem by starting to provide governance throughout the country: training, equipping, and deploying diverse, capable, and mobile security forces and building a functional economy that worked for more than just the few. Uribe and local mayors even attacked the cultural issues that had allowed cities like Medellin to develop a society or culture of lawlessness.

I inherited many of the functionaries who worked on Plan Colombia when I ran the Merida Initiative, a similarly structured program to rapidly expedite U.S. assistance to a Mexico under siege by traffickers and destabilizing actors. My chief of staff, Paul Mahlstedt, who spent a decade working on Plan Colombia, offered the following formula:

Strong bilateral political commitment: The strong support of the Pastrana government became even stronger under Uribe, who worked 24/7 and expected the same from his team. U.S. embassy personnel had exceptional access at all levels, and the Colombians considered us part of their team. Late-night meetings were often interrupted when senior Colombian officials answered their cell phone with *A la orden, Señor Presidente*.

Clear missions and authorities: Each program had a clear owner on both the U.S. and Colombian teams. Hard-side programs included new police and military units, a substantial increase in aviation, and eradication. Soft-side programs included human rights, civil-military relations, strengthening the Ministry of Defense, demand reduction, administration of justice, and adjudicating financial crimes. Later programs included "humanitarian demobilization" that encouraged thousands of FARC, ELN, and paramilitaries to abandon their ranks and be reincorporated into society, while allowing for the gathering of intelligence; training and equipping of seventy rural police units, for the first time facilitating the extension of law and order to the countryside; and rural programs for education, job training, and administration of justice.

Experienced program advisors and implementers: The program drew from retired military and law enforcement personnel with long experience in the region and often in Colombia itself. Because they were personal services contractors they were able to stay for significantly longer than their diplomatic or military counterparts. They were also able to take risks that would not have been possible with uniformed personnel. These advisors and program officers were able to embed with their Colombian counterparts—from vice ministers to sergeants—to design, develop, and implement programs within weeks, not years.

Expedited contracting: An often underappreciated component of programs of this kind is the tangle of contracting regulations that makes speedy delivery impossible. For the first eighteen months, until attention shifted to Afghanistan and Iraq, Plan Colombia enjoyed a period in which the supply chain worked with amazing rapidity.

Uribe used his first term to strengthen the security forces and pursue peace with the paramilitaries, taking the most accessible of the armed groups off the battlefield. By mid-2006 thirty-one thousand paramilitaries had been demobilized and violence was coming down while recovered territory was up. The security forces had doubled in size and now included much needed special units and greater mobility. The morale of the security forces rose alongside their capacity.

The Democratic Security program was popular with the Colombian people, who voted to change the constitution and allow Uribe a second term, which he started with large majorities in both houses of Congress. He continued the military offensive, and by 2008 the security forces caught some welcome breaks—in March alone one FARC leader was killed in a bombing run, a second was killed by his own security guards, and the movement's founding leader died of a heart attack. Then in July the government pulled off a highly sophisticated operation to rescue fifteen prominent individuals held hostage by the FARC, including three U.S. security contractors captive since 2003 and a former presidential candidate, Íngrid Betancourt. It was described by one journalist as "a blow to the FARC, boost to the Colombian security forces, and vindication of Plan Colombia."[11]

In 2009 Uribe pivoted from Democratic Security to the rebranded National Consolidation Plan, which the researcher June Beittel describes as "a whole of government program integrating security, development, and counternarcotics by consolidating state presence in previously ungoverned or weakly governed areas. . . . Once security forces took control of a contested area, government agencies in housing, education, and development would regularize the presence of the state and integrate the municipalities of these marginalized zones into Colombia."[12] U.S. support for the new program was dubbed the Colombia Strategic Development Initiative and was intended largely to "fill gaps" in Colombian government programming. Special emphasis went to the restructuring of the key judicial sector, a critical and undeveloped institution.

The push for state presence in ungoverned areas was more aspirational than real and ten years later would remain a key challenge. And the program was fraught throughout with human rights abuses, often on a large scale, and some financial scandals. But it was accepted in both the United States and Colombia as successful enough that Uribe was seen to be passing off a recovering state rather than a failing state to his designated successor, former defense minister Juan Manuel Santos, who could now build on the state's newly strengthened position to press for peace.

From Security to Peace

It had taken most of eight years to gain the upper hand on security, but Uribe had also begun an economic reform program that Santos continued, calling his administration's policy Democratic Prosperity. He would continue a hard line on security but stated in his inauguration address in August 2010 that the door to peace was "not locked"—perhaps not the ringing invitation of "open," but something to work with.

Santos continued to hit the FARC hard, especially its leaders, killing its top military commander a month into office in a bombing and a little over a year later its supreme leader, whose replacement would lead the organization into peace talks. Santos too began "to re-orient the Colombian government's stance toward the armed conflict," which he made tangible through a series of reforms.[13] In June 2011 Santos signed the Victims and Land Restitution Law to compensate the four million to five million victims of the conflict, a strong indicator to the rural-based FARC "that the Santos government shared its interest in addressing land and agrarian concerns."[14] He followed this in June 2012 with a legal framework for peace and set up congressional support and the means to pass further legislation that would be necessary to secure the peace, in the process undercutting much of the reason for the FARC's existence in the first place.

The two sides began formal negotiations in October 2012 in Oslo after many months of preparation—the first time in a decade and only fourth time in thirty years they were face to face. The talks then moved in November to Havana, where they would continue for over thirty rounds. Santos was reelected in August 2014; by then his priority was peace with the FARC. "Ultimately, the peace talks became the signature of the Santos government."[15]

There was a long list of grievances on both sides, and the talks required patient, skillful negotiators to work through them. The parties tried to build on the slowly developing goodwill. The FARC announced a unilateral cease-fire on December 20, 2014, that would be upheld as long as the military did not attack any of its fronts. Negotiators were helped by having Venezuela, Chile, Cuba, and Norway in support, and on February 20, 2015, President Barack Obama named as special envoy to the talks a former assistant secretary of state, Bernard Aronson, who would be able to shape U.S. policy and engagement in a way that supported the negotiation's outcome at a critical time. In February the FARC announced it would proscribe kidnappings; on March 7 the government and FARC organized a joint effort to clear land mines; and on March 10 the government committed to stop bombing FARC encampments. The government's general position was also bolstered both in the talks and with the Colombian citizenry by strong economic growth; the Colombian economy grew by 4 percent a year between 2010 and 2014, and the poverty rate slid from 45 percent in 2005 to 27 percent in 2016.[16]

The talks concluded in August 2016, nearly six years after they began. A signing ceremony on September 26 in Cartagena was attended by dignitaries from around the world, including Secretary of State John Kerry and UN Secretary General Ban Ki-moon, the two key international actors in securing the peace going forward. "The horrible night has ceased," Santos remarked, quoting a phrase from Colombia's national anthem, while his counterpart, Timolcón Jiménez (whose nickname is Timochenko), promised, "[Going forward] our only weapons will be our words" and asked in the name of the FARC for "forgiveness from all the victims of the conflict and for all the pain [FARC] may have caused in this war." The country was euphoric, but not without reservations.

Those reservations registered when the agreement was narrowly defeated in a referendum by Colombian voters in October, due in part to low turnout on a rainy day with competition from a major soccer match, but in part to the belief that the government had given away too much to insurgents who had brought the country three generations of misery. Four days later Santos was informed he had won the Nobel Prize, placing him in a somewhat awkward position but at the same time strengthening his hand as he and his teams blanketed the country listening to all sides to inform revisions to the agreement.

The government revised the accord and, after a brief period of renegotiation, had it ratified by Congress in November, the populace by then accepting that a bad accord would be better than no accord at all, and political parties who saw gain in opposing the accord not wanting to overplay their hand. The agreement was re-signed in a more modest and sober ceremony in Bogotá on November 24. The lengthy accord covered rural development and land policy, political participation of the FARC (the movement would get five guaranteed seats in each chamber of Congress for two terms), reintegration, drug trafficking, victim reparations, and implementation and verification.

The accusation that Santos gave away too much would dog him to the end of his term, and the next election would see this theme emerge as a popular one. But at the time the *Economist* made a convincing case that he "leaves his country a better place than he found it" in terms of poverty and income inequality, infrastructure, human rights, environmental protection, and especially signing a peace that put an end to fifty years of conflict.[17]

In his Nobel Prize speech on December 10, 2016, Santos accepted the award on behalf of all Colombians, "but especially the 220,000 killed in the war, and the eight million displaced." He cited scholars who believed this was the first peace accord "that has placed the victims and their rights at the center of the solution," reflecting the long consultations with those most affected by the conflict. And he cited the Kroc Institute for International Peace Studies at the University of Notre Dame, which suggested the agreement was the most complete and comprehensive reached in the past thirty years. He offered lessons for future peace agreements: learning from other peace processes, their successes and their problems; putting into play a very focused and specific agenda that doesn't drift to "all the problems faced by the nation"; discretion and confidentiality in order to prevent the process from turning into a media circus; maintaining the willingness and ability to fight and talk at the same time; securing the ability to make difficult, bold, and oftentimes unpopular decisions in order to reach the final goal; accepting the help of regional partners, even those with deep ideological differences; and agreement on a model of transitional justice that enables a maximum of justice without sacrificing peace.

I returned to work on Colombia six months later as director for Andean affairs at the State Department, a rare opportunity in my career to return to an earlier issue that I had a very personal interest in. I was chagrined that I had done nothing to pitch in during the war itself but happy that now I could help guide the U.S. team that was supporting the implementation of the accord. Santos has said in his Nobel Prize speech that "it is much harder to *make* peace than to wage war." We were quickly learning that *sustaining* the peace was also going to be difficult.

The most visible initial act of the peace process included the demobilization of seven thousand combatants in 2017 in an imperfect process that often left them adrift in a society they had never been a part of. There was always the fear that they would rearm, but a greater fear that they would drift off into criminal violence.

The peace accord was complex and would be expensive to implement. Having endured a "war tax" for decades, would the Colombian business community be willing to endure a "peace tax"? Adam Isacson of the Washington Office on Latin America cited $4 billion a year as a conservative estimate of what will be needed, about 5 percent of the government's annual budget, a "big fill for a country running fiscal deficits and suffering from price declines in principal exports of crude oil and coal."[18]

The special jurisdiction for peace, which would govern claims and grievances, would deal with a tangle of past human rights abuses in the midst of ongoing abuses and killings. Restitution of land, over 50 percent of which was mined, would be made to 360,000 families. There was still an armed group, the ELN, that had not yet made peace and in some areas was stepping up its attacks, finding safe haven in increasingly lawless Venezuela. And the peace accord had created an anticipated but unintentional spike in coca production, with areas under cultivation nearly doubling. But the most difficult part would be the establishment of governance in the countryside, with all the services that have never found their way beyond city centers. If the war lasted fifty-two years and the peace process six, consolidating the peace will be the work of at least another decade.

In July 2017 I attended the award ceremony of the Orden de San Carlos en el Grado de Gran Cruz to U.S. special negotiator Bernard Aronson. Colombia's Ambassador Camilo Reyes praised the bipartisan support from Washington that Colombia had received through the decades of its struggle and the strong leadership on both sides that had led to the successful conclusion. But he was honest in describing the two Colombia's, one urban and progressive, with jobs and services, and the other of the countryside, lacking in hope and opportunity. Riffing off President Santos at the Nobel Prize event, he spoke of Macondo, that mystical place in Gabriel García Márquez's imagination, of which Santos had said, "[It was as if] we ourselves were inhabitants of Macondo, a place that was not only magical but also contradictory." Reyes wondered which took more imagination: creating Macondo or trying to govern it.

"Eight years ago Colombia was the black sheep in the region and the world," said Santos. "Today Colombia is respected." It was a hard-won respect, and satisfying.

Staying the Course and Other Lessons Learned

As early as 2009 the U.S. ambassador to Colombia William Brownfield described Plan Colombia as "the most successful nation-building exercise that the United States has associated itself with perhaps in the last 25–30 years."[19] Given the next decade to follow, that statement still stands.

One measure of success is Colombia's ability to "export security," which it started doing in 2012 in a regional security initiative in Central America and the Caribbean, carrying out hundreds of training events involving over thirty-six thousand security personnel from seventy-three countries between 2013 and 2016.

What was it that made Colombia's resurgence work and made U.S. involvement so productive?

First was simple leadership. In Uribe and Santos Colombia had presidents who were both technically proficient and possessed of vision and a firm understanding of the core problems their country faced. They were self-aware enough to accept help from wherever it came—the United States, Cuba, Venezuela, Norway—and capable of channeling that assistance in the most efficient way.

Second, the U.S. never robbed these leaders of the ability to own the conflict and act as true patriots and nationalists, not stooges of outsiders. The respectful distance established early on by U.S. operatives and policymakers was never breached.

Third, both countries put their whole governments behind the project, not slipping into false machismo to favor hard power when other solutions were the real issue. They established a balance between fighting and developing, between police posts and courthouses, always building institutions along the way that could carry on when the fighting subsided.

Fourth, the parties put just as much effort into peace as they did into war. When the time came to end the conflict, the energy that had previously been used to prosecute the war shifted to creativity in finding ways to both design a functional agreement and entice the fighters to accept it.

Fifth, communities were involved in the peace, just as they had suffered during the war. There was an honest effort to include all parties to the conflict in finding solutions and in designing the peace in a way that would allow them to repair the fabric of a shredded society.

Sixth, there was an early acknowledgment that winning the war and consolidating the peace would be expensive. Both the United States and Colombia understood this and allowed for it throughout the conflict.

But all that was decades in the future. As I left Colombia in February 1980 I had seen firsthand, if not fully internalized, the importance of good governance over everything else. Dysfunctional governments with weak connections to citizens would multiply a host of problems and create a negative synergy that made everything harder. And there was a clear economic component to successful states, with communists and others exploiting very real grievances over land distribution and lack of economic opportunity that security forces alone would never be enough to talk people out of. Solutions would be clearer in the future, but the basic diagnosis remained fairly constant throughout my career—it was about a blend of security, the economy, and politics. But mostly politics.

After my missionary stint in Colombia I returned to college, where I focused on being a Cold Warrior, studying Russian history and the Russian language, and spending as much time as possible in the Robert E. Wells ROTC building. I was honored to serve as cadet battalion commander my senior year, earning the top George C. Marshall Award for distinguished service to the corps. The Soviets had just invaded Afghanistan and the Gulf was heating up. I was loath to miss anything and tried to position myself well. With no technical skills but little fear of heights, I volunteered for the 82nd Airborne Division. After the Infantry Officer Basic Course, Ranger School, and Airborne School, I was assigned to the 2/505th Infantry at Fort Bragg, North Carolina.

The 82nd of this period was the nation's strategic reserve, with one brigade at a time on a quick fuse, one of whose battalions was ready to deploy in eight hours. It was difficult to pin down a clear theater of operations, as we were a global force, but by then the notion of stopping the Soviets in a thrust across the desert was a persistent exercise favorite; I recall considerable work on the Anti-Armor Airborne Defense. After every exercise I would strongly recommend through command channels that we really needed dirt bikes to do it right since on foot we were limited in the number of positions we could cover; I suggested calling it the Anti-Armor Airborne Motocross Defense. Higher HQ acknowledged the logic but thought it sounded too recreational to justify.

While the deserts of the Middle East seemed a more likely field of battle than the forests of Europe, as Jimmy Carter passed the presidency to Ronald Reagan an even more likely theater became jungles, as we started to drift back into the mission of low-intensity conflict, something that had largely fallen out of favor since the end of the Vietnam War. The ghosts of Vietnam were quickly excised, and Reagan hit a nerve with his call to take up a more robust global posture and confront communism wherever it existed. While Carter had begun a major defense buildup, Reagan upped the ante, and we were soon in the throes of new equipment, more training, and increased readiness, along with much higher standards of entry. It was a heady time. Under Reagan we were ready to flex our muscles where necessary and, significantly for those of us in the Airborne, directly seek places where we could geographically reverse Soviet advances.

TWO

Grenada, 1983

Rescuing a Hijacked Country

Operation Urgent Fury

As paratroopers we didn't spend much time on geopolitics; it took all our energy to know whether our soldiers had all their gear for the upcoming training exercise. But we were aware that the overriding missions our country had taken on were pushing back and deterring communism while stabilizing the Middle East. Those two undertakings hit front and center one desperate weekend in late October 1983.

The evening of October 24 my brother called, asking if I had heard about the terrorist attack on the U.S. Marine barracks in Lebanon and the coup in Grenada. By midnight my platoon was at the Green Ramp staging area, where we were told our company, B/2/505th infantry, would be replacing a cohort company from the 2/325th Airborne Infantry Regiment that was deemed not fully trained (something they strongly disputed). My 3rd platoon was at full strength and had strong noncommissioned officers (NCOS), with Oesch as platoon sergeant, and Sullivan, Bray, Coulter, and Shaver as squad leaders. They were all in excellent shape, experienced jumpmasters, and were trusted by the men.

We soon got word that the objective was not Lebanon but an airborne operation into Grenada and that resupply was sketchy, so we should bring everything we could carry. As we were rigging parachutes we were given a five-minute look at a map of the Point Salines airfield, a single copy that was circulated around the battalion one platoon at a time. The men were somewhat unimpressed, as it didn't yield much detail, but confident of their abilities to improvise. We loaded up and soon were in flight, when I received a more detailed op order with a linkup point once on the ground. Paratroopers in flight are a bit like overturned turtles nestled and intertwined with 120 pounds of gear each. Rather than try to gather even the squad leaders, I made a sketch of the airfield, with a triangle at the northwest corner indicating where we should link up and what our sector would be, and passed it down the line with the text "Move to the northwest corner and link up with A and C Companies." It was the simplest op order I had ever given.

The jump in the end was unnecessary, eliciting both relief and disappointment. We landed and made an initial move off the airfield and linked up with a sister unit, for the first night watching a few battles on other parts of the airfield while the brigade assembled. We had been given strict rules of engagement and an injunction to treat the Grenadian people with the utmost respect.

A Cold War Outpost between East and West

Operationally Grenada was straightforward, but it did have a more complex local and geopolitical context. Like Libya, Grenada is one of those places that took on larger-than-life proportions because of the geography of the Cold War. It is a tiny island, the last of the Spice Islands before getting to Venezuela, and home to 100,000 laid-back people with a modest GNP based on tourism, spices, and international students. In the postcolonial scrum between the United States and the Soviet Union, with our competing models of free market capitalism versus international socialism, Grenada kept an open mind.

The country gained its independence from Britain in February 1974 and was governed initially by the strongest of its precolonial leaders, the eccentric, elitist, and somewhat unstable Eric Gairy, who had been serving as premier under the British. Independence Day was chaotic, with the country in the throes of a general strike led by Maurice Bishop, leader of the opposition party New Jewel

Movement, whose father had been killed sixteen days before. In the words of Mark Adkin, a British Army staff officer serving in Barbados who was involved in planning for the operation, "Never before or since had a British colony achieved its independence in such miserable circumstances."[1]

Gairy's was a petty dictatorship—brutal, corrupt, and self-serving—whose Mongoose Gang and Green Beasts rounded up and tortured political opponents. But for all Gairy's oppressive tactics, he was no Duvalier with total control over society, and the New Jewel Movement functioned as an opposition, gaining political support as frustration with the regime mounted. When Gairy left the country in March 1979 to attend a UN meeting he had called seeking a proper hearing on UFOs, he left instructions to round up members of the opposition. Preempting him, Bishop mounted a near bloodless coup, taking over the government and military with just one casualty. He declared a new era: "without Gairy, without corruption, and without brutality." Over the coming few years ten thousand Grenadians would flee the island, threatened by the new economic regime and realizing that one form of oppression had been traded for another. But Bishop was also no Duvalier and left just enough political space for his own undoing.

Bishop sought a new economic model, like many leaders of the time associating the Western model with the relative poverty his people seemingly couldn't escape. He also knew that his socialist revolution might need to be defended, so within a month arms shipments and advisors started to arrive. He signed an agreement with the Soviet Union in 1980 and with Cuba soon after. He took care not to provoke the United States with advanced weaponry but did want the kind of defensive arms that would make an invader think twice: anti-aircraft guns, mortars, lots of small arms and ammunition, and some armored vehicles. He expanded popular militias and could theoretically put one in four Grenadians under arms.

The People's Revolutionary Government was a fully communist elitist party, but from what we observed four years later the revolution never really took hold. Surrounded by large amounts of unused weapons and reams of propaganda posters, pamphlets, and booklets, the Grenadian people simply did not embrace the philosophy of their leaders.[2]

What the Grenadian people might have seen as a laid-back revolution and a tentative revolutionary leader, however, were seen much differently by Moscow and Washington. The Soviet chief of staff Marshal Nikolai Ogarkov told his People's Revolutionary Army counterpart, Maj. Einstein Louison, in March 1983 that "over two decades ago there was only Cuba in Latin America, today there are Nicaragua, Grenada, and a serious battle is going on in El Salvador." While the United States would try to prevent progress, there was no way imperialism could turn back history, Ogarkov said.[3]

But whatever importance the island held for the Soviets, when Bishop pressed for economic aid, in one case twenty thousand tons of fertilizer, it was not granted. With tourism as a source of hard currency on the decline, Bishop was finding his country squeezed. The socialist path was heavy on weapons, somewhat less generous on economic and commercial aid, and the Grenadians we met described the Cubans as arrogant and overbearing.

One project the Soviets were committed to was a nine-thousand-foot airfield that Bishop suggested in November 1979 would be used to expand the tourism industry. Its capacity as a dual-use facility became transparent when Deputy Prime Minister Bernard Coard signed an agreement in May 1980 giving the Soviets permission to land their longest reconnaissance plane, the TU-95.[4] It was also capable of accommodating the largest Soviet bomber. A Cuban construction brigade of 650 arrived with eighty-five pieces of heavy Soviet equipment and forty military advisors.

Upon taking office in 1981 the Reagan administration indicated to Bishop that it considered his ties to the Eastern Bloc a threat to the region. Apparently Bishop was unmoved and in July 1982 traveled to Moscow, where he was granted financial credit to build a land station that would be linked to a Soviet communications satellite.[5] To U.S. policymakers Grenada was now positioned as the southeast leg of a triangle of Soviet-leaning states that included Cuba and Nicaragua.

Reagan outlined specifically the geostrategic context of Central America and the Caribbean, calling it America's "fourth border." Cuba at the west end of the Caribbean and Grenada at the east end, he said, was part of a power projection by the Soviets to challenge our capacity to resupply Western Europe in case of an emergency. If forced to defend ourselves "against a large, hostile military presence on our border," he declared, "our freedom to act elsewhere ... and to protect strategically vital sea-lanes and resources has been drastically diminished." In a televised address he showed a classified picture of the airstrip and asked, "Grenada doesn't even have an air force. Who is this intended for?"

Reagan saw the situation in Grenada as part of an ideological struggle, a contest he suggested in a March 10, 1983, speech was the result of accumulated grievances and social and economic change that were challenging traditional ways: "New leaders with new aspirations have emerged who want a new and better deal for their peoples.... The problem is that an aggressive minority has thrown in its lot with the Communists, looking to the Soviets and their own Cuban henchmen to help them pursue political change through violence." He made clear that the United States would compete in this struggle.

Reagan would contain the Soviets in places like El Salvador, where he saw the embattled regime as a test for setting limits to the Soviet global advance. But he would also start to roll back Soviet encroachments, starting with Afghanistan, where he increased support to the mujahideen fighting the Soviet occupiers, and Nicaragua, where controversial support to the Contra rebels was in full swing. He laid out no clear plan of action with regard to Grenada, but Bishop knew he was on notice and may have started to rethink the whole project.

Although Bishop did not state his intentions, we know that in June 1983 he traveled to the United States, seeking meetings in Washington and New York with the idea of exchanging ambassadors and opening the door to economic assistance. In the background was a long-running battle with Deputy Prime Minister Coard, a harder line Marxist and longtime rival of Bishop's who was angling for a chance to oust him and take power.

On October 12 Coard confronted Bishop in a Central Committee showdown after skillfully garnering the support of the party and the army. It ended the next day with Bishop under house arrest. Coard did not realize, however, how strongly the people were still with Bishop, who was freed by a crowd on October 19. Bishop had the opportunity to consolidate his reestablished position by arresting Coard and the other plotters but, encouraged by his popularity and wanting to ensure he still had control of the security forces, instead went to army HQ at Fort Rupert. There Coard and the plotters were able to again threaten Bishop. In a confrontation with the crowd that had followed Bishop to offer their popular protection, thirty or forty demonstrators were killed and a shocked Bishop turned himself over to the hardliners to stop further bloodshed. Within hours he and his inner circle were executed.

It was not clear whether the Soviets took a position on the coup, but Cuba made clear that it would not intervene in "internal Grenadian matters." With Coard sliding into the background to disguise the power play from the people, Gen. Hudson Austin came forward to lead the new government. He announced to the nation that evening that the Revolutionary Armed Forces were forced to storm the fort to stop Bishop and a few others from wiping out the party leadership, the army, and the revolution itself. He would head a Revolutionary Military Council that would govern with "absolute strictness" and announced that anyone who sought to demonstrate or disturb the peace would be shot. The country was under martial law. Its laid-back revolution had finally given way to a proper communist dictatorship. The citizenry was stunned.

Reagan Acts

The United States had drawn up plans for an evacuation of the large number of American medical students on the island even before the coup but advanced quickly to consider more serious options immediately after Bishop was killed. On Friday, October 21 the nations of the Organization of Eastern Caribbean States (OECS), in a diplomatic model that would be used for several other interventions in the coming decades, invoked Article 8 of their charter and asked the United States for assistance: "The Authority proposes therefore to take action for collective defense and preservation of peace and security against external aggression by requesting assistance from friendly countries to provide transport, logistics support, and additional military personnel to assist the efforts of the OECS to stabilize this most grave situation within the Eastern Caribbean." The "additional military personnel" came in the form of Delta Force, Rangers, the 82nd Airborne, and the marines. The OECS offered a small force of constabularies who would be active in the training of the new Grenadian forces after the liberation was consolidated. The more unwieldy Caribbean Community was not able to muster a similar petition, but Community members Jamaica and Barbados signed on to the OECS petition.

The U.S. decision to invade was largely condemned by the international community and even by Prime Minister Margaret Thatcher of Great Britain. She expressed to Reagan on October 24 her concern that intervention in the internal affairs of a small country, "however unattractive its regime," would make things problematic elsewhere in the East-West struggle in the Third World, and that it would cause difficulties in the debate in Britain over the basing of cruise missiles there. "I cannot conceal that I am deeply disturbed by your latest communication," she told him. Reagan conceded that at this point he was informing her, not asking for advice.

As the invasion got under way on October 25 Reagan laid out its goals to the American people: "First, to protect innocent lives, including the 1,000 students; second, to forestall further chaos; and third, to assist in the restoration of conditions of law and order and of governing institutions." By then the expulsion of the Cuban and Soviet advisors and the return of a government friendly to the United States were givens. As Reagan expressed in a phone call to Vice President George H. W. Bush on October 22, "If we're going to go there, we might as well do all that needs to be done."[6] The operation was complicated by the bombing of the marine barracks in Beirut, Lebanon, on October 23, but Reagan was undaunted, stating that he would not "let a few terrorists dissuade us from doing what is right."

The strength of the opposing force was not clear. The 650 Cuban construction workers were supposed to be able to shift gears quickly to defend the revolution. And the Grenadian People's Revolutionary Army (PRA) had three thousand members on the rolls who were supposed to be augmented in the "revolutionary strategy" by "popular militias" that would foment resistance across the island. But the PRA had expressed concern with their performance for months. In one Worker's Committee meeting in March 1983 attended by Bishop himself, many leaders did not see the need for a militia, and some reportedly thought a better method of dealing with threats was to "pray," let "the army deal with defense," or exercise "very strong religious feelings." At 5:30 a.m. on October 25 a duet of male and female radio announcers implored the people, "You should report to your militia bases immediately.... We are under attack.... Defend our homeland! We shall beat them back! Them have to get a beating! ... Together with the People's Revolutionary Army, we will save our country."[7] The response was underwhelming.

The Price Some Pay

From the airfield we began a long clear-and-hold operation across the island, moving from strongpoint to strongpoint. As we moved off the airfield we bumped up against a sister company whose commander had just been killed doing a leader's recon on a Cuban base. Despite the overwhelming force we were a part of, we were not entirely certain what resistance we would face and how dispersed it would be. We were on a ridgeline the second day when the hilltop across from us lit up with perfectly spaced gunfire. We thought it was coming in our direction but quickly realized it was pointed at the valley below, where a jeep full of soldiers was recovering the bodies of four Rangers who had been killed earlier.

On day 3 we came across our first group of American students from the medical school. They were overjoyed to see us and wanted to join our column, apparently not sure when they would see another friendly face. They said they had been holed up in apartments and houses under martial law for ten days before we arrived. It was an unlikely but welcome encounter and reminded the troops why we were there. We chanced upon someone from Brigade who guided them to the airfield, where they would be repatriated to the United States.

By day 4 we were having more and more encounters with the Grenadian people. They were a bit reserved at first, not knowing exactly what was happening. But when they realized we really were there to restore security and democracy, they came out in droves. As we walked through village after village, they would line the streets or stand on their porches and applaud, coming down to the road to thank us for liberating them. When we bivouacked, they cooked for us. One woman was apparently so overjoyed that she could again practice her religion that she circulated religious tracts among the troops, asking if they had been saved and, if so, were they sure. It was a reaction American soldiers hadn't experienced since World War II, and it was deeply moving. In the words of a British staff officer serving in Barbados, "The U.S. military had won its first clear-cut success since the Inchon landing in Korea over thirty years before."[8]

We continued seeking out Cuban and Grenadian forces for several days, searching Cuban engineering encampments and some PRA bases and government buildings. Everywhere there were troves of propaganda, "Long live the Revolution, long live Grenada, Forward Ever, Backward Never" being the main theme. The sentiment felt out of place and forced.

There was sporadic and stiff resistance on various parts of the island by a mix of PRA and Cubans, but it did not last beyond the first few days. Notably the message to the militias did not seem to resonate; it was more common to find a uniform left on the side of a road than an active combatant. I took full advantage of this, swapping my deteriorating and by then heelless garrison jump boots for a size 12 pair of East German jungle boots (admittedly after exercising some of my own "strong religious feelings").

Castro was upset that his forces had not fought harder, reducing the commander to the rank of private and sending him off to Angola, from which he did not return. We had several encounters with uniformed PRA, the most stressful of which was a dance of sorts in a compound where one soldier had been hiding in the grass and was trying desperately to figure out how to surrender without surprising us and getting shot as we advanced. He succeeded.

After the initial week of targeted movements across the entire breadth of the island we began another several weeks searching for elements of the Grenadian revolutionaries, or more likely Cubans. As 2/505's commander Lt. Col. Keith Nightingale described it:

> By the end of the first day of the invasion, Austin's army had dropped its uniforms, put on civilian clothes and tried to fade back into the population. It didn't work. Virtually every small unit had the same story. They would arrive in a populated area . . . where they would be greeted by the populace as saviors, offered food, water and shelter. Very quickly, locals would point out the thugs who would be detained and flown to the rear for further interrogation and incarceration. This scenario continued throughout the period until all population centers had been screened and occupied by forces ranging from a squad to a battalion [command post]. The soldiers settled down and enjoyed a receptive population and its gratefulness.[9]

We covered all the country's mountains—Sinai, Qua Qua, St. Catherine's, the Grand Etang forest—in part believing if there were holdouts they would have withdrawn to the same areas escaped slaves took to in the eighteenth century, but in large part because we didn't want to miss anything out of simple inattention. We island-hopped to the second largest island of Carriacou and then to the tiny Petite Martinique, the most carefree of the Grenadines, five hundred people who were blissfully ignored by the revolution and the central government. In many places the presence of a medic drew people showing up at our encampment with ailments new and old and hoping for a solution. Private Williams reminded me that he was a medic, not a doctor, but I asked him to conduct a civilian sick call each day and do what he could.

There were also residual missions related to the earlier massacre around the fort. We provided security for the funeral of a young woman who was gunned down trying to protect Bishop. The troopers felt our service at the funeral was a particularly honorable task. The family was distraught but had come to terms with her death, seeing it broadly as service to her people. The mother did not want any members of the former regime present, and there was a near riot when some arrived. We put them back in their cars and sent them down the road. It was clear there were deep and long-standing wounds that had now been made worse and that it would take the Grenadians years to recover from all they had been through. And it was clear that having liberated the Grenadians from the coup plotters, as outsiders we would have little to do with their recovery process.

We were called on to capture those involved in the massacres, so on day 10 we exercised a rapidly planned cordon and search to capture the former regime enforcer Paul Sylvester (AKA Bully) on the island of Carriacou.

He was surprised anyone was still looking for him, but apparently a reckoning was to be had at the behest of the U.S.-friendly Grenadian leadership. We rounded up others who had been involved in the massacres and at one point attempted some of our own interrogations, on one occasion allowing some of the soldiers to slip into very mild abusive techniques. We quickly realized that interrogation is the business of professionals, a lesson America would relearn with the most painful consequences twenty years later in Iraq.

On November 23, a month in, we experienced our only casualty. After a night operation the troops were cleaning weapons in our police station billet when a .45 caliber pistol went off, drawing the attention of the platoon immediately to the yard where a machine gunner had accidentally shot Pvt. Dinesh Rajbhandary through the chest. We loaded Raj onto a door and put him on a jeep, taking him down to the medical facility, where he died on the operating table. Our medic Private Williams was distraught, believing he should have been able to save Raj in those first critical moments, even with his very rudimentary medical training. The doctor told him that the wound had severed an artery very near his heart; even if the incident happened outside the operating room it would not have mattered.

It was a devastating loss. Raj had always been the first to volunteer to walk point, the kind of soldier other soldiers wanted to work with and leaders wanted on their team. My most forceful image of him was in the Grand Etang Forest, where he led the platoon on a long movement through a glade when we bumped up against several PRA and he guided the platoon safely through the encounter. He was the son of a British mother and an Indian father and had joined the U.S. Army like so many of our generation, myself included, to find meaning and get his life on track. I wrote that night, "To watch one of my men slip from life was the dullest, sickest feeling I have ever experienced." He was the second youngest member of the battalion.

We sent Sergeant Shaver back to the States with Raj's body to attend the funeral service. I had written a long letter of sorts in one of the pocket-size green notebooks we used for operational planning. I wanted the family to know the kind of soldier Raj was, but just as important, what he had died for. By then there was no doubt on the island that the United States had done the right thing in sending in troops. It was, I wrote, as simple a rescue mission as one could conceive, and the Grenadian people would be forever grateful for what Raj and his family had sacrificed. Sergeant Shaver spoke of the nobility of the family and of Raj's friends, who were accepting his loss and what he had given his life for.

Few of us kept in touch with the family in the intervening years, but with the advent of Facebook one platoon member, Tom Maloney, got us all connected, and half the platoon convened in Raj's hometown of Lexington, Massachusetts, for the thirtieth anniversary of his death. There we met Raj's father, Uttam, his mother, Joan, and his siblings, Zoe and Kiran. We realized we should have done better when Zoe said the years were often lonely and they felt Raj's absence. The family was gracious beyond measure in receiving us and allowed us to participate in the rededication of a memorial for Raj at the local park, an impressive flagpole and plaza in a central location. It was then 2013 and we were ten years into two wars, so hometown ceremonies were more common. But for Lexington the significance of the loss of this extraordinary young man was undiminished. The mayor, townspeople, and the local vfw chapter, including veterans from World War II to Vietnam, came out for a very moving ceremony. They allowed 3rd platoon the honor of raising the flag. It was lost on no one that we were in Lexington, where American patriots first showed their mettle.

For many of us Raj's death began a period of intense introspection. And second guessing. For a year afterward the last thing on my mind before I retired at night, and the first thing on my mind when I got up, was what I could have done to prevent the shooting. More seasoned ncos were more philosophical. When you match men and ammunition for any lengthy period of time, one said, accidents happen. But it didn't happen on their watch. It was a reminder that that most clichéd of our American maxims, the one we reserve for hastily prepared July 4th speeches— "Freedom isn't free"—is accurate, at least for some.

What Did the Invasion of Grenada Change, and What Did We Learn?

While visiting a friend soon after the operation I found myself at Berkeley, where I saw a "Get U.S. Force out of Grenada" banner in the Latin American studies office. I was surprised to learn the operation was condemned by many in the United States; their operating assumption was that any intervention was wrong and should be opposed. It was roundly condemned by most international organizations, including the un, where a Security Council resolution that the United States vetoed and a General Assembly resolution it could not "deeply deplored the military intervention."

It was a confusing time. After Vietnam it was easiest to simply condemn any and all interventions, but when those interventions were conducted to stop killing, to restore democracy, or to prevent famine, is there still a right and a left? The question would get more complicated in the coming decades. Even at conservative Georgetown University, where I would later study, a prominent professor held that there was simply no way the Grenada operation could have been justified under international law. But international law, like domestic law, I reasoned with him, surely is intended in the end to protect the rights of the defenseless and to do the right thing on behalf of actual people, not simply follow a script.

The case for war, I thought, was best laid out by Stanley Arthur, a former British high commissioner in Barbados, who wrote, "The joint U.S.-Caribbean intervention in Grenada removed, not the People's Revolutionary Government of Maurice Bishop, which, although it had no strict constitutional validity, was at least initially popular, and was internationally recognized, but a totally unrepresentative and highly unpopular armed faction, which had no claims to legitimacy and could only be described as having hijacked the island in the wake of Bishop's murder. The temporary occupation of Grenada restored the right of the people to choose their own government, and at the same time removed what was seen as a major threat to the stability of the region."[10]

To the Grenadians it was even more straightforward. In 2013 I asked my friend Lou Crishok, then U.S. chargé d'affaires in Grenada, how the intervention was viewed. He said the anniversary of the liberation is celebrated as a national holiday, Thanksgiving Day. Lou explained why it is one of their most significant national holidays: "Following the liberation, Grenada has enjoyed forty years of peace and democracy. We will remember your fallen comrades in ceremonies here on the twenty-fifth."

U.S. forces stayed for another month after I departed to help keep order and train a new constabulary but were largely out by Christmas. A small contingent of other Caribbean states stayed for several years to help mentor the new force and guide the political process, and Great Britain assisted with advisors. As one of the advantages of still being part of the Commonwealth, Governor General Sir Paul Scoon set up an interim government that lasted for a year while the country prepared for elections. Gairy returned and retooled his old Grenada United Labor Party, which stood a good chance of winning the election of 1984. While cautious about direct involvement, the United States was not about to see the country return to where it had been before Bishop. Three rival parties, one consisting of Bishop loyalists and two smaller parties, were blended at the behest of other Caribbean leaders and with U.S. backing to form the New National Party, whose victory brought in Herbert Blaize as prime minister. The United States would include Grenada in its Caribbean Basin Initiative and was generous with assistance over the coming decade. To help with the tourism industry it also finished building the airport, which was christened the Maurice Bishop Airport when it was opened on October 28, 1984. And the medical school still functions, its graduates sprinkled across the United States in clinics and hospitals.

The kind of truth and reconciliation process that some recovering countries go through was not required in Grenada, since the military operation was a single incident that lasted only a short period of time. Twenty-four Cubans, sixty-seven Grenadians, and twenty Americans were killed. The various individuals who had been rounded up by us were jailed for a time, and then many were released. Some fourteen perpetrators of the coup, among them Austin, Coard, and Coard's wife, who was in some ways the steel behind the coup, were sentenced to be hanged after a three-year legal proceeding. In the end all were eventually released—Coard in 2007 and Austin in 2008, along with the two other longest-serving prisoners.

On the political side of the ledger the lessons learned were straightforward. Diplomatically you can't please everyone, but it helps to have someone, in this case the friendly Caribbean states, on your side. It also helps immensely to have the support of the people; the positive reaction of the Grenadian people bought grudging acquiescence from many, and in the United States gave the administration a needed boost. The decision-making process worked smoothly enough, with a capable national security apparatus able to manage several crises at once. Few who participated from Washington or in the field had any regrets.

There was a longer list of lessons learned on the military side, some of which may have been overanalyzed but which helped to retool how we fight and the ability of the services to fight together. The Goldwater-Nichols Act of 1986 that finally moved the services in the direction of a "purple" force and away from the stove-piped services that went into Grenada dealt with many of the communications, planning, and operational issues that had manifested. When we went to Kuwait eight years later we went with a much different conventional force, and the impact on our special forces was just as pronounced, something that would pay dividends in the wars to come. If the U.S. military is nothing else, it is a learning organization that tears apart old assumptions and assesses precisely what went wrong after each operation. In this regard there are few institutions like it in government.

I transferred soon after from the 82nd to 7th Special Forces Group, where I would participate in the Central American piece of our hemispheric strategy. In retrospect Grenada was one of the clearest things I would do in my career and remains so to this day—a rare black-and-white operation in what would be a haze of gray over the coming decades. And Central America would be one of the grayest.

THREE

El Salvador, 1984

Vaulting over Two Centuries of Development

"Left Behind": El Salvador's Long Game of Catch-up

If Grenada was to be an operation of several months, returning a small island to its natural roots, Central America and especially El Salvador would be a decades-long challenge of pushing against entrenched social, political, and economic forces to yield more equitable and functional societies. As Mario Vargas Llosa once wrote, it was not a matter of catching up a few decades but rather vaulting over several centuries. These were societies that were left behind in the 1700s.

The historian Walter LaFeber, in his classic work whose title says it all—*Inevitable Revolutions*—quotes the professor and author Adolfo Gilly as saying, "The war's purpose was not complex: it was to decide whether a very few could continue to dominate the many."[1] There was a Cold War overlay that caught the attention of the United States, but as a U.S. diplomat put it, "Even if it were not for Cuba and the Soviet Union, we'd have a revolution here."[2]

The domination in El Salvador by the few revolved largely around land. Its population density of 220 per square mile in 1980 was seven times higher than that of Honduras and Nicaragua, higher even than Haiti's. What evolved into one of the most repressive regimes in the hemisphere was largely about keeping the peace in a place where one study estimated the amount of land available to rural households declined from 7.4 to 0.4 hectares between 1872 and 1971.[3] The systematic concentration of land reflected a common dilemma in Latin America: to be competitive and earn hard currency, export crops had to be grown on large plots, but the concentration of land for export crops came at the expense of the peasantry. In most of Latin America it was possible, at least to an extent, to have both large *fincas* and small peasant farms. But in El Salvador it was more of a zero-sum game. As the journalist and political commentator P. J. O'Rourke pointed out, only partially tongue in cheek, to give each family the minimum acreage needed to support life would take six times more crop land than the country had.[4]

The politics of land tenure hit its first major road kill in 1932. After consolidating land for coffee plantations for decades and then seeing the price of coffee collapse, LaFeber comments, "the poor had little more to lose. Lines were being drawn for a series of struggles between the very rich and the very poor."[5] Agustín Farabundo Martí mobilized the peasants after a military coup truncated a stillborn democratic movement, bringing to power the strongman Gen. Maximiliano Hernández Martínez. The general ushered in fifty years of military rule, while presiding over the killing (and martyrdom) of Martí and thirty thousand workers and peasants in what is referred to simply as *La Matanza* (the massacre). The Salvadoran elites regrouped and spent the postwar period building an export-oriented infrastructure, which led to notable economic gains, nearly all of which accrued to them and their families. By the early 1970s the model was again starting to break down under its own weight.

The contest the United States was involving itself in had both an internal and an external component. Internally it was the long simmer of what in Special Forces we called "rising expectations," as the grotesque income inequality became more and more pronounced. By the mid-1970s political and insurgent organizations were challenging the regime both at the ballot box and through armed resistance. The human side of the challenge was presented in a period documentary, *Witness to War: An American Doctor in El Salvador*. As the prominent author and analyst Lars Schoultz describes the film: "In one scene a ragged Salvadoran peasant stands in a field with a large house in the background and, looking sadly into the camera, tells why he chose rebellion: 'I worked on the hacienda over there, and I would have to feed the dogs bowls of meat or bowls of milk every morning, and I could never put those on the table for my own children. When my children were ill, they died with a nod of sympathy from the landlord. But when those dogs were ill, I took them to the veterinarian in Suchitoto."[6] The anthropologist and activist Ellen Moodie explains, "The liberalization of the 1960s sustained growth in civil society and social movements. In the subsequent political closure of the early 1970s, these groups radicalized. But this time there would be no single *matanza* to silence their struggle."[7]

By 1977 the traditional military regime had lost its legitimacy after successive manipulations of elections, leading progressive officers to mount a coup in October 1979 to steer the country away from civil war. They forged an unsteady alliance between hardliners and reformers, trying to stave off the growing power of the popular organizations while maintaining the central position of the military in society. The center never really jelled, though, and the left was not impressed.

Bolstered by the fall of Nicaragua to the Sandinistas in July 1979, the country's guerrilla groups united under the banner of the Farabundo Martí National Liberation Movement (FMLN). The FMLN increasingly confronted the morale-deficient and base-bound army and carved out sanctuaries in many of the country's provinces. The military responded with mass roundups and in some places a scorched earth policy like Guatemala's. In the most egregious example, in May 1980, six hundred civilians were killed in the Sumpal River while attempting to escape into Honduras. Death squad activities increased, with five thousand killed in 1980 and twice that in 1981. The church increasingly sided with the left, and Archbishop Óscar Romero used his weekly sermons to memorialize the dead and demand social justice from the junta, until he was killed by an assassin while giving mass in March 1980. Lay leaders meanwhile had been forming Christian base communities in the countryside to both agitate for reform and provide an alternative model for agrarian societies.

Increasing numbers of Salvadorans sympathized with the insurgents and offered them active support. To moderate the face of the military junta, its leaders invited a Christian Democrat, José Napoleón Duarte, who had joined in March 1980 after returning from exile, to head up the body in December 1980. It was a shaky arrangement, and Duarte could not fully control the military or rein in the death squads.

Fearing the change about to take place in the U.S. administration as Carter passed off to Reagan, the insurgents mounted a "final offensive" in January 1981 with six thousand fighters, hoping to make the war's outcome a fait accompli as the Reagan administration took office. The offensive was an impressive show of force, in which two-thirds of the country was the scene of major military actions, a provincial capital fell to the insurgents, and a company of soldiers killed their commander and switched sides.[8] But the insurgency was ultimately beaten back and a semblance of order restored.

On the external side, the offensive did succeed in getting the attention of the incoming U.S. administration. Reagan and Carter were both concerned with communist encroachment in Central America, and Carter in January 1981 had reversed a four-year-old policy and authorized the resupply of lethal aid to El Salvador. Reagan was to increase aid several-fold to ensure the survival of the Salvadoran government as part of a dual policy that included supporting the overthrow of the Sandinista government in Nicaragua.

A February 1981 public white paper painted a picture of a progressive moderate government that was "working hard and with some success to deal with the serious political, social, and economic problems that most concern the people of El Salvador" but faced "clandestine military support given by the Soviet Union, Cuba, and their Communist allies to Marxist-Leninist guerrillas." The author dismissed any popular support for the guerrillas and was sloppy in places. Still, the administration stuck to its main premise: that communist encroachment in the hemisphere had to be actively confronted.

The Reagan strategy had military, economic, and political components. Militarily, the United States would dramatically increase assistance, taking account, as the activists Robert Armstrong and Janet Shenk put it based on personal observation, that by the summer of 1981 "it was clear that quick victory by either side was a mirage and that the Salvadoran Army by itself didn't have the means, the men, or the capacity to win the war."[9] When Capt. Michael Sheehan of U.S. Special Forces went as one of the early advisors to Chaletenango in 1981 he was told by his command to just try to help the unit hold on and stave off disaster. But help was on the way. Starting in 1981 and continuing for several years, the United States committed to a complete overhaul of the Salvadoran military.

The Cadets of the Barrios Military Academy into the Breach

In the summer of 1983 I played a small but central role in this overhaul when called to serve as an advisor to forty cadets from the Capitan General Gerardo Barrios Military Academy who were brought for training to Fort Benning in Georgia. The school was named after the founder of the professional Salvador military in the 1850s who was executed after coming up on the wrong end of a Central American wide political transition; we wondered if the naming was a kind of cautionary tale.

The Academy had been turning out fifteen to twenty officers a year in a highly controlled, very politicized, and garrison-bound program. We would train over four hundred officers in a single season in a blend of Officer Candidate School and the Ranger course. The intent was to turn out small unit leaders who could break out of their garrisons and take the fight into the mountainous jungle-like terrain the guerrillas controlled. It also included sessions on human rights and stressed the centrality of civic action in winning hearts and minds.

I was with the cadets 24/7 and got to know them well. They were largely from the educated middle class. One grew up in New

York and was in El Salvador on vacation when he was inducted
into military service while in a movie theater. I used him as my
anger translator. Their average age was nineteen, and most had five
months in the service. They normally would have had four years
in a spit-and-polish classroom learning how to conduct themselves
as a cacique in the countryside or the ops officer of the Presidential Guard. Now, in four months they would be thrust into the
field in one of the most brutal conflicts in the world.

They were somewhat reserved when they arrived but caught
on to our system of empowering NCOS and trusting the individual soldier to act with initiative. One used the word *convicción*
(conviction) to describe what motivates our soldiers, as opposed
to the *pena* (penalty), which they were accustomed to. And they
saw that it had broader implications in society—theirs relying
solely on the penalty of physical coercion rather than incentiviz-
ing working for the good of the group.

They were in extremely good physical condition, "gazelles," as
our battalion commander called them. We liked to pass the Ranger
students on our morning runs on the company street. And they
were immensely motivated, knowing that from a small program
we ran at Fort Bragg the year prior, sixty to eighty of their peers
had already been killed in combat, one of whom was the brother
of one of my cadets. They circulated some dark legends, the most
prominent of a lieutenant whose entire platoon was garroted
while they slept in a patrol base; he was captured and forced to
drive their corpses back to the barracks. What was a "small war"
to us was, proportionally, World War II to them.

I asked them to write a brief essay about themselves, including
something of their motivation for serving. A few said they were
drawn to the military lifestyle in the terms they had been taught
at the academy: *por la patria, vencer o morir* (for my country, con-
quer or die), "sovereignty and liberty, even at the cost of my life,"
that sort of thing. But most were seized with the current situation.
One said, "I see my people suffer attacks by the guerrillas, with
the destruction of towers, bridges, houses, machinery, haciendas,
roads, et cetera." Another wanted to guard against an "intrusion,"

and a third was tired of "living in a calamity." Peace was a common theme: "a country free and at peace," so that "peace prevails," a "desire to prepare myself mentally and physically to do my part to see my country free and at peace."

I had a longer discussion with one of my top cadets, Hector Alas-Luquez, the one who lost his brother the previous year. He spoke honestly, trying to summarize the conflict in ways an outsider would understand. He said that in the 1970s El Salvador had been a feudal country of rich landowners, a privileged military, and a government with disdain for human rights and the good of its citizens. The people saw in the guerrillas a kind of collective Robin Hood, taking from the rich and giving to the poor. But starting in 1980 the dynamic shifted. The government implemented land reform and banking reform and held credible elections. Meanwhile the guerrillas stepped up their campaign, destroying buses and roads and bridges. There was little work, and farmers couldn't get their products to market. Over time government forces were seen to be protecting people, "at least sometimes," while the guerrillas were "stealing from the poor and keeping it." And that was why he served.

There was one cadet who caught me off guard toward the end of the course. He was a thoughtful LDS kid, and we had attended church together most weeks. In a moment of insensitivity I asked him if he was ready to "get into the action." With a somber look he simply shook his head and asked, *Mi teniente, que estamos haciendo?* (Sir, what are we doing?) Unlike most he was sensitive enough to ask the "What is it all about?" question. He saw it as a bloody competition between two socioeconomic models. Everyone knew the society had to change. But he believed there had to be a better way to do it. It was probably a more common sentiment than we had picked up, and it gave me pause.

The cadets and I formed a unique bond, and they got me past the reticence I felt in accepting the assignment in the first place (not that anyone asked) because of the country's human rights record. In the end I saw them as young patriots, committed to keeping their country on the reformist path it had undertaken without

falling to a communist insurgency that would hopelessly compli-
cate everything, and frankly never reflected the will of the people.

They had worked intensely hard at each task at hand, always with
that legendary Salvadoran work ethic. I sent them off and wished
them well. We kept in touch sporadically, although I would not see
them again for eleven years. It was a long eleven years for most of
them. I had been a technician, training them on how to conduct
a patrol or ambush, lead soldiers, and integrate weapons systems,
but we all came to realize we were part of something much bigger.

Firing on All Cylinders

The arrival of the U.S.-trained units and the new officer corps, coupled with the addition of gunships and greater mobility, allowed the
Salvadoran Army to finally push the guerrillas into more remote
areas as it broke up guerrilla columns, reduced strongholds, and
ended their ability to mass. The Salvadoran military also started
various civic action programs and through training, mentoring,
and the inclusion of a new cadre of middle- and even lower-class
officers, improved the human rights picture.

While we were working on the security piece, the internal political and socioeconomic pieces were also in play. The economic
component of Reagan's program was as expansive as the military
buildup. The administration held that El Salvador's dependency
on a single crop and failure to diversify away from agriculture (just
20 percent of the economy was light manufacturing in 1982) made
it vulnerable to wartime disruptions and damages. This assessment
was affirmed by a 23 percent decline in GDP from 1979 to 1982.

To garner broad support, the National Bipartisan Commission
on Central America, led by a former U.S. secretary of state, Henry
Kissinger, issued its report in January 1984 calling for bold action
to meet the crisis in Central America with short- and long-term
economic measures.[10] In the short term the Commission recommended $400 million in balance-of-payments support to give gov-
ernments some breathing room, and over the long term $8 billion
to stimulate economic growth and pursue policies and programs
that would support a redistribution of wealth. The Caribbean Basin

Initiative became effective in January 1984, allowing for duty-free entry into the United States of a range of products. From 1981 to 1983 economic aid to El Salvador was three times higher than military assistance and followed only Israel and Egypt in the size of the program.

The administration also pushed for agrarian reform, with Reagan certifying that in 1982 20 percent of El Salvador's arable land was distributed and that by 1984 550,000 peasants, one-fourth of the rural population, benefited from land reform.[11] U.S. assistance and then a boon of remittances from new migrants to the United States led to GDP growth of 1.5 percent between 1982 and 1986. It wasn't a bull market, but it mitigated some of the damage of the war, and there were other creative programs that focused on schools, health clinics, and rural development. The Salvadoran Army also stepped up with modest civic action programs, although these often came on the heels of unpopular relocations.

While trying to reverse the dismal military picture and stave off economic collapse, the Reagan administration knew the most important long-term piece of the puzzle was political and called for a broad reformist agenda and improved human rights. In addition to land redistribution, the reform targets included banking, the judicial system, and the place of the army in society.

With the dramatic increase in aid came leverage, and Reagan used it to push for improvements in human rights. In October 1982 Ambassador Deane Hinton told the junta it must make progress "in advancing human rights and in controlling the abuses of some elements of the security forces" or risk losing U.S. assistance. Then in December 1983 Vice President Bush traveled to San Salvador to read the riot act to the government over continued death squad activities.

The last large-scale human rights violation had been the El Mozote massacre in December 1981, when as many as eight hundred peasants were killed during clearance operations, but smaller scale human rights violations would dog the army right up to the signing of the peace agreement. El Salvador remained a very raw society where violence was the most immediate currency of political discourse. But many would argue it was ultimately better than it would have been without U.S. involvement.

As it measures democracy, the United States generally looks to elections as the ultimate standard, and El Salvador was no exception. The administration would be supportive of a free and fair electoral process, while firmly guiding it to an outcome that would be acceptable to the U.S. Congress and helpful in resolving the conflict. In El Salvador this meant pushing for more moderate governments, as even during a raging civil war fought largely over socioeconomic inequality, the majority leaned to the right. In the March 1982 election, for example, even with a credible turnout, the right-wing candidate Roberto D'Aubuisson was elected. Knowing the backlash a right-wing government in El Salvador would cause both there and with skeptics in the United States, a parallel election for a constituent assembly led to his orchestrated replacement by the more palatable Álvaro Magaña, who would turn over the presidency in 1984 to José Napoleón Duarte, the previous leader of the moderate junta.

Magaña was not a great leader, but the country would not collapse, and he was considered a safe placeholder as better leadership emerged. Security, the economy, and the consolidation of democracy and human rights would be part of a long, long process of building a modern nation. For the time being, though, popular mistrust of the government and military remained high, and popular rage for change remained strong. With their external supply pipeline and captured weapons, the guerrillas could fight on by some assessments indefinitely. By the mid-1980s the military situation was at a total stalemate.

Counterinsurgency Rediscovered

While the war was in a holding pattern I was inducted into Special Forces, whose core missions of direct action, counterinsurgency (or foreign internal defense), and support to insurgencies paralleled the military component of our hemispheric strategy as carried out in Grenada, El Salvador, and Nicaragua, respectively.

Supporting, not countering, insurgency was the first mission of the early U.S. Special Forces units in the 1950s and 1960s, anticipating competition with the Soviets over Eastern Europe. Such support was also carried out in Vietnam, classically with the arming of the Hmong tribesmen in the highlands. Counterinsurgency was added to the Special Forces task list under Kennedy as North Vietnam stirred up insurrection in the south, and direct action was difficult to avoid since in creating Special Forces the army had massed some of the most skilled operators under a single banner.

Our focus in 7th Group, with the CIA taking on the Contra mission in Nicaragua, was counterinsurgency, by then a boutique mission not taught in any of the service schools, devoid of updated manuals, and without any prominent doctrine. But there were plenty of officers who had lived it in Vietnam, and we dusted off the old manuals.

The challenge was multifaceted. Coming out of Vietnam the U.S. Army had been burned by counterinsurgency and hoped never to have to do it again. This response was somewhat odd, since the counterinsurgency campaign was largely successful: South Vietnam in the end fell to conventional forces while the Viet Cong uprising in the south was spent and ineffective. But whatever the emotional reaction may have been to Vietnam, it was difficult to see a conventional way forward to the fighting in El Salvador. It was what President John F. Kennedy had described to the U.S. Military Academy graduating class on June 6, 1962, as "another type of war, new in its intensity, ancient in its origins—war by guerrillas, subversives, insurgents, assassins; war by ambush instead of by combat; by infiltration instead of aggression, seeking victory by eroding and exhausting the enemy instead of engaging him."[12] And it was making a comeback.

The Special Forces qualification course was great training, lavishly funded and creatively taught by Vietnam veterans. It attracted an older and more independent-minded cadre, with little patience for "big army." An A Team, the basic Special Forces organization, comprised a captain as commander, a lieutenant or warrant officer as executive officer, a team sergeant, an intel sergeant, two medical specialists, two demolitions specialists, two communications sergeants, and a light and heavy weapons sergeant. Members had a minimum of seven years of service, had the rank of sergeant or above, and spoke at least one foreign language. There was built-in redundancy, and given the independent environment teams worked in, everyone acted at a higher skill level, such that medics conducted field surgeries as if they were doctors and demolition sergeants worked like structural engineers. All were leaders, in peak physical condition, and as a team could train up to a battalion of irregular forces at a time or mentor a brigade in foreign internal defense. It was a liberating group to be in, but one with little tolerance for mistakes.

I was assigned to lead Operational Detachment Alpha 733 and immediately prepared for deployment to the Regional Military Training Center outside the northern coastal town of Trujillo, Honduras, where we had been training Salvadoran infantry battalions. Trujillo was a cheaper and less visible alternative to Fort Bragg and helped circumvent a congressionally mandated limit of fifty-five advisors in El Salvador itself. It was an idyllic setting, ten miles inland from a coast that included some of the better beaches in Central America, with jungle-filled mountains that rose straight up from the ocean before tumbling into hilly pine forests and meandering rivers on the inland side. For training purposes the place had it all: ocean and rivers for small boat operations, forests for conventional ops, jungle for patrolling, and swamps for infiltration. Trujillo itself was charming, in a Special Forces sort of way, with its one black-light discotheque and three restaurants, a Spanish fort that harked back to the days when it was the capital of Honduras and the final stop for gold shipments leaving the country, with an easily comprehensible and inviting culture, a mix of Afro-Caribbean Garifanos and Mestizo farmers.

In a seven-month deployment we trained a fifth of the Honduran armed forces in counterinsurgency and civic action and a new officer corps for Costa Rica's civil defense force. Costa Rica had been sitting out the war while the Contras used its territory as a sanctuary. The war came to them, however, when Sandinista mortar fire inadvertently killed two officers inside Costa Rica and the country realized it lacked a force that could even recover the bodies. The country's leaders decided it was time to quietly break with their nonmilitary tradition and at least train a small paramilitary force.

My share of the task at the Training Center was tactical training—running units through a rapid course of individual tactics, platoon ambushes, raids, and patrols, culminating with a company-size force-on-force exercise in the rugged Rio Claro Valley. We pushed the units hard defending bridges, cordoning and searching villages, and patrolling through the region's many valleys.

It was a training mission, and the threat was minimal. Still, we were reminded that none of our operations was cost-free. One afternoon during a punishing rainstorm a peasant from the nearby coast came to the base to report that he saw a plane crash into the ocean. As we unraveled the details we learned that our resupply flight, attempting a risky landing on the short runway in Trujillo, had clipped a wing with a wave while banking out to sea. It tumbled into the ocean, killing all seventeen on board. They didn't get a wall or a monument, probably not even a plaque. But they died in the service of their country, helping to sort out a part of the hemisphere the U.S. government believed was threatening.

I had excellent mentors in the art of counterinsurgency in this period, starting with Lt. Col. Reynaldo Garcia at Fort Benning during Salvadoran Officer Candidate School and again when I arrived in Honduras. The Cuban-born Garcia was trained at the military academy in Havana, fought against Castro, and was captured during the Bay of Pigs. He was eventually released to the United States and joined the Marine Corps and later Special Forces, fighting in Vietnam. His skill set was underappreciated until the conflicts in Central America broke out, when he was suddenly a hot commodity. He would go on to be the military group commander in Honduras.

Garcia was all about light, fast, low-tech small units. He advocated mules for mobility over jeeps, and 60mm mortars over 90mm recoilless rifles for firepower. These units needed to be able to saturate an area with patrols, raiding guerrilla encampments and ambushing and harassing them at every turn to limit their operating space. He had a full tactical-to-operational plan that he taught and mentored.

But Garcia saw the strategic picture as well, believing not in body counts but in effectively "outbidding the guerrillas." Killing guerrillas by itself, he said, "is like killing mosquitoes one at a time to get rid of malaria. You want to get rid of malaria? Get rid of the swamp. What breeds the guerrilla? First lack of respect for the population by the army and two, motivation."[13] To fix the first, stop abusing the people and meet their legitimate grievances. Garcia suggested the Central American governments "go to the large landowners and tell them unless they want to see their fincas confiscated in a half-assed land reform . . . they should: 1) build a school and hire a teacher; 2) build an aid station; and 3) pay the people a fair wage all year round."[14] Now let the guerrillas talk to the farmer and he won't have anything to say. Garcia also believed there was a certain breed of men who are destined to fight for someone, and we needed to get them to fight for the legitimate forces and simply treat them better than the alternative did.

A second mentor, Col. John Waghelstein, was the military group commander in El Salvador when I trained the cadets and would later be my group commander in Special Forces. He too spent hours with us in seminars and in the field sharing his experiences going back to Bolivia on the mission that captured Che Guevara, through Vietnam, and on to El Salvador. He required officers to read widely—histories like Edgar Snow's *Red Star over China*, Gerard Chaliand's *Revolution in the Third World*, practitioners like David Galula's *Counterinsurgency Warfare*, and the source documents: Guevara and Mao on guerrilla warfare, Giap's *Military Art of People's War*, and the Communist Party of Peru's "Develop the People's War to Serve the World Revolution," published in Berkeley, of all places.

Waghelstein warned that each insurgency is unique and defies "accepting those solutions that worked elsewhere."[15] He was convinced counterinsurgency would be with us for the foreseeable future, shifting from those who want to "shoot their way into political power" to groups with "drug-derived financing, or unextinguished ethnicity embers," one of the more prescient predictions made in 1994. But he stressed the commonality of three principles. First, keep it small. Reflecting on Bolivia, he said, "We did not take over the war, as sometimes tends to happen in those days, and our presence remained at a level that did not embarrass the Bolivians." He similarly believed that in El Salvador the fifty-five-man cap on advisors "helped keep the war as essentially a Salvadoran effort."

Second, Waghelstein believed military efforts must be backed up by real reforms. He was an active link to Col. Edward Lansdale's successful mission against the Huk insurgency in the Philippines in the early 1950s. The Huk leader Luis Taruc explained to Waghelstein in the 1970s, after his release from prison, that President Ramón Magsaysay's land reform undercut the Huk's recruiting base in northern Luzon, and the disbanding of the abusive militias and establishment of regular courts drew many to the government's side. Waghelstein helped guide the Salvadoran government to the first National Campaign Plan in 1983, blending economic, social, political, and military operations in two target departments.

Third was the simple primacy of human rights, "the one issue where it was demonstrable that those regimes that abused their citizens were much less likely to achieve positive popular support, a constant prerequisite for success in [counterinsurgency]." Waghelstein was uneasy, as we all were, with El Salvador's always imperfect and at times egregious human rights record but concluded that our engagement in the end saved lives and raised "the consciousness level of flawed allies."[16]

A third mentor I would work closely with several years later and who provided an intellectual bridge to the later insurgencies in Iraq and Afghanistan was the former assistant secretary of defense F. J. "Bing" West. His classic on Vietnam, *The Village*, covered a two-year period in the village of Bin Nghia, where a Marine Combined Action Platoon would live and fight with local provisional forces to wrest control of the area from the Viet Cong. First, West describes how the only terrain that matters in counterinsurgency is human terrain—the village, not the hilltop. Second, the political imperative goes to him who stays. The peasantry have little emotional attachment to either side, but considerable attachment to the one they think will be there tomorrow. Therefore the foreigners lose unless they can replace themselves with locals more capable than the local enemy. Third, like Garcia and Waghelstein, West paints a picture of limited numbers of U.S. troops well placed to draw out and bolster local forces, who do the bulk of the fighting. But the foreign force must be willing to die in large numbers; in West's village, seven of the fifteen marines were killed in action. Fourth, a foreign force must apply caution and restraint with firepower, which is useless or counterproductive if used indiscriminately. Ironically, this means the relative U.S. military advantage—high-tech, twenty-four-hour firepower—must be given up. And fifth, the cross-cultural imperative is essential. Respect and an affinity for your partner forces were the starting place for success. This was perhaps possible in Vietnam and Latin America, but it would prove difficult to implement in parts of the Muslim world, where U.S. forces were never able to integrate into communities.[17]

There were two other inputs to my understanding of counterinsurgency, both things I noted from observation but which took several years to internalize. The first was nationalism as a force for violent opposition. The Pulitzer Prize–winning journalist Stanley Karnow rehearses an incident in which U.S. Ambassador Maxwell Taylor scolded Vietnam's future leader Nguyen Van Thieu and others involved in the coup of 1964 as if Taylor "were still superintendent of West Point and they were a group of cadets caught cheating." He concludes, "The South Vietnamese leaders were competing against a Communist Movement that, having defeated the French, could rightly claim to represent the vanguard of Vietnamese nationalism." They could never preserve a sense of sovereignty when Taylor, "striving to push them into getting things done, behaved like a viceroy."[18]

The theme is more thoroughly developed in the work of Rufus Phillips, who was present at the creation of South Vietnam in 1954 and worked to help midwife the country through 1968 as one of Colonel Lansdale's field officers. Phillips writes:

> The "x factor" as Lansdale called it, was the human, political side of the war, about which Dan Van Sung, a perceptive Vietnamese nationalist, has said, "The anti-Communist fight in Vietnam is seventy-five percent political and twenty-five percent military. Yet, everything America is doing is directed to the twenty-five percent and nothing to the seventy-five percent." ... The official American view of the war missed the single most influential component—a South Vietnamese political cause worth fighting for—while the enemy, the Vietcong, framed every action as furthering its political cause against colonialism and feudalism, and for unification. ... We underestimated the motivating power of Vietnamese nationalism, and we failed to comprehend the fanatical determination of an enemy willing to sacrifice its entire people until only the Politburo was left. ... We thought in conventional World War II battlefield terms, when this conflict was at its heart a political one, a war of ideas and of the spirit.[19]

In El Salvador and Colombia we largely heeded this advice and were successful. But in Iraq and Afghanistan we returned to the Vietnam model, inspiring the *New Yorker*'s George Packer to entitle his 2009 review of Phillips's book "Why Rufus Phillips Matters."[20]

The second work that clarified much of what many of us observed on the economic side of counterinsurgency was Hernando de Soto's *The Other Path: The Invisible Revolution in the Third World*. De Soto suggested that the contest playing out across the hemisphere was not between capitalism and communism but rather between mercantilism and communism. He was not willing to credit the societies of Latin America, in which a bureaucratized and law-ridden state regarded the upward redistribution of national wealth as more important than the broad and equitable production of wealth, as being capitalist.[21]

De Soto concluded that to tackle the economic issues that were driving some of the populace to desperate measures, the government would have to lead the country into economic growth that promotes and protects property rights, facilitates access to business and transactions among individuals, and gives people the necessary confidence to save, invest, and produce.[22] In other words, they needed to embrace true capitalism.

Recently arrived in Honduras in December 1984, I could see there were "no simple solutions," although "the terms were clear enough: greater resources for the countryside, responsive governments, broad-based education." I had doubts about whether our version of open capitalism was right for Central America, given the rapacious nature of its economic system, and was convinced that instability would persist until they developed something resembling social democracies. However, as we learned more about the abject brutality of Sendero Luminoso in Peru and saw the genuine reforms in much of Central America, I conceded that what we were doing was as good as it got at that point, writing in February 1985, "The reforms have taken place," while the insurgents "have no legitimacy, no popular support, no grievances, and only want to destroy."[23]

By 1986 low-intensity conflict finally caught on and was all the craze in the policy community; the U.S. Department of Defense even got an assistant secretary for special operations and low-intensity conflict. Secretary of State George Shultz reviewed the range of conflict in a speech in January 1986, listing terrorism, democratic resistance in Nicaragua, insurgencies in Angola and Ethiopia, civil war and terrorism in Lebanon, the "rescue" of Grenada, and the struggle of the Afghan people against Soviet aggression. He pointed to ambiguity as the single feature they had in common and suggested low-intensity warfare was largely the Soviet "answer to our conventional and nuclear strength—a flanking maneuver in military terms."

Shultz pointed to three facets of our strategy. First, it would be an offensive strategy; we would "fight back." Second, we would mobilize nonmilitary tools, including the collaboration of governments, legal measures and sanctions, diplomacy, and security assistance, which Reagan believed "contributes as much to global security as our own defense budget." Third, it would apply new weapons, doctrines, and tactics to include covert operations.[24]

Our conventional forces had gotten all they needed with the new Air-Land Battle Doctrine supported by a new array of weaponry that would be on full display in the First Gulf War five years later. But we were also finding our footing at the lower end of the spectrum, blending political, economic, and military tools into a full spectrum of power to bring conflicts like El Salvador's to a successful conclusion.

A Viable Peace Deal

The point of fighting insurgencies was largely to get to a peace settlement in which progressive, viable, democratic forces prevailed. By the mid-1980s it was clear that with U.S. assistance and the marginal concessions to core political and socioeconomic demands, the rebels in El Salvador could not win outright. But with a continued inflow of weapons and an economic system that elicited such ingrained distrust, neither could the Salvadoran government. Over time the disparate guerrilla groups, writes the Latin American scholar Diana Villiers Negroponte, came to share the same goals: dismantle the Salvadoran government, destroy the existing security structures, and erect a new power and a new state.[25] With the election of Duarte in 1984 the guerrillas accepted the need to pursue dialogue and negotiation as part of a political strategy.[26] Through the offices of the church Duarte met FMLN leaders on October 16, 1984, at Las Palmas with a positive outcome. At a second meeting, in Ayaguelo, however, the process fell apart in shouting and both sides returned to the field.

But by this time international actors were emerging. Spurred by Nobel laureates, Colombia, Mexico, Panama, and Venezuela formed the Contadora Group, issuing a document of objectives in September 1983 to promote democratic action, end armed conflict, observe international law, and revitalize economies across Central America. The group was probably too ambitious for the time; its objectives were overly expansive, and the United States was concerned with unhelpful spillover to Nicaragua, where non-communist forces were too weak for negotiations.

A more successful effort that ultimately informed and shaped the final accord was started quietly by the Costa Rican president Óscar Arias under the auspices of the Contadora Group. He laid out a peace plan in February 1987 that called for a cease-fire, a national commission for reconciliation, amnesty for military officers and insurgents, dialogue, elections that would include ex-insurgents, and disarmament and demobilization of irregular forces. The five Central American presidents signed the plan in August 1987, winning Arias the Nobel Peace Prize and providing a long-range blueprint for peace.[27]

But in the medium term the war dragged on, the FMLN reminding the government with some frequency of its strength. In late March 1987 U.S. Special Forces Staff Sgt. Greg Fronius was killed along with sixty-nine Salvadoran soldiers when insurgents over-ran the garrison at El Paraíso, Chaletenango. Still, the FMLN could not permanently expand its holdings, even though it retained nine thousand men and women under arms and a presence in all fourteen provinces. The fifty-thousand-strong Salvadoran Army was also active nationwide but was criticized in a report by four U.S. lieutenant colonels who had served in El Salvador as being a nine-to-five force, lacking vision and aggressiveness. As former advisor Victor M. Rosello put it, "Both prize fighters fell in a heap from exhaustion."[28]

In June 1989 Alfredo Cristiani from the Nationalist Republican Alliance (ARENA) was inaugurated president, affirming again the rightward lean of the country. In early November, after months of preparation, the FMLN launched a major offensive across the country and on the capital itself, with attempts on the lives of the president, the vice president, and Assembly leadership. U.S. analysts believed it was an effort to raise doubts internationally about the government's ability to win the war, which the insurgents could translate into greater leverage in future talks.[29] The two thousand to three thousand rebels attacking the capital fanned out, and in many barrios, including upper-class neighborhoods, it took the army three weeks to expel them. Even then they remained on the outskirts of the city, poised for a second attack. The murder of six Jesuit priests, their housekeeper, and her daughter by a military unit on November 16 further damaged the army's credibility and accelerated demands for a political solution. The demands reinforced the fact of the military stalemate but also asserted the urgency in bringing the contest to a conclusion, with even wealthy Salvadorans feeling more exposed than ever.

In the end it was shifting leverage, not victory, that created the right conditions for peace. The conclusion of the Cold War eliminated the guerrillas' patrons, and the new administration of George H. W. Bush was less ideologically seized with Central America and more open to the UN acting as mediator.

After a month of preparation, in January 1990 the UN took the lead role in negotiations, but with considerable U.S. activity behind the scenes. According to Alvaro de Soto, advisor to the UN secretary general and a successful negotiator of the ultimate peace agreement, there were two key indicators that the parties were ready. First was the FMLN's Joaquin Villalobos stating publicly he wanted "a flexible, open, democratic pluralistic," not a Marxist, society. Second was Cristiani's declaration that negotiating with the FMLN was a goal of his administration, unlike Duarte, who would negotiate only if a complete ceasefire was in effect.[30]

De Soto called it a "textbook example" carried out in "laboratory conditions" of a successful peace negotiation, moving through peacemaking to peacekeeping and on to postconflict peacebuilding. He guided four sets of talks, culminating in December 1991 in New York City covering security force reform, demobilization, and land issues.

The parties initialed an agreement in the early hours of January 1, 1992. The United States, Villiers Negroponte suggests, "remained an impatient and interested observer" without actually leading or being directly involved in the talks.[31] With considerable fanfare President Cristiani, his cabinet, the *estado mayor*, and the FMLN *comandantes* signed the final accord in Chapultepec Castle in Mexico City on January 16, 1992. Many considered the outcome a total success.

A Postwar Often Worse Than the War Itself

In a 1959 cabinet meeting focused on how the United States should limit the appeal of the Castro government in the hemisphere, U.S. ambassador to the UN Henry Cabot Lodge suggested, "The United States can win wars, but the question is can we win revolutions?"[32] The United States had indeed won the war, but the revolution, such as it was, left many things undone.

The cruel math of the conflict was striking: 75,000 killed, 200,000 internally displaced, and a million, about a fifth of the country, having fled to the United States. Adding the conflicts in Guatemala and Nicaragua, the era was the bloodiest, most violent, and most destructive in Central America's post-1820 history.[33] But for all the grief, as Ellen Moodie sums up, "post conflict policy analysts have called the Salvadoran case among the most successful peace agreements in the post–Cold War period."[34] Defense Secretary Donald Rumsfeld and Vice President Dick Cheney even cited El Salvador as a model for Afghanistan and Iraq, as the analyst David Holiday puts it, "demonstrating how holding free elections in the midst of civil war or terrorist attacks will eventually weaken insurgencies and bring about democratic progress."[35]

There was a good deal about the peace accords that went well and left a lasting positive framework for the future. It allowed the FMLN to enter the political system and compete, "the most successful case in Latin America," according to one observer, "of a guerrilla movement transformed into a political party."[36] ARENA would continue to lead the country, with victories in 1994, 1999, and 2004, but with the FMLN playing a viable role in opposition while building a base locally. Participation varied wildly from election to election, but the electorate was motivated; in the 2004 election, as one example, 2.1 million voters went to the polls.

As El Salvador's socioeconomic problems and rising crime rate worsened, the country even decided to give the FMLN a chance, electing Mauricio Funes in 2009 and Salvador Sánchez Cerén in 2014. The country converged on the center as ARENA and the elites became more socially progressive, while the FMLN became more economically conservative. Throughout there was almost no political violence. For two sides whose legacy was the most violent period in the country's history, it was no small achievement.

The United States had played its political role well, supporting the UN in its key function as negotiator, supporting democratization and political institution-building for the parties, and advancing the reform process without taking over. The congressional limits on advisors had been helpful, ensuring that throughout it was El Salvador's war, not America's. As one American diplomat put it in 1990, "We don't want Cristiani to look like a U.S. puppet."[37]

The political transition also, Villiers Negroponte writes, ended the "historic political power of the Salvadoran Armed Forces and reduced them to a size necessary to respond to natural disasters." Taken with the entry of the FMLN into politics, this effectively "ended two centuries of landowning and military dominance of El Salvador. New forces gained the opportunity to lead."[38]

But beneath the surface were flaws that quickly manifested themselves. Villiers Negroponte points out that "the Chapultepec Accord omitted details concerning the process by which the FMLN combatants would be reintegrated into Salvadoran society, the transfer of land, and the availability of credit and training in new skills to men who had spent the previous years living by the gun. Alvaro de Soto considers this omission to be a 'significant casualty' of the accords and blames himself (as mediator) and the FMLN for not pursuing this issue."[39]

I joined the Foreign Service in 1991; after a two-year posting in Israel I was stationed in El Salvador in 1994 and had a good window on the initial postwar period. I met with two former guerrilla leaders in September 1994 and was pleased to hear that their main concern was the status of their migrants in the United States, not the war's aftermath in El Salvador. It was good to see them focused on mundane, temporal issues.

My family and I lived in the wealthy suburbs of San Salvador and even from our bubble in barrio San Benito could see the aftermath of the civil war and its horrific cost. But I accepted this result as necessary if things were ever going to change and wrote optimistically in October 1994 that I couldn't help but be encouraged by what I saw: widespread reconciliation, one of the most successful demobilizations in recent times, good economic growth, a rising middle class, and hope for the future. "Now if they can sustain this momentum until there is sufficiently broad political and economic empowerment so as to forever wrest from the elites the former control they had over the nation's capital and resources, we may have a real success story." Still, the "if" of broad political and economic empowerment was larger than I realized.

I invited the cadets I had trained at Fort Benning, now captains, to our home for a barbeque. They reported that none of their colleagues had been killed in ground operations, exonerating, I thought, our training. One had been killed in urban violence not related to the war, and Lieutenant Sosa, a helicopter pilot, crashed when flying too close to a tree line.[40] Captain Zaldana had left the army and was the chief of San Salvador's police force, in the throes of a massive new project. They were professional and well-presented, somewhat optimistic about the future, but realistic. They were grateful for the United States and our role and still concerned about a culture where people don't act out of social conviction but because of coercion. Above all they were completely apolitical. They were focused on managing either their piece of the security puzzle or their business interests, but they embraced a security force that was completely out of politics.

In the fall of 1994 I organized a roundtable for the Venezuelan jurist and UN official Enrique Ter Horst, who had taken over as UN special representative. Acknowledging pressure by donor nations to wrap up the mission, he said he hoped that Salvadoran institutions would be functional enough by October 1994 to close the UN mission. He had been working as an honest broker to deal with the many postwar disputes that were not publicly visible but needed to be resolved and saw the biggest threat as nonindemnified soldiers. He was concerned about the status of the police, citing their need for training, leadership, and equipment. But overall he believed the country was on track.

I took several regional trips to get a sense of how things looked on the ground, one to Libertad province along the Pacific coast and into the highlands. People there considered the right-wing ARENA Party the norm and were distrustful of the FMLN's ability to lead the country. There was no functioning jail or judicial system, and the police in every town in the province were without vehicles or gas. In one village the people came up with ways to provide the police with fuel, and in another there was one vehicle with no fuel budget for fifteen officers in a rural area. Crime was increasing rapidly; one small village pointed out that it was not just the rich who were being assaulted, but poor families as well. Still, there were bright spots. We met the president of the textile firm Hilasal, who was bullish on the orders they had from abroad for shirts and underwear. He showed us the medical clinic and school they were funding for workers' families, believing doing so made good business sense as it would attract better workers, but also doing so in support of a new spirit of social welfare among the wealthy.

Another window on the society was from my local church community, where I was the leader of the youth I mentioned in the introduction. Our youth were a funny mixture of optimism and despair. I wanted to take them camping to the cloud forest at Montecristo and asked if any of them had any gear. One answered, "Brother Mines, the only ones who have been camping in this country for the last fifteen years are guerrillas and the army, so no, we do not have any gear." But I had enough for all of us, and they were stunned at the natural beauty of a country that none of them had seen. They often let loose with their anxieties about the future, such as the *Este país no sirve* comment referenced earlier.

That phrase stuck with me. There was now a viable political accord, but the transition to a fully functioning state was a long way off. I wrote soon after that while we knew the country would never be Switzerland, El Salvador's hardworking and disciplined citizens certainly gave it the ability to land in a better place than when I first encountered the country in the 1980s. But I could also see it was a long road to fully excise its demons.

The accords had included a socioeconomic component, but it was something of an afterthought. Cristiani had argued that economic issues and alternative models should be debated at the ballot box after the FMLN entered politics, while the guerrillas focused only on the reintegration programs and land for their fighters. In any event it was difficult to build into an accord a new socioeconomic structure, particularly given international pressure to move forward on a neoliberal path. At its core, the policy analyst David Ucko writes, there was a "failure to address the social and economic imbalances that once provided the FMLN its recruiting base."[41]

It was a significant lapse. The political scientist Roland Paris quotes the former Central Bank president Carlos Acevedo as saying, "The success of the peace process in the long run will hinge on the country's ability to redress the great inequalities of wealth and power that imperil both economic and political stability." Paris goes on to say that the rapid economic liberalization promoted by international peacebuilding agencies "have enriched a very small portion of [the population] and left the most vulnerable sectors relatively untouched," working against the consolidation of a stable and lasting peace in El Salvador.[42]

The postwar economy had some bright spots, but always with caveats. From 1992 to 1995 international assistance equaled 3 percent of GDP.[43] I conducted a study of remittances in 1994 and found that they had surpassed coffee as the country's largest "export," at almost a billion dollars a year benefiting 800,000 people. Remittances were a large factor in stability, but migration also brought its own social issues, with broken families, torn local social fabric, and U.S.-inspired gang violence coming back to the country. And while remittances helped ameliorate poverty, the money mostly went to consumption, not investment.

Meanwhile unemployment remained stubbornly high; education did not improve markedly; and poverty, while by one measure decreasing, never fell below a third of the population. El Salvador also continued to have some of the highest levels of income inequality in the world, although the gap has closed slightly, from a Gini coefficient of 49.88 in 1995 to 43.51 in 2013.[44]

A sluggish economy remained steady under the FMLN governments beginning in 2009. Poverty dropped but was still in the 35 percent range; unemployment came down to 6.1 percent in 2017 from 7.7 percent in 2009, but with underemployment in the 35 to 40 percent range; and government spending rose from 13.5 to 15.5 percent of GDP, although still the lowest in a hemisphere whose average is 25 percent.[45]

These issues are structural and not easily solved. Researcher Elaine Freeman points out that between 2001 and 2010 Salvadoran businesses invested $8.7 billion abroad and tax evasion remains extremely high. In the fifth year of the first FMLN administration, 45.8 percent of Salvadorans believed the economy had worsened.[46]

The failure to move to a more equitable economic model led former combatants throughout the 1990s to remain pessimistic about the future and believe conditions had gotten worse.[47] This then played out against a security force transition that was abrupt and never completed. Demobilization, the analyst Charles Call writes, meant that "in the space of a few weeks, the dismantling of the FMLN and [government forces] had effectively cut the coercive forces available for deployment from some 60,000 to 6,000."[48] As many as 300,000 weapons ended up in civilian hands.

The new force was to be "softer" than what preceded it, with the military confined to the barracks and natural disaster duty, making the police the key security force. But the security force was lightly armed and tightly controlled the police to avoid the abusive behavior they had been part of in the past, and criminals quickly outgunned the new force. The rich could afford private security, so criminals turned on the poor. And the early crime wave had spillover effects to the economy at large. A close friend of ours who ran a textile factory was on the way to the beach with his American wife and children in early 1995 when criminals not only stole their vehicle but in the process made the entire family lie face down on the dirt road while they got away. They were not sure until the end of the incident whether they were going to be executed. The following Monday they were on a plane to North Carolina, never to return.

The weak economy, plethora of weapons, and demobilized killers opened a gap that never really closed, made worse by the rise of gangs, as the *Guardian* journalist Jonathan Watts describes: "These '*maras*' have their origins in the gangs of Los Angeles. When El Salvador's civil war ended in 1992, the United States deported thousands of illegal migrants back to their home country. Many brought back the violent street culture and mutual hatred that had shaped their existence in California. Over the past two decades, they have grown, evolved and wrecked more carnage in El Salvador due to the weak government, dire inequality, and a historical national tendency towards violence both in institutions and households." Violence, he writes, "has been normalized."[49]

The killing was at its peak in 1995, when there were 8,500 murders, more than double during some years of the war, a world-class 152 per 100,000 population (compared to 3.9 in the United States in 2013).[50] The number never subsided to anything approaching normal levels. In 2008 it dropped to 52 per 100,000, but rose to 76.6 in 2010, and by 2015 was at 108. It dropped slightly again in 2016, to 85, reportedly because of a gang truce.

This wasn't entirely the fault of a weak police system; the judiciary was only marginally effective, and prisons housed many times more than they were built for, with very weak levels of control. The archbishop of San Salvador was quoted in 2010 as saying, "Violence is undermining El Salvador and is capable of sinking the entire country."[51] In a 1999 survey, 55 percent of respondents cited crime as a justification for the toppling of the democracy.[52]

There is a social issue at work as well that is too seldom considered. We often look at nations like El Salvador in terms of sheer economics, believing that if good jobs are provided for young men they will not be criminals. But "good jobs" is not just an economic concept; it involves pride and belonging. There is simply nothing quite as humiliating as being a day laborer or landless peasant, utterly lacking in respect and personal empowerment, a situation made worse by the conspicuous consumption of the well-to-do. It is hard to get men and women who have tasted power to go back to a disempowered life on the farm or urban ravines, especially when they saw a life of crime as giving them status.

One gang member told the *New York Times* in 2016 he had been bullied as a youth: "[But] since I joined up, nobody screws with me."[53] The *Times* breaks down the economy of gang membership and shows how pitifully unprofitable it is for gang members, who in El Salvador are involved not in the transnational drug trade but in simple extortion, often from neighbors and bus drivers, several dollars at a time. But while extortion is not more profitable than legitimate work, it is, as one gang member said, easier than "cultivating vegetables and raising chickens."[54] So the gang system is pulling in "tens of thousands of grunts who are not seeking personal profit, only respect and a sense of belonging." One gang member summed it up in a notebook seized by authorities: "The day I die I want to be remembered as a strong street-level soldier, a committed delinquent, and at that hour that the shots ring out, I want to be marked 'present.'"[55]

I encountered a similar narrative in Ciudad Juarez when we were trying to build a new criminal justice system in Mexico as it went through a different but no less difficult institution-building transition while under fire. Juarez had topped Caracas as the most violent city in the world in 2010, and we were working with civic leaders and national and state security officials to try to bring the violence down. The mayor of the city told me of an encounter he had with gang members at a gas station. They were enriching themselves more than the Salvadoran foot soldiers but were still only marginally compensated. "Why do you do it?" the mayor asked. "Look," one said, channeling his best Pancho Villa, "it is better to live a year on your feet, than a lifetime on your knees." Life at a carwash, scrimping to get by, did not impress him. The gang members of that period in Juarez had a life expectancy of just a few years. But for those few years, they walked with swagger.

Este país no sirve. The gangs have sixty thousand members and operate in 247 of the country's 262 municipalities, compared to the insurgents' nine thousand combatants, who had a presence in all the provinces but were persistently active only in a few. By one estimate the gangs extort 70 percent of businesses, "dislodging entire communities from their homes, and helping propel thousands of Salvadorans to undertake the dangerous journey to the United States." The gangs also cost the economy as much as $4 billion a year. (U.S. aid to El Salvador through the entire conflict years was $6 billion.)[56] The analyst Jose Miguel Cruz recaps: "Central Americans have perceived the combined effects of political reforms, which replaced outdated institutions with inefficient ones, and economic adjustment, which slashed jobs and assistance programs, not only as a withdrawal of the state and its most fundamental functions, but also as confirmation that a better future awaits them elsewhere."[57] A recent survey showed that 40 percent of Salvadorans desire to leave the country.[58]

Lessons Learned: Making the Second Transition

El Salvador is one of the most tragic of the postconflict cases I experienced. The Balkans are always going to be a hotbed of unfinished ethnic business; Haiti and Somalia have deep-seated cultural and historical impediments to functional nationhood; in Afghanistan and Iraq we have made a series of mistakes in countries that would have been difficult in the best of circumstances. But El Salvador, with a textbook transition, proximity to the United States, high levels of energy, and a strong sense of nationhood, seemed like it should have had a better outcome.

One thing the international community could have done better was simply stay the course. As he left, de Soto warned, "A premature pullout in El Salvador could prove to be very dangerous. The job must first be finished. We are currently resolving the cause of the conflict in post-conflict peace-building, but we are far from completing this critical stage. Continued resource funding is essential, and the cost of peacekeeping is a mere pittance compared to the resources used during the war."[59] Villiers Negroponte told me she agrees, considering that collectively we simply did not finish the difficult task of building new institutions and helping to restructure society. There is the postwar, and there is the post-postwar.

The defense analyst David Ucko too believes "the quick dismantling of coercive capacity and the delayed establishment of new forces created a security gap at an acutely fragile moment." He points to the need to "ensure public security during the entire war-to-peace transition. It is not the case, as one might expect, that war-to-peace transitions bring ever-greater stability over time: often it is the exact opposite."[60] Analysts at RAND agree and believe armed civilian police observers would have helped fill the gap, in addition to more attention to the development of a functional judiciary, prison system, and police.[61]

Roland Paris argues that the international community has the sequencing wrong in working with postconflict societies and cites El Salvador as a prime example. He quotes the political scientist Kimbra Fishel, who makes the case that applying a "widespread structural adjustment policy has resulted in micro-economic difficulties which exacerbate the initial social and economic causes of conflict."[62] Paris concludes that peacebuilders should construct "the foundations of effective political and economic institutions *before* the introduction of electoral democracy and market-oriented adjustment policies," a strategy he calls "institutionalization before liberalization."[63]

Whatever could have been done better, there will never again be the levels of support for El Salvador that there were in the 1980s, so it is the struggle of Salvadorans now. They will need to effectively lead the country through a "second transition," as some have called it. But first, suggests Sonja Wolf, a researcher with the Center for Economic Research and Instruction, they need to get at the heart of elite resistance to democratic reform and discover whether debilitated institutions are limited by a lack of resources, expertise, or a combination of the two.[64]

We also need to recognize that the challenge itself has changed significantly. Villiers Negroponte points out that "in the 1980s, the challenge to citizen safety came from a powerful state, [but] now the challenge comes from non-state actors, such as the maras [gangs] and transnational criminal actors."[65] This is no small technicality and presents us with a malleable, resilient, and persistent enemy. Unlike the insurgent factions that had rigid leadership supported by foreign actors who would one day lose interest as their ideology went bankrupt, the new hemispheric threats are motivated by money and power. These are not values they can be easily talked out of, and coercing youth who have a fatalistic approach to life to begin with is going to be a challenge. It will require even more resources, more societal cohesion, and more creativity than fighting a war.

This is the challenge of the second transition. El Salvador along with the other Central American states is seeing this more clearly, and the United States, persistent to a fault, continues to seek creative ways to support their efforts. In 2015 the country, with U.S. support, launched Plan El Salvador Seguro, drawing in the private sector, NGOs, the international government, and the whole of government to attack the root causes of violence. The program has shown tangible progress.

El Salvador may yet arrive at a point of truly consolidating the coercive power of the state that so many bled for, or fled from, in a country worth living in. A state of which its youth will say, *Este país si sirve*.

PART TWO

Humanitarian Intervention and
the Fragile State Circuit

FOUR

Somalia, 1994

Resisting Nationhood

Darwinian Pastoralism Meets the Cold War

While I was serving in Israel in 1993, a cable hit my queue asking for one hundred volunteers to shore up the UN mission in Somalia as political, development, economic, and security officers, a deployment of diplomats to the field we hadn't attempted since Vietnam. The rationale was that with the end of the Cold War we would need more flexibility in deploying resources and personnel, and more than just military forces to achieve what appeared to be a wider range of objectives. It seemed intriguing, and I put my name in, along with two others.

Somalia was the first real test of the limits of post–Cold War humanitarian intervention. During colonial times the country had been divided between the Italians in the south and the British in the north and it remained one of the most rootless nations on earth, 70 percent of the population being pastoral nomads who followed their small herds. It has a desperate landscape. I would later write of Baidoa, known as "the city of death" during the famine, that it was "back to normal now, but normal for Somalia means the land mocks any attempt to plant and harvest and the sky sputters rather than pours. Granted, man has been uncooperative in what little the land could produce, bringing in foreign animals like goats that tear vegetation out by its roots, leaving the soil to be swept away. But even without man's mistakes it is still a cruel, tough, unyielding environment."

Somalia is the size of Texas but elongated such that it stretches the equivalent of Georgia to Vermont. Besides being one of the most nomadic on earth, its population is one of the most homogeneous. 85 percent are Somali Muslims and the rest Bantu. The south has rich agriculture belts, and the north was once the butcher shop of Aden, Yemen, which the British garrison depended on for its supply of meat. But all this was conditioned on a very tenuous balance of population and resources.

Somalia traditionally had one of the highest birthrates in the world, seven-plus children per woman, under the assumption that half would die. With the extension of modern medicines through humanitarian groups, that assumption no longer held true, and from the 1970s the country was in a perpetual population boom. We would later work to solve a local conflict, of which I would write, "The theme is people fighting over wells and grazing rights. As population increases this conflict naturally intensifies. No amount of international intervention will change this basic fact. It will solve itself when there are fewer human beings competing over scarce resources. This is the whole Somalia question in a nutshell."

This sort of Darwinian pastoralism also imprinted itself on the country's politics. After having a light colonial footprint, the Republic of Somalia became an independent state in 1960 as the British and Italian territories joined. In 1969 military officers led by Siad Barre staged a coup; Barre would rule the country for the next thirty-two years, pushing an "anti-clanism" philosophy (even going so far as to outlaw asking the question "What is your clan?"), while formalizing a system that favored just three of the country's clans, all related to him.

Somalia's prime location at the mouth of the Red Sea, where 11 percent of the world's petroleum transited, made it competitive terrain during the Cold War. The country fell in with the Soviet Union in 1974 as Barre developed what he called "scientific Islamic socialism." Ethiopia too was with the Soviets, but by 1977 the United States had started to lure Somalia away, helped by the Ogaden War in which Somalia tried to occupy the part of Ethiopia where one million Somalis lived. The Soviets withdrew support from Somalia in a nod to the more significant Ethiopia. By 1980 Somalia had fully switched sides, something I experienced firsthand when I befriended a Somali lieutenant at the Infantry Basic Course in Fort Benning who had been trained in the USSR the year prior. I told him he was the ultimate cold warrior. Cold War or not, he said, he was glad to be in Atlanta, not Moscow. The Cold War period had also started a trend of centralizing Somalia's resources in Mogadishu, thus drawing clans to the capital to compete for the new spoils.

Opportunity and Limitations in the Post–Cold War World

With the collapse of the Soviet Union the United States rapidly lost interest in Somalia. In early 1991 Barre's regime fell to rebel factions, who had been frustrated for decades at missing the spoils of government. The United States was embroiled in the aftermath of the First Gulf War and after evacuating the embassy in Mogadishu amid factional fighting there in January would not be a key player as the country spiraled downward.

The various factions vied for control, and fighting alternated with efforts at reconciliation. The contest for power came down to Ali Mahdi Muhammad and Mohamed Farrah Aidid, each with factions and fighters behind them. Efforts by the international community to reconcile the parties and build a government resulted in Ali Mahdi's being sworn in as president in August 1991, which was immediately contested by Aidid. The factions continued fighting, resulting in tens of thousands of deaths, in a scenario similar to what Kabul was experiencing: post–Cold War loss of interest by the superpowers taking the lid off long-standing fissures, leading to warlords competing for power in a country awash with weapons.

With the fighting came bottlenecks in the Port of Mogadishu for humanitarian aid, and starvation manifested by January 1992, with thousands dying in makeshift camps. The UN Security Council called for urgent measures to pacify the country enough to ensure the flow of humanitarian aid, and the UN Operation in Somalia (UNOSOM) was launched in April. At first the factions, including Aidid's, agreed to allow UN troops into Mogadishu to guard food convoys, but within weeks Aidid supporters claimed UN flights were transporting money and equipment to Ali Mahdi's forces. The flow of aid was suspended. UN military observers arrived in July to explore more forceful and urgent options as by August an estimated 1.5 million people were on the verge of starvation. A game of humanitarian cat and mouse with Aidid ensued as aid by then had become the country's main source of revenue.

UN forces attempted to open the aid corridors but were losing in a race against widespread famine. An old word, "technical," was coined anew for a machine gun–toting pickup truck that offered "technical assistance" to the aid agencies for the right to deliver assistance. After the surprise victory of Bill Clinton in November the Bush administration decided as its final act to lead a military intervention that would, in a limited fashion, establish enough order in the country to allow assistance to reach the people.

In a speech to the country on December 4, 1992, President Bush described a total breakdown of government in Somalia in which seven thousand tons of food aid was bursting out of warehouses while Somalis starved less than a kilometer away. He told the American people that only the United States had the ability to place a large security force on the ground quickly and thus save thousands of innocent lives. He promised the United States would limit its involvement by passing off quickly to a UN force, not staying one day longer than necessary.

There were some questions about U.S. interest in a place like Somalia to begin with. I believe many Americans, myself included, tended to see it as "humanitarian national interest." We simply accepted that while a country like China can do nothing while watching untold suffering, we cannot. Americans have often supported military action to stop a people from falling below a point of human anguish that we simply find unacceptable.

Still, this situation came with several inherent contradictions, the most glaring of which was the stated intent to quickly lose interest and turn the mission over to an organization that had already proven incapable of maintaining order on its own. And many wondered if, as in the past, we were underestimating the tenacity of our foe and the political complexity of what we were inserting ourselves into. But we did have the power to stop a famine, and that is no small thing.

My Brother and I against the World: The Somali Tar Baby

In addition to a difficult landscape and challenging history, Somalis had many perplexing societal factors that would play out negatively for them and for us. The late Dr. Said Samatar, a Somali professor at Rutgers, said in 2002 that the Somali polity is shaped by an overriding principle: lineage segmentation. It is best explained by the Arab Bedouin saying "My brothers and I against my father, my father's household against my uncle's household, our two households against the rest of our kin, our kin against non-family clan, my clan against other clans, and my nation and I against the world." In lineage segmentation there are no permanent enemies or permanent friends and no fixed loyalty, only "a permanent attention to the availability of self-improving opportunities." Segmentation, he concludes, "is a social system that results in, and sanctions, institutional instability as a cultural norm."[1]

The historian and longtime observer of Somalia Charles Geshekter explains how this played out at the national level: "Somalis once considered nationalism a force for integration and unification. Today, they remember the nation-state as a divisive force that provided no one with a safe environment.... Beyond redemption of the Somali lands [from Ethiopia], there were few national objectives that Somalis agreed upon. Relationships became expendable once clan lines were crossed.... By 1993, Somalia lost all sense of national cohesion or concern for the well-being of its people. No intellectual clarity, ideological principles, or political will existed to resurrect the country."[2]

There was a martial element to the Somali puzzle as well, as an Irish lieutenant who was posted to Somaliland when it was a British protectorate expressed in the 1940s: "The Somalis are a nation of warriors and poets.... It is natural in a country like Somaliland for the very strong and very brave to become heroes, even if their careers include unbelievable slaughter and cruelty. Most people can never defeat the killing environment of heat, drought, barrenness of country and poverty. But when a man rises up out of that environment, as the Mad Mullah did, they cannot but be tremendously impressed by him, even if he treats them badly."[3] (Samatar reminds us that the campaign of the charismatic rebel leader Mohammed Adbullah Hassan, the "Mad Mullah," between 1898 and 1920 led to a million deaths on the Somali side and precious few infidels.)

The historian and anthropologist I. M. Lewis amplifies this: "Political ascendancy . . . derives from superior fighting potential. In Somali lineage politics the assumption that might is right has overwhelming authority and personal rights . . . can only be defended against usurpation by force of arms. Political status is thus maintained by feud and war, and self-help—the resort of groups to the test of superior military power—is the ultimate arbiter in political relations."[4]

Two things I would add from my own observation. First is that to the Somali, everything is personal and everything is taken personally; there are no bureaucratic firewalls or protocol distancing measures between leaders. Everything there works on personal relationships and few problems can be solved without a face-to-face meeting. Relationships are constantly tested and limits constantly explored.

Second, the tenacity of Somalis can also be turned to good, which is why all the overseers on Isak Dinesen's Kenyan farm in her memoir *Out of Africa* were Somali, not Kenyan. They were the ones who could get things done, and they did so through personal dominance and organizational skills, not through direct resort to violence.

The American official in 1992 closest to Somalia was Ambassador Smith Hempstone in Kenya, who thought the whole operation was misguided. In a December cable to Undersecretary of State Frank Wisner he wrote:

> I must confess that I have been bemused, confused and alarmed at the Gadarene haste with which the [U.S. government] seemingly has sought to embrace the Somali tar baby. Aside from

the humanitarian issue—which admittedly is compelling (but so is it in Sudan)—I fail to see where any vital U.S. interest is involved. Statecraft, it seems to me, is better made with the head than with the heart. The first question that needs to be asked is how long the American public is willing to put up with a major, expensive U.S. presence in Somalia and how large a butcher's bill it is prepared to pay. I think it is safe to assume that a 30,000-man force could be landed in Mogadishu and other Somali ports with few or no American casualties. But . . . Somalis . . . are natural-born guerrillas. They will mine the roads. They will lay ambushes. . . . A sniper occasionally will knock off one of our sentries. If you liked Beirut, you'll love Mogadishu.

To what end? To keep tens of thousands of Somali kids from starving to death in 1993 who, in all probability, will starve to death in 1994? . . . Just how long are we prepared to remain in Somalia, and what are we prepared to do: Provide food, guard and distribute food, hunt guerrillas, establish a judicial system, form a police force, create an army, encourage the formation of political parties, hold free and fair multi-party elections? I have heard estimates, and I do not feel they are unreasonable, that it will take five years to get Somalia not on its feet but just on its knees.

. . . Finally, what will we leave behind when we depart? The Somali is treacherous. The Somali is a killer. The Somali is as tough as his country, and just as unforgiving. The one "beneficial" effect a major American intrusion into Somalia is likely to have may be to reunite the Somali nation: against us, the invaders, the outsiders, the kaffirs. . . . Do I have a better idea? Not really. I do not think Somalia is amenable to the quick fix so beloved of Americans. . . . Send an American envoy . . . to Mogadishu. . . . (I'll go if no one else will). . . . Encourage the Somalis who want peace. Leave them alone, in short, to work out their own destiny, brutal as it may be. . . . Inshallah, think once, twice and three times before you embrace the Somali tar baby.

Regards, Hempstone.

Given how far along planning for the U.S. intervention was it would have been unlikely for a single cable to derail it. And unless it had moved at lightning speed and had given an unimpeachable rationale for not intervening, these sorts of cables don't tend to influence decision making. But it is one of the classics of Foreign Service reporting, for whatever that is worth.

I later became close to one of the longest serving UN officials in Somalia, Leonard Kapungu from Zimbabwe, who was involved with the mission from the beginning. He described how the mission evolved from humanitarian coordination to national reconciliation, to a U.S.-led armed humanitarian intervention, to peacekeeping, to peace enforcement. "All these things could not have been planned when UNOSOM I was established in April 1992," he concludes. "We have therefore not been in control of events; *we followed where events led us*."[5]

Somalia presented outsiders with a mass of contradictions for which, even with two decades of hindsight, there are no good answers. It was impossible to see a way forward in the long term without a state of some sort to manage the country—providing security, building an infrastructure, and tamping down internal disputes so that, at a minimum, the people were not living in a constant state of famine. But building what Geshekter called an imported "ethos and organizational structure" in a country "with the largest nomadic population in the world" was destined to be a long, difficult process.[6]

We were entering a place where force of arms was the only real arbiter of power, where governance would be difficult to establish, and where life was cheap. And we were committed only in a very limited way to seeing it through.

1993: The Year of the Ranger

On December 3, 1992, a day prior to President Bush's speech, the UN Security Council passed Resolution 794, authorizing the creation of a U.S.-led Unified Task Force (UNITAF) under Chapter 7 of the UN Charter (allowing the use of force to achieve the objective), as opposed to Chapter 6 (allowing force only in self-defense).

This would be the first time a UN Security Council Resolution would be used to secure safe passage for humanitarian aid, and only the fourth post–Cold War UN-sanctioned military operation, after Gulf I, Cambodia, and the Balkans.

The Somalia operation would vacillate back and forth between Chapters 6 and 7 and was often referred to as 6.5. There was a desire to keep it in the peace-building realm but with the ability to use force if necessary. It was a gray area since Chapter 7 is usually reserved for compelling threats to international security, but it would have been impossible to achieve anything in a strict Chapter 6.

Operation Restore Hope began on December 5, 1992, with reconnaissance units on the beaches and harbor and the 2/9th marines landing in Mogadishu, where they set up camp unopposed at the port and airport. U.S. forces pushed out from the beachhead and were joined by forces from twenty-seven other countries as they established a presence in the four provinces of the country's southeast, the limit of their mandate. By the end of the year twenty-five thousand Americans and twelve thousand foreign troops were on the ground.

The UN at this point took a back seat on the security side but was still active politically. It added 3,500 civilian and military personnel and prepared for the transition of the operation in a few months' time. An Iraqi, Ismat Kittani, had taken over as the UN's special representative of the secretary general (SRSG) from the Algerian Mohamed Sahnoun on November 8 and was joined by the Guinean diplomat Lansana Kouyaté in early 1993. Kouyaté was a uniquely gifted diplomat who was simply ideal for the Somali landscape. His patience, persistence, and skill in unraveling the historic and cultural issues with the Somali clans was unlike anything I had ever seen. He was described by U.S. diplomat Steve McIlvaine, accurately in my opinion, as the equal of renowned U.S. peacemaker Philip Habib.

While the military forces pushed out into the countryside to secure the new humanitarian routes, the UN team worked to forge agreements among the clans that would make that security last.

They hoped to reach a point where the clan leaders saw their interests best served not by holding food hostage but by facilitating its flow. The modalities would remain unchanged for a year—as Kapungu put it, "Commencing with Ambassador Sahnoun we shuttled from one leader to the other; the leaders never came together. They were Somalia's leaders but they were enemies. Even those who shared the same objectives were never meeting."[7] As the shuttling continued there was always an outlier, which led to a period of renewed courtship and concessions. And usually the outlier was Aidid.

Kouyaté at this point took on the task of bringing these partial efforts together, resulting in the Addis Agreement of March 27, signed by all but the Somali National Movement, the controlling movement in Somaliland that by this time was seeking full independence. The process leading to the Addis Agreement was classic Kouyaté, shuttling between factions one at a time, building agreement between two or more, maintaining momentum and showing small gains, and finally leaving them with a text and an ultimatum. The agreement was signed by fifteen factions and was the most complete pact to date. It envisioned a rebirth of Somalia, with disarmament, cease-fires, new security forces, and four political bodies from the national to the district levels in a quasi-federal arrangement.

The U.S. exit strategy hinged largely on the ability to make a quick handoff to the UN, which would now take the lead militarily with a force of 22,000 troops and 8,000 logistics personnel and civilians, backed up by an American quick reaction force of 1,200. The UNOSOM II mandate shifted to a more fulsome political reconciliation and expanded the mission to the entire country.

Considered critical to this handoff was emplacing a trusted U.S. official as SRSG, something Washington policymakers thought would give them control over the mission and improve the quality of its leadership. It was a fateful decision that resulted in the appointment of Adm. Jonathan Howe. Howe was one of the most respected political-military figures in the Washington bureaucracy, with successful command at every level of the navy and successful leadership at every level of the national security apparatus. Missing from his résumé, however, were the interpersonal and cross-cultural skills needed to move the Somali clans, something that in fairness very few possessed. Howe took over March 19, and Kouyaté stayed on as deputy SRSG.

From the back seat, U.S. officials quickly began pushing the UN to do things that the U.S. force had not been able to do when it was in control. U.S. Liaison Office chief Bob Gosende pressed Kouyaté to ignore the warlords and focus on broader participation of civil society in the way forward, "lest the warlords will dominate and manipulate the political process at the expense of the Somali people." He also urged the arrest and trial of "war criminals like [faction leader Mohammed Said Hersi] Morgan and [strongman] Omar Jess" and the control of Aidid's radio station. Kouyaté disagreed firmly on the first point, stressing, "The reality in Somalia is that the warlords cannot be totally ignored, but depreciated, by expanding the participation of civil society." He asked how it was that UNOSOM with a much-diminished force would be able to achieve what UNITAF with its robust force could not, and assured Gosende that they were aware of the radio issue and would work on it, but short of a hostile takeover.[8] Kouyaté retained a clear sense of what was possible and kept close contact with the clan leaders throughout.

It was a very tentative arrangement, with multiple points of possible friction and unraveling. On June 5 Pakistani troops moving to search for weapons at Aidid's radio station were misconstrued by the militia to be seeking to shut the station down—understandable given its constant stream of anti-UN propaganda. The UN had a weak political section at the time, and the United States took a hands-off approach to day to-day UN operations. As a result, there was simply no one who could effectively blend the political and military sides of the operation and anticipate the reaction of the Somali factions and clans to armed UN actions.

Aidid's forces lashed out; twenty-four Pakistani troops were killed, and the commander of the unit was horribly mutilated. The

Security Council, recognizing the importance of a strong response not only for the Pakistanis and the UNOSOM mission but also on behalf of peacekeeping everywhere, passed Resolution 837 the next day. Many felt it was too hasty a response and fraught with problems. It allowed for "all necessary means" to be brought to bear against those responsible for the attack and singled out Aidid's faction. It also called for more troops as well as armored vehicles, tanks, and attack helicopters. Howe put out a $25,000 price on Aidid's head and cut off communications with him and his clan. Aidid already had disdain for the UN because of Secretary General Boutros Boutros-Ghali's support for his former enemy Siad Barre when the UN official was Egypt's foreign minister. Now UNOSOM was at war with Aidid, whose young rural Habr Gidr toughs had already established themselves as first among equals with the other Somali clans after being the muscle that brought down Barre and now dominated Mogadishu.

But others of the Habr Gidr were less interested in fighting and more interested in the spoils of the aid industry—the only thing producing revenue in Somalia at the time. Many of the subclan leaders sought reconciliation with the UN and Americans, and dozens of them, absent Aidid, gathered in a compound on July 12. When U.S. intelligence picked up the gathering the force commander suggested it provided an opportunity to take out the leadership of the Habr Gidr in a single attack.

Some seventeen helicopters ringed the compound, pummeling the house with sixteen TOW missiles and thousands of rounds of cannon fire. Fifty-four of those present, including elders, religious leaders, and businessmen, were killed, and dozens wounded. Four journalists covering the event were torn apart by an angry mob seeking any Western targets they could find.

Howe had opposed the attack, convinced by then the most productive policy was a more surgical approach to get Aidid without alienating the entire clan. But he relented when U.S. forces convinced him this was an opportunity to decapitate his nemesis. It was a catastrophic decision and again reflected the lack of skilled political advisors on the U.S. side and a total lack of coordination between the United States and the UN. Events by now simply took on a life of their own.

The attack galvanized the entire Habr Gidr clan against the outsiders. Its small hit-and-run ambushes evolved into more sophisticated attacks using improvised explosive devices, one of which killed four Americans on August 8, and another of which wounded seven two weeks later. Aidid's forces also began to modify their rocket-propelled grenades to take down helicopters as they by now accepted that the primary threat would come from the air.

Howe had been pushing for a force that could pull off a more surgical raid, and with the August casualties Washington finally conceded. It sent a task force that could provide an outer cordon of Rangers, a search team of Delta Force, and support from TF-160's helicopters. The fresh force began carrying out raids soon after arrival and had developed a straightforward template for their operations. But on October 3, while searching for several of Aidid's lieutenants, one Blackhawk and then another was shot down. The ensuing melee left eighteen Americans dead, one captured, and the overall mission completely transformed. The battle included the most intense urban combat by Americans since Hue in Vietnam and examples of sacrifice and courage that left me spellbound. Two Delta Force operatives, SFC Randy Shughart and MSG Gary Gordon, willfully gave their lives for their comrades and were posthumously awarded the Congressional Medal of Honor for their actions.

I had not been in touch with the Somalia team for months as I passed the time in Tel Aviv, but seeing the carnage of the street battles in Mogadishu and the face of CWO Michael Durant on television in captivity reenergized my desire to get there. I pressed Maj. Michael Sheehan, the military advisor to then U.S. permanent representative to the United Nations Madeline Albright, and he slotted me as Howe's executive assistant, managing military liaison and staff coordination.

The Somalia policy hit hard domestically, as few Americans seemed to know we even had service members at risk in Somalia. While Durant was still captive, the president reminded the nation of a time when "our consciousness said: enough," and outlined four purposes for our forces going forward: force protection, keeping the humanitarian lifeline open, preventing a return to anarchy, and facilitating agreements for longer term stability. He decried any larger political objectives. There was no way to dress up the incident, but his remarks did serve to put it in context and buy time for what would follow. He confirmed that all U.S. forces would pull out by March 31, 1994. That gave us three months to make progress on the reconciliation front.

But the immediate issue remained the recovery of Durant, which would require the service of the only American official who was trusted by the Habr Gidr. Ambassador Robert Oakley had a very close relationship with Aidid, as he did with all the clans, based on his earlier service in Mogadishu as ambassador from 1982 to 1984 and leadership of the earlier UNITAF mission; they even gave him an endearing nickname, referring to the space between his front teeth. Oakley arrived in Mogadishu on October 8 and over the course of the next few days met with members of the Habr Gidr who could get a message to Aidid. Footage the next day shows his vehicle leaving the compound unaccompanied and unarmed, driving off into the streets of Mogadishu, a testament to his courage and the understanding that personal accountability for the protection of "guests," once promised in societies like Somalia, would not be breached.

The journalist Mark Bowden has perhaps the best telling of the story in *Black Hawk Down*. He says Oakley told the clan that the battle was definitively over and the U.S. military was finished with the hunt for Aidid but wanted Durant released immediately. Clan leaders were "skeptical" of the first statement and "incredulous" of the second. Oakley promised to convey their request for a prisoner exchange to the president, but only after they released Durant. He then went on to deliver with clarity the situation they faced:

> What will happen if a few weeks go by and Mr. Durant is not released? Not only will you lose any credit you may get now, but we will decide that we have to rescue him. . . . The min-

ute the guns start again, all restraint on the U.S. side goes out. Just look at the stuff coming in here now. An aircraft carrier, tanks, gunships. . . . Once the fighting starts, all this pent-up anger is going to be released. This whole part of the city will be destroyed, men, women, children, camels, cats, dogs, goats, donkeys, everything. . . . That would really be tragic for all of us, but that's what will happen.[9]

Aidid got the message, and Durant was released several days later. It was one of the more effective and courageous acts of diplomacy I have witnessed. There is a truly boneheaded quote by a certain Sir Henry Wotton claiming, "An ambassador is an honest gentleman sent abroad to lie for his country." It rises to the top of the queue when searching for a definition of diplomacy: one hears it in speeches; it is used as an epigraph for chapters and books; and it makes absolutely no sense. Diplomacy is the art of telling the truth to foreign audiences in a way that will get them to see things your way and react appropriately. Oakley had done this—no one else in this case could have—and absent his intervention it is likely things would quickly have gone in the direction he suggested.

Delivering First Aid to a Rattlesnake

I arrived in Mogadishu via Nairobi in early January 1994 along with several other officers on loan from the Pentagon and staffer Adrienne Marks. We joined the very talented UN staff that had been working there for months and in some cases years. Disarmament, building a security force, hardening the humanitarian infrastructure, and, most important, political reconciliation were all issues to be worked aggressively in the three months that remained before the Western forces would withdraw.

The security gaps had been plugged with the arrival of the armor and c-130 gunships that had been denied the force earlier. On the political side plugging the gaps was going to be more difficult, but it appeared there was an opening to be exploited. Earlier estimates that Aidid's support in the Habr Gidr was diminished proved to be wrong; the clan had coalesced around him after the battles in July through October. The earlier compunction to avoid the warlords and hope they would be marginalized by an emerging civil society was off. And there was no more stomach for pursuing Aidid militarily and would not have been time for it even if there were. What was left was engaging him and attempting to draw him into a political process in which the clans agreed to build on a cease-fire and implement the Addis Accord.

But there was a more positive factor that was not obvious to many. Political Officer Don Teitelbaum at the U.S. Liaison Office believed that as painful as the October battle had been for us, it had decimated the Habr Gidr forces, which until then dominated the clan terrain through superior fighting numbers and sheer recklessness. The hundreds killed on the "Day of the Ranger" left them seriously depleted vis-à-vis the other clans, and from this weakened state they could be forced to the table and possibly into a multiclan governing structure.

The challenge, though, was that the conflict between the UN and the Somali warlords had become personalized, so that Aidid and others refused to deal with Howe. Real progress would come only after Howe was gone, which was becoming clear to Washington and New York.

Meanwhile we worked on a "regionalization" strategy Sheehan developed, in which we would press initiatives in the rest of the country that could both bolster a larger settlement and put pressure on the spoilers. It occurred to me at this point that there may have been a simpler way of managing the whole thing. By the end of 1993 we had spent $100 million on humanitarian assistance and $1.3 billion on military operations. This imbalance prompted a question that would return in the post-9/11 conflicts: Was there a way to simply pay off the warlords with massive bribes if they would allow humanitarian assistance to flow into their respective areas? We never knew what their price was because we never explored the option, but I suspect it was a lot less than $1.3 billion. A little less virtue and a little more funding flexibility in many cases might produce a less painful outcome.

UN and U.S. officials were also starting to look more assertively at what would be the right governing model for Somalia. I wrote on January 9:

> The challenge now is to cause the Somali people to either return to a loose confederation of tribes, or to become a nation with a central government. There is wide disagreement on which should happen. The reality will undoubtedly be somewhere in between. There must be something called a central government if nothing else so that they can send the UN home and have a national currency, flag, and airport. But how much power that national authority would have is subject to intense negotiations ... and given the tribal and nomadic nature of this people, and their suspicion of each other, [it should probably] not go much beyond the currency, flag, and airport.

In Howe's remaining month we got out of the office a fair amount. One visit was to a school where we found smiling, well-fed, clean kids attending classes. It was a simple visit of the kind ambassadors do all the time, but a year ago these kids would have been in a camp awaiting starvation. For all the pain of the preceding year, some things had improved dramatically. In addition to shaking up the military balance favorably, Teitelbaum believed, the international presence had had a major impact on living conditions more generally, coupled with environmental factors that were now working in our favor. With the fighting subsiding in most of the country and aid flowing, and with the end of the drought, farmers were able to get a crop in, and then another, and shepherds were finding better forage for their herds. The worst of the famine was over, and it would not return in anything like the conditions of 1992. Somalia would always be one bad harvest away from disaster, and there would often be some hunger in some parts of the country, but we were over the hump.

We got out to see troop contributors frequently, in one case attending a rotation of units at the Pakistani camp, a fortress in the middle of the city that had been the U.S. lifeline on October 3–4. The Pakistanis are proud peacekeepers and have a long tradition of participation in international missions. I was struck by the thirty flag bearers from troop-contributing nations, all flying their nation's colors in this godforsaken place they had come to help. They stood at attention as the Pakistani national anthem was played, cognizant of the heavy price this contingent had paid in June 1993, when they lost twenty-four soldiers in an ambush, and its willingness to stay with the mission after an incident that would have brought most forces home. I found it moving.

Visits to other units were also instructive, at times even inspiring. It is thankless work, peacekeeping, unappreciated in most nations at home and perfectly despised by large circles in the United States. Incidents involving the spread of disease, as happened in Haiti, or sexual predation, as some peacekeepers are being investigated for, and failures like Rwanda have tainted the concept. But it has succeeded more often than not, providing a shred of hope and opportunity in societies that have completely broken down.

After one visit to the Indian contingent in Bosaso I wrote, "The Indians have done by far the best work here. They are natural peacekeepers, mixing easily with the people, never patronizing or belittling them, never threatening, but always with the specter of force in the background if it is needed to coerce. They have a myriad of small projects going on, schools, a clinic, construction projects. Although they have one of the largest troop concentrations in the country they have yet to take their first casualty. They have mastered the art of civil-military relations in a way that most contingents never do."

In mid-January we got out to a few villages, starting in Garoe, midway between Mogadishu and the northern coast. It was a classic Somali town—a collection of mud huts and a few stone buildings, surrounded by nothing but scrub brush and dirt across a desperate horizon. It was intimidating flying into these towns where we had no presence and the local militia met us with "technicals" and machine gun–toting young men. But they were the law, and they took us to the local town council, which could be gathered on short notice. The council members were cordial but blunt: "UNOSOM has been here before, made promises, and kept none of them. Why do you keep coming back?" We thought it was a good question and didn't stay long. We didn't come back.

We found a more welcome reception in Eyl, further up the coast in historic Puntland. It has a stunning landscape of cliffs and valleys that reminded me of the American Southwest, with pristine white sand beaches disappearing into gorgeous blue-green water. UNOSOM had a small presence led by an Australian diplomat who had been happily exiled there.

I recorded, "The Somalis seem to look at us with a combination of bewilderment and surprise, but it is an extremely personable place, few people pass us, or each other, without a nod or a wave. Also extremely verbal culture, people always talking."

The buildings there were primarily Soviet but with some residual Italian villas and an old Italian consulate. It was an oasis town, and I noted, "The village has a small stream that runs through it, and one becomes quickly conscious of what a difference water makes to a community's psyche. Other villages, without anything but brackish well water, seemed listless and slow. But Eyl exuded life, color, vegetation."

Another seaside Puntland village that raised our spirits was the northern coastal town of Bosaso, just around the corner from Somalia's knee, on the border of Somaliland. We went through the standard tedious meeting with the district council as they recounted their many needs and appeals. A sad state of affairs, I thought, for these once proud nomads to now be wards of the international community and with a sense of not only dependence but entitlement.

But there we also met one of the true good guys, the general and erstwhile governor Mohammed Abshire Musa, who had spent twelve years in Siad Barre's jail after getting crosswise with the dictator while head of the national police. Like Ali Mahdi he had a quiet demeanor and an almost gentle disposition. He was not going to be a player among the jostling warlords, but as a statesman he had real potential. He spoke English well and we talked a good deal about his vision for the future. He was honest about the chances for success but believed that if we would get out of Mogadishu and start to focus on developing regions like his, we would find greater success than getting pulled down into the marsh of the capital. Harry Truman intrigued him, so I had my wife, Cecile, send my copy of David McCullough's biography, which I gave Abshire at our next meeting. He was a hopeful character and the darling of the international community, but difficult to replicate.

We toured the port that evening, one of the country's major-class ports built in the 1980s to manage the export of livestock to the Gulf. Absent a national or even local authority to run it, the local militia took care of security and the local political party charged the fees. It was raw capitalism at its best, the ultimate in free enterprise, and while it definitely had its limits, I recorded, "Surprisingly things work relatively well. Cargoes are secure and ships can dock and leave in a relatively orderly fashion."

Our final stop was another fishing village, Alula, right on the tip of Somalia's knee. The terrain was somewhat like the Sinai, with sharp but small mountain ranges and deep wadis; it is the only place in the world where frankincense flourishes. Alula was sleepy but had a good vibe. A faith-based NGO was trying to help restore the fishing industry that had existed before the civil war. Somali men, they said, found it unmanly to fish, so a key source of protein from some of the richest fishing beds in the world was going unharvested. (The Somalis did, however, believe it was okay to raid the fishing boats of other nations and hold their crews for ransom.) The NGO seemed to have a long road ahead, but a recent cursory glance shows that by 2012 there was indeed a fishing industry out of Alula. Like all things in Somalia maybe it was just a matter of time, and timing.

U.S. officials from the Liaison Office were working feverishly to get a police program up and running, which, like everything, had a political background that was difficult to skirt. Any arming and organizing of men in Somalia would be seen by the warlords as a threat to be controlled, and armed groups were to them a zero-sum game. But we needed to start somewhere, and a $25 million drawdown of surplus U.S. stocks brought in 5,000 rifles with 1.8 million rounds of ammunition, 3,000 .45 caliber pistols with 500,000 rounds, 5,000 handcuffs and nightsticks, and several hundred vehicles. The program was up and down for weeks, with U.S. vehicles on the verge of being withdrawn for lack of an agreed upon plan for their use. Seized with the thought of losing vehicles of any kind, faction leaders finally reached an agreement and the force was deployed. It provided limited security in the Mogadishu area but never really hit its stride.

All Roads Lead to Nairobi

Howe was recalled to New York on February 10 for consultations and did not return, leaving Kouyaté as SRSG. He and Ambassador Oakley, there on a brief visit as the administration's envoy, believed that with persistent and effective jawboning with the right leaders, there was a chance for limited success.

Kouyaté sought out Aidid in Nairobi, knowing that he would always remain both spoiler and lynchpin to a future agreement. It was the first meeting with UNOSOM since May of the previous year and Kouyaté characterized it with a parable from his mother tongue. If your finger is in the mouth of a madman, the way to get it out is by tickling the madman; when he laughs, remove your finger quickly. "Such is our relationship with Aidid," he said, "but don't tell him that until I get my finger out of his mouth."

On February 16 they started by clearing the air; Aidid insisted there was no need for UNOSOM at this point, and Kouyaté, acknowledging his view, simply moved on, raising regional peace conferences, the establishment of development committees, assistance to war victims, and control of armaments. Aidid, always trying to advance his clan at the expense of all others, pitched a new framework in which the political alignment would be formed around who fought against the Barre government and held territory during the revolution. Kouyaté, again acknowledging the suggestion and moving on, stressed the importance of including the northwest in any engagement, lest the natural drift toward separation, already in play, continue. Kouyaté briefed Aidid and said he would include his people on the security and police committees, and they established a mechanism for closer contact on day-to-day issues.

The pipeline was now open, and with future meetings in the coming weeks Kouyaté would skillfully maneuver toward a larger conference that would bring all parties together. Part of what Kouyaté faced was the urgency of showing political progress sufficient to warrant a new mandate when the Western forces pulled out at the end of March. With international skepticism as high as it was, he knew that the whole mission could simply fold.

Kouyaté continued to meet with Aidid and the other clan leaders separately and focused on getting them all to Nairobi for a large peace conference. But there were local conflicts that continued to threaten the process. The Kismayu-based political officer Ken Menkhaus was one of the foremost experts on Somalia and had come on board early in the UN intervention. He had assumed he would be part of the team that would put Somalia back together; now he feared he was watching it all unravel. He predicted that Kismayu would blow up again soon and that the faction leaders going forward would have less and less control over their own militias. The young men were traditional camel thieves, he said, and "no faction leader is going to get them to put down their weapons for the sake of a peace treaty."

The historian and diplomat John Drysdale similarly wrote, "Fighting and politics are synonymous, and looting has its roots in the enormous tonnage of heavy and light weapons sent to this country by both East and West during the Cold War. These arms have fallen into the hands of the 'Morian'—urbanized camel boys (turned unpaid, uncontrollable, demobilized militia) whose pastoral tradition is to loot (in this case camels) for quick assets and for the greater glory of their clan—with violence if necessary."[10] Menkhaus said the clans had been circling each other for the past several weeks and were itching for a fight. Kismayu was clearly one of the local conflicts that would have to be solved before anything larger could be achieved, and so Kouyaté built it into the structure of the Nairobi talks. Nairobi was turning into the last chance for peace.

The process of corralling the faction leaders and channeling their energy reminded me of what a sheepdog does in getting the sheep into a pen: three are almost in and a fourth bolts, so off the sheepdog goes to get that one, and when he returns the other three have now drifted. The trick is to get them all in a pack and keep them there. In early March Ali Mahdi and the leaders of the twelve clans aligned with him flew to Cairo for a conference without Aidid, who was in Addis Ababa at the time. Kouyaté, knowing Aidid would fly off the handle when he learned of the snub, flew to Addis to meet him, calming the waters by telling him Ali Mahdi needed some international attention after all the focus Aidid had received lately.

Kouyaté then got the Ali Mahdi–aligned Group of 12 to fly to Nairobi when they returned from Cairo, at which point Aidid was already there. We put them up in a four-star hotel with all the amenities, thinking the allure of a nice few days with lots of press coverage would help to seal the deal. Kouyaté asked me to stay behind and round up the rest of the faction leaders and then join him in a few days. The immediate issue was Kismayu, but as it turned out once we had everyone in Nairobi Kouyaté realized this might be the only opportunity to work the national accord, so he jumped over regional issues altogether.

The number of arrivals kept growing, but in a week we crested at seventy faction leaders, so, with no more additions, I joined the last group and made my way to Nairobi. Kouyaté was in his element. We staffed the upcoming meetings as he shuttled between factions in large groups, one-on-ones, and small conferences, all the time building a consensus on the way forward. We split up the secondary leaders, and several of us were tasked with forging agreements within some of the factions that had split, to then channel them into a more workable formulation. On one occasion I worked with an Indian diplomat and army officer to unite two subfactions. We met with four of the junior leaders in a hotel room, explaining to them the task at hand and leaving them alone for the rest of the morning. I returned to the room during lunch only to find that they had indeed reached consensus to strip the bathroom of all its fixtures: nozzles, handles, towel racks. If nothing else we had found a joint project they agreed on, and when they returned in the afternoon we were able to finalize the agreement.

Kouyaté's shuttling continued incessantly. The clans held out for more concessions, and he was starting to wear down, wondering if it was simply not possible to reach consensus. Word filtered back to Mogadishu that the clans were deadlocked and the fear of renewed conflict spread across the country. At this point a group of Somali women, quite an independent and strong-willed bunch, whatever stereotypes might abound, reportedly sent word to the leaders in Mogadishu. If there was any expectation of resuming normal conjugal relations upon return, they warned, the leaders had better not show up without an agreement. It was some welcome track II pressure and seemed to help.

But we weren't there yet. Kouyaté continued to whittle away the differences and at one point wondered if we shouldn't just take whatever the leaders were ready to offer and get something, anything signed. By then, however, we were well past the middle of the month, and I suggested that if we didn't show solid progress we might lose the new mandate, which would be debated in days. I urged him to keep trying. Kouyaté agreed, but eventually got to a point where he could simply do no more. He had drafted a minimal agreement committing the parties to restore peace, hold a preparatory meeting in April and a national reconciliation conference in May, and establish an independent judiciary and local authorities. Anything less than this would leave the process in total drift and the international community unsatisfied.

Kouyaté left the agreement with the leaders on March 23 and told them they had until the end of the day to agree, or we were returning to Mogadishu. He had already used this gambit at least once and they didn't take the threat seriously, but this time we reinforced it. At the end of the evening the hotel staff gave each of the faction leaders instructions for checkout and made clear the bill from henceforth would be on them.

Kouyaté spent the evening visibly relaxing. In midevening he told me and my team to stand down; there would be no agreement, and we would return the next day. I went to bed a bit dejected but was sleeping soundly when a call came at 2:00 a.m. They have agreed, the chief of staff said; get the ceremony on track for the morning. We worked through the night to get together a script, speech, and copies of the final agreement.

Later that morning, we arrived at the UN facility at Gigiri, where we had planned a visually rich outdoor ceremony. Kouyaté accused me of trying to replicate the recent Camp David accords. In our symmetrical Western way we had placed nine chairs on each side of the podium for the party leaders, who would blend in a show of unity and reconciliation. Upon arrival, however, the factions immediately reset the chairs, placing three on one side for Aidid and his people, and fifteen on the other side for Ali Mahdi and the Group of 12. So much for conciliatory symmetry. We had also hoped to call the leaders in one at a time for dramatic effect, but once they had the seating as they wanted it, they stood their ground, lest some international again try to get them into an unacceptable lineup.

Kouyaté and his entourage entered and took their place at the head table, observing some symbolism that I believed was important. I wanted it to be clear that Kouyaté was more than just the referee, that going forward he would lead them and make demands. Kouyaté spoke briefly, followed by Aidid, then Ali Mahdi on behalf of the Group of 12. Then the Somali Democratic Alliance leader Mohamed Farah Abdullahi from Somaliland read the declaration; we wanted Abdullahi to have a prominent, or at least a visible role to give Somaliland a stake in the proceedings. When it was time to shake hands Kouyaté took no chances; he grabbed Aidid and Ali Mahdi at the wrists, shoved their hands together, and raised them high in a symbolic gesture of unity. It was as good as it gets, and probably was the event that bought another several years of support from the international community. It was not in the end enough to create a country, but it may have saved thousands of lives.

Pullout and What We Learned

The next day the last of the U.S. forces pulled out. My colleague Adrienne Marks went to the bluffs overlooking the beach to watch the departure and found it sobering. "I was on the beach at 0730 this morning," she wrote,

> the same beach on which the Marines landed almost sixteen months ago. An Amphibious Ready Group, eight Navy ships with over 4,000 Marines embarked, ready to carry the rear guard down the coast to Mombasa. Army Cobra helicopter gunships circled overhead. By 1030 an American Marine colonel had passed responsibility of the airfield to an Egyptian officer with a ceremonial handshake. And at 1130 the last armored personnel carriers, proudly flying the Stars and Stripes, clanged close their hatches, bounced across the beach, and headed out to sea. The final words of the last U.S. officer: "I might get seasick on the way to Bosnia. You better get out while you can."[11]

Adrienne was reminded that Admiral Howe had said on more than one occasion that we had taken on Mission Impossible. But like me she couldn't help but note the successes:

> Hundreds of thousands of Somali people have been rescued from starvation—there are no more walking skeletons. The country's infrastructure is slowly being rebuilt, the seaports and airports are functioning, livestock is being exported to the Middle East, District and Regional Councils are being formed, police are being trained. And the leaders of the warring factions signed an agreement establishing a timetable for a national reconciliation conference and elections. They are talking rather than fighting and finally realize it is ultimately their responsibility—not that of the United States or the United Nations—to rebuild their country.

The glass might not have been half full, but it wasn't completely dry either.

I wasn't too far behind the contingent, returning to Mogadishu for a few days before departing myself. Kouyaté strongly requested that I stay, and but for the firm agreement I had made with colleagues in Tel Aviv who were covering for me I would have done so. I felt a tinge of guilt for leaving him and remained somewhat seized with the mission, but it would have burned more career bridges than I could successfully rebuild. As I look back with twenty-three years of hindsight as Somalia continues to alternate between embracing and resisting nationhood, I'm not sure what another year would have produced anyway.

I wrote my own postmortem of the operation a few months later, with the lessons I thought we should have learned from it. First was questioning President Clinton's campaign mantra, "It's the economy, stupid." That may work for stump speeches but requires a quick pivot on January 20, when new presidents take office. In the end few people get killed building our economy, but the risks in foreign policy are ever before us. Second, it is impossible to hand off a mission to the UN in a matter of months and expect it to succeed. The UN has real limitations and should not be set up for failure. Third, we don't decrease risk by decreasing troop levels and need to send a force that is appropriate to the mission. Fourth, in Somalia one will not reach a political settlement at the exclusion of one clan. More generally, and this more than anything else was what I would take away from Somalia, it is all about the politics—get that right, and security and development will take care of themselves. We have been almost as resistant to that lesson as Somalis have been to nationhood.

Several days after I returned to Israel the Rwandan genocide broke out. The world community was too traumatized by Somalia to respond, something that would haunt U.S. policymakers for years. I doubt it haunted the Somalis, who tend not to be too sentimental and are slow to take accountability. It was their gift to their cousins to the West.

The Somalia mission sputtered along. In September 1994 three Indian officers were killed in Baidoa. I felt somewhat responsible. Maybe we shouldn't have worked so hard and instead just let the mission fold with the Western forces six months earlier. But in August 2000 a president and government were finally formed. They struggled hard, and after 9/11 we regained interest in Somalia as fear of ungoverned spaces rose and Islamists took hold in parts of the country. In 2006 we backed Ethiopia in an intervention to shore up Somalia's transitional federal government and have been involved in keeping terrorism at bay while supporting an eventual government ever since.

The international community truly is relentless. A new Somali Parliament was inaugurated on August 20, 2012, in a joint session of the two houses, leading the UN secretary general to comment, "The Somali people have waited twenty years for peace to take root in their country. Now is the time to begin a new chapter in their history."[12] Twenty-four percent of the upper house and 23 percent of the lower house were women. The rebirth of Parliament ended the transitional period and led the country closer to a stable and functional government, which the United States recognized in January 2013, the first time in twenty years a Somali government was granted U.S. recognition.

In an interesting connection between the two countries, a fifty-four-year-old dual Somali–U.S. citizen named Mohamed Abdullahi Farmajo had been selected prime minister in the transitional government in 2010. He was working in the Buffalo, New York, Housing Authority at the time and came to Mogadishu as a diaspora delegate. Upon taking office he immediately declared war on the jihadist militant organization Al-Shabab, rearranged the security force chiefs, and replaced the Mogadishu mayor amid increasing piracy and another famine. Farmajo served for only a year but returned as the country's president in February 2017, based in large measure on the success of his tenure as prime minister. The country continues to face immense problems with insecurity and poverty, but it has an elected government dealing with the issues and has held together.

On one of my visits inside Somalia I observed a UN contingent holding back a demonstration of some sort, when a Somali man with a flag on a pole maneuvered his way in front of the demonstrators. He started to wave the flag, but then every few minutes dipped it to drag across the ground. He is acting out his frustration with what has happened to his country, my interpreter said.

The crowd cheered when the flag went up, gasped and sighed collectively when it fell.

We can talk all we want about postmodern tribalism, but in the end no one really has a better idea for civic organization than a flag that represents a functional government and proud nation. Not even Somalia.

FIVE

Haiti, 1996

With a Lot of Help from My Friends

A Deep Pool

When foreigners write about Haiti their titles are telling: *Written in Blood, The Tumultuous History, For Whom the Dogs Spy, Best Nightmare on Earth*. Even when writing about helping Haiti the best they can do is *The Uses of Haiti, Killing with Kindness*, or *How the World Came to Save Haiti and Left Behind a Disaster*. Haitians are no less critical of their own narrative although more prone to ultimately find redemption than despair: *God Loves Haiti, Miracle on Voodoo Mountain*, and *Haiti: The Sleeping Economic Power*.

But the titles are only the opening salvo. Don Schulz, a U.S. Army War College professor of national security affairs and one of the more constructive chroniclers of the country's recent past, explained that Haiti's "self-destructive political behavior" is marked by "authoritarianism, paternalism, personalism, patronage, nepotism, demagogy, corruption, cynicism, opportunism, racism, incompetence, parasitism, rigidity, intolerance, rivalry, distrust, insecurity, vengeance, intrigue, superstition, volatility, violence, paranoia, xenophobia, exploitation, class hatred, institutional illegitimacy, and mass apathy, aversion, and submission."[1] I'm not sure if Schulz was shooting for exhausting or exhaustive.

The journalist and longtime observer of Haiti Bob Shacochis puts a lighter spin on his list: "Like a disturbing dream, Haiti brimmed with contradictions. It was archaic, alarming, fabulous, and strange, home to a state of permanent upheaval and permanent transcendence, a nation with an accomplished artist and incipient dictator in every family."[2] And the novelist Herbert Gold, one of the many foreigners who came to Haiti young and never really left, further lightened the mood, saying that his first weeks in Haiti "marked out the elements of an inexhaustible set of interlocking puzzles: unimaginable poverty, unpredictable appeal; friendship and fear; a culture which was impenetrable and profoundly hospitable; desperation and humor; corruption in politics and generosity in friends; a collaboration and suspicion between classes unlike anyplace else."[3]

Indeed, of all the places we have lived Haiti has received the most effort by outsiders to explain it but in the end simply has to be experienced to be understood.

Soon after our arrival in the early fall of 1995, where I would work in a new postconflict section of the embassy, Cecile and I often just looked at each other and wondered what we had gotten ourselves into. We had added our fourth child, Daniel, between tours, and the kids initially found it jarring to leave their comfortable home in San Salvador. But at their ages—five, three, two, and two months—everything is one big adventure and they adapted quickly.

They loved to go for walks on the trails and roads above our house, the former residence of Haiti's last dictator, Raoul Cédras, which the U.S. government had rented as part of the deal to get him to leave. It was located high above Port-au-Prince in Pegueyville, an hour's jarring drive from the embassy. On these walks we would often peek behind the walls of motel-size homes that had been *dechoukajed*, a uniquely Haitian word for "pulled up by the roots," which was what happened to oppressive elites when there was a popular reckoning. The rule was you could not loot, only destroy, and there were several houses in our neighborhood that had been on the wrong side of the most recent struggle. Goats filled the streets and ambled through houses that were now occupied by squatters who had creatively taped together dozens of extension cords and connected them to power lines.

Our new home was large and oddly designed, with floating staircases and multiple split levels. It was difficult to get comfortable in, and I often wondered what it had looked like with the Cédras furniture in it. But no amount of furniture could have brought it up to standard for a minor industrialist or small-time drug lord in Colombia. Our house manager, the poet and writer Alex Laguerre, explained that the Cédrases simply didn't have enough time to steal much, and frankly, there wasn't all that much to steal.

Through it all Cecile somehow held us together, as Shacochis said of the Haitian people, "rising stoically or even playfully to Haiti's challenges." She kept the house running through power outages, theft, water shortages, and medical calamities; kept the kids safe from six-foot snakes, gunshots during birthday parties, and the occasional voodoo spell; and still took a local orphanage under her wing, saving two lives and improving the life chances for dozens of young women.

Dechoukajed. It was a word we would never forget. There was an air of gentleness and friendliness among the Haitian people, whom most outsiders find it difficult not to like. I can think of only once when I felt genuinely threatened there. But we also could see that we were stepping into a deep pool of history that included sustained and persistent violence. I never thought it would be directed at us, but it was a form of political discourse that would impact much of our work.

A Tortured History of a Vibrant Culture

The executive summary of Haiti's dysfunction is commonly told through statistics. Ambassador Bill Swing spoke in 1995 of the "vicious cycle of poverty, population, and environment"—a loss of thirty million trees a year, a 30 percent drop in GDP over four years, the highest birthrate and the lowest use of contraception in the hemisphere. Haiti's quality of life indicators bore this out; compared to the rest of the hemisphere its infant mortality rate was double, average earnings a tenth, illiteracy rate three times as high, and life expectancy ten years lower.[4]

The political history that produced this mix of madness and grace is also often recounted numerically. In 190 years of existence Haiti had twenty-one constitutions and forty-one heads of state, of whom seven served more than ten years, nine declared themselves head of state for life, and twenty-nine were assassinated or overthrown.

History has given Haiti very few breaks. And like few places on the planet, most of the above indicators are explicable only by understanding that, as Shacochis put it, "Haiti, much like the Balkans, is a place where history has a parasitic lock on the present."[5]

One commentator reminds us that Haiti's contact with the outside world began when Columbus dropped anchor to praise this "most Rousseauian of isles."[6] There was a 1915 *National Geographic* in circulation around the embassy with a politically incorrect period piece entitled "Wards of the United States: Notes on What Our Country Is Doing for Santo Domingo, Nicaragua, and Haiti."[7] It offered a compelling picture of the tragic attraction of Hispaniola for the French in the late seventeenth century, when they wrested the western half of the island from Spain as a bargaining chip: "When Nature was distributing her gifts to the islands of the earth Haiti seemed a favorite child, for she bestowed upon it a fertility of soil, an abundance of rainfall, and a wealth of mineral resources that left little to be desired." Realizing the blessings of this "tranquil abundance," however, would require a "firm yet gentle, beneficent guidance."[8]

Firm and gentle and beneficent guidance has not actually been a part of the Haitian experience.

By the time the French arrived the Taino Indians had been decimated and African slaves imported. The economics of slavery in Haiti were among the most brutal in the world, with French plantation owners coming to believe it was cheaper to work slaves literally to death and import fresh ones than allow the relatively more measured system of the Americans and British. Their moral grounding and math skills both were equally lacking. By the end of the eighteenth century there were 500,000 slaves and 50,000 freemen, 30,000 of the latter mulattoes. The result of this system of utter brutality was that the slaves of Haiti had nothing to lose, and beginning in early 1790 had learned through a series of failed efforts how to organize for revolt clandestinely and with furious urgency. They also raised up, as the historian C. L. R. James puts it in his masterful account of the period, *The Black Jacobins*, a line of great leaders in "profusion and rapidity."[9]

The final revolt began in earnest in July 1791 around Cap-Haitien. James describes the scene:

> Each slave gang murdered its masters and burned the planta-
> tion to the ground.... From Le Cap the whole horizon was a
> wall of fire.... Like the peasants in the Jacquerie or the Lud-
> dite wreckers, they were seeking their salvation in the most
> obvious way, the destruction of what they knew was the cause
> of their sufferings; and if they destroyed much it was because
> they had suffered much.... For two centuries the higher civ-
> ilization had shown them that power was used for wreaking
> your will on those whom you controlled. Now that they held
> power they did as they had been taught.[10]

Out of this swirl of destruction emerged Toussaint Louverture, a charismatic and brilliant leader who carried on the struggle for a decade with statesmanship and vision. Toussaint was tricked into captivity and died in France, while new leaders, less enlightened, continued the struggle, winning Haiti's independence definitively in 1803. Jean-Jacques Dessalines rejected the chance to move beyond the war with the help of the French who remained, and carried out massacres at Cap-Français, Port-au-Prince, and Jérémie, while prohibiting white men from owning land. The country would likely have had a different future under the more moderate and unifying hand of Toussaint. Like so many places I have served, a single leader can often make a difference for decades or longer, for better or worse.

Analysts Chetan Kumar and Elizabeth Cousens point to four potentially destructive legacies from this period: the ascendancy of the Creole aristocracy, precipitous and brutal changes of lead-ership, the violent tactics of Haiti's founding leaders, and the

protracted wars that destroyed the island's flourishing plantation economy.[11]

As I experienced Haiti two other issues were arguably even
more important. The first was resistance to social order. Dessalines
declared himself Emperor Jacques I, provoking his assassination
in 1806 and dividing the country between Henri Christophe, who
declared a kingdom in the north, and Alexandre Pétion, who established a republic in the south. Christophe's plan was to maintain
the plantation system and build a magnificent palace by using
work gangs. He succeeded at both, albeit with a system that to
the average peasant looked much like the previous regime, with
thousands dying in the process.

Pétion took a different approach and broke up the colonial
estates into smallholdings, which peasants worked as subsistence
farmers. The loss of export crops led the south into extreme poverty and its government into a state of perpetual bankruptcy. Still,
tens of thousands fled the prosperous oppression of the north for
the anarchic liberty of the south. In both cases the mulatto elites
came to dominate the government and the cities, while the black
lower class sought refuge from their predations in the countryside.
Much of the country's history would revolve around the chase by
the elites to plunder from the impoverished masses.

While the Haitian Revolution was fought over resistance to
slavery, it also established a tradition of fleeing to disorder rather
than accepting the cost and compromise of civic organization
and order. And at an even more extreme level than I have experienced in other societies newly liberated from repressive regimes,
this had a deadening impact on civil society, which as the political
scientist Robert Fatton argues, "rather than constituting a coher-
ent social project ... tends to embody a disorganized plurality of
mutually exclusive projects."[12]

The second issue was the isolation imposed on Haiti from outside. Haiti was from its beginning "shipwrecked in the exclusive
harbor of western civilization."[13] Part of this was self-imposed, the
prohibition against whites owning land, for example. But much
came from countries that simply did not know what to do with

this independent republic of former slaves. France did not recognize Haiti until 1825, and then only after an agreement to a stunning amount of reparations that Haiti did not finish paying until 1887. South and Central America shared no common language and culture with Haiti, and even the English-speaking countries of the Caribbean found little to bond with. Britain recognized the new country in 1833, but the United States, fearful of the symbolism of an independent black republic born of a slave revolt, did not establish relations until 1862. Haiti was completely on its own; it had no mother, no father, no aunts and uncles, not even distant cousins. It was to be a chillingly destructive isolation that would make everything more difficult.

All this played out over the coming century as these largely destructive political and economic tendencies became firmly rooted. Ambassador Swing uses the term "domestically colonized" to describe Haiti's plight. "At various times," he writes, "a small group—the army, a family, a 'President for life' or a clique—has taken power and held the rest of the society hostage ... colonizing the country from within."[14] This is described elsewhere as a phenomenon of "state vs. society."[15]

The 1990s was not the first time the United States had tried to stabilize Haiti. In 1915 U.S. Marines were sent by President Woodrow Wilson to quell the chaos surrounding a particularly violent coup and protect American commercial interests, at the time in competition with German businessmen whose presence in the hemisphere was disconcerting. During the occupation U.S. officials disarmed the old army and formed a gendarmerie that was much smaller and concentrated on internal security. The United States stayed for nearly twenty years, achieving much in the nation's infrastructure but less in building a sustainable political system and economy, which were still at the mercy of coups and elite machinations.

The various streams of Haiti's history came to a head when François Duvalier was elected president in 1957 and immediately began to consolidate power in a reign of brutality that cost as many as sixty thousand Haitian lives. Known as Papa Doc, he sought to make his regime "coup proof" by creating a Palace Guard directly responsible to him, closing the Military Academy, and developing a parallel intelligence service and corps of enforcers, the Tonton Macoutes. Under Duvalier there was no separation between police and military, and he set up 565 "section chiefs" with hundreds of "attaches" that the analyst Rachel Neild explains "dominated the lives of Haiti's rural majority . . . imposing arbitrary taxes, making illegal arrests, and demanding payment to release or feed . . . prisoners."[16]

The regime of repression Duvalier created surprisingly outlasted him; at his death in 1971 he was replaced by his nineteen-year-old son, Jean-Claude, called Baby Doc, who carried out the same range of policies, albeit much less effectively. Baby Doc was overthrown in a popular uprising and in February 1986 fled Haiti for France, where he would live in exile until returning to Haiti in 2011.

Enter Aristide

In Duvalier's wake there were six provisional governments in five years until a former Catholic priest named Jean-Bertrand Aristide was elected president in late 1990. Aristide was a firebrand street preacher steeped in liberation theology who garnered widespread popular support and challenged the established political and economic order. He was championed by the journalist Amy Wilentz, who was one of the first to identify his popularity, convinced he would finally give Haiti the chance it deserved. U.S. government analysts, who ignored him at first, came to believe he would only perpetuate Haiti's nightmare, albeit from the extreme left rather than the extreme right.

Aristide's election and the threat of his socioeconomic policies to the entrenched elites and the army led to a military coup on September 29, 1991, in which Gen. Raoul Cédras became head of state.

The reaction of the international community was swift but relatively ineffectual. The Organization of American States (OAS) immediately condemned the coup and so began a long process of UN and OAS involvement in trying to use instruments short of force to depose the generals and restore Aristide. The Cédras regime became expert at parrying the international community's blows by accepting minimal intrusion and oversight but never giving up the real levers of power. The International Civilian Mission in Haiti was established in February 1993 to deploy civil rights observers and facilitate dialogue among the political parties and was later expanded to a joint UN mission. Absent serious reforms by the de facto government, the UN imposed an oil and arms embargo in June 1993, which finally brought the generals to the table.

Cédras agreed to meet Aristide under UN-OAS auspices in late June 1993, leading to the Governor's Island Agreement on July 3. Aristide would appoint a new commander in chief to replace Cédras, the parties would agree to a prime minister, and the UN would oversee the modernization of the armed forces and police. The New York Pact two weeks later dealt with political factions and parliamentary blocs, and with the ratification of Prime Minister–Designate Robert Malval the UN confirmed its willingness to suspend sanctions.

To maintain momentum, the mandate of the newly formed UN Mission in Haiti (UNMIH) was to provide police and military observers and instructors to train and mentor a new police force and modernize the army, a task on par with political reform in importance. Special Representative to the Secretary General (SRSG) Dante Caputo and a small staff arrived on September 8, 1993, and by early October fifty-three military and fifty-one police advisors-observers were in country, and 220 military personnel were set to arrive on the USS *Harlan County* on October 11.

The timing could not have been worse, given the events of October 3–4 in Mogadishu, which emboldened the opponents of the agreement while drastically increasing America's aversion to risk. Armed civilians were at the port to greet the ship and harassed the waiting diplomats and international personnel. Given the need for a permissive environment for the force to be even marginally effective, and no indication of good faith by the regime, there was no reason to force the issue and the ship withdrew. The bulk of UNMIH personnel were likewise withdrawn over the coming weeks, but talks continued. Sanctions were reimposed and removed in pieces along with the ups and downs of the political process. As humbling as it may have looked at the time for the international community, the dance was all part of the process required to get to a point of using force. This was especially true as the project relied on the good offices of countries and a hemisphere that were allergic to foreign intervention in the first place. But even to them the limits of diplomacy not backed up by credible force were becoming clear.

An American Commitment to Democracy and a Need for Stability

The United States was absent during the Rwanda crisis in 1994 because that tragedy was simply too close to what it had experienced in Somalia, but Haiti was harder to ignore. The president would later lay out three reasons to intervene: (1) to stem the flow of migrants into the United States, (2) to ensure the forward consolidation of democracy in the hemisphere, and (3) to show a willingness to keep U.S. commitments. While only the first aimed for tangible results, those were quite tangible, since there were 38,000 Haitian migrants interdicted in a six-month period in 1991, with another 300,000 internally displaced and effectively looking for the opportunity to leave. Rumor of a change in asylum policy in June 1994 led 10,000 to attempt to flee by boat in a matter of weeks. Such numbers were not sustainable.

But the other two reasons were also compelling. Democracy had been consolidating in the hemisphere for the previous two decades and there was a certain positive synergy to it; a reversal would have larger human rights and security implications. And U.S. credibility would be suspect in more than just the hemisphere. This is clear when one looks at the impact of the Somali pullout on Al-Qaida and later terrorist groups, who came to believe they could chase America out of a region by inflicting casualties.

The international community's response to Haiti was also in the context of the short-lived post–Cold War world before Russia reconstituted its traditional bellicosity. This was a rare window of opportunity to work certain issues with easier UN Security Council support and an international system that was more pliable than it had been before or would be later. Procedurally there would still be advantages to using a heavy initial U.S. force that transitioned to a less pugnacious UN force. This model would help provide the shock and awe that shifted the political and security dynamic irretrievably, while better sharing the cost and risk over time.

By late August official U.S. patience with the process was breaking down and Americans' resistance to intervention was also softening.[17] Certain constituent groups of Americans, such as the Congressional Black Caucus, were pushing the president to act, initially without military intervention, but later accepting this as the only option.

After a U.S. offer similar to what was used in Somalia a year earlier, the Security Council passed UN Resolution 940, permitting member states to use all necessary means to oust the military regime and restore "legitimate Government authorities." It was the first time the UN had authorized military force to restore democracy and the first time the United States had sought UN approval for military intervention in the Americas. It gave life to the "assertive multilateralism" that Permanent Representative Madeleine Albright had conceptualized in New York.

Through all this the de facto government continued to bargain, somehow believing in this high-stakes game of chicken that the United States would swerve first. In mid-September, with the U.S. Fleet steaming toward Haiti and the 82nd Airborne Division in staging areas, President Clinton sent former president Carter, former chairman of the Joint Chiefs of Staff Colin Powell, and Senate Armed Services chairman Sam Nunn to negotiate with the junta. Cédras had blustered earlier to CBS that the landing of U.S. troops would trigger "a massacre starting with a civil war."[18] But the reality was sinking in.

The talks, some of which were held in the living room of the Cédras mansion where we would take up residence, were blunt, and the three Americans made it clear they were there to discuss how, not whether, the trio would be leaving the country. But behind Cédras was an even tougher negotiator, his wife, Yannick Prosper, the brains of the Cédras financial mini-empire. She said at one point she would rather die with her children than see her husband forced from power in a U.S. invasion, and on her ten-year-old son's birthday no less. She eventually softened her stance, but on the question of how well they would live in exile, she drove a hard bargain.

At one point they offered to sell their houses to the U.S. government for $650,000, which, given the late hour and the cost of an invasion, seemed reasonable to the negotiating trio. But while the idea might have been compelling, someone still had to come up with the coin, and neither the Pentagon nor the State Department had a line item in their budget for purchasing properties from former dictators. The offer was therefore withdrawn and other solutions sought. The State Department finally offered to rent the properties for $6,000 a month to be used for embassy staff. In the end whether the entry of twenty thousand marines and paratroopers would be hard or soft came down to finding a landlord within the U.S. government. The crisis was averted, and the troops landed successfully on Monday, September 19, 1994, and began the mission of stabilizing the country.

After the passage of amnesty legislation on October 10 and the departure of the de facto government, Aristide returned on October 15 and assumed office. Ever the poet, he told the crowd, "We have to swear seventy times seven times that never, never, never, will one drop of blood fall in Haiti. We all want peace. Let all weapons be silent. To all of those who question their dreams, remember Oct. 15. To all of those who are discouraged in the pursuit of their dreams, remember Oct. 15. . . . Today is the day that the sun of democracy rises to never set. . . . Today is the day that the eyes of justice open to never close again. . . . Today is the day that security takes over morning, noon and night."[19] The International Civilian Mission in Haiti returned, and the UN mission started to get organized.

The Mission Begins

Toward the end of September the UN secretary general had noted that the great majority of the Haitian population welcomed the multinational force but might be developing "unrealistically high expectations of what it would do."[20] U.S. Special Forces teams, who were the first to fan out across Haiti in what would become the largest U.S. foreign internal defense mission since the Vietnam War, were also finding this to be the case. Tracy Kidder was a journalist embedded with an "A" team centered around Mirebalais as they sought to create the stable and secure environment their exit strategy required. "They were given responsibility for a thousand square kilometers of Haiti's central plateau," he reported, "an area that contained about a hundred and fifty thousand people, scattered among about a hundred towns and villages, many reachable only by horse."[21]

Kidder describes their initial meeting in the village of Coudgoye, where hundreds of citizens had gathered to meet with the team: "They wanted the Captain to build them a new school and provide schoolbooks and pay the teacher's salaries; to construct a better road than the rutted dirt track that now connected their village to the district's main road; to repair their dam and irrigation system; to bring them electricity. And surely, some in the crowd thought, the Captain would arrest their former oppressors, the Macoutes."[22]

I similarly commented in a letter after debriefing some of these teams, "They are the glue that is keeping this country together. They have been the police, judge, fire department, city council, water works, religious affairs office, disaster relief agency, public information disseminator, and county jail, all rolled into one. There are a host of UN and assorted agencies out there, but it is Special Forces that has made things work." As one Haitian observer put it, "The people are suffering with hope."[23]

The U.S. coalition continued to work, while the UN advance contingent grew, and there were no major security or political incidents to speak of. The incredibly skilled former Algerian foreign minister Lakhdar Brahimi took over from Caputo in September 1994 and would lead the UN mission for the next eighteen months. I got to know Brahimi well and considered him one of the most effective international peacemakers and nation-builders in the world—calm, politically astute, and with the ability to draw in factions and leaders to a political process. He exuded confidence and empathy, a rather odd but useful mix of traits.

Maj. Gen. Joseph Kinzer was selected as the force commander, keeping the United States involved in the mission even though U.S. forces would be largely withdrawn. Kinzer was an excellent choice, with wide command and staff experience and a sense of humor about the restrictions of commanding a multilateral force.

On January 18, 1995, the president of the Security Council formally reported that a secure and stable environment existed in Haiti and that the climate was right for a handover from the United States to the UN. The handover ceremony on March 31 was attended by Presidents Aristide and Clinton and the UN secretary general, an unusually dramatic show of confidence in and support for the country and the new UN mission.

Internal reporting within the UN, however, showed that beneath the surface there was still an air of instability. UN field officers saw no serious danger to the existence of the government and a generally positive picture on demobilization, human rights, and electoral preparations. But the collapse of all organized forces created a security void that contributed to a marked increase in banditry and criminality throughout the country.

The security situation, UN officials concluded, "was very fragile," and on January 17 the secretary general laid out for the Security Council a number of factors that could lead to future instability, including disaffection of the former military, paramilitary networks, the availability of arms, rising frustration over the inability to prosecute human rights abuses, tension over the upcoming election, and lack of economic progress for the impoverished majority of the country.[24] An understanding of this looming instability caused the United States to maintain a contingent of three hundred soldiers as U.S. Support Mission Haiti. It was ostensibly an engineering unit working on civic projects, but more than anything it was a reminder to Haiti that the United States was still fully committed and that behind these three hundred soldiers there were thousands more a phone call away.

Building Institutions with a Limited Toolbox
and Just Enough Lumber

By the spring of 1995 the embassy was gearing up. The State Department had not come to terms with the wide range of "operational" as opposed to "representational" and "reporting" functions that are required for these missions and did not have a personnel system to rapidly shift the right people to support them. But seeing a need, I offered my services by curtailing early from my assignment in El Salvador.

I described our mission in Haiti from the start as a train without a throttle. In addition to our main lines of effort in shaping and supporting U.S. programs for the new police, judiciary, and prison system, I soon saw a somewhat ill-defined task involving identifying and heading off large-scale instability. I noted in a letter that there were still a lot of "what if's." "What if Aristide doesn't give up power? What if the police force proves incompetent and public order completely crumbles? What if the elites simply wait out the departure of the American troops and stage a comeback?" Accurately conveying to Washington where we were on the instability curve—not provoking an overreaction but not allowing an underreaction—would play out constantly during my tenure.

It started early. On November 7, 1995, Jean-Hubert Feuille, a newly elected member of Parliament and Aristide's cousin, was shot and killed. Aristide assumed the political worst and delivered a eulogy at Feuille's funeral that included calls to "go to the neighborhoods where there are big houses and heavy weapons" to disarm "the big men." Brahimi called for calm, but it was difficult rhetoric to pull back and the masses would always listen to Aristide over an international.[25] By the time the incident had run its course seven were killed and dozens wounded and several houses burned down. We experienced the crowd's wrath firsthand the day after the eulogy, when we were confronted by a machete-wielding mob while driving to church. We were able to talk our way out of their efforts to search and threaten vehicles, retreating to Pegueyville and the kids' preferred church service: staying home.

It was a stunning display of something that would afflict the country for years: the sheer popularity of Aristide and his inability to put that popularity to good use. The historian Philippe Girard writes, "The Haitian poor professed a love for Aristide that was as passionate as it was exclusive. . . . Their only allegiance was to Aristide himself."[26] Aristide, I wrote after the incident, sometimes forgets that he is a head of state and reverts back to being a radical parish priest stirring up his followers.

But I also wondered if there wasn't more calculation behind his way of intimidating the right and demonstrating that "people power" was a force to be reckoned with. "If I were a revanchist leader," I wrote, "I would think twice about acting, which seems to be what is happening." A year later I observed that the ex-military took seriously the threats by popular organizations that if they "burn tires in protest they will quickly find those burning tires around their necks." It was a constant struggle to build institutions fast enough that they could manage security and deliver justice before impatience led to the enlistment of a mob that would undermine what progress had been made in a vicious dysfunctional cycle. Progress would always be marked but tentative.

Demobilization and Reintegration

The concept for the army had evolved from Aristide's first term. Initially he thought he would just leave it alone and try to control it, then after the coup decided it would be limited to 1,500 soldiers, and then following pay riots in December 1994 determined to eliminate it altogether. Aristide was haunted by the incredible brutality meted out against the Haitian people and the ex-army's now transparent threat to democratic institutions, concerns we shared. But unlike Aristide we were also worried about what would happen to the ex-soldiers when they were suddenly unemployed.

As a bridging mechanism the international community urged the establishment of a seven-thousand-man Interim Public Security Force formed of six thousand ex-military and a thousand returning refugees. They would be switched out one for one as the new police were trained, so it was a temporary gig but it provided a margin of stability while the other balls we had in the air landed.

Meanwhile USAID and the International Organization for Migration provided six months of training for demobilizing soldiers in auto mechanics, plumbing, carpentry, electrical work, refrigeration, and masonry. At the end of it they would get a tool box and a diploma. I was sold on the importance of the program after I watched a riot by three hundred ex-soldiers over lack of pay, noting in a journal on September 9, "I haven't seen that many angry young men since I drove through the Gaza Strip. They were different than the average Haitian, had a crazed look about them, a look of unpredictability, the potential to hurt someone."

The ex-soldiers took the training seriously and said they would do their best to apply their new vocation, but they were skeptical about their chances for new employment. I confirmed the validity of that skepticism by speaking with a host of potential employers. The civilian and business world had no incentive to hire ex-soldiers; even if an employer could ignore their past, many said the ex-soldiers simply didn't have the necessary skills.

I concluded two things. First, the former soldiers were getting good training for jobs that probably didn't exist. But second, this would nonetheless not be a core driver of instability in the short term. Washington was surprised by the first and consoled by the second. Both points turned out to be accurate, at least for the next three years. But they were also very short-sighted, as many of the former soldiers would become part of the rising crime rate and increasing gang violence that hit the country later, and a handful would be involved in serious political violence. Potential spoilers, we could see, needed a long-term place to land.

Prison and Justice Systems

One of the places where the rank evil of the Duvalier system and the dysfunction of the Cédras period were on clearest display was the prisons. The central prison had been built by the United States in 1915 for five hundred inmates. The first time I visited it held eight hundred, of whom three hundred were squeezed into the main block in the center of the facility, a single room fifty meters square. The prison was such a travesty that one intelligence officer, driven by pure conscience, had broken curfew to expose it, leading to his court-martial. I toured the facility from the safety of the catwalk and noted that for the large bloc, there were no cots, no mattresses, no functioning sanitation, and no way to even let the prisoners into the yard. The prisons in the countryside were mixed. I visited Les Cayes in the fall of 1995 and found only marginal overcrowding and decent sanitation. But at one point in Jérémie prisoners could go for days without water, while Gonaives held two hundred in a facility built for half that.

I could see the obvious problem was funding; politicians don't want their fingerprints on prison construction because it simply doesn't play well with taxpayers. But there was a much larger issue at play. The journalist Elizabeth Rubin reports that when U.S. civilian police advisors arrived at one Haitian police station in November 1996 they found some twenty detainees jostling for space in a filthy holding cell about the size of a news kiosk. An American advisor summed up: "They're all thrown in together, and they haven't seen a judge."[27]

They haven't seen a judge. We heard that constantly. As many as 90 percent of the prisoners were in pretrial detention, and it was set to get much worse because the police were starting to get organized and make more arrests. But there was not yet a functional justice system to process cases and either convict or release prisoners.

Justice advisor William O'Neill observed of this period, "Haitian justice lacks everything: financial resources, materials, competent personnel, independence, stature and trust. Court facilities are a disgrace, courthouses often indistinguishable from small shops or run-down residences. . . . No judge or prosecutor in Haiti, until mid-1995, had received any specialized professional training."[28] Law schools were similarly inadequate. And some judges were actually illiterate, more like village elders than judicial officials, put in place because of the respect they had earned in their community.

The dysfunction was established in the postrevolutionary period when a commission drafted a Haitian civil code that replicated France's Napoleonic Code. Several major problems persisted because of this earlier system. First, it was possessed of an impossible complexity that could be sustained only in a society with highly educated and motivated officials with ample resources. Second, as a former justice minister, Jean-Joseph Exumé, put it, the judiciary in Haiti has always been politically weak: "We have a judicial body, but not the judicial power."[29] Third, the system was ignored for so many years that it never cohered. Duvalier established an arbitrary system of justice meted out by the Tonton Macoutes and his section chiefs, while "the justice of the peace does not know what is going on in the hills."[30] Finally, there were practical problems, such as lack of bail, which led to large numbers awaiting trial in a criminal court that convened only twice a year.

An informal system continued to a point under Aristide, with a local supporter or appointee taking over the role of regional strongman, and Aristide on some occasions exhorted his followers to simply deliver street justice themselves in the absence of a functional judicial system. But while Aristide did maintain some old-school tendencies, he was supportive of our efforts to develop a judicial system, stating in 1994, "The second cornerstone for both a peaceful democratic society and a prosperous economy is . . . the establishment of an independent judiciary that is able to fairly arbitrate conflicts . . . and provide adequate protection for private sector activity, property rights and fundamental human rights."[31]

For prison reform we had a $1.2 million program administered through the UN Development Program by a talented French former prison director. The program evolved to be a mix of technical assistance and infrastructure enhancements, the latter driven by my concern that the early emphasis on technical assistance alone was going to lead to training guards how to secure prisoners whose cells had no doors, or properly manage sanitation in a prison with no bathrooms. After a horrific incident in which a prisoner lost a leg due to gangrene brought on by malnourishment we also added a kitchen to the package; my guides always showed me its progress when I visited. Another early reform was the establishment of a separate prison for women and juveniles.

The prison system was one of the more tangible programs and evinced slow progress, with a physical infrastructure and people who could be looked after. But the justice system was a more amorphous beast that required a much longer period of support to be at all effective, something we found was simply at odds with the impatience of the international community, especially the United States.

When I arrived, we had a very skilled team from the Department of Justice, led by a Haitian American, Carl Alexandre, whose native creole helped with the challenge of managing the day-to-day issues of supporting the current system while training new judges and building a new system. It is noteworthy that wherever America works, it draws on its rich immigrant population in a way few other nations can.

The teams had some initial successes, building on and later blending with the efforts of U.S. Army Civil Affairs, which had deployed a team of eighteen judges, court clerks, and lawyers under Maj. Gen. Donald Campbell, a New Jersey superior court judge. The army reservists had developed a good rapport with Justice Minister Exumé and his officers as they fanned out to assess and advise the country's four hundred courts. They made recommendations on which judges to keep, prevailed on the minister to increase judges' salaries from $80 a month to $320, and mentored the judges and their staffs.

I was impressed by the skills of these Civil Affairs officers and came to see them as America's natural nation-builders. They came in with critical skills, a command structure, and, most important of all, the requirement to deploy under any conditions and to any location, an ability that is difficult to find in most other organizations. They were highly respected by the judges and lawyers and often had unique reach back to resources and people in local communities in the United States.

With $18 million in funding the U.S. Department of Justice renovated the former military academy and turned it into a magistrates' school, now a permanent institution, and worked with the Ministry to develop judicial training at the law school. For the first time in Haiti's history an Office of Judicial Supervision was established to monitor the performance of judges and prosecutors.

Significantly the teams thought through the bottlenecks and decided that if they couldn't heal the entire justice system, they could at least apply some tourniquets. In a July 1997 cable with the self-congratulatory title "Explosion in Haiti's Prison Population Averted by [U.S. Government] Legal Aid Programs and Modest Improvements in Justice System," I noted that in just a year we had slowed the increase in prison population to one-sixth of what it had been.

We did it by focusing on those cases where the individual had already served longer in pretrial detention than his sentence would have been had he been convicted. This got an astounding number released. We also worked on the case management system to get at the many prisoners who were simply lost in the system, and provided mentors to tie it all together. It was a bit Kafkaesque, if that term hasn't already been overused in Haiti. In months we had secured the release of three thousand prisoners. And while 300 a month were coming into the national penitentiary, some 250 to 275 a month were finally being processed out.

It was a small victory and it was not clear how sustainable any of it would be. I implored Washington not to prematurely see this program as sustainable, suggesting it was averting a humanitarian disaster and should be continued for several years until it could be institutionalized. I commented in a journal during this period, "People now say they hope 1997 will be the year we hoped 1996 would be. Probably will say the same thing about 1998."

Building a Police Force

For the early period of our tenure the police were the centerpiece of the U.S. effort, following the formula "no police, no security; no security, no democracy." In most transitions the requirement was to reform and upgrade existing security forces, so a clean sweep in Haiti would prove to be a challenge.

The short-term plan was for the twenty-three thousand members of the international force in September 1994 to be slowly replaced by Haitian security forces until the new police were fully fielded, complete with special units, by July 1997. To help with the transition during the U.S.-led phase of operations the former police commissioner of New York City Ray Kelly brought 670 international police monitors from twenty countries, including Benin, Jordan, Argentina, Bolivia, Pakistan, and the Caribbean Community, in October 1994. They patrolled with the interim force from twelve bases across the country, mentoring, monitoring arrests, overseeing treatment of detainees, and generally keeping the peace.

Kelly later stressed to me the importance of a long-term mentoring relationship with the new officers at all levels and for all functions. He compared the new Haitian police to the force in New York City, which had many second- and third-generation officers, a city with a culture of policing, an established academy, and older officers to mentor their younger peers. Haiti would have none of that, and while he hoped it would not take three generations to get there, he knew it would take a lot longer than six months. In March 1995 the long-term police monitoring mission was taken over by UN civilian police, led primarily by Canada.

We noted in our embassy briefing that the Haitian National Police (HNP) would be lacking in the three E's: equipment, experience, and encadrement (leadership). Our solution was to provide $8 million in equipment, prolong the UNMIH mandate to provide deeper experience and mentoring, and offer $64 million over five years to establish an academy, train 5,200 officers, and develop specialized units. It was a credible plan but required constant vigilance, extreme flexibility with resources and assistance, and a long game.

The first class of 375 graduated in June 1995 after four months of training from American, Canadian, and French trainers. The academy would turn out a steady stream of graduates, hitting the full contingent of 5,200 by mid-1996. For most of the cadets the first time they handled a firearm or drove a vehicle was upon entry into the force.

The new officers would be paid wildly above the national average, $330 a month, on the assumption that higher salaries would avert corruption.[32] It was probably the right decision, but it did make the force expensive, constraining the numbers of officers that could be fielded. The trade-off between salary level and numbers would be constant; Schulz pointed out in April 1996 that the country needed between seven thousand and twelve thousand security personnel to provide a marginal degree of security.[33] Our Haitian counterparts balked even at the lower figure, in part over cost and in part to keep the number of armed men in the country to a bare minimum. In the end it was hard enough to make the 5,200-officer force effective enough that no one pushed back, but in retrospect the higher numbers were probably what was needed, and today the target is fifteen thousand.

Getting the force's leadership to a good place was a struggle, as it was in all the new institutions. The effort to enlist officers who were untainted generally meant that they had no security experience whatsoever. The first chief, an ex-divinity professor named Adrien Rameau, was appointed by Aristide just ahead of the first class of HNP cadets in May 1995 and quickly found himself out of his element. After an incident in which a small girl was killed and the twenty-four-man contingent of Cité Soleil chased out of their station, he told SRSG Brahimi that he "didn't want to tell the police what to do." (If the new HNP were having a difficult time breaking with Haitian tradition, so were its citizens.) Brahimi firmly reminded him, "You *are* the police," which seemed to come as a bit of a shock.

Rameau was relieved several days later, and after a second candidate was rejected by the Senate, Pierre Denize took over. Like Rameau he came to the job with a lack of experience—he ran a drug rehab center—but unlike Rameau he was a solid leader and a quick study, took advice, and could be tough when necessary. He earned the respect of most of us and stayed on for several years.

I started to get out and meet with the police in the field as they deployed, amazed at some of the early progress. In late September I wrote, "It is encouraging to see how they are received in the communities where they are deployed, the first time in this country's history that it has a security force whose main objective isn't cracking heads."

In December 1995 I commented on the experience of watching two U.S.-trained officers monitor a polling stating during an election: "[They were] one of the strongest symbols of the changes taking place here. Eight years ago the equivalent would have protected armed thugs who attacked polling stations and threw the election, now they are deployed all over the country not only to provide physical security, but ensuring the integrity of the process (they questioned me aggressively and made sure I was there as a legitimate observer, not a partisan)."

After the successful handover to the UN in February 1996 I similarly commented that it was an incredible feat to have demobilized the army and trained a five-thousand-man police force from scratch in less than eight months, the largest project of its kind in recent history. All similar programs—in El Salvador, South Africa, Panama—had an army in the background to maintain security and did not involve these large numbers.

Still, there were persistent challenges. In a September 9, 1995, meeting with the UN civilian police chief, we were told that the new police were having a difficult time seeing themselves as servants of the people along traditional Western models of policing, and quickly fell into the Haitian model of using their position for personal gain.

In late October I made a trip to the southeast claw to review our programs in Les Cayes and Aquin. Seeing both the half-empty and the half-full parts of the glass, I commented, "The police are enthusiastic and well-trained, but without equipment, vehicles, and communications." At one rural police station we found the ten or so officers living in people's homes because the station house was not completed; one said he felt like he had been "parachuted" into his duty station. They had no communications and only one vehicle. The vehicles for all the police were small Toyota pickup trucks that sat very high on the chassis and tended to flip easily on gravel roads. With no way to repair or maintain them, we ended up with a veritable graveyard of damaged and wrecked vehicles in a matter of months. The U.S. military, as was often the case, filled the gap by building and staffing a vehicle maintenance facility. And there were always gaps to be filled.

In addition to the problems of fielding this new force we also had to contend with domestic politics in the United States, with political sniping at the policy leading to holds on funding and at one point the threat of walking away from the program altogether. Bipartisanship that yielded clear timelines and a consistent funding stream would have been most welcome by those of us executing the policy.

Things on the street continued to be rough and the police often responded poorly. We had good outreach and oversight through the civilian police contingents, but it was never complete. Between July 1995 and November 1996, the HNP killed at least forty-six civilians and wounded fifty more. They had taken a few casualties themselves, but their frustration when encountering opposition and the lack of the full spectrum of law enforcement capabilities and capable backup were leading to increasing confrontations with crowds and civilians.

One case garnered international attention. On March 4, 1996, HNP responded to a demonstration and killed a demonstrator after he slapped an officer. Nine demonstrators were arrested and taken to the HNP's Ministerial Security Corps HQ, one of them surfacing the next day with a bullet in the chest after the others had been released. Residents of Port-au-Prince's Cité Soleil slum gathered to demonstrate over the killing, blocking National Route 1 and reportedly using a broken bottle to attack a police officer. For the next few hours various police and ministerial security officers swarmed Cité Soleil, searching for members of the Red Army, a local gang. There were detentions, shootouts, and extrajudicial killings, leaving eight dead and at least eleven wounded. It was a mess.

Cité Soleil is one of the most crowded slums in the hemisphere, a place where people were funneled from both north and south as a kind of dumping ground of those who had run out of options. Worse than much of the city, it did not have enough water and practically no sanitation, only rivulets of run-off between the houses.

The police station, which we visited often, was at the very end of the community, on the water, presumably so that the officers could make a waterborne getaway if necessary, but helpful in keeping them fully in the community, not on the outskirts.

I found Cité Soleil an intriguing but suffocating place, where the crush of humanity made you want to simply get out, even into the chaotic streets of Port-au-Prince, to breathe again. We found the families of the March 4 victims and got their side of story for congressional investigators. But more important we realized the police needed a boost.

Frustrated that we had not been able to contribute to the civilian police force because we have no federal police, U.S. officials hit upon the idea of allowing local U.S. police officers to take a leave of absence from their force and be contracted as a U.S. contingent. So in early November I returned from the United States with the first seventeen Haitian American officers from LAPD, Chicago, NYPD, and Boston. I commented, "The Haitians see them as returning sons, who have been abroad to learn and experience something of the functioning world and are now returning to impart some of that experience to their countrymen." All of us were struck by their size; nothing like twenty years of U.S. nourishment to physically separate them from their peers. The contingent would grow to fifty and was one of our most successful programs. The men had professional gravitas, and being native Creole speakers gave them a huge leg up on their counterparts from French-speaking countries. The UN contingent was initially skeptical of them, as their swagger and demands could be exhausting.

Then, on November 11, Augusto Tavernier from the NYPD and Yves Orno from Boston were enlisted to join a Canadian RCMP and two French gendarmes to fly to Isle de Gonaives and resolve a distress call from an HNP contingent. The helicopter dropped the five off and, to their surprise, promised to return only the next day.

They moved to the HNP station, easy enough to find since one of its buildings was on fire, where they encountered a crowd of four hundred who had surrounded the compound and were brandishing knives, machetes, and Molotov cocktails. Incensed over a series of incidents that included killings, sexual predation, and corruption, the crowd's strategy was to wait until the officers were out of ammunition and rush them. They had burned down the courthouse on the way to the commissariat, which they saw as being no different from the previous regime. The U.S. officers surmised that the only way any of them would get through the night was by visibly disarming the HNP and ensuring the crowd the officers would be taken in for disciplinary actions. The crowd also insisted they produce the Uzis and shotguns (it seemed they knew the weapons inventory) and that the UN officers go to the morgue to see the body of a young man they accused the police of killing.

This satisfied half the crowd, but two hundred or so stayed on, at one point adding a Rara band complete with drums to keep the throng riled up and alert. The U.S. officers managed the crowd for the entire night, negotiating and cajoling and making assurances. Relief finally arrived the next day in the form of a small UN military contingent and twenty more HNP with the district commissioner, who promised the town an accounting would be forthcoming. The crowd allowed the contingent to leave but pelted them with rocks on the way out to make the point that they would rather have handled it themselves. Without the Creole-speaking U.S. officers, the Canadian RCMP assured me, the entire HNP contingent would have been killed.

The U.S. contingent was not a panacea; several were sent home for disciplinary issues, generally related to going native in their treatment of civilians or to insubordination. But it made a difference—there is simply no substitute for the neutral international player to keep everyone on the straight and narrow and the tough-minded mentoring that our guys provided.

And a Special Investigative Unit

Alongside mainstream police development, certain incidents demonstrated the need for special units. The right-wing politician Mireille Durocher Bertin was murdered on March 28, 1995, several days after forming an anti-Aristide political party and days before President Clinton's visit to Haiti. The case quickly took on political overtones as U.S. congressional opponents of the Haiti policy made it the centerpiece of their attempt to discredit the administration's efforts. As a supporter of Cédras, Bertin was lionized by the American right, who shared her sentiment that the country would have been better off had he stayed in power.

Given the void in law enforcement, a substantial team of FBI agents came to Port-au-Prince to investigate and in December were ready to pass the case on to local investigators. We formed a Special Investigative Unit (SIU) that, working under a U.S. advisor, handled this and other cases until either the leads ran out or it was clear that the case was so politically sensitive it would never be solved.

The SIU became somewhat proficient at investigations, and the close mentoring it received in these early years helped develop some of the security force's better leaders. Its first commander, Mario Andresol, went on to lead the police with effectiveness from 2006 to 2012, during probably their toughest years, with little political backing and a rise in crime that spiked dramatically with the mass escape during the earthquake of 2010. He turned over his duties with the accession of President Michel Martelly and, in a very Haitian story, has gone on to be a very popular and successful fashion designer—naturally, his supporters say, for a man who was arguably the best-dressed man in Haiti. There are few shortcuts to that patient development of leaders, along with the other many things for which there are also few shortcuts.

And a Coast Guard

Another successful program that similarly had to do with mentoring, resources, and longevity was to create the Haitian Coast Guard, overseen by Cmdr. Phil Heyl, who was passionate about building new units and improving their capacity. He had $1.1 million in U.S. security assistance funding for four twenty-five-foot Boston Whalers, spare parts, and refurbishment of the base at Killick. He also had a very healthy training budget and the ability to send leaders and technical personnel to U.S. schools while bringing trainers to Haiti, augmented by partners from Canada. The demilitarized Coast Guard would be an arm of the police that combined shoreline policing with search and rescue.

Unlike the police, the Coast Guard's forty personnel came from the previous force. The unit held up longer than most and went on to produce several excellent security sector leaders, including Charles Pierre, who would lead the police effectively several years in the future, and Reginald Delva, who was sent to West Point and would later become the country's interior minister. But the force itself eventually fell into disrepair. By 2007, a time when as much as 8 percent of U.S.-directed cocaine was being transshipped through Haiti or the Dominican Republic, the Coast Guard was down to two boats and with little political backing was largely overwhelmed.[34] It has since made a comeback, and U.S. and Canadian assistance continue to improve its capabilities, which have been helpful during recent natural disasters. The early foundation laid in the 1990s did not survive intact, but it was never entirely swept away.

The Indispensable Palace Security

First among equals because of the impact it could have on stability broadly was the Palace Security Force. As we would find in Afghanistan fifteen years later, this was the one place the entire project could come crashing down in a single incident. I persistently made the case that palace security should be the very last piece of security assistance we withdrew, arguing to Washington that it was "one thing if they don't pick up the trash or make the power work, quite another if they make mistakes in the presidential security arena that leads to [President René] Préval getting killed." It really was a single-bullet regime.

That emphasis was not misplaced. Eight years later, when right-wing parties sought to depose Aristide, they claimed on the radio, "The fight in Port-au-Prince will not even last one hour ... [because] the people who are going to help us get [Aristide] are already with him."[35]

A small team of U.S. soldiers from the 101st Airborne Division who were a combination of mentors, trainers, and liaisons and, most important, the final line of defense in the event of a coup were brought in to base at the palace. They recognized that the raw material they were working with and the vast gray area of local political and cultural factors left some uncertainty about what they would be leaving behind.

We continued to monitor and manage the security at the palace, keeping U.S. security contractors and State Department diplomatic security officers there trying to build an effective unit while providing that essential inner cordon. But there wasn't a clear place for it in the Haitian security force organization, and loyalty was a fickle thing, so personnel were subject to constant rotations and distrust. It was also tricky to correctly calibrate the proper weaponry—arm them too heavy and they are a coup in waiting; too light, and they can't fight off an attack.

By mid-August 1996 there were coup rumors that gave even Préval concern. Washington responded by sending a small contingent of the 82nd Airborne in late July to work with the U.S. Support Group, and a heavy platoon of marines augmented the embassy three weeks later. The show of force reminded nefarious actors that when we say we are still in the game we mean it, and when we say we are just over the horizon, the horizon is not all that far away.

The chatter regarding threats continued. Then, on August 24–25, in reaction to the arrest of twenty ultra-right-wingers accused of plotting against the government, a hit squad from the opposition attacked the Legislative Palace and a nearby police station with rocket-propelled grenades and rifle fire. The attack was relatively ineffective but caused the police to flee. The guards at the palace, who were now jumpy, soon ordered a car that they thought was casing the place to stop, Haitian style, by shooting in the air. After the expenditure of a thousand rounds they realized the driver was involved in nothing more than bad timing as he showed visiting relatives around the city.

Préval, meanwhile, was awakened by the firing. Joseph Moise, Préval's security advisor, who himself spent over a year in the palace jail as a security prisoner under Duvalier, went to Préval's room to brief him on what had happened. There he found the president standing in his room, two bandoleers of ammunition draped across his chest, an Uzi in one hand, a Galil in the other, and a pistol in his belt. Before Moise could speak, Préval said simply, "The bastards took my country once, they won't take it again, even if I have to fight myself." I remarked in a journal on the quiet nobility of this soft-spoken leader who no one, including Préval himself, was sure would be up to the job. "He is honest, sincere, lives a simple life, and has the best interest of his people at heart."

The incident ended well enough. But then, all good things in that environment were fleeting. A few days before this, unidentified gunmen had assassinated two right-wing politicians, and by early September there were indications that the Palace Security Unit was involved. In our zeal to protect the palace from the people, we had neglected to protect the people from the palace. Seeking to head off the assault on the policy that was sure to come, a bevy of U.S. and Canadian high-level officials arrived to impress on Préval the importance of getting ahead of the story with investigations and restructuring. Préval agreed to allow a larger foreign contingent to come in and essentially take over the Palace Security Unit. They would protect him but also assist the SIU with a full investigation of what had happened and carry out a parallel investigation of their own. It would be an all-consuming issue and another major effort we would be working with for the next year, and another one that would never quite take hold.

The timing of the issue was less than optimal, coming immediately before a contentious second-term election for Clinton, which Senator Bob Dole was contesting, in part by attacking the president's foreign policy record and ensuring Haiti was not in the success category. In the October 6, 1996, presidential debate, Dole suggested, "Saddam Hussein is probably better off than he was four years ago. Réné Préval is probably better off than he was four years ago." But, he asked, "are the American people?" We patiently responded to each inquiry; in one case our house manager, Alex Laguerre, and I went into the slums of Cité Soleil to find the widow of an attack and ensure she was taken care of.

Clinton won the election, and the congressional attacks subsided a bit, but only a bit. The policy and everything we did would remain under U.S. political assault continuously, making time-lines shorter, funding tentative, and any effort to build long-term capacity more difficult.

The security forces never fully turned the corner on the road to self-sufficiency but, through many ups and downs, kept improving. As SRSG Ter Horst put it, "There's little mystery that building a new institution takes time. Just as you can't produce a human being in less than nine months, it is difficult to produce a police force in less than three years."[36] We were leaving behind a vast unfinished project, but there would be many others who would keep it moving forward in the years to come.

The Politics and Economics of Instability

The security and judicial institutions were always just one part of that unfinished project, but we were forever judging whether they, and the country, would hold up without an improving econ-omy, which was itself often held hostage by political forces. Aris-tide's stated objective was captured in the reasonable expectations "From misery to poverty with dignity." But reaching this modest goal would require more than just rhetoric. The real need was for functional institutions, a fact borne out by the many Haitians who flourished abroad and realized that "misrule, not laziness," had held them back, as Girard puts it.[37]

Haiti was behind the curve in every possible way. During the three-year embargo leading up to the intervention, Haiti had lost eighty thousand manufacturing jobs, only a quarter of which would ever return. The agricultural economy after the intervention had been undercut by cheap foreign imports intended to reward the poor but serving only to make agriculture unprofitable. I overflew the northern claw in the spring of 1997 and was shocked at the desolate terrain: "It looked almost exactly like the scrubby land-scape in Somalia, and is about as unyielding in terms of crops. The only sign of production one sees from the air are the black circles where the peasants have been burning what few trees there are to make charcoal, which is shipped to Port-au-Prince." Rural inhabitants flooded the cities, adding to the already high unemployment.

Getting Haiti from misery to mere poverty would take considerable foreign assistance for the medium term, and in principle foreign donors took seriously Préval's plea to "provide jobs or there will be an explosion." But foreign assistance was increasingly difficult to sustain as donors became fatigued, Haitians stewed over required reforms, and the country encountered limits in what it could manage. The immediate question was how much tough love to apply in insisting on privatization of state-owned enterprises, and how to balance that with the impact it would have on already high unemployment. The common formula of insisting on deep reforms was not universally accepted in the case of Haiti.

The former ambassador Robert Oakley and the analyst Michael Dziedzic, for example, concluded, "U.S. policy makers and international financial institutions need to strike a balance between withholding economic assistance as an inducement to reform, versus the injection of funds essential for economic revitalization and political performance. Denial of assistance could undermine domestic confidence in the Preval government to such an extent that it becomes too feeble to adopt or implement the very reforms being sought by the international community."[38] Schulz similarly argued, "The neoliberal economic package being imposed on the government will likely prolong the current socioeconomic hardship . . . and may lead to a disillusionment with democracy."[39]

The issue did indeed lead directly to political instability. Former president Aristide had broken with Préval largely over privatization (while also wanting an independent power base), starting the breakaway party Fanmi Lavalas in mid-1996. By March 1997 the secretary general of the original Lavalas Party blamed Aristide for acts of violence that left fifty dead in six weeks, including eight police officers, suggesting the violence was intended to "interrupt the process of institutionalization."[40] Schulz called it an "economic coup d'état."[41]

Aristide countered in a press conference that the government itself was directing the violence, suggesting, "Insecurity is one means they are using to cow us and make us accept [the new economic plan and extend the international presence]." It was never clear who was behind the violence, if anyone. But all sides understood that instability could be used as a political tool, to many possible ends.

In addition to sequencing of reforms, there were problems with absorptive capacity. After a donors' conference I commented, "Haiti does not have the means to spend the money which the international community would like to give it. The ministries are so lacking in qualified people, the government is so unable to plan and organize, and there is such a lack of urgency on the part of anyone that millions of dollars is waiting for a time when the country can successfully spend them, or in some cases be used elsewhere." In one of those many moments of despair, I commented in a letter, "Having failed to provide for its people, this government cannot even organize itself sufficiently to help others who will help its people." It had, I concluded, been a very long week, as so many weeks were.

It may have been reasonable for the international community to expect adherence to this neoliberal framework, but in the end it didn't work. Stubbornness on both sides led to such a breakdown that Haiti got neither privatization nor assistance nor institutionalization, losing half a billion dollars a year in foreign aid from 1997 to 1999.

The feud between the two Lavalas factions led after the poorly attended elections of April 4, 1997 (90 percent of the populace stayed home), to Aristide's Fanmi Lavalas controlling the Senate while Préval's mainstream Lavalas controlled the Chamber of Deputies. The Parliament was hopelessly divided, and by October the country was without a government when Prime Minister Rosny Smarth resigned. "During the remainder of Préval's mandate," Girard writes, "political rivalries would wreck Haiti's transition to democracy and the Haitian people, as always, would pay the price for their leaders' fractiousness."[42] But it would go on far beyond Préval's mandate, and in fact was just the beginning of a series of crises that would last the better part of a decade.

My last few months in the spring of 1997 were a blur as we continued to work the full range of issues at an accelerated pace. I was given a Superior Honor Award a few months after I left by Assistant Secretary of State Jeff Davidow, asking quietly during the photo shoot if I would have to give it back if the thing went sideways. He said he thought things "going sideways" in Haiti was a bit of a relative concept, so I should plan on keeping the award.

Haiti was a difficult place not to love, but a hard place to help. I think Ambassador Swing, speaking through official press guidance, spoke for most of us when he was asked whether he was disappointed in the results after his departure. He said during his four years in Haiti he had witnessed the successful intervention of twenty-one thousand U.S.-led troops; the first peaceful democratic transfer of presidential office; the beginnings of economic modernization, including successful privatization; and the development of democratic institutions. He acknowledged the challenges that remained for Haiti: economic growth, enduring political institutions, encouraging a culture of tolerance, judicial reform, and solving political assassinations. He was honored to be there during a momentous transition to a more functional Haitian society and had played a large role in ensuring support for Haiti's modernization. That transition, he said, is now in progress.

In short, he did what he could, which is what we all did. And yes, that transition was in progress; it just wasn't clear then how long it would take.

Muddling Along through Political Crisis to Earthquake and Back to Political Crisis

The struggle to create stability continued. Bob Manuel, with whom I had worked closely when he was Haiti's secretary for public security, was chased out of office by Aristide in the fall of 1997 and went into exile. His successor was killed within days, leaving one observer to conclude, "Haiti confirmed its international reputation as an impenetrable, irretrievable hotbed of political violence."[43] I later came across him in Afghanistan in 2002, where he was a UN official working on the elections there. Manuel was a very talented guy and it struck me as unfortunate he was trying to help Afghanistan develop stability when he was needed at home.

Aristide was reelected in 2000, adding exasperation to the growing fatigue of donors. The peacekeeping mission by then had been reduced to a few hundred police advisors and was closed out in February 2001, when Aristide took office. Far from the widespread high-level turnout for his second inauguration, few leaders showed up this time. The country topped Transparency's annual survey of the world's most corrupt nations in 2004 as Aristide's always erratic behavior went from the pernicious to the bizarre. He used the bicentennial of Louverture's death in 2003 to demand that France reimburse Haiti for the indemnity it paid to the French upon independence, plus interest—a figure he calculated at $21 billion. He relied increasingly on popular justice and vigilante groups, especially the "*chimères* gang," a criminal group led by a notorious thug, allowing the nation's security institutions to atrophy. Aristide's international shunning was matched by increasing internal isolation.

In the fall of 2003 Aristide started to lose control even of his own *chimères*, with demonstrations hitting the country on a scale not seen since the time of Baby Doc. By February 2004 there was a full-scale revolt in play, as the *chimères* had switched sides after the mysterious death of their leader and were now taking town after town in the north. When they threatened to march south, the United States and France convinced Aristide that the jig really was up this time and facilitated his exile, followed by a brief intervention by Canadian, Chilean, French, and U.S. troops that turned back into a peacekeeping mission in June 2004.

The fabric of the country had completely unraveled. As Girard puts it, "Under Aristide, Haiti had been undemocratic. Now that he was gone, the country was ungovernable . . . a political patchwork ruled by local chefs de guerre, Aristide devotees, remnants of the army, or in the case of Gonaives, chimères warlords."[44] The new UN Stabilization Mission in Haiti kept such order as it could, at least in Port-au-Prince, and where possible delivered humanitarian assistance, losing ten peacekeepers by 2006.

After a two-year caretaker government Préval was reelected and governed with relative effectiveness for five years, from 2006 to 2011. GDP began to grow again, rising to 2.3 percent in 2006, 3.4 in 2007, and 1.2 in 2008. But in Haiti no good trend can flourish; the country was hit hard by four tropical storms in 2008, and then the historic earthquake in 2010 that killed 200,000 and shattered the country's barely recovering infrastructure. A cholera epidemic brought to Haiti by a UN contingent killed another 10,000 that year. But the earthquake sent images of human misery around the globe that bought the country a stream of goodwill on an order that was in some ways without precedent in the hemisphere.

The security and judicial systems we tried to develop are still struggling to take hold, largely because the comprehensive legal reform required to anchor them was slow to occur. By the time of the earthquake in 2010 the population of the central prison had gone from 1,500 to 4,500, and there were 10,000 prisoners nationwide. When the earthquake hit, most of the prisoners in the central prison escaped and set off a crime wave that has become a part of Haiti's current urban reality. The UN Periodic Review from 2011 reports that between 80 and 90 percent of all prisoners in Haiti had not been tried, and defendants spent an average of 408 days in pretrial detention, while the backlog in cases was worsening. The earthquake also caused widespread loss of files and the destruction of forty-nine judicial buildings, further diminishing judicial activity.[45]

But undaunted, Haitian officials working with UN advisors have over the past five years redoubled their efforts, and a new Criminal Code and Criminal Procedure is currently before the Parliament for ratification. This major milestone required the political stability of the past few years to complete. Meanwhile UN advisors have mentored and guided the development of a legal framework for the Forensics Institute, internal rules for the evaluation of judges, a decree on the promotion and advancement of police officers, a law on legal assistance, some 112 judicial acts, and policy guidelines on prison management. The judicial system also gets special attention to address the issue of prolonged pretrial detention and prison conditions and overcrowding.[46]

Brazilian and other police trainers, including an NYPD contingent, have shown incredible resolve, doing the gritty and dangerous work of continuing to mentor and train the police and oversee a considerable amount of joint patrolling and special attention to gang violence, organized crime, arms and human trafficking, and border management. The judicial and security system remains a largely unfinished project, but the groundwork has been laid for future success and there is considerable forward momentum.

The economic picture would continue to struggle. Haiti slid from 150th in the Human Development Index in 1998 to 163rd in 2014. This was, however, a mixed picture, as life expectancy was up by 11.9 years between 1980 and 2014 and mean years of schooling by 3.5, while GDP per capita had decreased by 42 percent. Overall the vast improvements in much of the world had left Haiti behind.[47]

Two presidential administrations have followed, of Michel Martelly, from 2011 to 2016, who I remember as Sweet Mickey, a Kompa singer who founded the Farmer's Response Party, and Jovenal Moïse, his designated successor, beginning in 2016. Transitions have been peaceful and largely orderly.

The period 1995 to 2017 makes one generation. I wondered if building a security system might take three generations after all, as Kelly suggested. In any case, it was always going to take longer than the six months that was originally allotted.

Did We Do Any Good? Lessons Learned

True to the spirit of the unfinished project Haiti remains, I have in my papers an unfinished essay that I started soon after my departure. I called it "Haiti—The Case for Semi-Dependency" and argued that "our Haiti policy [was] failing" because of two divergent trends: underestimating what needed to be done and overestimating what we had done. This, I argued, has led for some time to thinking that we are almost across the finish line, while in fact we are just getting started, skewing our actions in favor of security-related policies and programs at the expense of the building of economic potential and civil society. I thought such thinking derived from false assumptions and false comparisons about what it would take to instill liberal capitalism and responsible democratic government in such a fragile and battered country. Haiti, I said, did not simply need the restoration of its elected president and the development of his security forces; it needed a comprehensive program for the building of society. I knew the country would continue to require a lot of help for a very long time.

There was a book that obsessed our Haitian American naval attaché as he tried to puzzle together what it would take to build a new society in Haiti, comparing it to his experience in Central America. In *Pericles of Athens and the Birth of Democracy*, Donald Kagan writes of "the shadow of Pericles." In Pericles's funeral oration the compelling image is one of citizens who "were willing to run risks in [Athens's] defense, sacrifice on its behalf, and restrain their passion and desires to preserve it."[48] Kagan suggests three essential conditions for the flourishing of such a democracy: good institutions, a body of citizens with an understanding of the "character" of democracy, and a high quality of leadership, at least at critical moments. "At times, the third qualification is the most important and can compensate for weaknesses in the other two."[49]

Kagan warns that if the world's newly free nations see democracy chiefly as a quick route to material well-being and equal distribution of wealth, they will be badly disappointed, and democracy will fail. "To succeed ... they must see that democracy alone of all regimes respects the dignity and autonomy of every individual, and understand that its survival requires that each individual sees its own well-being as inextricably connected to that of the whole community." Above all else, "the new democracies will need leaders of the Periclean mold."[50]

More than mere institutions, for Haiti to succeed it needs a new social contract. Slowly and painfully, that social contract is being written. In the end I believe Haiti simply had to live through the challenges of the past twenty years to expunge its fascination with demagogues, to value the worth of each citizen, and to overcome its horrific past. It was never going to be easy. Or quick.

We had learned a great deal about preparing UN contingents for deployments, about civil-military integration, about building police and other institutions, about guiding a fragile political process. But we had not learned that cases such as Haiti's are the work of a generation, and will take the better part of a generation of patient nurturing and support, to get to a place of self-sufficiency and stability. Do we have a generation in our political system? We do, apparently, as twenty years on we are still there. But it would be easier if we settled in for the long haul upon arrival rather than going in fits and starts through what was always going to be a very long process.

SIX

Darfur, 2007

Beating Back a Genocide

When the World Says Enough

One of the perverse downsides of certain missions is an inability to take credit for success because there is a larger political imperative for keeping the success quiet. We also sometimes succeed at the primary mission, but then are frustrated that everything else didn't get fixed alongside it. Sort of like replacing the carpet in the living room, and then being agitated that the family room carpet is still worn out. This was the case in Darfur, where the international community was galvanized with the images of genocide and united to stop it. It largely succeeded in this endeavor but was unable to trumpet the success in order to maintain pressure on the Khartoum government. It also found that sustaining this very tentative success would require a long process of developing a political framework among the Darfur rebel groups. While the genocide had clear culprits and victims, the political way forward played out in a haze of gray and continues in that haze today.

But we did help stop the genocide.[1]

An Unforgiving Landscape Made Worse by a Nation at War with Itself

A good Foreign Service officer can capture the essence of a place with a single phrase. "Sudan," my mentor Andrew Steinfeld said, "is where the Arab world comes crashing into sub-Saharan Africa." And so it was. Sudan is one of Africa's many unlikely countries, where three very different regions have been assembled together in a makeshift political arrangement. South Sudan is Christian and animist, green and fertile, populated by sub-Saharan African tribes, and has most of the country's oil reserves. Northern Sudan is Muslim, a mixed African and Arab populace, and has sought clumsily to play a leadership role in the Arab world. Muslim Darfur in the west was the home of the Fur Sultanate, by 1800 the most powerful and dynamic state within Sudan's modern borders, an "African kingdom that adopted Arabs as valued equals," as one commentator put it.[2] The north in 2006 was home to sixteen million citizens, the south nine million, and Darfur six million.

Historically the north saw South Sudan as a place for plunder—ivory, slaves, and later oil—and sought to impose an Islamic system there to maintain the country's cultural and legal integrity. This led the south in 1983 to reignite earlier struggles for independence. The central government in the north similarly saw Darfur as a place of plunder, when it was not being ignored. So Sudan by the mid-twentieth century consisted of a Muslim Arab north with traces of Africanness seeking to impose its culture and will on the rest of the country, a Christian and animist African south with oil seeking independence from the north, and an African Muslim west ignored by the rest of the country. This was hardly a recipe for success, and things played out badly for all sides.

Independent of its conflict with the central government, Darfur also contained its own fraught political and environmental tensions. The prominent Darfur experts Julie Flint and Alex de Waal describe it as "a forbidding place, with landscapes of elemental simplicity: vast sandy plains, jutting mountains and jagged ridges, and occasional ribbons of green along the all-too-rare seasonal watercourses. A village, sometimes comprising no more than a cluster of huts made from straw and branches, may be a day's ride from its neighbors."

But, they continue, "Darfur's people are resourceful and resilient. Extracting a living from this land requires unrelenting hard work and detailed knowledge of every crevice from which food and livelihood can be scratched. A woman living on the desert edge will know how to gather a dozen varieties of wild grasses and berries to supplement a meager diet of cultivated millet and vegetables, along with goat's or camel's milk. Nomads move 300 miles or more twice a year, ranging even further in exceptionally wet or unusually dry years. 'Settled' people move also, migrating to open up new areas of farmland."[3]

With as many as ninety tribes Darfur was an independent kingdom until 1916, when it was absorbed into Sudan, then part of the British Empire. The early interplay between two key historical economic groupings, the Baggara, or "cattle people," and the Abbala, or "camel men," would play out with horrendous consequences in the first part of the current war. Fighting among the various tribes of the Baggara—Tunjur, Zaghawa, Berti, Birgid, Massalit, and numerous smaller groups—would be the region's undoing in the second phase.

The property distribution system during the Fur dynasty period led to the Baggara receiving land under a system loosely associated with the various tribes. Their Abbala cousins, Flint and de Waal explain, "moving as nomads in the densely administered northern provinces, occasionally received small estates, but had no jurisdiction over huge swathes of territory. To this day, many Abbala Arabs explain their involvement in the current conflict in terms of this 250-year-old search for land, granted to the Baggara but denied them."[4]

Darfur was neglected by the central government from the start, with development beginning only after 1945. By this time the province had been reduced to a footnote economically, and even its cultural contributions to the Sudanese nation were downplayed. Still, the Darfur tribes went along with a Sudanization program, becoming increasingly assimilated. By the 1980s, however, as Flint and de Waal write, "the complaint of most Darfurians was not that the process of 'becoming Sudanese' denied them their own unique cultural heritage, but that the government in Khartoum was not treating them as full citizens of the Sudanese state." Darfur "was a backwater, a prisoner of geography."[5] There was also an increasing element of racism in the treatment by the Arab central government of their black compatriots in Darfur and the south.

The ascendancy of a hardline president, Omar al-Bashir, in 1989 gave the Islamists the upper hand and pitted the Sudanese government against both the established regional Arab order and its own southern and western citizens. Bashir sided with Saddam Hussein in Iraq and supported wars of destabilization in the region, later taking isolation to a new global level by hosting Osama bin Laden when he was ejected from Saudi Arabia in 1992.

The regime had also begun a strategy of using local militias as a bulwark against the independence-minded southerners, arming and empowering local tribes who could be incentivized to fight for their own interests. Sudan endured crippling isolation and turned inward, largely oblivious to what the world thought about its scorched-earth policies toward the rebellion in the south. But it was accepting of some pressure, as the ejection of bin Laden in 1996 at the behest of the United States demonstrated. Darfurians continued to seethe with frustration toward the central government, but by then they were dealing with urgent local problems. Supported by Khartoum, increasing numbers of armed Arabs, under environmental pressure as their traditional grazing areas were blocked or taken over, were starting to push an agenda of quasi-apartheid. They raided and plundered non-Arab villages while armed groups in Darfur sprung up in self-defense against the marauding horsemen.

Early in 2000 a number of factors came together that would produce the conditions for the mass slaughter to follow. In May a challenge to the government emerged in the form of a roughly assembled document, 1,600 copies of which were distributed around the country and government. *Black Book: Imbalance of Power and Wealth in Sudan* laid out in searing detail how the government was behind systematic policies to disadvantage the south and Darfur; senior government jobs, for example, were in the hands of three tribes representing only 5.4 percent of the population.

Darfurians started to organize militarily and politically to both stand up against increasing attacks on their people and overturn the established discriminatory order in Khartoum. One of the *Black Book*'s authors, the Islamist Khalil Ibrahim, assumed the much-used phrase "justice and equality" for a rebel movement that came to hold the clearest and broadest political position of the emerging rebel factions. He sought to overthrow the central government and restructure the country into its original six political regions with a rotating president from all six.

A second group, initially the Darfur Liberation Movement and later the Sudan Liberation Army (SLA), would prove far less cohesive. But unlike Ibrahim, who resided abroad, its leaders lived in Darfur and represented a greater cross section of tribes, giving it many more fighters. Both groups found that self-defense on the part of the Fur and other tribes could quickly be turned to active rebellion, but they could also be challenged militarily by the armed Arab groups whom they had been bumping up against for years.

Some analysts mark the beginning of the rebellion as July 21, 2001, when Fur and Zaghawa fighters met and declared a solemn oath on the Quran to work together to foil Arab supremacist policies in Darfur.[6] The fighters dramatically raided garrisons and police stations, alarming a central government that was already struggling to hold on to the south. The movement's political agenda was not set, so many of the attacks were for the primary purpose of acquiring arms for self-protection. But through leadership conferences and a meeting with the South Sudanese rebel leader John Garang, the group crystallized, becoming the SLA/M (Sudan Liberation Army/Movement). On March 16, 2003, it issued a political declaration that called for a new Sudan, led by a secular government on principles of equality, decentralization, and self-determination. Unity in the movement would be elusive, with fundamental problems of ethnic divisions, conflicting personalities, lack of leadership skills, and rapid growth.[7] The Justice and Equality Movement (JEM) and SLA were united just long enough to start a war.

The war intensified in the spring of 2003. On April 25 a joint SLA-JEM column of thirty-five land cruisers stormed the garrison town of El Fasher and destroyed four Antonov bombers and a number of helicopter gunships, killing seventy-five soldiers and taking another thirty-two captive, including the garrison commander. The incident shocked Khartoum and the security establishment, who noted that Garang's Sudan People's Liberation Movement had never carried out an attack on this scale. Newly armed, the rebels continued to pummel the government across a broad swath of territory, killing 500 soldiers in Kutum in May, another 250 in Tine in July, and launching a surprise attack on Mellit. Khartoum feared losing the entire province. The government sacked commanders and turned operations over to military intelligence, which had the ideal weapon.

The Arab Janjaweed, or "devils on horseback," were numerous, easy to mobilize, and well-led under the militia leader Musa Hilal. While there were security officials who recognized the inherent political nature of the conflict and the legitimate grievances of the Darfur rebels and wanted to negotiate and offer reasonable concessions, the hardliners won out and developed a simple military strategy. They would arm and empower the Janjaweed and set them loose on the unforgiving terrain of Darfur, first against the rebels, whom they started to push up into the mountains, and then against the civilians. The horsemen burned villages, killing and raping as they went, and destroyed the water sources upon which life depended. The air force did its part by randomly terrorizing villages and offering aerial support to the Janjaweed when they faced armed opposition. Military intelligence, meanwhile, broke down any political support for SLA-JEM through arrests and harassment.

As refugees flowed across the border Chadian officials became alarmed and negotiated a humanitarian cease-fire in N'Djamena on April 8, 2004, between the government, SLA, and JEM. The agreement also provided an opening for a small group of 3,300 peacekeepers, mostly Rwandan and Nigerian. But the killing and the destruction of Darfur's livelihood continued without letup, and the situation was turning into a humanitarian crisis. UN Security Council Resolution 1564, issued on September 18, 2004, welcomed the African Union to expand the international mission and asked other nations to contribute. The peacekeeping mission reached a troop strength of seven thousand by April 2005.

Civilian losses in Darfur were by then staggering, with as many as 200,000 killed, approaching two million displaced, and another 200,000 having fled to Chad. Some 10,000 a month were dying, according to UN figures, and the International Crisis Group estimated in mid-2004 that 350,000 were at risk of starvation and disease. A large web of NGOs and private and religious organizations united under the banner "Never again" were clamoring for more action, stung by the flaccid international response to Rwanda a decade earlier. The United States supported a firm response and in September 2004 declared what the Sudanese government was doing in Darfur "genocide," thus putting America out in front even of the UN, which continued to declare the action "mass murder," arguably a more legally accurate term.

Not everyone agreed with the introduction of peacekeepers. De Waal warned at the time, "Those who are clamoring for troops to fight their way into Darfur are suffering a salvation delusion. It's a simple reality that UN troops can't stop an ongoing war, and their record at protecting civilians is far from perfect.... The crisis in Darfur is political. It's a civil war, and like all wars needs a political settlement.... Fix the politics first, and the peacekeeping will follow."[8]

In April 2005 the dynamic shifted when, after two decades of fighting, the government finally signed a peace agreement with South Sudan's rebels. Many hoped this would segue into an accord over Darfur, and intense negotiations followed. The plan was first to unite the Darfur rebel groups, and then for the rebels to sign an agreement with Khartoum. But in the end only one of the rebel factions would sign the 115-page agreement, leading to a new series of problems.[9] The SLA had by then split into the faction of Minni Minawi (SLA/MM), which signed the accord, and Abdul Wahid (SLA/A), which did not. JEM, holding out for a far more expansive restructuring of the government, also sat out the accord.[10] The signing ceremony for the Darfur Peace Agreement on May 5, 2006, included representatives from the African Union

(AU), European Union (EU), UN, Arab League, and several countries. It was intended to lock in the gains of the negotiations while
allowing negotiators to quickly circle back around to the nonsignatories and get them to join. This would turn into an elusive mission but at the time was a not unreasonable way forward.

The Architecture of Peace and Relief

I deployed to El Fasher in West Darfur as part of the newly created Bureau of Conflict Stabilization Operations to head up the
embassy field office there. This was just before Christmas 2006
and after spending a few days in Khartoum, where I was able to
meet with Minni Minawi at his compound in the heart of Khartoum.[11] Minawi was tall and almost elegant-looking, appearing
to me very unlike a rebel leader, with none of the wear that generally comes with years of hard fighting. He had charisma, and I
was told his tactical skills were such that he could easily attract
and retain fighters. Like nearly every rebel leader I met with, I was
taken aback by his effusive praise for the United States and what
we had done for his people. The large-scale killing had stopped
and there was a lifeline of humanitarian assistance. He knew that
this would not have happened without the United States.

But he also expressed extreme frustration with how the peace
accord was turning out. Rather than being the first of several signatories, he said, he felt isolated and abandoned, or, as one of his
people would later tell me, "like we have been dropped down
a deep hole and forgotten." He was also feeling more and more
estranged from his fighters and would have a difficult time controlling them if he could not provide the basic supplies and food-
stuffs they needed to survive. It was a good introduction to the
frustrating mission we would face trying to take a shaky agreement and expand it into something comprehensive.

When I arrived in Darfur I found the compound we occupied
in the desert just outside the main AU base on the outskirts of
the frontier town of El Fasher was far more comfortable than I
was expecting. It was a typical Sudanese homestead, with an open
courtyard, several bedrooms along one wall, an outdoor shower

and sink, and an office/rec room. It also had a lighting system that made it look from a distance like a little league baseball field.

I told Cecile that I thought the best time to do these sorts of field missions was "six months in, when the amenities are in place but the local populace still has a sense of humor about us being here." My job would be a mix of negotiations, reporting, observing, representing, program work, and providing a platform for VIPS who needed to show the flag or get up to date with the factions and dynamics of the peacekeeping mission. Whatever you do or do not know, Ambassador Cameron Hume told me as I departed Khartoum, in ten days you will know more than the rest of us, so don't hold back.

By the time I arrived there was an impressive architecture for managing the crisis. The African Union was in place across the region in twenty-four outposts, with company-size units that were supported logistically by a U.S. contractor. Each base also hosted a U.S.-contracted military observer, a retired officer or senior NCO who would help with operational planning and intelligence. They were tremendously effective, living in austere base camps for months at a time, several over a two-year period. The AU contingents and their observers were tasked with monitoring the ceasefire, conducting "presence patrols" to reduce incidents of violence, and as much as possible protect civilians, commonly women collecting firewood or water. They also helped to supervise the law enforcement system, such as it was, inside the camps. For a stopgap measure the patrols produced a relative level of stability.

The AU HQ was a few hundred meters from our compound and staffed by officers from across Africa, with a sprinkling of EU military and political officers. It was led by MG Luke Aprezi from Nigeria, with Brig. Gen. Frank Mushyo Kamanzi, a Rwandan who served in the force that ousted the Hutus, as his deputy. Aprezi was a solid officer whose difficult mission of protecting civilians in the field constantly bumped up against the need to ensure as few casualties as possible. It also bumped up against the challenge of covering an area the size of Texas with a modest force. Aprezi said the harshness of the land made it relatively straightforward to monitor and control—his opponents had few places to hide because of the openness of the terrain, and scarcity of water channeled them to a few critical points. Still, he said, his force was simply stretched too thin to cover even many basic tasks, such as protective patrols for camps.

Other pieces of the U.S. architecture included a small contingent of USAID personnel, DynCorp contractors who provided some logistical support to the AU mission, and a small cell of military personnel. The Americans were the leaven in the loaf of this complex arrangement.

The NGO and international community was also robust by then; my informal phone list had over two hundred contacts from an alphabet soup of agencies—OCHA, FAO, UNICEF, UNMIS, UNMAS, UNDSS, WFP, WHO, UNDP, ICRC, IOM—as well as single-nation NGOs that numbered in the dozens: Oxfam, Relief International, Jesuit Refugee Services, CHF International. Cynics criticize the "aid industry," working in conflict zones with their SUVs and high salaries, but what I saw was tough, committed, and in many instances hopelessly idealistic people bringing a touch of humanity to a place that was unmoored from civilization and sinking fast.

By the time I arrived the mission had outgrown the AU capacity and the international community had been pressing the government of Sudan to allow in an AU-UN hybrid force that would greatly expand the capacity of the beleaguered AU force to go beyond its current mission and begin to protect civilians proactively as opposed to simply reporting on attacks after the fact. And it would greatly enlarge the area of operation.

The government also had a robust presence in El Fasher, with a national intelligence unit that we dealt with frequently and a large array of police, military, and special units. The dynamic with the Sudanese government was somewhat fraught. While the United States continued to publicly pressure the government of Sudan on the issue of mass atrocities and the UN force, I needed to work closely with them on the ground to develop the space we needed to facilitate the unity of the rebel factions. It remained a politically complex environment and required a bit of dexterity to navigate.

I saw value in this field presence within days. Making peace requires hard work that goes beyond a declaration or a conference. It includes the gritty, detailed tasks on the ground: manifesting our country's interest, engaging with all sides, reassuring, reporting, and shaping the political environment. It often goes against the interests of numerous stakeholders, and on a higher level includes directed force, the threat of force, sanctions and international pressure, and negotiations. But it starts with people on the ground, and the closer they can get to reality, the more effective and well-calibrated the policies will be.

Our share of the task was to report on the status of the AU mission and make recommendations on where to improve their functionality, with an eye to the hybrid mission; represent the United States on the Cease-Fire Commission; meet with rebel commanders and faction representatives and seek to help unify them into a solid negotiating bloc; oversee the Darfur Peace Agreement Secretariat, a small facility for meetings and reconciliation outreach; and report on the political, military, and humanitarian dynamics. Getting to this point of stability in Darfur, I wrote at the time, was all part of a "long and frustrating process," but at least there was now something to work with, and most pieces were in place.

Our base town of El Fasher had about 100,000 inhabitants, although good population figures were hard to come by. (One of my translators suggested two million, a figure that would make Herodotus blush.) There were an additional 70,000 in the Abu Shouk refugee camp and 40,000 in the As Salaam camp, effectively doubling the size of El Fasher proper. It was a hardscrabble town of one paved street that splits two ways midway through, with one-story brick and concrete homes beyond low walls, a huge open market, a soccer field where kids appeared to congregate without actually playing any soccer, and a small seasonal lake on the edge of town that served as the local car wash. A camel-racing track outside of town hosted Friday-night races. In addition to playing host to the international community, El Fasher was a market town and transportation hub, with dozens of trucks a day driving in to cleverly dug depressions, the width of a truck, so that goods could be loaded at ground level.

There was also a university, whose opening I attended. It attracted several thousand students from across Darfur and had seemingly high entry standards. The opening ceremony included a formal procession by the faculty, a jazz band, and speeches by civic leaders on the importance of higher education. I spent a good bit of time at the university and found it on par with what one would have found in many parts of Africa and South Asia, a crazy anomaly given the image we had of a Darfur of nonstop violence and genocide. I would see the students sitting by a tree studying as I walked up in the desert above our compound on weekends. For many locals, life simply went on.

We also visited the refugee camps frequently, as every visitor needed to go there and it was just a short walk from our compound. They were a veritable study in what it takes to sustain life: water, food, basic shelter, and waste disposal; all the rest is luxury. Camps were started when an accumulation of people fleeing after their village and water source had been destroyed gathered next to a village or AU base. The international community would then formalize their presence in a recognized camp. Abu Shouk was one of the first and oldest of the camps; As Salaam was added in November 2004, when as many as thirty thousand people arrived from the Tawila area. Every time we visited the camp there were dozens of women and children waiting in the new arrivals area, some saying they had been there up to thirty days. One aid worker explained that the system ensures they were not residents from El Fasher who just wanted to score a ration card but genuine displaced persons with nowhere else to go. "This refugee thing," I wrote, "is one long exercise in patience and endurance."

The camp itself was laid out on a grid, with main roads and secondary alleyways. The grid was numbered in blocks, and each family was given a fifteen-by-fifteen-foot plot of land, on which they essentially re-created the lifestyle they had left behind, minus the farming and herding. They were initially given a tarp for shelter, but most incorporated that into a traditional thatched hut. We visited one family with Governor Bill Richardson, then a presidential candidate, which consisted of a woman in her forties with ten children. Five of the kids slept in one hut, five in another, and the matriarch had her own small hut, next to a small food prep area. The woman said she wanted to return home but would not do so until there was an assurance of security; even in the camp she felt safe on her plot but less so going to collect firewood outside.

For every block there were latrines dug with a maze of tarps for privacy. There was a water pump for every few blocks, which were constantly in use all through the day. The whole area depended on one large underground lake that filled during the rainy season and then was drawn down for the rest of the year, leaving many wells on the "banks" of the underground lake dry. There was increasing pressure for water from the camp and from El Fasher, which drew from the same source.

Education in the camp was provided in nine schools, and there were nineteen "child-friendly spaces," something less than a playground as we know it but a place for kids to play. There were several well-stocked and -staffed clinics, including one we visited run by the Cooperative Housing Foundation from Maryland with a full range of services up to minor surgery and including psychosocial counseling for victims of conflict and sexual assault. This last was a particularly important service, if easy to overlook. *Newsweek*'s Rod Nordland reports in January 2007 of meeting with women from Abu Sakin village when they finally reached the As Salaam camp. Three women, ages thirty-six, twenty, and fifteen, told of being "taken away at gunpoint the night before the Janjaweed attack on their village while their men looked on helplessly. The women were kept in the Janjaweed village, where they were assaulted repeatedly for two days, one 15 times and another 6." We're going to rape you until you don't come back, their attackers said, the same tactic used by Serbs against Bosnians. They knew the perpetrators, who they said attacked them because "we are blacks and they are Arabs," treating them "like slaves."[12]

Governing in the camp was done by a series of traditional sheikhs leading councils, with other organizations for women, youth, and elected block representatives. Security ebbed and flowed, largely determined by whether the rebels were stocking weapons and, if so, whether the government patrolled the caches, leading to invariable tensions.

I wrote at the time that while the camp was taking on permanent airs, "on another level it [was] still a very tentative existence."

Leaving a village in flames in this terrain, where even in good times survival is on a knife's edge, knowing the innate cruelty and power of those who burned you out, makes going back a less than appealing option. And relying on the good will of others for all the basics of life, not having real control over any aspect of one's life leaves one with an existence of constant hesitation. They are between the world they left behind, which they cannot return to, and any sense of stability in the world they are trying to move on to. That they take it as well as they do is a tribute to this people's inborn toughness and good nature.

The Cease-Fire Commission and Broadening the Peace

Getting beyond the tenuous existence these refugees were experiencing would require two things: first, taking a short-term cease-fire mechanism and broadening it to establish a longer-term settlement; second, inducing the rebel groups to unify and negotiate a new arrangement for Darfur with the central government. The immediate means for the former was the Cease-Fire Commission, led by Force Commander Aprezi, in which the parties, the AU, observer representatives, and the government of Sudan met biweekly to go over violations and "name and shame" the violators. It was a moderately effective mechanism for developing some accountability for misbehavior and guiding the actions of observers and peacekeepers.

General Aprezi was a large man, over six feet and probably 240 pounds. He commanded respect by his presence alone as well as the forces under his command, and came across very balanced, an honest broker. The factions were aware of the limitations of his forces but appeared not to want to provoke or test him. He often used the line "I can't want peace more than you do," while positioning his forces to keep the humanitarian lifeline alive.

When the body was established the assumption was that it would primarily cover violations by the Janjaweed against civilians, but as the situation on the ground evolved things became a free-for-all and accusations were blaring in all directions. Some ten or so attacks per week were brought to the commission, presumably a mere snapshot of what was going on across Darfur. One commission meeting covered two attacks by Arab militias on Abu Shakeen, a hijacked NGO vehicle that was later recovered, an Arab militia attack on Dolor village, an attack on an AU convoy to Kutum, the shooting of an AU soldier, the abduction of women by armed militia near the Kassab camp for internally displaced persons (IDPS), the theft of camels and one killing by JEM near Wadi Sunut, the sniping at an AU patrol near Tui Village, fighting between the government and SLA/M at the Mawasha Animal Market, the alleged killing and wounding of students at the Tagadum Basic School by Janjaweed, the theft of vehicles from the World Vision Guest House in Khor Abeche by forty armed men, a government aerial attack on Deim Bishara, and the ambush of an SLA/M patrol by an armed militia. It was like the monthly rap sheet for the entire state of Texas. Each incident was investigated, perpetrators named and shamed, and some pushed to the Second Chamber (where JEM came in, since they would not participate in the First Chamber, which was guided by the Darfur Peace Agreement they had refused to sign), or to the higher level monthly Joint Commission in Khartoum.

The Joint Commission brought together more senior representatives from all sides to review cases that couldn't be resolved in the field. In early February the Joint Commission was held in El Fasher for the first time. It was designed both to show progress in building a secure and stable environment and to bring the deliberations closer to where the violations were taking place. It was a good snapshot of the situation on the ground and the challenges we faced.

In the February meeting Aprezi noted a decrease in Janjaweed activity, an increase in the government of Sudan's military movement, intertribal fighting that he credited the government with helping to solve, a deteriorating humanitarian situation related to an increase in vehicle theft and attacks on compounds, and rising instability on the Sudan-Chad border. He sought structural changes to the commission and reviewed the government's disarmament plan, declaring it inadequate. His assessment demonstrated the challenges of working through a multilateral framework and the requirement for extensive behind-the-scenes pressure and even more extensive patience.

Two notable individuals on the Joint Commission were the UN's Darfur Peace Agreement implementation chief Sam Ibok and Gen. Mohammed Ahmed al-Dabi, presidential assistant for Darfur. Ibok reminded me of Lansana Kouyaté in Somalia and other African diplomats who could call out the parties more effectively than their Western counterparts. He implored them to end the meeting with a positive message for the people of Darfur. Al-Dabi we understood would be posted in Darfur and was given a role to play coordinating security arrangements. What was not clear was whether he was being placed to run interference for an intransigent government or to help move the process forward. A year earlier that would have been obvious, but by now the international community and elements of the Khartoum government were oddly on the same page in wanting to see a politically united rebel movement that could join the peace process. At the same time, however, the government was not heartbroken over the rebels' inability to unite, and if they did unite, Khartoum hoped for a weak movement that it could dominate in the talks.

Through all of this we knew we were getting just the tip of the iceberg in what filtered up to us, so I sought more detailed assessments from the field. There each sector had its own set of challenges and opportunities, its own tribal and historical stew, and often local issues that had nothing to do with our grand national plans. This diversity added tremendously to the complexity.

Our military observer from Muhajeria sent a spot report in mid-January in which he detailed a Janjaweed attack on a village in his sector: "The attacks occurred early in the day, beginning with a small team of Janjaweed entering the southern fringe of the town and setting flame to several tukuls/huts. The Janjaweed then retreated into the bush to wait. When the villagers came to extinguish the flames the Janjaweed, > 80 of them, came fast on camels and started shooting the villagers. The Janjaweed then completed their burning of the rest of the village."

This had been a clearing attack to prepare for the main attack on the large village of Muhajeria, and the observer was frustrated that the AU sector commander interpreted the mandate to preclude a forceful response, contrary to the more liberal understanding of many national observers. He had been through two major attacks on Muhajeria, but said, "This one feels different, almost final." It was already cutting into the credibility of the Darfur Peace Agreement, with SLA/MM faction commanders commenting that the accord was no longer viable in a situation where the only signatory was supposed to watch a major village be pillaged. Unwilling to accept a passive response, the observers saw 120 of the SLA/MM combatants leaving to defend the village.

For all the negative things some of the rebels were doing elsewhere they were often involved in these sorts of protective measures. In late January an observer reported that his government-controlled Kabkabiya sector had a significant presence of SLA/MM fighters. When one column of these fighters stopped by the headquarters on their way to defend the village of Abugamra (for which he could not even find a grid coordinate), some five thousand villagers congregated quietly in front of the HQ to pay homage to their fighters. The observer remarked that in seventeen years in Africa it was the most remarkable thing he had seen, a "prime illustration of control and respect and not one of fear." The rebel commander even took the government representative into the crowd, where, as the color drained from his face, he was able to interact with the villagers under the protective presence of the rebels.

Khartoum was one step closer to Sudanese reality than New York; I was one step closer than Khartoum; the observer was one step closer than I—but all the foreigners were still one large step away. The Kabkabiya observer concluded with a long lament, "The IDPS are tired and want to go home. The factions are perplexed and have no leadership. The government is content that the situation is under control. The villagers are still starving and suffering from no medical attention. The nomads, Janjaweed, government, rebels, and all the rest are still fragmenting and grasping at straws in an attempt to dominate territory. The cycle continues, and the general perception of the population is that it is life as usual." He did add that the humanitarian assistance was appreciated by those who received it.[13]

Some sectors were very undramatic. The Nyala observer, for example, commented that all was calm and the only violations were theft of livestock. At other times the African Union Mission in Sudan force was blamed for the violence it was not empowered to stop in the first place. On December 9, 2006, a group of merchants requested a medevac from the Geneina base after a commercial truck was ambushed. When the helicopter landed at the town of Sirba it was met by a heavily armed group of residents who accused the AU of siding with the government and delivering "nothing but reports and empty promises." The cease-fire team was told they could either board the aircraft and be shot out of the sky or accompany the citizens to the site of the ambush. Their visit revealed two trucks burning and dozens of dead. The villagers had no clear solution but wanted to visibly express their frustration with the whole process. The team was forced to spend the night at a local police station and was evacuated the next day. The Geneina base also had a large angry mob descend upon it to make the same point. Much of peacekeeping takes place in this underpowered arena of reporting and wondering whether anything is truly being accomplished.

But there were also proactive peacemaking missions carried out in many sectors that at least temporarily staved off disaster. The South African commander of the Kutum sector, Lt. Col. Gary Lloyd, took the faction representatives and the government reps from his sector to a field southeast of Kutum to get to the bottom of recent attacks by competing nomads and agriculturalists that uprooted thirty thousand people, of whom only two thousand to three thousand showed up in camps, as reported in *Newsweek*.[14] Lloyd's group met with the villagers and their leaders, who were skeptical that either the five hundred AU soldiers patrolling an area the size of the Benelux countries or the resource-strapped rebels could protect them. They had found a tentative home elsewhere, and it would take real assurances to get them to go back. But with the attacks on aid workers the humanitarian lifeline to their new location was tenuous.

Lloyd was determined to expand the parameters of safe conduct, enlarge the talks, and lock in a cease-fire agreement while ensuring the belligerents respected humanitarian access. It would take a series of one-off local arrangements and continuing to try to keep the Janjaweed at bay. And the new UN force he hoped would help expand their capacity. So even as he admitted that his force was unable to fully protect people, didn't have enough resources to satisfy all their needs, and were becoming targets themselves when "blamed for unfavorable outcomes," Lloyd concluded, "Without us, it would be pure chaos."[15]

By this time the urgency and importance of local accords was becoming clear. There might not be a national accord for years, but even if there were, there would still be hundreds of local contests to reconcile and settle. As Nordland put it regarding Kutum, there was "just enough water to support either the ... Arab nomads ... or the agriculturalists."

We were at times called upon to witness and validate these local processes. On March 11, 2007, I flew to Abu Sikkin, seventy kilometers northwest of El Fasher, to attend a ceremony for a peace deal that had been brokered between local mediators for the Tunjur and Arab tribes. The mediators were part of an organization that called itself Open Hand and had conducted dozens of negotiations over the preceding several years.[16] We arrived at a hall in Abu Sikkin where dozens of local leaders, civil society representatives, and a small women's component were seated. The governor of Darfur, Osman Mohamed Yousif Kibir, whom I had gotten to know fairly well as an honest broker, presided over the event.

He praised the group for tapping into Darfur's long tradition of reconciliation and committed the government to making the deal stick. The agreement was signed by the leaders of the four groups and called for strict rules on carrying arms, compensation for losses, the prohibition of aiding and abetting outlaw groups, and empowerment of local leaders to enforce the deal. It was an impressive accord, and we wondered if the method could be replicated elsewhere.

The commission had more conventional tasks as well, among them monitoring air activity. One morning in early February I clambered aboard one of the contracted MI-8s with the French Cease Fire Commission's vice chair, the SLA faction rep, the Sudanese government rep, and a small contingent of soldiers. We dropped by the AU base at Nertiti and picked up a squad of Rwandans who were closer to the terrain than our guys and found ourselves flying over one of the most striking parts of Sudan. Jebel Marra reminded me forcibly of the American Southwest: large pillars jutted up from the desert floor in some places, canyons sliced through the desert in others, and massive plateaus stood like tables in defiant isolation. The area is much higher than El Fasher and has richer soil and more rain. There were orchards with apples and fields with grains and tomatoes and corn, many cascading down steep terraced mountains, few with noticeable irrigation. It was a far cry from the four inches of sand and brick hard crust around El Fasher.

After ninety minutes we saw the first abandoned village, a sobering and eerie sight. Across a grid of rutted roads were carefully laid out yards with pens for animals, huts, a well—all that was missing was people. I considered that this scene was repeated across the whole of Darfur, thousands of ghost towns filling with dust and sand, and within a few years set to disappear altogether.

Our directions to the sight of the bombing were somewhat sketchy. The Russian pilots always took on these missions with a mix of dedication and good humor, knowing that as often as not no one really knew precisely where we were going, but they were going to do their level best to get us where we needed to be. The copilot called for a guide among the passengers, and because the government rep was closest to the cockpit he took us to the nearest Sudanese Army base at Rokkero, where we landed in the soccer field. The doors opened and he disappeared into the headquarters, at which point we realized he actually had no idea we were going into rebel-held territory and not to investigate some of his reported violations on friendlier turf. After much cajoling and posturing by the French vice chair, himself indignant about the whole wrong landing zone bit, we lured him out of the HQ and reboarded the helicopter, allowing the rebel rep to guide us to his people's territory, which was remarkably close.

We landed in a wheat field at the base of a ridge line with no sign of activity. But within minutes several rebels descended the rocky scree on the side of the ridge and greeted us. They were dressed in a variety of uniforms and carried an assemblage of antique weapons, no two of which were the same. But the uniforms and the weapons were clean and well cared for and the men were lean but spirited. They were not expecting us but said they would show us the site of a bombing. We eventually found our way to a dry creek bed, where there was evidence of an ambush, and nearby an abandoned village where there was indication of an aerial bombing. The government was effectively using Sopwith Camel technology, Antonovs cruising low over a village and soldiers throwing mortars out the back. The rebels had collected over a dozen, some that had exploded after hitting the nose cone and a number of duds, which would make sense, as that is not really how mortars are designed to work. It was almost comical, except for the fact that the village was, in fact, abandoned. The advantage, I wrote, "is still with the government, since in this environment it doesn't take much firepower to terrorize, and that is all they are doing—terrorizing civilians and getting them to flee their villages, in support of the Janjaweed with their similarly crude tools of random shooting and rape."

I spent some time with the rebels to get a feel for what it would take to get them to stop fighting. One guy in his early thirties was dressed in a dark Banana Republic–like suit with a Crocodile Dundee hat. He seemed out of place in the bush, very pensive, serious, educated. He had studied at the University of Khartoum, where, like many of his compatriots, he came to the conclusion that the government was systematically denying his people their rights. He joined the rebels in 2003 and had been in the field ever since. But he was not itching for a fight; none of them were. They were tired of fighting and just wanted to get on with something else. Farming? I suggested, as we were in the middle of an orchard. No, not farming they said. We want to continue to be soldiers, in the national army or police, although one enterprising young man suggested he would like to serve in a European army, and another wondered if the United States had any openings.

It was the familiar challenge of finding something suitable for former fighters. The Darfur Peace Agreement provided for a total of 4,000 former movement combatants to be integrated into the Sudanese Armed Forces, 1,000 into the police, and 3,000 demobilized, leaving a gap of 3,400, not untenable when considering the scale of the conflict. But because all of this required an end to hostilities, these plans remained aspirational.

The trip did not yield any immediate response, but it was clear that just having a mechanism for getting all faction reps to the site of these incidents, and meeting with the armed elements in the field, did have a positive impact on the conflict. If nothing else it demonstrated interest and showed that the local fighting had a broader context and there was at least an effort being made to maintain balance between the belligerents. But there were other interventions that had a more immediate impact on events on the ground.

On March 1 I traveled with other Cease-Fire Commission members to the village of Bahr Umm Durman in the Muhajeria sector. We arrived via MI-8 near the village with all faction reps and were greeted by soldiers and military observers from the sector. The conflict in question had begun with the killing of a young man at a water point by former fighters turned bandits from the SLA/MM, which quickly escalated into an attack on one of their vehicles by locals. They then fortified themselves in the village and were forcibly ejected by the actual SLA/MM faction, leaving as many as thirty villagers and bandits and five SLA/MM fighters dead in the crossfire.

The village also accused the SLA/MM faction of looting during the ejection, taking pieces of the water pump, the television from the community center, personal items from homes, and livestock. A delegation of tribal and government officials from El Fasher had already laid the groundwork for reconciliation by working through the core issues of compensation and assurances, and the AU and military observers had stopped what could have been a mass exodus by developing a new paradigm for cooperation between the community and factions. But the village wanted to be more clearly under someone's overall security umbrella, and as we sat down in a large circle with the factions, community leaders, sheikhs, traditional leaders, and AU reps, the head of the Popular Committee said bluntly, "We want our stuff back."

In the end it was an imperfect but largely successful model of how the system was supposed to work, with rapid intervention by the government and factions, an accounting for the perpetrators and some recognition of the victims, and an AU-brokered local model for reconciliation going forward. It was also an example of the fine work of our military observers, who as far as I know never received even a nod of public praise for their service. They were the backbone of an entire force and, with severe restraints on what they could do, worked heroically in very difficult circumstances to stop a genocide.

But I came away with larger concerns, as it was by then clear that the Minni Minawi faction was in near total meltdown, affecting the entire architecture for peace. Nordland commented of this time that there was no difference between the signatory and nonsignatory factions in terms of violations, and in many ways the signatories were worse. I spoke with some of Minawi's fighters, one of whom was no older than fourteen, and called the commander out on using young fighters. He said he had told the subcommanders not to bring the young fighters to gatherings with internationals. But they are the most fearless fighters, he added, and it was difficult to keep them out of the force. They looked like a rabble, without uniforms or a chain of command.

These concerns had been growing since December, when former fighters from the SLA/MM faction took over a compound at Gereida, home to one of the largest IDP camps in the country, stealing vehicles, radios, and supplies and raping an American aid worker. These actions caused the evacuation of the sector's seventy-plus humanitarian workers and a near shutdown of international assistance.

The force commander and I came down hard on the SLA/MM rep, and Khartoum came down hard on Minni Minawi. They denied responsibility, claiming the perpetrators had been members of a breakaway faction, but no one was buying it. Part of controlling a sector, we told them, is controlling what goes on there. They did not react with the thorough assumption of accountability we wanted, but the message got through. At the same time we saw the limits to imploring not backed up by force. We had to accept that given what our countries were willing to risk in Darfur, this was as good as it gets.

The issue came to a head, though, when two Nigerian peacekeepers were killed in a carjacking by SLA/MM fighters on March 5. Aprezi was livid over the incident and determined to insist to Minawi how jarring it was that the only signatory to the Darfur Peace Agreement was also the most belligerent. Minawi's faction was defensive, claiming innocence until the investigation was complete, but Minawi himself was in a more humble mode when the force commander and Ibok met with him a few days later. He conceded that his faction was in deep trouble and he was shedding fighters because of his inability to provide them with any form of livelihood. When they were fighting, Minawi said, they could raid to stay viable, but at the end of the day "peace doesn't pay," and his forty-five thousand fighters had dwindled considerably.[17] Those who remained he could no longer control. As angry as he was over the death of his peacekeepers, Aprezi conceded, "If there is no Minni, there is no Darfur Peace Agreement."

The SLA/MM faction that had signed the accord was expecting a lifeline when they came in from the field, which was not forthcoming. The issue was one of those quirks of budgeting and bureaucracy. The *New York Times* columnist Nicholas Kristof pointed out that by March 2007 the United States had spent $2.7 billion on Darfur. It would be a bargain, he thought, to invest several hundred more million in peace. He suggested pledging to finance reconstruction and compensation schemes as incentives to wary Darfuris to back a peace deal.[18] It is not something we are accustomed to, but these operations simply require extreme budgetary and operational flexibility. The rigidity of our system, which in this case had no budget stream for providing humanitarian assistance to combatants, led to a significant missed opportunity, and more violence.

The Elusive Rebel Unity

The second key to long-term stability—inducing the rebel groups to unify in order to negotiate with the central government—was then and remains today an essential first step in solving the conflict. The extensive architecture for monitoring and maintaining the cease-fire was not matched by a parallel architecture for this longer-term but critical task. Since the Cold War, when one superpower or the other would simply demand unity as a price for support, this had become a very ad hoc enterprise. All we could do now was monitor the rebel's intentions and seek openings that could be exploited to induce unity on a broader scale.

As early as October 2005 the International Crisis Group wrote that unless reversed, the slow implosion of the rebel movements threatened "to extend the tragic situation in Darfur indefinitely. The growing divide within the movements, particularly the [SLA], has opened the door for Khartoum and various regional actors to pursue their own agenda and further weaken the rebels. . . . Splintering the SLA and JEM would likely lead to the prevalence of warlordism throughout Darfur and make a political solution to the crisis impossible." They stressed the importance of internationally supported field conferences to induce SLA and JEM unity, the critical first step in a durable peace.[19]

In contrast to the south's unified movement under Garang, Darfur started with two guerrilla movements in the late 1990s: the Islamic JEM and the more general Sudanese Liberation Movement (SLM). But from the beginning they started to splinter, over personalities, geography, and negotiating positions. The SLM evolved into the SLA by 2003, which splintered during the Darfur Peace Agreement talks in Abuja at the beginning of 2005, with the SLA/MM signing the agreement and a nonsignatory faction that later splintered again into SLA/Abdul Shafi and SLA/Abdel Wahid. Impatience on the part of foreign negotiators may have led to pushing for an agreement when not all parties were prepared, thus helping divide the movement.

To make it more complicated some of the nonsignatories split with their leaders and went over to the peace camp, and some of Minawi's fighters wanted to keep on struggling, so by the time I arrived there was also SLA/Free Will, SLA/Darfur Peace Agreement, and SLA/Peace Wing. JEM also had a peace wing that broke with its leaders and joined the peace camp, and from there they fractured even further, as times encouraged by the government, which may have believed it could more easily pick off small groups than a united front. Added to the mix was foreign money and support from Libya, Chad, and Eritrea.

The essential first step was a series of commanders conferences to start to build a concept for unity. In early January 2007 UN field officers attended a meeting in Umm Rai with 150 field commanders trying to solidify a new umbrella movement but which served merely to lay bare the challenges of doing so. There was competition among commanders for the lead position and politics were in play, with the internationally favored Dr. Sharif Harir dismissed by many on the ground as being out of touch. As the gathering got under way there was a rumor of a competing gathering by a prominent commander who reportedly had signed an agreement merely to attract more forces to his faction.

It was messy, but not without a way forward. The cease-fire reps insisted there were really just two groups that we needed to concern ourselves with, sla/National Redemption Front, a unified group of the nonsignatories to the Darfur Peace Agreement, and jem—unite them and the others would come along. I was further encouraged by a Darfurian with deep experience with the rebels and peace process. Over dinner, he said they were not like the rebels in the south, who fought Viet Cong–style for twenty years and would endure untold casualties before yielding. The Darfur rebels, he told me, were exhausted, as were their people. It is much easier to fight on in the forests and mountains of South Sudan than in the deserts of Darfur. There was immense pressure from their people, especially those in IDP camps, to get back to the table and reach a settlement. He was hopeful, assuring me, "It's not a distant hope: the political differences are small." I wrote in late January, "Exhaustion, in these cases, is our best ally. And I think the Darfurians are close. Now we just have to keep wearing down the government of Sudan." There was, to use the scholar and diplomat Richard Haass's term, "ripeness" in this conflict. But even a ripe fruit needs to be picked, peeled, and eaten, or it just falls to the ground and rots. And we were still in the picking phase.

We met frequently with the factions' political and military leaders, who were eager for Western, especially U.S. contact and began every meeting by expressing appreciation for what the United States had done for their people. In one gathering with twenty-five sla/mm, jem/Peace Wing, Sudanese Liberation Movement/Peace Wing, and sla/Free Will representatives, the groups expressed disillusionment with the Darfur Peace Agreement and told of a worsening situation in the field, which disincentivized the nonsignatories. They also accused the government of maintaining a constant sense of crisis to justify its military campaign and help divide the rebels. In short, I reported, "the key message is that we need to create the conditions whereby peace is more inviting than conflict, something many of these factions are starting to question."

I asked Governor Richardson during his visit in mid-January to press the Sudanese government to allow the rebels to hold a commanders conference, and he was successful, at least on paper receiving assurances that they could go forward. The rebels made plans for pickup at four locations, from which they would be moved to a central site. It was not to be a perfect gathering, as some commanders had moved to Chad for an alternate meeting, and it would not include JEM. But hopefully it would get the core of the SLA back together.

Managing the gathering, however, was problematic. The Ministry of Foreign Affairs agreed to the conference up front, as did Bashir's Darfur advisor, but it wasn't clear whether the Ministry of Defense was entirely on board. I raised the issue with the government representative on the Cease-Fire Commission in late January, passing on rumors that gathering sites were being bombed. He first assured me the sites would not be bombed, but later asked if he could rephrase that: "I cannot say the gathering will not be bombed, but I can say it will not be deliberately disrupted," thus allowing for a rogue element of the air force to carry out an aerial attack not ordered by the government. It was less than reassuring, but the rebel commanders continued to attempt to make it work, and we looked for ways to support them.

In late January I accompanied the force commander on a field mission to the JEM faction in the Jebel Moon Mountains in the north. The landscape was similar to Jebel Marra, but with larger tracts of mountains that at one point in the flight extended all the way to the horizon, blanketed in clouds, with just the tips of the peaks breaking through. We had left in two helicopters, Aprezi and his entourage in one, and me with the others in the second. The commander's helicopter took a diversion to Geneina to pick someone up, and so ours arrived first. We disembarked to a long row of rebel fighters, and before I could explain anything, they were feting us with a pass in review, weapons drill, and salute. I returned their salute crisply, explaining as it ended that I was not in fact the ranking member of the delegation and that the force commander was inbound. They stayed in line for a few more minutes, but in the spirit of being a true insurgent force, when the second helicopter didn't arrive promptly, they took to sitting on rocks and lounging in a field. By then they had decided to forgo repeating the ceremony and simply congregated under a tree for the meet-up.

It was a valid and useful exchange, they pressing for more humanitarian assistance for their people, we pressing them to guarantee security for expanded humanitarian access. They insisted on getting their people out to the field on the Cease-Fire Commission, but the government was clear it would not entertain this until they signed the Peace Agreement, so they offered to join the Second Chamber for nonsignatories. Neither side expected a breakthrough, but there was real value in the exchange: it kept JEM in the game and showed them respect.

In the end peacemaking is no different from a political campaign, with hundreds of stops and engagements and speeches and pressing the flesh and building coalitions and heading off adversaries and messaging. In this and dozens of other encounters we were building momentum and laying the groundwork for the larger peace we sought while making small agreements along the way.

Afterward

I departed in March, leaving my colleague Eythan Sontag to keep the mission alive. There was not a system for keeping U.S. officers in the field, so when Eythan returned some months later he did so without a replacement. The field mission closed altogether a year later when the threat was deemed too great to justify a presence.

There were three larger goals for Darfur when I left, articulated by Special Representative Andrew Natsios to the U.S. House Committee on Foreign Affairs: (1) achieve a durable peace through a resilient settlement that is agreed to by all the parties voluntarily; (2) ensure the protection of noncombatants and the humanitarian aid flow; (3) get the UN in to expand the AU operation. The third goal was achieved by the end of the year with the establishment of the UN African Union Mission in Darfur (UNAMID) hybrid force. It was a robust mission of nearly 20,000 military personnel and another 3,800 police, with nineteen formed police units of 140 personnel each. They would expand the reach and capacity of the peacekeeping force to patrol and provide presence, as well as enhancing self-protection, the need for which was highlighted when rebels overran an AU base and killed twelve peacekeepers in September 2007.

Since then there have been ups and downs in the search for peace, with temporary respites in violence, restructuring of rebel alignments, and new peace processes, all punctured by outbreaks of hostilities. The flow of refugees throughout has been largely one-directional; there is no indication that any have returned home in large numbers. The elusive search for rebel unity continued, with nine groups announcing a union in November 2007, but continued splintering after that. JEM, maintaining its focus on national instead of local issues, mounted an impressive attack on Khartoum in May 2008 that left one hundred government forces and ninety rebels dead, but it was pretty much a one-off attack.

The war in Darfur became regularized, leading Gen. Martin Agawi, head of the UNAMID force, to tell the BBC on August 27, 2009, "The real war, as such, was over, with banditry, localized issues, mostly conflicts over water and land, what remained."[20] When compared to the large-scale fighting characterized as genocide several years earlier, Agawi was right. But these localized conflicts could nonetheless flare up fast and continue to cause significant loss of life and displacement.

The Darfur Peace Agreement fell away as an organizing mechanism for peace when Minawi's group denounced the agreement and declared his faction in a state of rebellion against the government, moving to Juba in South Sudan at the end of 2010. Negotiations on the new agreement, similarly imperfect and not inclusive of all rebel groups, led to the signing of the Doha Document for Peace in Darfur in July 2011 between a rebel umbrella group—the Liberation and Justice Movement, comprising ten smaller groups—and the government of Sudan. It came five days after the agreement with South Sudan, and it appeared at the time there might be synergy between the two. But having fought Khartoum in a united front the south would similarly soon devolve into a morass of factional fighting that has, if anything, taken the attention off Darfur.

Similar to the Darfur Peace Agreement, the government wanted other groups to sign on to the Doha Document for Peace in Darfur, but SLA/Abdul Wahid, JEM, and Minawi held out, with Minawi by 2013–14 being the most active rebel group. The flare-ups could be intense; 450,000 were displaced in 2014 alone, adding to the over two million long-term displaced.

Throughout, the UNAMID mission did what it could to achieve its three benchmarks as laid out in 2014: achieve an inclusive peace process, protect civilians and manage unhindered humanitarian access, and prevent or mitigate community conflict. The 2016 report of the UN secretary general states that there was no major armed conflict in Darfur during the reporting period, although it remained volatile in the absence of progress towards a comprehensive agreement addressing the root causes of the violence. It surmised that hostilities decreased as a result of the government's military offensive, which limited the armed rebellion to a small part of the Jebel Marra Mountains. It noted that there were also fewer intercommunal clashes than in previous years, although the security situation was affected by seasonal competition and unresolved disputes over water, land, and resources.[21]

In the midst of this seeming stasis, there is occasional good news. Soon after I left, a giant aquifer was discovered in Darfur that could forever change the critical issue of water, one of the greatest sources of conflict. It has yet to be mapped and developed but is a reminder that technology and luck can provide a break in a conflict. The government has prepared to enhance Darfur's infrastructure, perhaps begrudgingly and perhaps to improve its own ability to move troops, but laying the ground for an improved economy and connectivity to the rest of the country nonetheless. In 2015 a road connecting El Fasher to Khartoum was completed by a Chinese construction company, cutting the drive time from three days to fourteen hours, with more roads in the planning. New airports and runways have been completed in Geneina and Zalingei, and local traders are talking about returning Darfur to its traditional place as a trading hub, with new markets for their thirty million head of sheep, cattle, camels, and goats. A two-year project to hook up Darfur to the country's electricity hub was started in 2015, and mining possibilities are being explored by international companies. It is all very preliminary, and not exactly a good faith effort, but it is a long way from the large-scale killing of 2003–4.

What We Learned

By this time in my career there was something familiar about Darfur—another intractable conflict fraught with environmental, historical, ethnic, and cultural challenges that were going to take decades to unwind. But in the meantime I had developed very modest standards and so considered the intervention in Darfur as having a positive outcome: the international community set out to stop a genocide, and it succeeded. I also considered it a mission that was still very much in play and could one day result in a successful longer-term outcome. I do not believe any of that would have been possible without international intervention. But all that said, there were a number of obvious areas where the international community could have done better.

In terms of the architecture for conflict resolution and peace, several issues stood out. First, on a macro level the mission proved that the AU could conduct a reasonably complex mission, if properly supported with U.S. and European augmentees in the areas of operations and intelligence. There was a definite ceiling where it simply exceeded the capacity of its collection of national forces to conduct certain operations, but there were also things the African contingents and their political and uniformed leaders could do that the Westerners could not. These primarily involved interactions with local leaders, mastering the complexity of tribal and ethnic politics, and at times calling out warlords and the government on nonsense that might have gotten past a true outsider. When the AU exceeded its capacity, a joint AU-UN force could be made to work, building on the natural advantages of the AU but adding more robust Western capacity.

Second, there was a need for flexible funding for peace. To date the international community has spent around $25 billion in keeping the peace and maintaining a humanitarian lifeline in Darfur. The United States spent more than $2.7 billion in FY 2005 and FY 2006 for Darfur-related relief programs, most of which was tightly scripted and came with little flexibility. It is worth asking if a lifeline of $10 million to $20 million to the Minawi faction in 2006, which would have allowed his group to truly come in from the cold, wouldn't have been cheaper than mounting the massive peacekeeping operations that were required when the faction devolved into bandits. Conflict resolution and peacekeeping simply require some walking-around money.

Third, we need to have people in the field, really in the field, for lengthy periods of time. Marianne Nolte and Hideo Ikebe in the UN system were good examples. Both spent years in Darfur and have no peers in the U.S. or European systems. Nolte wrote in 2008, "For international intervention to be effective, what is required are political officers who have mastered the Darfur portfolio, who are prepared to work and stay in Darfur for an extended period, and who are ready to win the trust of the fighters by listening rather than talking and who have political skills to assist the rebels move from the expression of collective grievances to the articulation of a political platform."[22]

Fourth, we do not have all the tools we need in terms of conflict resolution. My current assignment, as an interagency fellow at the U.S. Institute of Peace, has opened my eyes to a whole world of training and organizing to resolve conflicts and lock in the gains of conflict resolution. Much of this is done through on-the-ground facilitators. Training and empowering and in many cases funding local facilitators is a key component of such conflicts and can pay real dividends, especially in terms of localized conflicts and maintaining humanitarian access. On a higher level the international team for peace is sporadic and comes with a very thin bench.

On the conflict itself, we must focus first on its inherent political nature. The International Crisis Group concluded in 2015, "The government remains wedded to a military approach and is reluctant to pursue a negotiated national solution that would address all Sudan's conflicts at once and put the country on a path of a democratic transition." The Crisis Group stressed that "Darfur's different conflicts cannot be addressed all at once or in the same way." It spells out the many "spiraling communal conflicts," each of which have local roots, and all of which benefit the government and its "divide and rule" tactic, which "keeps the Darfur elites busy with local conflicts and away from power struggles in the centre." The Group stresses the importance of involving as many armed groups as possible in "parallel peace processes, including local inter-tribal conferences; Darfur regional security talks; and the national dialogue."[23]

Second, and to this end, we should follow Nolte's advice and "professionalize and structure more rationally our engagement with the rebels." She describes this engagement as "amateurish and incoherent" because of the "successive waves of special envoys, politicians, ambassadors, senior UN officials, and other foreign VIPS" who drop into Darfur for a visit, extol the virtues of peace, and disappear. Whenever I met with her she stressed that whatever we did it had to be based on solutions "from the inside, not imposed from outside." And to do that, we had to slowly and systematically build confidence. "The rebels are not well educated or sophisticated but have developed a well-founded mistrust of international intervention in their affairs," she would later write.[24] Nolte further believed we should conduct negotiations in Darfur, not abroad, simplify the process and remove nonessential participants, and identify and promote the next generation of leaders. In general we need to get as good at conducting peace as we are at conducting war, and have a structure and the people who can carry it out.

Third, we need to simply settle in for the long haul. The Colombian Civil War lasted fifty-two years, and it will take another decade to fully disentangle the various sides and return life to normal for affected villages. Darfur's has been going on for seventeen years by one measure, over twenty-five by another. To have a region like Darfur on international life support for decades is unseemly, but frankly sustainable, even for the decades it will take to reach a political agreement.

During my last week in Darfur the UN Development Program organized a cultural festival for the ten tribes of Darfur, which I hosted at the Peace Secretariat. It was quite moving. Dancers from each tribe took the stage and with great energy played out their national narrative. There were the Dinka transplants from the south towering over the others, the Islamic Hawza—migrants from Nigeria who settled in Darfur on their way back from the Haj centuries ago—in flowing white robes. Hakamati, Arab, Dinariah, Fur, Tama, Zagaw, Kein, and Umregbath. They interspersed the dance with poetry readings and speeches from local notables. It was an impressive array of color and movement, the first time in anyone's memory that all the tribes had assembled in one place. Their enthusiasm for peace got the best of me. After being introduced as the American ambassador and thinking it would be unfair to correct the record (after all that dancing they deserved the ambassador), I told them I had come on an official diplomatic mission but found something much more personal: a people who were generous and friendly and had a rich cultural tradition that I was quite moved to see on display in the interest of peace. I told my son that it reminded me of how civil wars usually end: the parties eventually just get tired and give up. And that is still where we are—holding off the worst until something better makes itself available. And that, by my standards, is a valid and commendable goal. It had better be, because for now it is as good as it gets.

1. Third Platoon, B/2-505, on patrol, Grenada, October 1983.

2. Training exercise with Honduran and U.S. forces, Rio Claro Valley, Honduras, spring 1985.

3. Cadets of the Salvadoran military academy at Fort Benning for combination Officer Candidate School, Infantry Basic Course, and Ranger School, July 1983.

4. Given the dangers on the ground, all movement around Mogadishu was by air, January 1994.

5. Somali warlords arriving in Nairobi for peace talks, March 1994.

6. In addition to keeping the family on track in Haiti, Cecile supported the Good Samaritan Orphanage with job training, food distribution, a well, and medical assistance.

7. The arrival of a Haitian American civilian police detachment improved our advisory capacity, with Senator Mike Dewine, 1996.

8. Reconciliation talks between villagers and the SLA/Minni Minawi rebel faction, Bahr Umm Durman, Darfur, spring 2007.

9. UN/AU/U.S. outreach to JEM rebels, Jebel Moon Mountains, Darfur, spring 2007.

10. Rebel fighter at the Ceasefire Commission field mission, Jebel Marra Mountains, Darfur, February 2007.

11. JEM rebel fighter, Jebel Moon Mountains, Darfur, spring 2007.

12. President Hamid Karzai of Afghanistan at the Loya Jirga, June 2002.

13. With Governor Abdulkareem Barjas Al-Rawi (center) at the Ramadi, Iraq, governorate compound, fall 2003.

14. Demonstration by civil society and new political parties in support of national unity and peace, Ramadi, Iraq, January 2004.

15. Currency exchange in Iraq, fall 2003. Saddam bills were taken out and new bills celebrating Iraq's historic achievements were in.

16. Iraq's Al Anbar Provincial Council election, women's caucus, March 2004.

17. Presiding with provincial judge (left with microphone) at one of ten caucuses in Iraq's Al Anbar Provincial Council elections, March 2004.

18. At business conference in Al Anbar, Iraq, January 2004.

19. Karakul skin market, Mazar-e Sharif, Afghanistan, one of the exports we hoped would make a comeback with new trading opportunities, spring 2013.

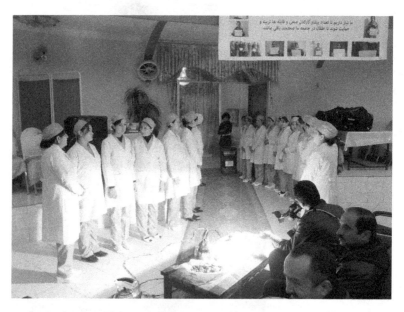

20. Graduation of class of midwives, Jawzjhan province, one of the many things that vastly improved Afghanistan's public health system by 2012.

21. Meeting with the governor of Samangan province, Afghanistan, perpetually neglected because it was peaceful, 2013. I was unable to explain the concept of the mouse that roared.

22. Nowruz festival in Mazar-e Sharif, Afghanistan, one of the first major challenges for the new security forces, 2013.

23. Transport across northern Afghanistan was spotty.
Waiting for a helicopter in Kunduz, fall 2012.

PART THREE

9/11 and the Challenge of Ungoverned Space

SEVEN

United States, 2001

Waking Up to New Threats on 9/11

The Twin Towers

We were just past the one-year mark in a posting to Budapest when the 9/11 attacks occurred. I was finishing my reserve duty in support of a large special operations exercise across Hungary that coincidentally included most of America's Tier One forces. I had heard a number of times the complaint from my Special Forces comrades that there wasn't enough "real work" in the world—too many exercises, too many restraints. That changed in a single morning.

I was with Joint Special Operations Commander Gen. Dell Dailey on September 11 as he briefed chargé d'affaires Janet Garvey on the concept of operations for the exercise when a staff officer entered the room. He whispered something to the general, who asked if there was a TV nearby. "That was no accident," he said as he watched the footage of the first plane hitting. In minutes Dailey had put in motion plans to backhaul his units to their bases, and in hours his staff had begun contingency planning for operations in Southwest Asia.

I focused on my share of the task in Budapest. Given their history on the receiving end of military intervention, our Hungarian allies had a natural aversion to military action on foreign soil. But they were both supportive and sympathetic, wanting to prove themselves in the NATO alliance, and President Péter Medgyessy would stretch their help as far as he could.

I started to think through exactly what we had woken up to on September 12, which no one was remotely prepared for and which had no doctrinal framework. In the spring of 2000 I had cofounded with several other special operations officers under the skillful leadership of Mike Fenzel the Council on Emerging National Security Affairs (CENSA); it gave me a good platform for debate and publishing. I had been frustrated, as many were, with our failure to develop a doctrine to replace containment after the fall of the Berlin Wall and for lack of anything more original had offered "neo-containment" in a speech to CENSA in the spring of 2000. I posited that the main threat we faced was the possession of weapons of mass destruction (WMD) by "relatively small nations, large reckless nations, and possibly sub-national groups." I outlined the need to confront with clear programs and policies the breakdown of the bipolar world and the potential dispersal of WMD technology and components across the globe.[1]

Confronting the Post-Westphalian World

On October 11, 2001, I completed a fresh essay for CENSA, "The Bush Doctrine: Sovereignty and Accountability in the New Nuclear Age," outlining a more urgent and fulsome neo-containment policy. I saw a geopolitical revolution in which, "for the first time in history, military power will frequently be unrelated to a country or group's resources, population base, and technological skill." I suggested the slippage of WMD to subnational groups was the prime threat we faced, drawing from Richard Butler's *The Greatest Threat: Iraq, Weapons of Mass Destruction, and the Crisis of Global Security*. He wrote, "Weapons of mass destruction are fundamentally different from other threats to peace. They cannot be the subject of politics as usual because of their capacity to destroy everything. They constitute both the greatest threat and the greatest exception."[2]

I proposed as a "Bush Doctrine" the need to strive "for an international system in which all parts of the globe are effectively governed, and all governments are fully accountable for what happens on their territory." I dismissed the pure "international posse model," in which we ourselves traversed the world seeking to contain and eliminate bad actors, arguing instead for strengthening the capacity and accountability by sovereign states to control the potential dangers on their own territory.

I saw the strategic objectives of the campaign as eliminating the ongoing threat by capturing bin Laden and dismantling his network, sending a message of total resolve to future threats, and draining the swamp in which terrorists dwell. I took it as a given that we would dismantle the Taliban regime, but also that Iraq needed to be confronted over its WMD program. In what seems horribly naïve now, I believed that regime change in Iraq, if managed skillfully and quickly, would be less inciting than the persistent bombing campaign and sanctions we had been carrying out for a decade, which were leading to mounting generational resentment and rage. In my defense "skillfully" and "quickly" were the operative words.

A balancing essay in February 2002 drew from Amin Maalouf's masterful work, *The Crusades through Arab Eyes*.[3] I outlined the skill and caution we would need to apply as we ventured forth so as not to be labeled crusaders in the Muslim world, sparking the very reaction we were trying so desperately to eliminate in the first place. "If this campaign has a center of gravity," I suggested, "it is minimizing the anti-Western radicalization of young Muslim men, who form an endless queue of potential terrorists, while shoring up popular support for friendly governments in the Islamic world—without whose assistance the campaign can never succeed."

I urged short campaigns and "limitations in the time and depth of a military reaction" in both Afghanistan and, if necessary, Iraq, with just enough stay-behind support to ensure we could buy or bribe our way to stability. "The Frankish Kingdom lasted some 200 years from the fall of Jerusalem until the last of the Franj were finally expelled," I concluded. "For the last 50 years, the kingdom consisted of a small number of Europeans clinging desperately to the coast around Acre. They held on through sheer military prowess, and only after they were expelled came to realize that their presence had helped galvanize the Arab world into a cohesive whole that eventually made a run at the heartland of Europe itself." The balancing act of doing enough to ensure our protection without provoking a violent reaction to our presence in the process may have been beyond our ability to manage.

I also came to see a larger historical framework beyond the localized issues in the Middle East. What we were facing was the emergence of the post-Westphalian era, best articulated by Michael Ignatieff in his Gifford Lectures in 2002 and further developed by Phillip Bobbitt in *The Shield of Achilles: War, Peace, and the Course of History*.[4] The core concept was the erosion of the nation-state as the organizing entity for international relations, as established in the Peace of Westphalia in 1648. As Bobbitt puts it, "For five centuries only a state could destroy another state. . . . We are entering a period, however, when very small numbers of persons, operating with the enormous power of modern computers, biogenetics, air transport, and even small nuclear weapons, can deal lethal blows to any society. Because the origin of these attacks can be effectively disguised, the fundamental bases of the State will change. . . . Because it may not be possible to determine the source of the incursion, strategies of retaliation and deterrence, which have served us well in the past, become less useful."[5]

Deterrence for five centuries was the key concept that the nation-state system provided to international order—when a state arose that was a threat to peace and stability it could be confronted by other states and its behavior modified. If it resisted deterrence it could be defeated, and a new state built that could be deterred. It wasn't great, as the bloody twentieth century attests, but it was a system.

Two emerging trends, a horrifying vision of which we were given on 9/11, were upending this Westphalian world. One was the rise of apocalyptic terrorism. For centuries terrorism had been a technique the RAND analyst Brian Jenkins called "armed propaganda," a means to influence the behavior of states. It occurred within the Westphalian system and was limited by the fact that terrorists killed for attention, not merely to kill. They were largely rational actors with goals and an end-state, however unlikely that end-state may have been.

The Aum Shinrikyo subway attack in Tokyo was the first terrorist attack not tied to any political objective but simply intended to kill as many people as possible, carried out by an organization with apocalyptic ends. With the rise of Al-Qaida we were entering similarly uncharted territory. Al-Qaida had a vague end-state, the restoration of the caliphate and the expulsion of infidels from Muslim lands, but it was so vast and so ill-defined that the practical means of achieving it were simply to kill broadly, provoking the West anywhere and everywhere and hardening the cultural and geographic line between the saved and the damned. We were experiencing the rise of apocalyptic terrorism, terrorism without limits or restraints.

The second trend was the increasing availability of the implements of small but highly lethal weapons, which was a simple reality as technology spread. "If weapons of mass destruction become available to terrorists," Ignatieff writes, "we may move from a pattern of high-frequency–low casualty attacks to a low frequency–catastrophic casualty pattern. . . . Liberal democracies are thus faced with an enemy whose demands cannot be appeased, who cannot be deterred, and who do not have to win for us to lose."[6]

He then asks what losing looks like, concluding it would effectively be the disintegration of our way of life: "A succession of mass casualty attacks, using weapons of mass destruction, would leave behind zones of devastation sealed off for years and a pall of mourning, anger, and fear. . . . We would survive, but we would no longer recognize ourselves or our institutions. We would exist, but lose our identity as free peoples."[7]

Confronting this new threat would come from strictly limiting the availability of the scientific knowledge and materials to build weapons of mass destruction, and of the weapons themselves. It would come from reducing the operating space of terrorists—their ability to move, to finance operations, to communicate, to plan in safe havens, to train. And it would come from reducing the virtual space terrorists operate in, the ideological world of supposed Muslim pain and suffering and humiliation at the hands of infidels. The imperative of nation-building to Ignatieff, and to many of us, was clear: "Strengthening honest government in burdened societies, helping them to deny sanctuary to terrorist groups, has passed from a merely desirable goal to an essential one."[8]

It was a tricky world operationally, since a clumsy move to reduce *physical* operating space in one area—eliminating safe havens or rounding up terrorists—could have the unintended effect of increasing their *virtual* space, the ideological and propaganda arena that feeds new recruits to the cause, inadvertently creating more *actual* space elsewhere. The need was for a dynamic multilateralism, a clear strategy, and flawless execution, with staying power across all lines of effort.

In two short months we would move largely alone into Afghanistan in what was hoped would be a very brief punitive expedition.

EIGHT

Afghanistan, 2002

Starting from Scratch

Getting There

The world watched intently as the military campaign to corner America's attackers began. Few of us predicted the rapid rout of not only Al-Qaida but their Taliban hosts as well, raised as we were on the long slog the Soviets endured in Afghanistan. But we had not considered the ferocity of opposition to Taliban rule by many Afghans, the strength of the new generation of U.S. air-power, and the simple fatigue of Afghans after a quarter-century of war and privation.

The rapidity of the U.S. counterattacks took both military and State Department planners by surprise. From the first introduction of an eight-man CIA Special Activities team into the Panjshir Valley on September 26, 2001, to the fall of Kabul on November 13 was less than two months. Not since the opening salvos of World War II had war moved this fast. Scrambling to catch up, a diplomatic effort ran in parallel, led by the very capable Lakhdar Brahimi, with whom I had worked in Haiti, and Ambassador James Dobbins, who had been our special envoy to Somalia, Haiti, and the Balkans. Both understood the imperative of getting the political piece of the transition right, and Dobbins was seized also with the criticality of ensuring that Pakistan and Iran stay out of the way. Both men were realistic about the resources, forces, and time that would be required, all a factor of ten or so greater than what was ultimately allocated.

A generous cross section of Afghan society, convened in Germany for talks, produced the Bonn Agreement, which established a six-month interim government on December 5. Hamid Karzai would lead twenty-nine ministries (half going to the Northern Alliance) as chairman, and the participants agreed on a plan to reestablish the judicial and legislative branches and draft a new constitution. Significantly, the agreement also called for a Loya Jirga, or Grand Council, in the coming months to validate the new government and lay out the course for the future.

I contacted Dobbins and offered my services, and he slotted me in for the late spring of 2002 as the economic and commercial counselor at the embassy in Kabul. When I arrived in June one of our best Central Asian hands, Robert Finn, was at the helm, and there were some improvements to the embassy itself, which in December had exactly one desk, one phone, and one computer.

The embassy yard was a hodgepodge of tightly configured trailers and new construction. The flagpole in front had two memorial plaques. The first was from 5th Special Forces Group, the first military unit into the compound in December, and included a piece of the Twin Towers buried beneath it, a useful token of what this was all about. The second was a memorial to Ambassador Adolph Dubs, who was killed in Afghanistan in 1979 during a kidnapping, a reminder of the risks that came with the place. The embassy's front door had taken a hit at some point in the preceding years, and the bulletproof glass was shattered but still intact, adding to the war zone aura. I was billeted in one of the oil field containers, which was comfortable and private enough. Many others were in a group underground bunker, and there were dormitory trailers going up for the legions yet to arrive.

We had a small office for five of us; it was tight, but I had a shared desk and a laptop, which was more than I was expecting. There was some internet connectivity at that point, but classified information could be moved only with difficulty and we worked largely on Hotmail. The food on my arrival was what they had been eating for the previous six months: cornflakes and boxed milk for breakfast, rice-meat-vegetables for lunch, and soup with a stack of naan bread for dinner, prepared by two mechanics from the motor pool. We had a fleet of vw Passats that were veritable period pieces from the 1970s but which still functioned and blended in well with downtown traffic. Recreation was a tree with chairs surrounding it set up in the courtyard, although at that point we could still get into town and did so frequently.

I reported to Deputy Chief of Mission David Sedney, who gave me a list of things to get started on that was revealing of the magnitude of rebuilding a country that had slipped from the sixteenth to the fourteenth century and now needed to be brought into the twenty-first.

Travel around Kabul told the story well. It was a ruined city inhabited by a traumatized people. Most of what functioned had been built by the Soviets; for all their faults they were impressive if boring builders. There were rows of Soviet bloc apartments, ministries, roads, the university, dams, bridges, irrigation systems, and factories. But their departure had produced one long story of deterioration. There was hardly a building that did not bear the scars of the factional fighting following the collapse of the Soviet-backed regime in 1989. It got even worse under the Taliban regime, with their self-imposed austerity and lack of access to capital.

The inhabitants lived in generally squalid conditions. On one visit to a health clinic we saw children with indications of advanced kwashiorkor, their mothers despondent and clearly protein-deprived themselves. In practical terms the city had only one hotel, and real estate was at a premium. Even a basic support infrastructure for personnel involved in the rebuilding process would have to be built from scratch.

The countryside was as bad if not worse. On the outskirts of Kabul and the agricultural belt around it we were shown the shattered irrigation systems, complete with minefields that left whole swaths of otherwise productive land fallow.

On one trip around town we stopped by the National Museum in front of the heavily scarred palace. The museum had two floors, with perhaps twenty rooms and a courtyard. As a crossroads country, Afghanistan is a cultural treasure trove—Greek, Bactrian, Pashtun,

Ghazvanid, Timurid—and a wealth of different religious expressions, including Buddhist, Muslim, and Kushan. The museum reflected the destruction the country had endured for the past twenty years. Prior to the civil war it held 100,000 pieces, but 90 percent of them were looted during the factional fighting, and the Taliban destroyed many of the rest.

The guard and curator were part of a team that had done heroic work to protect as much as they could from the Taliban regime, whose obsession with human images led to smashing statues and tearing up paintings. The museum team spirited many items to other parts of the city, hid some behind false walls, and argued with the enforcers over their interpretation of the Quran, convincing them not to put many pieces to the hammer. With the liberation they were starting to put the museum back together but left many of the smashed statues in boxes where the pieces could one day be reassembled, at least those that had not been turned to sand. They put these boxes on display to show the depredations of the Taliban as a cautionary tale.

Elsewhere a display case held twenty or so paintings that had been torn up and left in that condition, a bed of canvas pieces. And then there were the anomalies. A large water container with Islamic inscriptions was left intact, with no human images to offend the sensitivities, but so was the bust of a girl's head.

It was like walking through a morgue; after ten boxes of pulverized statues I had seen enough. I waxed poetic in a letter home, suggesting that it was the worse for the bases of the statues left in place, "symbolic of how [the Taliban] had attempted to reduce civilization to rocky stumps." I concluded that "the hero was the caretaker and his assistant, the former a professor who stayed with his stuff and did the best he could to protect and preserve it for reassembly, all without a salary and with no support. If civilization has its enemies it also has its protectors. Need to make sure the protectors have the larger guns."

We also tried to get a sense of the rest of the country. On the margins of the Loya Jirga we met Mohammed Arif, a six-foot-plus leader in his early forties from the village of Gayan, on the Pakistani border. His proud identity was on display in the size of his turban. It was clear from his grizzled features that he could have been transported back a hundred years and his life would have been little different than it was in 2002, focused on prayer, farming, and fighting. His only documentation was a Xerox copy of a military ID card, which he proudly indicated showed that he was a "model jihadi fighter" during the anti-Soviet campaign. His involvement in the jihad, Arif said, was what continued to earn him respect and what helped him win election to the Loya Jirga at his relatively young age.

Arif described his mountainous village as completely isolated from the rest of the country. Ninety-nine percent of the people there were illiterate; there were no newspapers, television, or any connection with the outside world other than BBC and VOA radio, which they devoured. The region's economy, Arif explained, was fully dependent on agriculture, primarily cultivation of nuts and fruits. Drought had hit the region hard, destroying current crops and causing people to cut trees that would have yielded exports in the future. Competition over scarce land and resources also led to fighting between neighboring villages, a Hatfield-and-McCoy–type battle that had led to as many as four hundred deaths and five hundred wounded in the past sixty years.

According to Arif, the Taliban had collected all heavy weapons, but most jihadi fighters kept their personal guns, so the majority of men had at least one firearm. He was concerned about coordination with U.S. military forces in the area and said that competing villagers were trying to disadvantage their rivals by selling false information that would lead to raids and captures.

Arif believed the first priority should be security and questioned the current government's capacity. "If they can't secure Kabul, how can they secure the provinces?" He was concerned that Kabul continued to be the "kingdom of the Panjshiris" since its capture by the Northern Alliance and criticized the UN as too weak to fulfill its promise to make Kabul safe without factional influence. "The Northern Alliance took Kabul by force, and it retains it by force, reinforced by [the International Security Assistance Force]."

At the same time Arif didn't see how a Kabul-based force could ever come to his province and suggested, "It would cause a civil war." Conversely, he didn't see how the men of his village would ever join a national force, which he believed would be controlled by the Northern Alliance. For his region to be connected to the central government, Arif said, Kabul would need to extend itself in building projects—schools, roads, infrastructure that would demonstrate its ability and willingness to serve the people.

We saw each other several times and developed a close relationship. I always sensed that he was both curious and hopeful about these foreigners who had washed ashore, knowing how much help his people needed. But I also sensed there were tight limits to how our assistance could be channeled, and he would think nothing of fighting us if his terms for the relationship were violated.

Arif summed up a good deal of what would play out for the next decade: anger over civilian casualties; mistrust of the central government by an isolated periphery; fierce factional and ethnic conflict, with the Pashtuns on the losing end; a flat economy; and a willingness and ability to fight anyone when things didn't go their way. There would be much work ahead.

But despite the obvious challenges, the refugees were returning home, a million by the time I arrived and another million by the end of the year. The Afghans I met had no sense of entitlement at that point; they were grateful for what came their way but expected little. That would change dramatically by the time I returned a decade later. One of the things I noted was that everyone seemed to be going somewhere: pushing a cart, selling something on the street, cycling to a job site. There was tremendous energy and focus, a kind of "it can only get better" attitude that seemed to permeate Kabul. The Afghans were not entirely trusting of the wave they were riding, knowing the innate selfishness and incompetence of their leaders and the fickleness of the foreigners who periodically came to help. But they were going to do as much as they could, as fast as they could, to take advantage of the new opportunities that had suddenly, unexpectedly come to them. And we were there to help tie it all together, harnessing that energy and, without saying so, building a new country. We hit three primary lines of effort—the economy, the security forces, and governing—which I have found is always the cleanest way to divide up the challenge of postconflict stabilization.

An Economy Starting from Nothing

Task 1 for me was to get a feel for the state of the economy and the most obvious points of entry for our assistance. I had a remarkable translator, Kanishka Bakhshi, who was born in Kabul just after the Soviet invasion and had effectively never known peace. He would be my window on a complicated society and remains a close friend. As we set out in one of the twenty-five-year-old Passats to survey the Afghan economy, we found it summed up by a female Loya Jirga delegate when she answered the question "What do you need?" by simply saying "We need everything."

Construction Sector

Sensing that infrastructure was the essential element for progress across the economy, we started by looking at the construction sector. I summarized: "After twenty-three years of conflict Afghanistan has developed very refined skills in the art and method of destruction but has all but lost the skills for construction. As with most of its business sectors Afghanistan's construction sector is almost completely starting over."

We found a few construction firms, some better capitalized than others. When I asked one owner of a small firm about his machinery, he said he had a large, medium, and small cement mixer. Another had one dump truck, and a third an old crane. When I asked the manager of a Turkish firm about heavy equipment, he said, "The country has two excavators, and they are both right here in my yard." He explained that nearly all machinery was either destroyed or sold off during the factional fighting, and what survived ended up in Pakistan along with most industrial machinery.

Technical skills were also lacking, although we did find a generation of older engineers who had been trained by the Soviets and were skilled in the basic management of construction projects. I concluded, "[The sector] needs equipment, materials, and a new class of engineers, architects, and foremen. What it currently has is extremely innovative and industrious workers and managers, a lot of work to do, and a host of local companies that are trying desperately to get back into business." It was clear the foreign firms would be doing most of the substantial projects for the foreseeable future, with the expeditionary-minded Turkish firms leading the way.

Manufacturing

We spent days trying to penetrate what was left of a manufacturing and processing sector, whose apparent absence was deceptive. In fact as we ventured out we found some welcome surprises. Twenty years of privation had taught Afghan businessmen to make do with very little, and there were many Afghan entrepreneurs in Pakistan waiting to bring their capital and equipment home.

All the industrialists we met were self-capitalizing. We surveyed one raisin plant, outfitted with equipment that a businessman had taken to Pakistan twenty years earlier but had packed onto trucks and returned to Kabul after the fall of the Taliban. His machinery was held together with chicken wire and duct tape; when an engine gave out, he replaced it with a car motor. We also saw three plastic shoe factories, all with equipment recently repatriated from Pakistan, and all similarly held together with wire and tape.

Occasionally we came upon a factory that defied the circumstances. One thirty-something executive's family had four factories in Pakistan and had made a fortune making thread during the Taliban era. They loaded up a million dollars' worth of new German- and French-built machinery and returned it to a factory on the outskirts of Kabul that employed 50 people, with plans to expand to 150 if the security situation held. I was surprised at how early in the transition he had come back, but he called it a measured first step, confessing that they had never been comfortable in Pakistan. He needed engineering support for the machines, a constant supply of power, and security, all common themes.

Workers were beginning to congregate in a USAID-funded industrial park looking for jobs, one guy saying he would rather work for ten rupees a day in Kabul than a hundred a day in Peshawar. It was more encouraging than we expected, more so than in the construction sector. Our messages back to Washington (in retrospect somewhat optimistic) reported the "rising hope of Kabul industrialists tied to the success of the Loya Jirga" and CEOS who asked the government to provide only security and a constant source of electricity—"they will do the rest."

While in relative terms there was more industrial activity than we expected, we still wondered if it would ever match the rising expectations of a seriously deprived people who had just been untethered and needed jobs. There were a dozen other key switches in getting the economy moving, and every one of them had to be turned on.

Foreign Investment

Many of the other inputs to economic activity we knew would need to come from abroad, and we tried to facilitate more foreign interest in the economy. I didn't see any conventional capital coming in for at least the next five years, but we tried to be creative in presenting the environment and clever in pointing out the opportunities to potential investors.

To this end we met with a Siemens Westinghouse executive from Germany who was looking at water-driven power plants. He had developed a sobering chart that showed who had built the country's seventy or so hydropower plants, a hodgepodge of U.S., German, and Russian and other Eastern European companies and governments that would take years to sort out. A team from the U.S. Overseas Private Investment Corporation enlisted my help in getting an agreement with the government for a Hyatt hotel project loan, which we thought would be a positive signal to the investor community. And we worked on securing funding for the U.S. Geological Survey to remap the precious minerals and oil and gas under the ground, something we and the Soviets had both done but that needed updating.

I spent a good deal of time with the acting CEO of Ariana Airlines, Jahid Azimi, a former MIG pilot. He was seeking to rebuild the airline to its glory days in the 1970s, when it had direct flights across the region and into Europe and Asia. He was enthusiastic and professional but admitted he was in over his head and sought help. At the time Ariana had four aircraft, the rest of the fleet having been destroyed by U.S. bombing during the war. India had committed to provide three Airbuses, but they would not be arriving until the fall. Meanwhile every flight on every route was full, with service to Dubai, India, and Iran, as well as a full schedule of domestic flights. Azimi casually asked me what he was supposed to be doing with all the money that was flowing into their coffers from the full flights and full schedules. I asked what the maintenance plan was for the aircraft; when he gave me a blank look, I got him connected with technical advisors who developed a maintenance schedule.

But providing that maintenance was tricky, given low profit margins and security concerns. Into the breach stepped an Afghan American businessman from Miami with a penchant for making deals in difficult places. The Afghan diaspora, we found, were some of the best investors—scrappy, tough, and creative. His solution to both maintenance and new aircraft was to have Afghanistan buy a seized Colombian aircraft at auction in Florida, fly it to Peru, pick up a crew of maintenance techs, and continue onward to Kabul, where the plane would enter the fleet and the techs would perform the maintenance on the other aircraft.

All went well until they stopped in the Bahamas for fuel. The authorities there called in the U.S. Drug Enforcement Administration when they saw a Colombian aircraft with thirty young techs from Peru, flying to Dubai and ultimately Kabul, with large boxes of jeans (on which they were told they could make a killing in the local market), all so soon after 9/11. Drug Enforcement agents did an aggressive search of the plane and released it when they didn't find anything, but by then it was barely operable. It limped into Dubai and couldn't go on. The mechanics finished the trip on a commercial flight and got started with the maintenance checks on the existing fleet in Kabul; the plane caught up later.

As part of a secondary deal, the techs stayed at the Serena Hotel for free in exchange for their assistance installing a phone system. Where some saw devastation, our friend from Miami saw nothing but opportunity.

Building Ministries

I worked closely with the ministers of commerce, finance, and civil aviation and tourism, giving me a window into the challenges and risks of leading in Afghanistan. Sayed Mustafa Kazemi from Parwan led the post-Bonn Commerce Ministry. He was a pleasant guy, with lots of street smarts and a basic level of education. Because I needed to present his bio to some Washington officials he would be meeting I first walked through it with his assistant: born in 1959 in Parwan, where he attended secondary school, university in Kabul with a degree in engineering in 1979, then in 2001 minister of commerce. I asked about the somewhat lengthy gap. Yes, well, the guerrilla struggle, then the civil war, then the fight against the Taliban. I realized that not only were we starting with a pre-industrial economy, but his generation had effectively lost twenty years of experience in business, education, and outside contact. And I realized we needed advisors for all ministries, a service we were simply not prepared to offer. To their credit, the new ministers were quick studies and accepting of help. Kazemi continued to serve in various capacities until he was killed in a bomb blast in 2007 in Baghlan province.

The one minister who probably least needed advisors was Finance Minister Ashraf Ghani, who had worked for a decade at the World Bank and served on various international faculties. But given the criticality of the Finance Ministry we provided advisors, and he was quite pleased with the assistance. What Ghani best understood was how far the country had to go and how underresourced our joint operation was. He worked overtime trying, largely in vain, to better coordinate the various packages of donor assistance that were starting to arrive. He understood there was a window for showing progress to the Afghan people that would not be open forever, and if it closed, everything would be more difficult.

Some ministries were simply tough neighborhoods. One minister for civil aviation and tourism was assassinated in February 2002, by one account beaten to death on the tarmac by hajj-traveling pilgrims who heard a rumor that he was taking their plane for a personal trip to India. Mirwais Saddiq, the son of the Herat-based mujahideen leader Ismael Khan, took over. One of the first things we did with him was locate the millions of dollars in fees that had been collected on Afghanistan's behalf for commercial planes overflying the country in the years when there was no government to receive them.

At that point any revenue stream was most welcome, although any revenue went fast. I wrote at the time that the unique location of Afghanistan made it a natural crossroads for trade, the connector between Europe and South Asia, and between Iran and Pakistan. Creating an infrastructure for collecting revenue would go a long way to funding the reconstruction, which was later formalized in plans for energy transit and the New Silk Road project. Saddiq was killed two years later in an exchange of gunfire in Herat.

The final cabinet-level member on the economic team was Central Bank president Anwar ul-Haq Ahadi, who had a PhD from Northwestern and was teaching political science at Providence College when the Taliban regime collapsed. He came over on a temporary basis, knowing that with the current dearth of expertise his skills and leadership were much needed; he told us, however, that having kids in the United States made it difficult for him to stay on too long. In the end he stuck it out, serving later as finance minister from 2004 to 2009. He was invaluable to keeping the economy on track.

Banking and Currency

For decades a prime piece of real estate on the Kabul River had been set aside for currency trading, thriving to a greater or lesser degree under different regimes. It was formalized at one point in a three-story U-shaped building, housing two hundred large traders with burlap sacks of bills stacked around their desks on the top stories, smaller traders on stools and benches in the courtyard, and microtraders out in the streets. Millions of dollars a day were traded in a combination of afghanis, Pakistani rupees, U.S. dollars, and Dostum notes (bills printed for the Northern Alliance during the civil war).

When asked what was the most lucrative period, one trader replied that it was the communist period, because the markup for dollars was so high; a colleague countered with the Taliban period, because of the intensity of cross-border traffic and Pakistani visitors. But the majority said the current period was best, because of a 35 percent increase in volume over the previous three months and stability in the system. While a regular banking system would put many of them out of business, they recognized the inefficiency and limitations of what they were doing and were eager to see the country's economy come out of the gray zone and begin to interact with the world.

In late July the first phase of this legitimization took place. Fifteen trillion afghanis (1,800 tons of old bank notes) were rapidly phased out of circulation, as we flew 800 tons of new bills out to fifty sites to trade in the old bills. For the first time since 1989 the country would have a single currency and a central bank that functioned. It was a remarkably efficient process, in which old notes were declared invalid after a reasonable trade-in period and three zeros were lopped off the prevailing 42,000-to-1 exchange rate. The populace expressed confidence in the new currency, inflation was kept low, and the exchange rate stabilized. It has fluctuated between 42 and 52.4 on the foreign exchange market since then. There were a lot of problems with the economy, but the currency and exchange rate were not among them. "A complete banking system it isn't," I reported, "but it's better than before."

By mid-June the mood regarding the economy was optimistic but tentative. The currency and banking system were in place, some foreign aid was arriving, and the government was finding its footing. But the hurdles still to be overcome were massive.

The United States later authorized $3 billion over four years in reconstruction and expanded peacekeeping, a figure that, given what we ended up spending on the fighting to come, was short-sighted. There was simply too little of everything to effectively build an economy, and many opportunities were lost as the security situation deteriorated. Building an economy from scratch is expensive and slow and requires a large transfer of technology and expertise, none of which was in our tool box to offer Afghanistan in 2002, and much of which could not have been absorbed by the Afghans if it had been available. But we would muddle through. And when I returned ten years later, I found many hard-fought advances.

Building Security Forces Where Everyone Has a Gun

The security picture for this early phase in Kabul was deceptively good. The city had fallen to the Northern Alliance, and there was never any question of who was in charge, as the posters of Ahmad Shah Massoud on every street corner and in every police station affirmed. This systematic and visible security helped anchor the reconstruction, but unfortunately it also reinforced the shutout of the Pashtuns that would come back to haunt the country politically.

It was another story out in the provinces, however, where we knew warlords and militias still ruled. Ismael Khan in Herat, for example, invited high-level guests to the city and feted them with a parade of his forces, complete with tanks and armored personnel carriers. He gave no indication of buying into a national force, and others were in agreement.

At this point there was no way for the new government to rapidly bring these forces under its purview, as it had neither the resources nor the command structure to control them. And with the United States declining to support an international peacekeeping force, others had no way to help. So these forces were largely left alone, with the hope that they would keep the peace until a national force could be trained and, in the interim, help in the hunt for residual Al-Qaida forces.

Army and Police

My experience with the new army went back to January 2002, when we received a démarche in Budapest asking for excess stocks of Soviet-era uniforms, equipment, and weapons. The Hungarians provided a full shipment of their excess equipment, pleased to get a positive mark in the war on terror at such low cost. I always wondered whether anyone caught the irony of equipping and dressing the new Afghan force in the uniforms of its defeated foes. There was also the morale issue of winding up this new force for the crucial duty of holding the country together but not even entrusting them with a new, pride-instilling national uniform and new equipment.

The first eighteen months were to yield a force of seventeen infantry, four support, and twelve border guard battalions of about 350 soldiers each. The long-term plan was to build an interethnic army of sixty thousand over the course of five years, while assisting in the modernization of the Ministry of Defense and General Staff, Kabul-based military academic institutions, and central logistics structures. Given the resources allocated, it was ambitious but still far lower than what was needed.

The first rollout would be of a Kabul-based corps of five infantry battalions, with other units being pushed out to the provinces later. Specialty training in logistics, signal, armor, artillery, and other disciplines would follow.

I visited a sparse base on the outskirts of Kabul to observe the training. Special Forces trainers commented on how many Afghan recruits had been fighting for years without ever knowing what the siting mechanism on the top of their weapon was for. Many apparently went through the jihad, factional fighting, and combat with the Taliban using pure "spray and pray" techniques. The training paid off. More capable soldiers were being deployed, and they were part of a national, not a local force.

The United States was reluctant to commit more frontline Special Forces trainers to the effort, but France took up some of the slack, and Germany and other NATO partners joined later. In what now seems like a pittance, given that our contribution to build an Afghan army would grow as high as $10 billion a year during the surge and over fifteen years would tally over $70 billion, donors agreed at the Geneva pledging conference to contribute $290 million and the United States an additional $70 million.

The modest budget and slow rollout would have real and immediate implications on the ground, as a vacuum developed. As one example, the budget allowed only for a $50 monthly salary for recruits, $70 a month for NCOs, and $150 a month for officers, none of which were competitive with what local strongmen could pay. Even with later increases they would not compete with the Taliban. In November the U.S. Congress offered the administration even more than it sought, $1 billion to expand the peacekeeping force beyond Kabul. But the aversion to peacekeeping and the greater aversion to nation-building were still deeply ingrained, and little support was given to the congressional proposal.

The first battalion of the newly formed Afghan National Army graduated to much deserved fanfare just prior to the Loya Jirga and was responsible for providing security for the gathering. It was the first mission of a united Afghan Army and one they took seriously. In addition to actively guarding the compound, they were deployed to secure against threats from the commanding heights above Kabul. They were recognized at one point by the leadership of the convention and given one of the strongest ovations of the entire week. The Special Forces team said they constantly drove home the essentiality of an interethnic mix in training and modeled it in their own unit behavior, but they could see it would be a generation before such a mix was natural.

By July the second battalion rolled out, and the pace continued with a new battalion every few weeks, always trying to stay one step ahead of threats. In early July unidentified gunmen shot dead Vice President and Minister for Public Works Haji Abdul Qadir as he left the Ministry. It was a reminder in this case of how opaque the security situation was. Qadir came to the post with several enemies, some financial and some political, and it was never clear if his assassination was due to terrorism or a message to the government. It did remind us of how vulnerable Karzai was, and that there was no good security plan for him when the current U.S. protective detail ended its service. Ambassador Finn reminded Washington of the "one bullet" nature of the regime, and I arranged for a plan to be put in place for a contract security team to take over when the active-duty construct expired, a move that paid off when Karzai was nearly assassinated in Kandahar in November.

Civilian Casualties

Another incident highlighted the conflicts inherent in our mission of hunting down terrorists while standing up a nation. On July 1, 2002, U.S. aircraft supporting Special Forces teams in Oruzgan province came under what they perceived to be ground fire. The planes returned fire and killed seventeen persons in a wedding party, including the bride and groom. The popular understanding was that our forces had simply misread celebratory gunfire. It was the kind of thing Karzai would have to explain to his people again and again over the coming years, as it was simply the nature of the conflict that collateral damage would occur with some frequency. But this one was particularly bad, given its location in the heart of the Pashtun south and that it was a wedding party that by one account wiped out an entire family. Karzai traveled to the site and sat patiently with the elders and the family members, expressing condolences and promising to reel in his international partners. He delivered strong messages all around.

To discuss compensation the military sent up a team, accompanied by my boss, Michael Mctrinko, who was uniquely suited for this kind of thing, with his fluent Pashto and cultural awareness. He quietly and patiently engaged, sitting with the village elders for hours, grieving with them, until he was finally able to get to the point of the visit. A compensation plan was drawn up, and the region could move on from the incident. There was no way to rush it, and in the end no amount of money could make it right, but a reasonable amount, if properly delivered, would help.

A Platform or a Partner?

While the pace of the rollout struck me as slow, I wondered if there wasn't another way to look at the whole thing. We were understandably obsessed with cornering Al-Qaida and getting bin Laden, missions that we could entrust to no one other than U.S. forces, using Afghanistan as a mere platform for conducting these missions. But over the medium term I cabled to a high-level U.S. Defense Department official that Karzai was asking whether Afghanistan was ever going to move from platform to partner in the war on terror. I believed this was destined to be the defining issue in our bilateral relationship.

A future model, I suggested, drew from the Salvador experience, in which we determined that long-term success could ultimately come from centering security for the country squarely on the Afghan government, with coalition forces taking as their key mission improving the capabilities of the Afghan forces, to include officer training and special units. The current militias could be federalized in partnership with U.S. advisors. Such a program could fill the security vacuum and enhance our long-term effectiveness in the war on terror, while giving Karzai the reach into the provinces he so badly needed.

Starting in about 2007 we would put considerably more emphasis on training and equipping the forces, which came to number over 200,000 by the time I returned in 2012, the United States incurring the cost for the bulk of it. We also developed a village security program in 2012, which filled the gap in rural areas. But the security gap we left between 2002 and 2007, the lost window of opportunity, when the shock and awe of the war created the will for a national force that we did not support, would haunt all our other efforts. Of all the missing tools in our tool box, training and equipping security forces has always struck me as the most glaring.

The Loya Jirga Provides a Way Forward

As in all transitions, security and economic development in the new Afghanistan were just the peripherals; no amount of economic development could compensate for a dysfunctional political settlement, and no amount of force could compel legitimately unsatisfied players. If it was to succeed, Afghanistan needed a political agreement that brought all the parties together in a comprehensive framework that would meet their collective needs.

One thing Afghanistan had going for it was a universally accepted mechanism for convening the nation whose results would be widely accepted. The Loya Jirga, Pashto for "Grand Council," lives in Afghan lore and is as much a part of the political consciousness of Afghans as the town hall is to Americans. Historically such gatherings were infrequent, usually reserved for large national issues such as the ratification of a constitution. When one uttered the term "Loya Jirga," there seemed to be no question what the protocol was for convening it, what it would look like, and what it should yield. It was this almost mythical process that all Afghans accepted as their way to choose those who would rule them.

Selecting the Candidates

To begin the process the UN secretary general established a commission under the chairmanship of the Afghan legal scholar Ismail Qasimyar and two deputies, including the law professor Mahboba Hoqomal, who would become vice president of the gathering and serve in Karzai's cabinet as advisor for women's affairs. Joint Afghan-international teams working under the UN Assistance Mission Afghanistan blanketed the country and developed the list of 1,700 delegates for the gathering.[1]

Commission members traveled to villages, where, through consultations and caucuses, they established twenty or so leaders, who then gathered to select their district delegates. All 362 districts were given at least one seat, with larger population centers having more. In some cases there were large gatherings to select the delegation—one meeting in Takhar had six thousand participants—but others relied on simple consultation with a group of elders.[2]

To Western eyes it might not have looked fully democratic. There were sporadic complaints of strong-arming during the selection process, and the common refrain during the Jirga of too many warlords. But for a country so battered and truncated to be able to convene 1,700 delegates, among them two hundred women and covering all ethnic and social groups, was nothing short of a miracle, and the Afghans saw it as such. In a northern gathering the Uzbek warlord and U.S. ally Gen. Abdul Rashid Dostum, one analyst said, had "probably his first ever experience of anything similar to a democratic process, where . . . he couldn't be absolutely certain that he would come out as a winner."[3]

Setting the Tent

The Loya Jirga in June 2002 was the first convening of the Afghan nation in decades, and the first real convening of the global community in Afghanistan after 9/11. There was not a single building left in Kabul that could hold the delegates, so the Germans brought in a huge Oktoberfest tent (whose usual purpose we did not advertise). They set it up on the grounds of the university with a sea of chairs, a sound system, and two huge screens to show the proceedings. A host of smaller tents for delegation meetings was scattered around the campus, and contractors worked feverishly to renovate the dormitories where delegates would be billeted.

The UN lead would be Special Representative Lakhdar Brahimi, who knew the importance of putting an all-Afghan face on the event, staying well in the background and ensuring that his officers were similarly not directly visible throughout the process. In opening remarks he reiterated to the delegates the critical role they were playing: "The world has followed the suffering of Afghanistan for twenty-three years and the eyes of the Afghan people are watching over you as you decide its future." He implored them not to turn the event into a scramble for positions but instead to unite the country and ensure that all Afghans felt represented.

The chair throughout would be Qasimyar, looking as if he was in far over his head, as scrums broke out among delegates who often rushed the podium while he looked haplessly on. But his scholarly status and low-key approach, clearly set on accommodating everyone, may have been what the gathering needed to show inclusion and goodwill.

On opening day my interpreter Kanishka and I spent a good deal of time in the parks and cafés of Kabul, watching and listening to the proceedings with groups of men, students, and a few burqa-clad women, with whom we could interact through their closest male relative or at least a random Afghan male. They spoke in hushed tones of the Loya Jirga, riveted to the event that brought such hope for the future.

To showcase ethnic balance up front, the Tajik Panjshiri interior minister Yunis Qanooni spoke on the first day, taking up a common theme of putting the nation above personal privilege. He told the delegates, "I am ready to give up my post because of you. Chairman Karzai can give my post to anyone he chooses." It was not entirely heartfelt, as he was later involved in a scramble for positions, but the theme came up frequently.

King or Karzai?

Some 80 percent of those we talked to saw Karzai as the only real option to continue to lead the country. They assumed the stability and progress of the previous six months was no accident and hoped the same team would continue. There were those among the older generation, however, who were hoping for a restoration of the king, Mohammed Zahir Shah, waxing nostalgic for the peace and stability experienced during his reign. One rumor circulated that as many as eight hundred of the delegates supported restoration. I noted that the contrast between the king and Karzai in simple capacity for governing could not have been greater. UN and U.S. special envoys later worked the issue behind closed doors, persuading the king to renounce any intention of being available to lead the country.

As always, Karzai was confident and stylish. (One observer remarked that his turban had never been taller.) In the first of many speeches Karzai's key theme was national unity. After travels throughout country, he said, he was pleased with the progress he had seen, the initial fulfillment of his dream of a free, united

Afghanistan. To thunderous applause he declared that after a long period of fighting and discord "Afghanistan is back." As urgent issues that deserved the body's attention he cited improving education, building security forces, establishing diplomatic relations, enhancing commercial opportunities, controlling corruption, curbing the cutting of forests, and strengthening the banking system.

He warned that the war was not yet over and that security would not be assured until all weapons and militias were brought under the control of the national army. But as a nod to reality he also praised the "living heroes," most of them with active militias: "Brother" Burhanuddin Rabbani, Ismael Khan, and General Dostum. Dostum had told Karzai he wanted to "change his clothes" and give up his military command for politics. Karzai also gave credit to those who had fought against the "tyranny" brought by outsiders, namely communists, foreign agents, and Taliban. He singled out his father, Abdul Ahad Karzai, and Shah Massoud and the mujahideen commander Abdul Haq as victims of Taliban depredations.

Election Day

The day for voting on the new government was relaxed and upbeat. The outcome was well known, but delegates were intent on seeing it play out fairly. The day began with speeches by the four candidates for president: Karzai; Dr. Masouda Jalal, an official with the World Food Program; Deputy Minister Mir Mohammed Mahfooz Nedahi, an army officer; and Glam Fareq Majidi, who in the end did not make the threshold and was dropped. Jalal drew strong applause from the female delegates after a well-delivered speech, a welcome display of gender politics in the new Afghanistan.

There was some back and forth on whether the vote should be secret or by public acclamation, but Qasimyar reminded the delegates that they had opted for the secret ballot the day before. Qasimyar then issued stern instructions to the delegates to avoid the problems of earlier sessions: "Some persons circled more than one candidate, and some even circled all the candidates." Not realizing his microphone was still on, he crabbed to security, "Don't let them come near," now wise to the tendency of the delegates to mob the podium. Qasimyar's final counsel to the delegates was this: "It is you who will finally put aside the period of destruction and move the nation forward."

The delegates went to their respective voting areas and cast their ballots. I described the scene as "taking place in Afghan fashion—an organized chaos of queuing, kibitzing, and much milling about. Kabuli delegates waited patiently in multiple long lines, some sitting cross-legged on the floor and chatting. Two ballot areas were mobbed with voters, as Western camera crews scrambled atop tables to gain close-up shots without being swamped by the human tide. There were no frayed tempers and many smiles and intense discussions. At the front of the tent, delegations posed for photos with leaders, many seemingly more intent on bringing home personal photos with Karzai, Marshal Fahim, the Northern Alliance commander whose forces captured Kabul from the Taliban, the popular Panjshiri politician Abdullah Abdullah, or others than on the voting."

Many delegates took the secret ballot fully to heart, one Turkmen leader later telling me when I asked who his delegation voted for, "This is democracy, and in a democracy you do not tell people how you voted." This led me to comment, "If anything is clear, it is that Afghans have embraced political expression and have a firmer understanding of democratic principles than their leaders anticipated."

At 9:00 p.m. the votes were counted and the results announced. Karzai had won 1,289 out of 1,550 votes, Jalal 171, and Nedahi 89. Although Karzai's win was something of a given, the delegates were nonetheless euphoric. Karzai offered brief remarks, praising both the process and his opponents, and was heartily embraced by the delegates when he dismounted from the podium. As always, he gave specific praise to the international community that had made it all possible. I wrote, "That Afghans were able to carry out a peaceful, almost polite, election less than a year after the end of twenty-three years of war was an impressive accomplishment for them, the international community, and the United States." In retrospect this conclusion was wildly understated.

The Question of Religion and State

The delegates soon came back down to earth. For the rest of the week Karzai generated more complaints than compliments, and "scrum" replaced "euphoria" as the operative word.

On day 4 the issue of religion and state was raised forcibly by the hardline Islamist and former mujahideen commander Abdul Rab Rasul Sayyaf. Sayyaf was allegedly the one who first invited Osama bin Laden and now called for an Islamic state under sharia law committed to permanent jihad. Notably he wanted to add "Islamic" to the name of the Transitional Authority. He was waved off by a good number of delegates but one female delegate who supported him asserted that she was not enamored of Western influence and that Afghanistan should stick to its unique culture.

Sayyaf was rebutted by Sheikh Muhammed Asif Mohseni, the most powerful Shia cleric in Afghanistan and the leader of the Hazaras in the anti-Soviet struggle. Mohseni called for a more moderate and tolerant vision of Islam, largely because he did not want to see the Hazaras under the Sunnis' thumb. He was not a social progressive, as his later drafting of a widely criticized Shia family law showed, but in this case his opposition to Sunni dominance worked in favor of a more moderate or at least more diverse religious system. He received by far the largest ovation of the day's proceedings.

A third individual, Governor Gul Agha Shirzai of Kandahar, drew vocal condemnation when he opposed the name Islamic Transitional Authority for the new government. He claimed the Taliban had discredited the use of Islam in a political setting by its perverse religious interpretations. Governor Haji Qadir of Jalalabad calmed the crowd by offering support for the Islamic inclusion. He pointed out that the entire structure of the Loya Jirga was Islamic, its elected leader was Muslim, Afghanistan's culture was Islamic, so why would they not include "Islamic" in the country's name? Another delegate affirmed the point. As incredible as it was to see people voting and taking their destiny in their own hands, he said, "equality will bring unity, but only in an Islamic system."

The final speaker was Sibghatullah Mojadidi, the first president in the 1992–96 mujahideen government. He closed the session by urging the delegates to transcend ethnicity and take proper actions under good leadership. "When Mohammed was in Arabia," he said, "it was the least of the nations, but out of it came a great nation—Islam. With God's help, Afghanistan can similarly transcend its current state."

The nomenclature "Islamic" would stay attached to Afghanistan through the transitional period and into the establishment of the permanent government, joining only Iran, Pakistan, and Mauritania in being so named. The name raised some concern in Washington, but in the end there were simply more pressing issues, and outsiders needed to carefully pick their battles.

Cries from the Heartland

The crowd was patiently respectful, but delegates had a lot to say so several open sessions were built into the proceedings. It was a time for venting (most commonly against the warlords), for reconciling, for laying down markers about the future, for commemorating those who had died in the long struggle for peace, for expressing hope, for praising. In the hall there was intense focus on each speaker, and throughout Kabul—in cafés, homes, and parks—people were riveted. It was the cathartic experience, the national group therapy that the new nation had been waiting for.

The speeches were ultimately forward looking, seeking to find a common ground for reconciliation. This became clear when delegates went beyond abstractions to point fingers. One delegate was shouted down and chastised by the moderator when he questioned the bona fides of Afghans with dual citizenship. Another drew angry shouts when he railed on Pakistan. The most disruptive speech was from an antiroyalist who attacked the king, leading one man to jump on the podium and denounce him. Qanooni took over when Qasimyar could not restore order and solemnly reminded the delegates that twenty-five million Afghans were relying on them to chart the country's future. Unity, reconciliation, and closure were the key themes.

But the delegates also raised practical issues. One female delegate declared, "Guns should be replaced by pens," and a dozen delegates argued that demilitarization should be the government's first priority. Others said the only armed groups should be the national army and police. Infrastructure was a common theme, with a call for a road from Kabul to Herat, the replacement of a key bridge whose destruction cut a province in two, and better allocation of aid to distant provinces. As one delegate told me, they were delivering a "Dear Mr. Karzai" letter and hoped he was listening. He was not, as he had been off doing sidebar meetings to establish the government, but after some complaints he returned several times to hear the speeches.

Business and commerce also got some play, with delegates calling for the exploitation of mineral wealth and an increase in exports. One urged an end to local taxation by warlords, and another the establishment of a functional central bank. One representative from abroad called on the Afghan diaspora to return. Minorities of small communities expressed their specific concerns: the Kuchis for land they were never given; the Turkmen for the Tajiks and Pashtuns to treat them like the "younger brothers" they are; and some Pashtuns for the release of Taliban prisoners who were "cooking in containers." Women, mine victims, returning refugees, widows, all waited patiently for their chance at the mike.

Women Take the Stage

It was a new day too for Afghan women, although we were not sure how deep-seated it was. We noted that the women of the Jirga immediately removed their veils and walked about freely once separated from the male escorts who had dropped them off (and conveniently were not allowed on the grounds). Whenever instructions were given, however vague, the women would immediately caucus and develop their collective position. Many would then go to their respective regional caucuses and try to spark some activity. (When left to the men, caucus opportunities generally turned into a long smoke break.)

As the week went on, the Jirga groups became increasingly cross-gender, the men often listening while the women took lead roles in discussions. When voting, the women comfortably joined their male colleagues to cast their ballots.

Female candidates exclaimed that the candidacy of a woman for president was "unbelievable," as was the large female representation. "We are happy to vote after five years as prisoners in our own homes, and we are proud of the lady candidates," one woman told me. Two Afghan American delegates (one of whom my colleague realized was his dental hygienist from suburban Washington DC) said they cried when they cast their votes: "Seven months ago, who would have believed we women would have this much freedom, much less be able to vote in the Loya Jirga." They called it a historic moment, one filled with emotion.

A constant theme for the women was demilitarization and disarmament, which they all supported and which explained the king's relatively greater popularity with women. "He is the only one who did not fight during the last twenty-three years, and all the others helped destroy Kabul. Who else can say that?" asked one woman. The most common complaint concerned the number of former commanders still in the cabinet and obviously headed for senior positions in the new government.

Other women looked beyond this single event to the future. A burqa-clad staffer at the Ministry of Communications saw it as a first step but cautioned, "Only the presence of a lady minister will ensure women have full equality and opportunities." And she thought it was far too early to tell how successful the new nation would be.

There was a clear gap between the countryside and urban areas, with most of the urban women expressing more optimism than their rural counterparts. And then there were the detractors. Rabbani's newspaper ran an article the week of the Jirga asking if the prominent female Hazara candidate Sima Samar was the "Salman Rushdie of Afghanistan," defying Islamic tenets by her very presence. And the fundamentalist Sayyaf reportedly threatened Jalal's family for her having had the temerity to run for head of state.

The women of Afghanistan, we reported to Washington, would have "a long road ahead toward full participation in Afghan society." But it was a start.

Selection of Government, Parliament, and Ministers

Three key items of business remained: the structure of the government, the establishment of a national parliament, and the selection of ministries. Karzai worked overtime to get all of them to a good place, but he didn't have much to work with and decided the best course was to defer to selected councils to do the work for the future. The delegates accepted the proposals, but their enthusiasm was waning.

Frustration mounted further as reminders of the raw power struggle that were still to play out in the regions were on display, regardless of what was decided in the Loya Jirga. Former president Rabbani, whom many Afghans blamed for fueling the factional fighting but who retained considerable authority, took to the podium at one point and called for a more active role for the mujahideen in governing. By then disillusionment had set in among many delegates, one of whom, a farmer from distant Badakhshan, told me, "The only action we have taken was to vote for Chairman Karzai. The rest of the Loya Jirga is no good. I had hopes we could act to resolve our problems. This has not happened." Another delegate agreed, stating that she thought they would be voting in a new parliament and cabinet. By then there were also rumors of intimidation, and Karzai himself called out those who had been threatening his supporters. The presence of former warlords was probably the most constant complaint, and many were starting to believe the gathering was a rubber stamp for decisions made behind closed doors.

But on the last day Karzai managed to pull it together. With considerable support from U.S. Special Envoy Zalmay Khalilzad, Brahimi, and other internationals, he had compensated the losers in the Loya Jirga and given ethnic balance to the new government. From the interim cabinet's ten Pashtuns, eleven Tajiks, three Uzbeks, and five Hazaras he chose a more balanced configuration of fourteen ministers, with the promise that future ministers would also accurately reflect the country's ethnic makeup. He took a vote by a show of hands and accepted it as a mandate.

He then announced his three vice presidents, Tajik Mohammed Fahim, Hazara Karim Khalili, and Pashtun Haji Abdul Qadir, all former Northern Alliance commanders, the last of whom would be assassinated several weeks later. Again he asked for a loose validation, which he received. Critics later argued that this should have been a more formal process, but under the circumstances it appeared adequate to us. It was a sort of controlled democratic gathering from the start.

Karzai closed the session by outlining his vision for the country's progress in the human, social, and economic spheres, speaking of education and economic development. He insisted on security being fully in the hands of the central government and spoke of the importance of the state protecting the country's religious heritage. He urged the delegates to continue the business of helping to form the national assembly.

The mood was good in the end. A stocky Pashtun delegate happily stated that he had not expected the Jirga to go so smoothly after twenty-three years of war, especially for a people with little education and experience in such things. He stood among a group of grizzled veteran mujahideen, a vibrant yellow and black turban wrapped around a straw bowler perched atop his head. "We are the free people of the Afghanistan-Pakistan border," he said. "We're all on the same ship now. If it sinks, we all go down together."

The United States and the United Nations had a generally positive brand at this point, and our interlocutors did not perceive U.S. involvement as too heavy-handed. "There wouldn't be a Loya Jirga without the United States," one merchant said, "so how can we talk about the U.S. being too involved?"

Lessons Learned and the Way Forward

The delegates returned home, some happier than others. The historic gathering was at an end. Over the final meal I was seated next to a Pashtun delegation from the south and asked their views on how it had turned out. One of the full-bearded members looked at me and shrugged. He was not interested in a conversation and looked as though he had had enough of foreigners' bright ideas for one week.

I tried to wrap it all up for Washington by clarifying the winners and losers, wanting to strike that balance between being hopeful about what had been achieved while stressing the immense work that remained to be done and the fragility of the accomplishment:

> The Emergency Loya Jirga was a tentative success, with winners, losers, and a slate of unfinished business, some of which developed during the meeting itself. Key winners include President Karzai, who gained legitimacy and emerged the indispensable, if embattled leader of Afghanistan; Marshall Fahim, who retained control of the defense ministry and picked up a vice presidency; the international community and especially [the International Security Assistance Force], whose security measures and presence were deeply appreciated; and the Afghan people, who came together with unprecedented unity and empowerment. The big losers include Interior Minister Qanooni, whose reduction in status increases the potential for instability; the Royalists, who were summarily dismissed through the Jirga process; the Pashtuns, who failed to break the Northern Alliance hold on power; and conservatives associated with former President Rabbani and religious leader Sayyaf.
>
> The slate of unfinished business includes the issue of religion in public life; the increased vulnerability of the regime as a result of cabinet spoils; the much-desired but undefined Shura (parliament); and the center-periphery divide, which has the potential to close but more reason to widen. In the end the Loya Jirga was a beginning, not an end, and capitalizing on it will require constant focus, resources, and effort.

It was the last sentence that we hoped would be Washington's focus. Americans had become so enamored of democratic processes that we were inclined to shutter the shop after a successful vote. This was not the time for shuttering, however; we had a clear window of opportunity, but we were just getting started. There was no single thing the country needed; it needed it all. We had learned enough in previous operations to know that a full-on push to develop indigenous security forces that were mobile, well-trained, well-led, and respected was essential, and it would take resources, advisors, and equipment to get them there. The economy was still fragile and the country would need considerable assistance, targeted at key sectors. And the political process would require highly skilled guidance over a sustained period. It was difficult to see how this could be managed absent a full peacekeeping mission throughout the country.

Yet even with all this there was going to be a long period of violent adjustment as the various peoples accustomed themselves to democratic processes and as the Pashtuns reasserted themselves and found their place in the new Afghanistan. For that there was probably no shortcut.

NINE

Iraq, 2003

The Cornered Sunnis of Al Anbar

What Else Is Out There

By the time I left Afghanistan the United States was already turning its attention to other perceived threats. The chilling fear that permeated American society after primitive terrorists brought down the Twin Towers raised the legitimate question "What else is out there?" And as threats went, Iraq was legitimately high on the list, having sought nuclear weapons for decades, used chemical weapons against its own people, and cavorted openly with terrorists. The problem was the administration took a very limiting view of the range of options that could have been deployed to defang Iraq and by then was enamored of the decisive regime change option after its apparent early success in Afghanistan.

Planning for regime change in Iraq began in 2002, and by the fall the administration had made its case for coercive actions while allowing the weapons inspection regime to play out for several more months. But it became clear that Saddam Hussein would never allow weapons inspectors the kind of access that would be required to satisfy the United States because he was concerned with threats from neighbors if they knew he was disarmed. On March 17, in frustration with Iraq's game of cat and mouse, the Bush administration declared the game over, and on March 20 initiated hostilities. The Ba'athist regime crumbled even faster than the Taliban, and on April 9 Baghdad and Basrah fell to U.S. and British forces.

On April 21 Lt. Gen. (ret.) Jay Garner, the chief of the Office for Reconstruction and Humanitarian Assistance, arrived in Baghdad with an under-empowered, understaffed, and underresourced cohort that was ostensibly to manage civil administration in the newly liberated Iraq. Garner described himself as a lame duck from the start, and indeed a week after his arrival was informed that a new entity, the Coalition Provisional Authority, would come in to replace him, led by Ambassador Paul Bremer. Garner had planned to execute a rapid and forceful handover to an Iraqi authority, while Bremer planned on a slower transition that would only over time and in phases yield a sovereign Iraqi government and democratic institutions. Neither model could fully contain the early and aggressive entry of Iran into the Iraqi political sphere nor the intense factional animosity. The United States was embarking on a grueling decades-long regional scrum with only the resources and plans for a six-month sortie among friends.

Free Iraqi Fighters and a Respectful Dissent: Let the UN Manage the Transition

My first Iraqi mission predated my arrival there. In the lead-up to the war a curious program was carried out in Hungary to train a corps of Free Iraqi Fighters—Iraqi exiles gathered from around the world to serve with military units as interpreters, guides, liaisons, and civil affairs specialists. The Hungarians agreed to host the program at Taszar airbase, and a civil affairs unit came in to train the first tranche of fifty, mostly from the United States and Europe, with hope for several thousand more picked up in the Iran-Iraq border area. The latter could not be marshaled in time and the window to pick them up closed when the fighting started.

In retrospect, considering how much assistance we would need on the ground and how long the occupation would last, it was probably somewhat short-sighted not to have done whatever was necessary to collect this last group. But military planners, and Cmdr. Tommy Franks in particular, did not see much value in diverting military resources to postwar issues. In the end some of those trained went on to be helpful during the occupation and others were hired as translators. The camp closed and the trainers moved to Kuwait to get ready for the real operation. It was one of the few tangible preparations for the postwar phase of operations.

It was both exhilarating and exasperating to watch the liberation of Iraq: exhilarating to see how quickly the regime crumbled, exasperating to see how little prepared we were for the postwar. But prepared or not it appeared there was a huge core of Iraqis ready to move on and who had the energy to build a new post-Saddam society.

In May I sent some thoughts on the postwar in a "dissent channel" message to the State Department, a venue developed after the Vietnam War to ensure all views on an issue were considered. I started by simply stating that this was going to be a whole lot harder than anyone seemed to realize, and cited the range of tasks and historical precedents for the challenge of postconflict reconstruction. But the key to it all, I suggested, was the political piece. I knew that we could make a lot of mistakes on the security and economic and humanitarian fronts, but we had to get the politics right or we would be facing an uphill battle for years.

I then listed a series of reasons why I thought the UN could do a better job than a U.S. administrator of managing a political transition—among them neutrality, experience, longevity, marshaling of international resources, and a firewall for the United States when things go wrong. I also suggested the UN would simply bring in a more talented leader than we would, citing Lakhdar Brahimi as an example of the caliber of individual available in the UN peacekeeping system. I was haunted by Somalia, where a weak political team and inexperienced leadership shattered any chance at success. In response Policy Planning Director Richard Haass was honest in telling me that the train had left the station and there was very little space for new ideas, particularly involving the UN. We would have a coalition administrator, and he would manage the transition. Having failed to shape the operation at the outset, I then turned my sights to supporting it on the ground. I offered my services and was given an undefined posting with the Coalition Provisional Authority (CPA).

Getting to Ramadi

The U.S. State Department of this period was not accustomed to staffing war zones and had none of the structures that were later developed to deploy large numbers of Foreign Service officers in the field. It was also not exactly clear how much space the Defense Department was going to allow other agencies in the first place. It was the kind of environment I thrived in.

While waiting for onward movement in Kuwait, with blast furnace heat raging outside, I made some blue-sky notes in a journal:

August 2003, Going in Position to Baghdad

The natural resistance of an Arab people to occupation is insurmountable. The Iraqis will always resist the occupation even if there are pockets of periodic acceptance. The key is to buy enough acceptance in enough of the country to achieve our objectives, and to limit the possibility of a wholesale jihad vs. the United States in the center and south—the cumulative impact of raids and curfews and shootings.

—Limit the geographic occupation to those places where our presence is necessary.

—Delay privatization of the economy. Massive public works projects.

—Show a clear way forward politically that includes an Iraqi-selected national body, delaying will tend to strengthen the already hardening lines.

—Short and long-term building of security forces—police are at the heart of the new Iraq, must be well-trained, disciplined, well-equipped, and mentored. Should be the biggest and most ambitious project we have.

—Create zones of stability. Show that in these zones aid, resources, and investment will flow and U.S. forces will leave.

I arrived in Baghdad two days later and was dispatched in front of a massive gaudy palace topped by gigantic busts of Saddam in British field kit, reinforced inside by a dramatic bas motif of

Saddam riding in a chariot beside Nebuchadnezzar. He was Iraq's newest conqueror, and he was everywhere.

The CPA was an interesting mix of people: a few Foreign Service officers who had self-selected to work the mission based on the appearance of need, a few British civil servants, and a bevy of young White House and Pentagon staffers who saw Iraq as a minor rite of passage.

Ambassador Bremer by this time wanted all hands in the field and assigned me to be governance coordinator for the Sunni province of Al Anbar under Mike Gfoeller, one of the State Department's best Arabists. Deputy Administrator Andy Bearpark, who had long experience in the Balkans and elsewhere, explained that I was soon to have a staff of ten civilians, augmented by civil affairs personnel, but for the time being would be a team of one. We would be forming what amounted to a shadow government, he said, at once governing a province and moving forward a political process that would ultimately lead to Iraqi self-government. A team of ten, Bearpark conceded, would be light, the first of many understatements I was to hear. Still, he did everything he could to support us and was one of the few bright lights in the CPA.

Hillah was an hour or so by road to the south through palm tree–rich countryside. It was a friendly area without a hint of threat, and as our security contractors hit traffic there was none of the pushing cars off the road that would come later as the threat increased. We simply waited along with everyone else.

As an Arabist, Gfoeller knew that having swept away Saddam's artificial regime we were left with what preexisted the Ba'athists: the tribes. He engaged tribal leaders constantly and sought to build a political structure where their traditional place was secure along with an emerging civil society.

The Starting Lineup

When a map is just a map, military planners can do all sorts of things on it—move men north, south, east, and west to get over rivers, around mountains, through deserts, and skirt civilian population centers. When fighting insurgencies, however, that civilian population becomes not just a hindrance to the fight but a center of gravity that cannot be avoided. Tribal politics, history, social stressors, religious convictions, employment options, the status of women, educational alternatives, and power, how and where it is exercised, all combine in a thick stew of cultural geography. Suddenly the mere challenge of rivers, deserts, and mountains looks appealing by comparison.

What we would experience in Al Anbar was the collision of history, culture, and four distinct groups: the Americans and their international coalition, the 5 percent of Iraqis who supported them, the 5 percent who unalterably opposed them, and the remaining 90 percent who were waiting to be influenced. The ultimate loyalty of the 90 percent would decide the contest.

The Good Guys: Americans

For the first several months of the war and its aftermath Al Anbar was just a piece of the map. The 82nd Airborne Division liberated the province and set the initial conditions for the occupation, getting off to a rocky start in Falluja when seventeen protesters were killed in April 2003. In May the 3rd Armored Division relieved them but was replaced by the 3rd Armored Cavalry Regiment (ACR) in June, which would then join the 82nd Airborne Division when they returned in September. That makes four units in six months, in an area where personal relationships were everything.

I arrived in early September, when there were fewer than ten thousand soldiers from the 3rd ACR operating in all of the province, a third of Iraq. The 3rd ACR commander, Col. David Teeples, was glad to have a civilian on board, hoping I was the first of many who could start to take over the nonmilitary tasks. While they would clearly have preferred operating their tanks and Bradleys across broad swaths of terrain, I was impressed with how well their units managed civil administration and how dexterous they were with limited resources. They took me in and made me part of the team.

Working alongside the 3rd ACR was the 1/124th Battalion of the Florida National Guard, which arrived in Ramadi in May and stayed in place as units swirled around them. The unit officers' day jobs in Florida were as police and city administrators, and they brought street smarts and trainers to the task of pacifying Ramadi that was impressive and encouraging. Col. Hector Mirabile engaged fully with tribal leaders, leading one local sheikh to comment to the press that they were "making him a member of [their] tribe" for the respect he showed them.

My key implementing partner was the 304th Civil Affairs Brigade out of Philadelphia but drawing from New Jersey and New York. When I arrived they were barely scratching the surface of what needed to get done, overseeing payroll, basic services, supervision of city managers, and paying stipends to ex-soldiers. If they could get people paid, they reasoned, maybe public services would muddle along and anger at the occupation would be kept to a minimum.

With the arrival of the 82nd Airborne Division in September the capacity increased dramatically. From one major and a translator we moved downtown with a team of twenty-five and started to build a government, with vastly increased capacity and experience.

On the CPA side I was joined in September by Harry Christian, who would manage security, contracting, and team planning; Paul Mades, IT guy and logistician; and Lt. Cmdr. George Younes, a naval officer who threw himself into everything from tribal negotiations to weapons recovery. Also part of the civilian team was Research Triangle International democratization specialist Vassil Yanco, whose long experience in international negotiations for the Red Cross and UN made him an invaluable asset in helping manage the political process.

Good Guys: Iraqis

There were no flowers in the streets when the coalition arrived in Al Anbar. But there were Iraqis who were willing to work with us, some tribal leaders even suggesting that properly empowered they could have liberated Ramadi on their own. The good guys included initially sheikhs and tribal leaders, imams, and bureaucrats, and we would later add members of civil society and business leaders. It was always a limited number of individuals but over our tenure reached deeply and broadly into Anbari society.

Most of the tribes of the Anbar governorate derive from the Dulaym Tribal Confederation, which first appears in history in 600 BCE, when it migrated from Yemen to the Arabian Peninsula and Iraq.[1] The Dulaym Confederation breaks down into several dozen tribes and subtribes, all geographically based but many with linkages to other parts of the province and some outside of Iraq.

The coalition was another in a long line of outside powers that imposed themselves on the province. Al Anbar in fact means "the warehouse," derived from the time when it supplied Persia's Sassanid troops. Tribal leaders were faced with core questions that played out daily in their interaction with the coalition: How long would we be there, and what would we leave behind? Did they want to be the leader who cooperated with the occupiers, or the one who resisted? These were perpetual questions for the province that produced Prince Dhari al-Dharer and his son Khamis, who assassinated a British officer in 1920 and sparked the uprising of that period.

The picture is further complicated by the fact that, as expressed in one U.S. Army tribal study, "Sunni tribal behavior is highly interdependent . . . a result of a complex web of tribal loyalties and betrayals, and of competition over limited resources. In Saddam's Iraq, tribes frequently broke rank with each other, and individuals broke rank from within the tribe, to take advantage of the regime's favor. When trying to secure the cooperation of Sunni tribes in post-Saddam Iraq, there will likely be multiple tribes involved, and each tribe must consider the patterns of behavior of all of the others."[2] Not quite as multifarious as Italian family politics, but complicated.

Against this complex backdrop we kept in mind that Saddam was not a native son of Anbar but a Tikriti, a fact that manifested in the shabbiness of the infrastructure and community services (but which were far less shabby than the community services and infrastructure in the south). Anbar's restiveness played out in 1995 when an Iraqi Air Force general and Anbar native, Mazlum al-Dulaymi, was executed by Saddam over a question of loyalty and his tribe rose in a brief and apparently not particularly well-planned uprising. Two thousand Anbaris were killed as the revolt was put down. Saddam, concerned about losing his grip even in the Sunni areas, then tried to make amends by showering resources on the province while tinkering with the tribal structure.

We dealt with dozens of sheikhs throughout the province, but our three most consistent interlocutors were Dulaym Sheikh Majid al Sulaiman, who many accepted as the "Sheikh of Sheikhs," Ammer Abdul Jabaar Ali Sulayman, and Deputy Chair Bizi'e Njriss al Gaoud of the Albu Nimr subtribe in Hit. Ammer and Majid were generally fairly conservative and slow paced, all about prestige and commercial advantage, while Gaoud was consistently full of ideas and energy.

In addition to the tribal leaders were key nontribal leaders whom the sheikhs empowered after the fall of the regime to manage the transition. The most prominent of these was Abdulkareem Barjas Al-Rawi. Barjas was a police major general when the coalition arrived with only peripheral Ba'athist connections and was well placed to take on the job of Ramadi mayor and later governor. He claims descent from the Rawa clan that emigrated from Saudi Arabia and has occupied the land between Ana and Qaim for the past four hundred years. His is a prominent family of consensus builders and mediators, "rich in morals, not money," as he put it.

Barjas was a rare linear thinker in a land of circularity, and his long years working in police leadership gave him quite good administrative skills. He had a vision of a tolerant, pluralistic Iraq under an Islamic framework. He once pointed to several traditional sheikhs we were meeting and explained that a tolerant governing system was the only thing that would work in Iraq because the people are so diverse. He defended his meeting with wild-eyed imams on another occasion as his way to keep track of them. He was the right person to lead the province, and I developed a very close friendship with him.

Along with Barjas the most surprising individual we worked with, an anomaly among the imams, was the reformist Dr. Khalid Sulaiman, born in 1965 into a family that often ran afoul of Saddam. Unlike most imams Sulaiman worked closely with us. He had spent time in the Gulf and Jordan and founded a progressive Muslim institute to explore the nexus between Islam and democracy, publishing booklets such as *The Need for a New Islamic Political View* and *The Islamic World and the New World Order*.

Sulaiman's demeanor was always one of intense calm, a man at peace with himself and the world. Shocked by the bastardized version of Islam that led to the attacks on New York and Washington, he developed a proposal, "Toward a World without Terror," to undercut the roots of political and religious violence. "Following the tragic events of September 11th," he wrote, "it is incumbent upon all intellectuals from all religions . . . to come together and lay out practical plans to face this catastrophe of terrorism that is threatening mankind." He proposed a comprehensive plan to uproot terrorism, engage the political elites, bridge the gaps between religions, and lay the foundation for democracy in all societies.[3] Coming as it did from the heart of the Sunni Triangle, it was an extraordinary document from a unique individual. Sulaiman was part of a small, restless, hopeful class of people in Ramadi and Al Anbar that wanted change and was willing to sacrifice for it.

The Bad Guys

Our encounters with the bad guys were less substantive than those with the good guys, and were usually short, oblique, and violent. They were ever evolving as well. The insurgent campaign was just starting in earnest when I arrived, the nexus of three groups: former regime elements getting organized to lend a violent voice to their frustration with the country's upended power structure, young men who wanted to make a name for themselves by throwing what they could against the occupiers, and, later, foreign fighters. But it was a very hazy mix, even for those who spent long hours analyzing it. Ex-regime elements had prepared caches of arms and ammunition with which to fight a rear-guard action during the war but were overwhelmed by the rapidity of the coalition's advance; they were starting to pull them out now for the post-war. And the greatest concentration of losers and weapons in the new Iraq was in Al Anbar.

We saw these attacks evolve from potshots to small improvised explosive devices (IEDS), then to larger ambushes and attacks on aircraft and finally mega-IEDS. One of the first large attacks was one morning in early September when we felt the buildings shake and heard glass rattle on base from an explosion across the river. A small convoy of Humvees was passing along a road enclosed by banks on both sides, when a series of artillery shells that had been embedded in the banks, ten on each side, exploded. Only three went off, but the recovery team found the others, daisy-chained together, in what could have been a catastrophic incident. One soldier was killed and one wounded in their unarmored Humvee.

Suicide bombings carried out by foreigners took place in the early summer of 2003 in different parts of Iraq, but the first sui-cide bombing by a native Iraqi occurred in September at a check-point outside the university in Ramadi. A young man approached two of our soldiers erratically; they confronted him; and he blew himself up. Fortunately he did not get close enough to do them any harm, aside from splattering them with his blood and body parts. He was a local mentally handicapped youth who had report-edly been persuaded to conduct the attack by "outsiders." We were assured by local officials that no Iraqi would offer himself up will-ingly as a suicide bomber, which indeed did take several years of radicalization before it became common.

In a case of bad geography, the most potentially violent prov-ince also had an open border with the countries that were allowing young men to join the jihad. Like so many other bits of the occu-pation, border security was simply not something that CPA had the attention or resources for. And the province had unguarded weapons stocks that were stunning. One could fly over abandoned military bases and see stacks of artillery shells, bunkers filled with ammunition, and crates of RPG rounds for miles. It was a Weapons "R" Us bonanza, impossible for the small units covering the prov-ince to fully control. By the time they were completely secured, enough ammunition had been removed to continue a guerrilla war for years. The minimalist occupation force that looked so revolutionary on the Washington cocktail circuit was looking less revolutionary by the day.

Camp Life

It was natural that the coalition had taken over Saddam's sprawling palace complexes as bases; they came with large amounts of fenced-in real estate and huge empty buildings and were generally on the outskirts of cities and unoccupied. In Ramadi there were twin palaces for Saddam's sons, one for Uday and one for Qusay, on either side of the Euphrates just west of town. These were identical complexes, about two miles square, with one four-story palace in the center, a sprawling administrative building next to it, and smaller buildings and guard towers sprinkled throughout. They were lavishly furnished; when an Iraqi contractor was asked what it would cost to level one of the destroyed palaces, he said he would do it for free if he could keep the marble he pulled out of the rubble.

The modern army is accustomed to building out a "city" in short order, as troops fill every building and alleyway with billets and equipment. Within forty-eight hours of arrival troops look like they have been there forever; within twelve hours of ending an operation, it looks like they were never there. I staked a claim to a motor pool administrative building near the entrance to the base. The rooms were air-conditioned, and although quarters were four to a room we eventually replaced cots with beds and were comfortable, especially compared to my civil affairs counterparts, who were sleeping forty to a room in a barracks that resembled a basic training billet. I admired the tenacity of these senior New York City executives who were willing to put up with the privations of this lifestyle.

The Civil Military Operations Center

My daily place of work was the Civil Military Operations Center (CMOC) in the governorate building in downtown Ramadi. CMOCS are the public face of our military operations, fully accessible to citizens and local leaders, where civil administration is managed and claims for damages processed. As the operation evolved they also became the place where governance and democracy support took place. A well-run CMOC took the hard edge off the occupation and provided both an outlet for citizens' anger and a channel for involvement in building the new Iraq. The CMOC emerged as a place for civil service training, contractors conferences, constant meeting with sheikhs and notables, and infrastructure planning. When security improved, it was often the simple result of a well-functioning CMOC.

Game On: Power, Police, and Political Process

We surveyed the stabilization playing field and how we would influence this complex society, from whose homes insurgents could move to emplace IEDs, or conversely whose willingness to participate in the political process would discredit the opposing forces. It was the hard edge of what we now call postconflict stabilization and reconstruction. We had fought our war, a war of massive movements and shock and awe; our opponents were now getting geared up to fight theirs, one of deception, IEDs, and ambushes. The postwar phase of operations was every bit as intense and urgent and violent as the war and it would require even more dexterity, resources, and imagination. We were fighting to develop a viable political future, security forces, and an economy before we lost the opening we had been given by the crash of the regime. We were fighting for Iraq's center. And we now know that time was already starting to run out.

I sketched out what would be our campaign plan for Al Anbar, focusing on the three *P*'s: electric power, police, and political process. To squeeze out the insurgents and solidify the new democratic regime we needed to generate electricity, which initially I thought was synonymous with restarting factories and generating jobs. We needed to train and equip large numbers of security forces of all types and at all levels, with a special emphasis on police. And we needed to ensure that the citizens of Al Anbar were fully vested

in the national political process and had a local democratic political process that they were part of. Power generation, we soon realized, was not enough to create jobs, so we changed this to simple
job creation. And alongside the political process we saw a need
for reconciliation of ex-Ba'athists, the spoilers who could not be
left outside the political process. So we ended up with jobs, security forces, and political process/reconciliation.

In my first meeting with the 82nd Airborne Division commander Maj. Gen. Charles H. Swannack Jr. I outlined these broad
themes and where we stood in each area. His campaign plan similarly consisted of four lines of operation:

1. Establish a stable and secure environment.

2. Reestablish key essential services to prewar levels.

3. Foster job opportunities and economic growth.

4. Establish an effective and representative government.

Swannack and I were effectively of one mind on things. I don't
recall our ever being very far out of sync.

Forget about the Power Grid and State-Owned Enterprises: We Need Jobs

Traditional Anbar Economy and Potential

As he had with civil society Saddam had made a total mess of
the Iraqi economy, some 90 percent of which the state controlled
directly or indirectly. Iraq has always had the potential of a balanced and successful economy, with a highly skilled populace,
strong educational values, access to capital, and great soil. (Prior
to the Iran-Iraq War, Iraq had twenty-two million date trees.) It
is also the epicenter of some of the most important trade routes
in the world, linking Iran with the Middle East, Turkey with the
Gulf. If it did nothing but grow dates and collect duties Iraq would
have been better off economically than half the planet.

But the curse of oil changed everything, underwriting Saddam's destructive wars with Kuwait and Iran and providing him
an arsenal that was among the most expensive per capita in the

world in the 1980s. It also allowed him to reorder society, with the capital to reward certain regions, families, and individuals, while punishing others.

As outsiders we had a small window on Iraq's military power and political structure, but the economy was a complete mystery. It was only with the arrival of the civil affairs units that we began to have decent assessments of the state of the infrastructure and commerce, and it was not an encouraging picture. Given the First Gulf War, sanctions, bad central planning, and the brief but destructive recent war, the Iraqi economy was in a shambles, and the further one got from Baghdad, the worse it got.

In Anbar the traditional economy centered on agriculture, small and medium-size factories, and trucking. The Euphrates flows through the province into Syria, and when the coalition arrived there was evidence of irrigation systems that spread the agricultural wealth of the river as far as twenty miles from its banks. There was also a large lake, Habbaniyah, in the north, which gave a large swath of the province a very high water table. Water for agriculture could be accessed through drilling or the lower tech version of digging a thirty-foot-deep trench with a front-end loader and installing a pump. These rectangular holes were spread all over the northern part of the province, surrounded by green fields of grains and rice.

Within weeks of my arrival I began to meet the business community of Al Anbar and was encouraged to learn that we had people to work with, albeit a bit out of date and with tremendous needs. There were construction moguls, investors, and traders, exactly the kinds of business people we needed if this thing was going to work.

Some, however, would require more assistance than others. In a meeting with angry Falluja businessmen in late September, I found a city that was never really under Saddam's control whose people lived comfortably off pensions and military contracts and enjoyed restaurants that drew a crowd from Baghdad. A very high percentage of the residents were ex-military, and a pocket of the city was the domain of ex-officers. They complained bitterly about a lack of attention and resources.

One of the businessmen complained about the recently announced new investment law, which allowed for foreign ownership of Iraqi enterprises. He was concerned that "the Jews" would come into Iraq and make of it a "second Palestine." I hadn't heard anyone refer to "the Jews" since my days in Ramallah and hadn't expected it here. Another said he was in the process of establishing a "holding company" and expected the new government to require all business in the province to go through his or another local company.

I gave them my complete assurance that no Jew, Christian, or Buddhist was going to be buying up anything anytime soon. But I implored them to stay the course so that together we could build an economy that worked for them.

I could see that Fallujans, more than any other citizens of Anbar, had an inflated sense of their own importance, a raw stubbornness and arrogance, and would always be the fulcrum of the province's stability. I wrote to CPA main that the up-and-down nature of coalition infrastructure projects in Falluja was accurate and funding low relative to other locations. "But the scale of what would be needed to restore this province to its Saddam era glory is immense—full employment, priority in government funding for projects, precedence for Fallujans for government posts.... We need to do more to complete visible projects in a timely fashion and ensure we advertise these projects, but it seemed dishearteningly clear from this conversation that ... there will always be a glaring gap between expectations and reality."

Between the seemingly limitless potential and the seething anger of things not moving fast enough we set about working to improve the economy within the parameters we were given. We had some ability to get things done locally without guidance from headquarters, but it was never as much as we would have liked. At this point we were seeking a large jobs program, while contenting ourselves with extracting as much project money as we could and keeping the state-owned enterprises viable. We were focused on short-term stabilization more than longer-term economic restructuring, and like most other provinces we soon found ourselves at odds with HQ.

Which Comes First: Security or the Economy?

The Fallujans raised a chicken-and-egg issue that was debated incessantly in CPA: Does security flow from a good economy, or a good economy from security? They were fully with the former, arguing that the reason things were unstable in Falluja was that for the past five months there had been no real improvement in the city. We too were sympathetic to this view, but CPA had a different mind-set.

My direct contact with CPA main was somewhat limited. Once a month Ambassador Bremer brought governance coordinators and senior commanders to Baghdad for a one-day conference, where we were joined by members of the CPA staff and senior Iraqi officials. These were extremely useful, and given the prohibition by CPA security on travel to Al Anbar by Ambassador Bremer and any of his deputies, it was the only contact we had with him.

In an early meeting in the fall the CPA head of economic development, a former submariner on loan from the Pentagon, laid out the CPA plan for suppressing salaries to around $10 a day. His rationale was that we would price ourselves out of the international marketplace if salaries were too high. Maj. Gen. Raymond Odierno, at the time leading the 4th Infantry Division in Tikrit, pushed back hard, arguing for fewer economic principles and more good-paying jobs that would get the young troublemakers off the street. The room was full of nods of approval, but the focus was unchanged.

At the next meeting, in November, Ambassador Bremer reviewed the next wave of economic measures. This was no longer just about suppressing wages but a full blown neoliberal shock program to steer the economy away from the distortions of a state-controlled petro-economy. As he laid out the new policies—selling off state-owned enterprises, monetizing the food basket, suppressing wages, opening up the investment regime—a wave of discomfort swept the room. There was no mention of the one thing all of us needed to provide—jobs—but there was a constant reference to the Hungarian transitions to capitalism, with which I was very familiar, having just come from Budapest.

When it was our turn I pointed out this was a gross misreading of the Eastern European transitions. Hungary went through a very painful transition with the Bokros Plan, which set its economy right, but only after four years of allowing the new political reality to settle, during which most pieces of the economy were left largely in government hands with the social safety net intact. What I argued for was simple stability—get the economy back to where it was before we arrived, build on it, and when everything else was stable, work on a transition to true capitalism. Bremer acknowledged my views but was not moved by them.

When we drifted back to the subject later in an intervention by Maj. Gen. David Petraeus, Bremer responded, "We do not have a security problem because of a bad economy, but an economic problem because of weak security. If you all will get the security problem under control, the economy will turn around. We cannot let Iraq turn into a petro-state with a wildly distorted statist economy. The next year is going to be tough as we implement the policies that will get the economy on the right track. People will lose jobs and families will lose some of the security they are accustomed to. But you all need to stay focused on keeping your provinces secure." This time it was clear the discussion was over. There was nothing more to say, and we returned to our respective provinces and got back to work.

State-Owned Enterprises without a State

When looking for economic potential the state-owned enterprises were difficult to avoid, and both coalition officers and the CPA gravitated to them soon after arrival as one place to get people back to work. Few were functional and all would need help. In addition to sustaining and possibly even creating jobs, I also wanted to fight the image that with our arrival things had gotten worse. We were writing a narrative about the new life we were bringing to the province, and the state-owned enterprises were a very visible symbol of the prewar economy.

There were a smattering of factories across the province, although many towns had no industry whatsoever and survived solely on the yield of agriculture and its derivatives. Glass and ceramic factories in Ramadi took advantage of the high silica content of the soil to produce plate glass, bottles, toilets, and sinks; Haditha had a dormant cement factory and produced some asphalt and tires; there were small factories in Falluja for cement (at a quarter capacity), asphalt, and bricks; and Al Qaim, Hit, and Kubaisa had cement plants. While there was a bit of private enterprise and factory-run decision making, most factories sold their product to the government, were operating at a fraction of their capacity for lack of raw materials and power, had wildly distorted prices, and inflated employee rosters that Saddam had used to buy tranquility. It was a command economy with no one issuing any commands.

Governor Barjas told the team as early as June, "All the factories in the province are ready to go back into production. What is lacking is electricity and propane." Power was the most common issue for all factories. But when we looked further we found a more complex picture, an onion with lots of layers. As I told Steve Hedges of the *Chicago Tribune* in early November, "There's not a single, fully functioning, fully viable factory in this province. It's 10 years of sanctions; it's the whole isolation."[4]

Phosphate and Glass

The onion with the prize for the most layers was the Superphosphate Fertilizer Plant (known as SPP) in Al Qaim on the Syrian border.

The SPP was the largest and most sophisticated enterprise in the province and one that even in Ramadi received a good bit of attention from locals because of its importance for fertilizer production. We thought that it would be symbolically important to restore the plant, which would employ several thousand.

Our team on the ground had done an initial assessment in early May 2003 in which it found that the most glaring problem was the conveyor belt that transports raw materials up to the processing plant. Once that was fixed, though, they realized there was a destroyed railroad bridge, a need for two fully operational transformers, and two new pumps for the mine at Akashad, which was flooded. Some things had been destroyed during the First Gulf War (there were suspicions it provided some components to Iraq's nuclear program), some during Operation Iraqi Freedom, and some simply broke down.

And beyond all the various repairs, the director said, before anything was going to work he needed 20 kilowatts of electricity per day and a stable flow of natural gas. There was also some discussion about whether the natural gas the plant needed came from Kirkuk by way of Haditha and Baji or via a transmitting station with a convoluted arrangement involving Jordan and Syria.

And even if all these details—power, natural gas, repair of all plant components, new railway bridge—could be successfully worked out, there was, according to a May 23 report, a need for raw materials, "primarily ammonia (from Baiji, or Basra—more expensive), urea (from Baiji), natural gas and sulfur (from Kirkuk), and raw phosphate (from Akashad)."[5]

The team was there to assess, and assess they did. But they knew, and when I arrived I knew, that we did not have a fraction of what it would take to work through this bramble bush of issues and problems. One captain physically relocated there and worked the issues as his only job. Yet in the end, we were no closer than when we started. I don't know if the SPP ever got up and running, but by the time I left in the spring it was still on our "to do" list. It was an onion with one too many layers.

Closer to home, and ultimately more successful, was the Ramadi Glass Factory. Italian engineers said Anbar's soil had among the highest silica content in the world; hence a glass factory was built in Ramadi in 1959 and a ceramic factory in the 1980s. According to a July 2003 civil affairs assessment, these two factories together employed 2,300 people. When running at full capacity the glass factory could produce 750 tons of sheet glass, 180 tons of tabletops, and 800 tons of bottles and jars per month, and the ceramic factory churned out floor and wall tile, toilets, and sinks.

We diverted the power the factory needed, and with some skillful workarounds the plant manager was somehow able to get the Swedish-produced bottle machines and the Soviet plate glass machine up and running by November 2003. We made it a big deal when the factory was finally spewing out black smoke again from one of its two massive stovepipes, showing the citizens of Al Anbar that what we broke, we would fix, that life was returning to normal, and that the factories of Ramadi would again produce glass and ceramics. Eventually someone might come to Ramadi and close that glass factory as an unviable enterprise. But not now. For now, it gave us billowing black smoke and people going to work each day. It was still just a fraction of the economy, though, and there were a lot of other sectors to get to.

The Need for Power

In my early meetings with community and business leaders the issue of electric power seemed so pervasive that I initially adopted it as one of the main planks for Anbar's restoration. It was another multifaceted issue that had no simple solution.

One of the early CPA decisions was to allow products to flow in from neighboring countries duty free. While valid in retrospect, like many right decisions it nonetheless had numerous unintended consequences. What this meant in practical terms was that consumer goods that used large amounts of electricity—refrigerators, air conditioners, TVs—were suddenly affordable for many Iraqis who couldn't have touched them under the old regime. At the same time much of the power grid had been damaged in the war and the system for maintaining it had collapsed. Like the state-owned enterprises, the aftermath of ten years of sanctions had eroded a system that was marginal to begin with.

The Haditha Dam that produced most of the power in the province had six turbines, only two of which were functioning by the time the coalition arrived. But the grid was also convoluted, and it was not just a matter of getting one facility up and running; the entire system—power generation, transmission, and distribution—had to be sorted out. It also needed to be a national solution, since the entire grid was intertwined. And in addition to the technical issues there was a security element. Every time we drove from Ramadi to Baghdad or out to the west we saw towers that had been toppled not by insurgents but by thieves who cut and rolled up the wire to sell for scrap.

As with politics in general, the local officials sought local solutions so as not to remain at the mercy of distant and often disinterested national leaders. The Provincial Council in August drew for me an explicit connection between electricity generation and security and recommended the acquisition of large gas generators. This, they said, would free Anbar from being at the mercy of and receiving only the leftover power generation from the central grid. The governorate electricity specialist said that 137-megawatt gas generators that would cover two provinces could be brought on line in two to three months. We could buy more cheaply from Syria or Jordan, but to do so we would need to reconfigure the grid.

By the fall we were receiving smaller generators through CPA procurement which could power factories and provide some electricity to towns—one for the SPP, two for brick factories in Falluja, and two for the Al Faris Factory between Falluja and Baghdad. They were helpful, but not the megagenerators we needed for full power generation. There was a reluctance to spend limited reconstruction funds on large generators when there would one day be full power from the central power grid that would make them redundant. So we would have to wait for the central grid to come on line. Increasing power generation would be a slow and steady project nationwide, and over the course of several years it did come to finally exceed prewar levels. But even then it did not of itself eliminate unemployment. We realized we simply needed a more direct way to generate employment and turned to project funding as a possible solution, another area that had the dual benefit of providing jobs while visibly showing improvements to the infrastructure.

Commanders Emergency Response Program, Project Funding,
and De-Saddamization

One of the best ideas to come out of the wars in Afghanistan and Iraq was the Commanders Emergency Response Program, or CERP, project money that was provided to commanders in the field to spend on infrastructure and employment-generating projects and expand the number of individuals who had a positive stake in our presence. It was a rolling fund that, within reason, could be used as fast as money could be spent.

CPA had a parallel program whereby governance coordinators were given a budget to dispense in project money. It was flexible in how it was used, going to local councils for projects they had identified, and could be disbursed up front to capitalize a project. Harry Christian put a good deal of structure into the process, adding a bid board and contractors conferences to formalize how we managed contracts and to help Ramadi-based contractors compete with the more sophisticated Baghdad companies. We managed our funds to a very high standard; I still have a disc with the spreadsheet that included building renovations, work projects, and small construction projects.

But the projects were always complicated. Every day on my way to work I passed an eyesore of a building that had been partially destroyed by a missile during the liberation, a symbol to many of our ability to destroy things without the subsequent ability to rebuild in their place. I was determined to take the building down and replace it with a park dedicated to peace and asked Harry to put the project out for bid. It was a bit ambitious, maybe even utopian, and quickly bumped up against Anbar reality on many levels. Midway through the contractor selection process we realized we were working around the tribe whose traditional land had been confiscated by Saddam to build the intelligence headquarters we were tearing down. In consultation with the governor and the local military unit we maneuvered the contracting process to a good outcome and got the building torn down, although the process ultimately snagged on the construction of a park.

The process drew out a new ally, Sheikh Hamid Rashid Mahenna, whose traditional robe, leather jacket, and red-and-white keffiyeh conveyed the look of a traditionalist who is also a player. He was snarly to deal with at first, demanding and unreasonable and entitled, clearly partial to how Saddam ran contracting by simply disbursing money to his favorites. I got to know Mahenna well, mostly over dinner at his compound, and came to like him. He put on a nice spread, as all the Iraqi businessmen did, a welcome change from the mess hall. He was somewhere on the ADHD spectrum, up and down, never sitting still for very long, punching in with a historical tidbit, then leaving to make a phone call. We talked about his family's history in Ramadi, how they were part of the anti-Saddam uprising after the killings of 1995 and had been punished for it. His clan was now starting to reestablish its place in the provincial leadership. Most of what we were doing was a crapshoot at that point, and we needed to be rolling a lot of dice on a lot of different tables. Mahenna was one of those tables.

In the end we got the Ba'ath Party headquarters torn down and built a new ally. I never did get my park. We found several local architects who caught the vision and submitted bids, one of which was quite compelling—complete with gardens and walkways on several levels. But somewhere along the way he got spooked about implementing it, and we were left with an empty field. And in Ramadi we got safer streets.

In other places success was more elusive. There was always a good bit of market chaos involved in our contracting, depending on which units could prepare the best proposals and security conditions. In the fall our civil affairs unit came up with a program to link projects more closely to local councils, which would help to better direct the funding.

The place that screamed loudest for attention was Falluja, by far the most lethal city in the province. When I met with the deputy civil affairs commander about how to increase funding there, I could see the absolute fatigue in his face. He matter-of-factly walked through each proposal: "This one we tried to get to and were hit by an IED. This one the guy who pitched it to us has been killed, so we can pull it for now. This one doesn't read well, but it is in a critical area and we should take a chance on it. The girls school, I don't trust the contractor but we really need the school." The Fallujans and the unit assigned to it were right, we had been neglecting Falluja, and we did what we could to turn that around, but with only marginal success.

There were general problems with how the CERP program worked nationally and it was a very inexact way to generate employment, but I remain convinced it was the right approach. Projects have got to flow freely, and everyone with the task of inducing stability in such a place needs some walking-around money.

Strengthening the Private Sector

While we may have had sequencing issues with the CPA on the free market question, we did want to see the development of free market entrepreneurship. In my initial provincial assessment, I wrote about the need to induce a shift from the kind of slick dealing that benefits businessmen personally "but leaves little in its wake, to enterprises that will employ large numbers of people." Maj. Dave Menegon, the civil affairs officer in charge of private sector development, looked for a structural way to do so.

Menegon dismissed the Ramadi Chamber of Commerce as more a patronage organization than anything but found real promise in the newly formed Young Businessmen's Association. Menegon's enthusiasm and vision for this organization was infectious and impacted all of us, but especially the Iraqis, who desperately needed someone to reinforce their hope that it was possible to achieve something better than what they had.

We developed a two-day business seminar with the young businessmen that would help us get Al Anbar better connected to the central government, draw out the business community as a pillar of civil society, and garner support for security and the rapidly evolving political process. Below a banner that read "With our Abilities and Energy, We Will Build the New Iraq," over 150 Anbar businessmen and community leaders came to the recently refurbished provincial council hall, where they listened and networked for two days. It was somewhat quixotic and in retrospect we were getting way ahead of ourselves, what with a shooting war still ongoing and all. But as one of our military colleagues said, "If you are in the middle of a chicken-and-egg thing, it is better to be the chicken." We wanted to push a vision of prosperity amid peace and cooperation, hoping to move things in a virtuous cycle of progress rather than staying stuck in a destructive cycle of violence and loss.

In the opening session a young engineer reviewed the province's human and natural potential, the Ministry of Justice covered the legal climate for business development and the new investment law, and we discussed how to improve the potential for commerce. Ministry reps from water, agriculture, electricity, trade, and industry and minerals were for the first time held to account for their actions. Businessmen offered them solutions, some practical and some simplistic, for opening up the western desert to agriculture, getting electricity to full capacity, and improving the trade routes to Syria and Jordan.

The conference provided a window on the Anbar business community that we had not had until then. It was discouraging on the issue of existing capacity, encouraging in will and enthusiasm. I suggested to CPA that there was a need for engagement and stage-managed linkages to break Al Anbar out of the semi-autarky it had been in for the past several decades, capacity building at all levels, and a stronger dialogue and interaction with Baghdad-based ministries and the Governing Council.

We had laid out a vision that was compelling, inspiring, and right for Al Anbar. But we knew, and they knew, that it would not be realized for many years. And while we had to work on multiple tracks, we all knew that the track we most needed to succeed was simply large-scale employment. We had learned that no amount of state-owned enterprises, additional power, CERP funding, and conferences was going to tackle the large-scale unemployment that afflicted the province. We needed long-term jobs, lots of them, and we needed them in a hurry.

No Substitute for Public Sector Jobs

CPA was hardly oblivious to the issue of job creation; two of their eight economic principles dealt with the issue head on. In addition to the general growth of the economy, this was supposed to happen through the projects that would be brought to bear via the $17 billion supplemental budget from Congress, which a Treasury Department study estimated would create 1.7 million jobs in 2004. And for more immediate job creation each province was provided funding for 7,200 menial jobs for two months, a program that would roll over if it was successful.

The problem was that job creation through projects was even more indirect at this level than it had been at ours, so success would be very sporadic, with most jobs going to the stable provinces through Baghdad-based contractors. And the 7,200 jobs were not particularly helpful to overall stability, as we knew the guys who would sweep streets were not the same guys who would take shots at the coalition. We needed more and better jobs, and we needed them for longer.

This was constantly reinforced in meetings with local notables. Falluja leaders on November 3 said that life was economically worse under the coalition, and Governor Barjas stressed the problem of ex-Ba'athists whose status had taken a 180-degree turn with the coming of the coalition. The mayor said insurgent groups were paying between 250,000 and 500,000 dinars to attack coalition forces, and while most citizens opposed the attacks there was a ready pool of unemployed men willing to carry them out.

In mid-November Central Command commander Gen. John Abizaid came to Rifles Base to read the riot act to some of the same Falluja leaders and seventy others from around the province after a large attack on the coalition. They sat silently, with rapt focus, maintaining eye contact throughout, as was common with Iraqis, who rarely looked at their sandals to avert personal attention. When he opened the floor they let loose with a flood of complaints and suggestions, jobs being the most persistent theme.

By December a Sunni strategy was evolving to try to get ahead of the increasing violence, and in trying to shape it we pitched a plan called Producing Stability through Job Creation. "The key issue we face in Al Anbar," we suggested,

> is one of political and economic disenfranchisement of people who once were on top and now do not know what the future holds. . . . What we have done over the past six months . . . has

been a recipe for instability. Through aggressive de-Ba'athification, the demobilization of the Army, and the closing of factories, the Coalition has left tens of thousands outside the economic and political life of the country. Added to this pool of angry disoriented men with too much time on their hands is a wealth of readily available weapons and an open border. The mix has been highly destabilizing.... The populace not involved in attacks has allowed them to take place and has turned a blind eye to the rat-lines that traverse the border areas to Baghdad.... This has left CPA officials and military units in the field in Al Anbar to effectively run interference for an empty policy. Political engagement substitutes for results, information operations substitute for resources, and meetings replace real change.

... We are working hard to grow the private sector in Al Anbar province ... but the simple reality is that the private sector will not be viable as a largescale employer in Al Anbar at least through 2004. It will require at least six months of consistent stability to attract private investment [in retrospect a wildly optimistic estimate] and private investment when it comes will take another six months to produce new jobs.

In the meantime we appealed for thirty thousand new public sector jobs, specifying, "These jobs are not a diversion from private sector growth, they are a prerequisite for it."[6]

We broke these jobs out by the groups requiring attention: 4,000 ex-Ba'athists, 20,000 ex-career soldiers, 8,000 ex-officers, 1,700 intelligence and secret service officials, tens of thousands of unskilled workers and conscripts. Our plan called for individuals to be employed at mosques, on public works, for highway, pipeline, electric line, and fixed site security, and as border guards. We also asked for an equitable slice of the New Iraqi Army with a Ramadi recruiting station and several brigades based in the province. We estimated the cost of the program at $38 million in salary and another $27 million in equipment for the first year.

Anticipating the reaction from Baghdad, we acknowledged, "The program violates every principle of free market economics. But if we fail to produce stability in the next year there will never be a free market in Iraq to worry about. If we succeed in producing stability in the next year, the free market will eventually take hold on its own. Stability is an absolute precondition to economic growth."

As with so many ideas during that time, no one ever told us no, but the program was never funded. General Abizaid took a modified version of our proposal with a $10 million ask for Anbar to President Bush in early November and the president was sympathetic. A note from the meeting said he "stressed that it is important to attack the security challenges with resources— 'massive amounts of money' and asked, 'Why only 10 million?'" Someone in the meeting said it sounded like I had prepared his talking points. It never filtered down, but we still had one sector where we thought we could channel the concept of public sector jobs, and it was one that we needed help with in its own right: the security forces. With our limited autonomy and some control over resources we would do what we could.

Building Security Forces While Fighting an Insurgency

How to Beat an Insurgency

I wrote a former mentor in the fall of 2003 that although we were working on a broad-based political settlement, past experience led me to expect great difficulties: "We are dealing with an urban insurgency of the kind that successfully fought the British for decades in Northern Ireland and caused them to quit Palestine, and continues to defy the Israelis throughout the West Bank and Gaza. The widespread opposition to the occupation will always make broad military options problematic." I cited the Colombian M-19 and Uruguayans Tupamaros as examples of successful campaigns against urban insurgencies but suggested these were cases of very small cells with extremely limited popular support, "nothing like what we [were] facing in Al Anbar."

In mid-January 2004, reflecting on the continued unrest in Falluja, I wrote, "The best way to fight an insurgency is not to

have to fight it in the first place by solving the political problem that caused it. The second best option is to deputize someone else to fight it. And the third way is to fight it yourself." I
suggested we focus on the first two before getting sucked too
far into the third.

We are all prisoners of our experience, and mine was with the
largely successful buildup of the Salvadoran armed forces, the
failed attempts to develop a new national force in Somalia and
Haiti, and watching the painfully slow rollout of the new Afghan
security forces against a backdrop of rising instability the year
prior. Swannack and I shared the view that a rapid buildup of a
full-spectrum Iraqi security force alongside a positive political
and economic picture was the only way to manage rising instability, especially with a U.S. force just large enough to conduct
a holding action. Swannack maintained an aggressive posture
in containing terrorist attacks and dismantling cells, but he was
cautious to calibrate military operations so that they were not
provocative. He and I both knew there was ultimately no shooting our way out of this.

Managing Our Own Security

Security issues quickly turned personal as we were operating
in the same insecure environment as everyone else. Unlike the
economy, where no matter how high unemployment might
have been, my check still hit the bank each month, security
was unpredictable.

We fell under the security umbrella of the civil affairs unit, but
because we often traveled alone we had amassed our own small
arsenal for protection. In the summer of 2003 one of the civilian
base security managers was concerned with my occasional solo
travel in an unarmored Suburban, so he gave me a 9mm Eastern
Bloc pistol with seven bullets. He said it was one of a kind; there
was no resupply. I didn't test-fire it, deciding I didn't want to lose
even one of my limited rounds. Harry later acquired a few AKs,
which we carried in the vehicle and into the governorate building each day. There was no shortage of rounds for these, although

I did worry about team members who had never fired one before and wondered if they would do more harm than good if we had to use them. We never did.

Our team was, however, on the margins of several attacks. We traveled to Baghdad by road on average once or twice a month. Air travel was generally safer, although in November a Chinook carrying soldiers going home on leave was shot down over Falluja and seventeen were killed. Going by air also did not allow us to return with supplies and carried the risk of being stranded, so we moved on our own or with a convoy.

On one occasion Harry, George Younes, and I were running behind but not part of a military convoy when we saw a massive IED explode just in front of us, creating a thirty-foot volcano spewing rock and dirt. The randomness of the IED has a psychological impact that is difficult to overstate; it is the ultimate insurgent weapon, hindering the movement of the occupying force, often eliciting a reaction from them toward civilians, and leaving the victims fearful and shaken. We edged our way up and got to the convoy to offer our assistance. Two soldiers had been injured but none critically, and miraculously no one were killed.

The two worst parts of the road were just outside Abu Ghraib and anywhere around Falluja, where high levels of anticoalition sentiment abutted the road. We were returning from Baghdad in November and came upon the aftermath of an IED on the Baghdad side of Falluja. A Bradley Fighting Vehicle had been hit and by the time we arrived was on fire, its sides burning white hot, having seared down nearly to the tracks. There was no way to recover the vehicle's ammunition, so the unit had cordoned off the area and was simply letting the Bradley burn down.

We were stopped by a young Latino soldier, perhaps nineteen. He looked slightly disoriented but explained with clarity what had happened and directed us to pull over and wait. His uniform was covered in dried blood; one of his companions in the Bradley had lost a limb and then died before he could be evacuated. I tried to imagine the scene inside the vehicle as they fought to save the life of the young victim. But it was the soldier's quiet ability to carry on in the aftermath that moved me. When civilians experience such things, we are allowed months to recover and regroup. Soldiers have no such luxury; they must move on. I realized that those of us who do not wear a uniform were being served and protected by men and women who were simply better than us—more disciplined, stronger willed, less self-centered. I was in the midst of a new Greatest Generation, and it was inspiring.

We also faced the dilemma of whether to travel with military convoys or alone. Military convoys were effectively IED magnates, but Chevy Suburbans were not far behind. Harry eventually purchased a few nondescript vehicles that we could travel in without attracting any attention, our heads wrapped in kufiyahs or turbans. We used the vehicles sparingly for trips around town and especially into Falluja, which always required special planning, if not an advance prayer meeting. Sometimes Harry, whose ingenuity knew no bounds, would stage a vehicle and we would switch cars in the middle of a movement.

In early December the safety of the base itself, usually our only true redoubt, was shattered when a delivery truck exploded on the main company street. It sent truck parts slamming through buildings and knocked soldiers off their feet. The explosive device had been hidden in the gas tank so was not detected. There were rumors the attack had to do with a contracting dispute. The young soldier escorting the truck was obliterated along with the driver; there weren't even any body parts to send back for burial. He was, as I recall, a young father. Several days later the 82nd held a memorial service for the soldier. I had been to a number of these, but somehow this one cut deeper. It was held outside the destroyed palace, close to where the attack had taken place. A picture of him on a black box with a pair of jump boots and a rifle formed a shrine that allowed the soldiers to file by and lock in one last memory after remarks by his commander and some friends. I wept openly, as did many of those in attendance. Major General Swannack was the first to file by as the ceremony ended, and I saw how moved he was as well. He would attend sixty such memorials during his tenure there and mourned every loss.

The Challenge of Building a Security Force on the Fly

The layers of mystery we found in the economy were not an issue when it came to the transparently broken security forces. Upon my arrival the governor informed me there were 7,180 street police and 1,105 traffic police. Some of these were ghost employees and some were not coming to work for lack of uniforms and equipment. There was a total of ninety-two vehicles, and most police stations had been ransacked. Police officers shared AK-47 rifles, and the traffic police had fewer than sixty pistols. Most officers were not veterans but were brought in based on the recommendation of a sheikh, a community notable, or another officer. Local coalition military units had vetted some, and 2,200 had been given a three-day training course. The force, I reported, was "structurally broken, and need[ed] a major infusion of new recruits, training, mentoring, and equipment to be functional." We were starting largely from scratch.

I tried to draw attention by suggesting the safety of U.S. soldiers was at stake, adding, "This is the most serious issue we face here, and is directly related to the ongoing deaths of American soldiers in this sector. It will not wait until a slow roll-out of future police programs but needs focused attention now."

We requested a very modest program from which we would move on to the more complete force we really needed. I asked for authority to recruit and pay an additional 2,250 police officers, the majority recruited from the military; a two-month training program; twenty international police advisors; seven hundred vehicles; and a uniform, a weapon, and gear for each officer. We also requested authority and resources to develop special units: intelligence, crowd control, a special investigative unit, SWAT, highway patrol, power line security, and border guards.

I ended the appeal by waxing bureaucratically poetic as I tried to put it in context:

> The relative cost of such a program should be considered in light of planned troop deployments. We are in the process of increasing our force by 8,000 soldiers, something which will

bring less stability than the removal of 2,250 ex-soldiers from limbo through their induction into the police force. We have reached a military stalemate here that will not be broken by a larger force—attacking the coalition is too easy and weapons are too plentiful for our opponents to be defeated by a force of any size. They can be co-opted however. Reducing, not increasing, the bellicose presence of the coalition, and replacing it with more support for basic Iraqi institutions such as the police, is key. Give me this program, fully funded, and it will pay for itself by saving on troop deployments in 12 months.

We estimated the requisite equipment would cost some $30 million and was not something we could procure locally. The pitch never sunk in. The CPA police advisor, former NYPD chief Bernard Kerik, saw himself not as the head of a large-scale international police training effort but as the interim Baghdad city police chief. He spent days in meetings and nights out patrolling. Baghdad neighborhoods were undoubtedly safer for his efforts, but the country did not get a police force. There was a plan to train thirty-five thousand officers in Jordan in an eight-week program over the coming eighteen to twenty-four months, and to train existing officers in Baghdad, Basrah, and Mosul in a three-week program. Plans were also under way to train customs police, border guards, and other specialty units and for 2,200 police advisors. But it was all aspirational based on future funding and was on a very slow timeframe.

In response to our constant entreaties two police trainers were assigned to do an assessment, and several of our police officers eventually went to Jordan. We never saw any equipment. But we would do what we could with the resources at hand.

The Al Anbar Public Security Academy

We were fortunate that many members of the 124th Infantry were police officers in their civilian lives, and several were trainers at the Miami-Dade police academy. Using $1 million in CERP and CPA local funds we refurbished an Iraqi Army training camp across the Euphrates, and by mid-October the Al Anbar Security College was training three hundred cadets at a time in a three-week course. In addition to teaching the core skills, this was an opportunity to instill in them a spirit of community policing, an approach that programs in the Balkans and Haiti had shown would be critical to success.

It was always a very tentative effort. We knew and the trainees knew that they were not grounded in a long-term national effort and that their future was uncertain. Without a parallel international structure of mentors at each police station, it was also an incomplete system. But it filled a few gaps in a few places.

Give Us the Tools: The Sheikhs Make an Offer

Given the entrepreneurial landscape we were working in, which included soldiers armoring their own vehicles with scrap metal and the building of new, unsanctioned government bureaus, we were always looking for creative new security forces. Most of these revolved around using local leaders to recruit and train young men from the tribes.

One sanctioned but unorthodox unit was the Iraqi Civil Defense Corps, a nationwide program to create rural security forces that would work with military units in the field. They were drawn from the ex-military, heavy on officers and light on NCOs, and had to rely on inconsistent CERP funding to function. I attended several of the Corps graduations and could sense a distinct lack of pride and capacity. We had taken a military that was not particularly effective in the first place, rehired it, and set it up with fewer resources and less training and consequently lower morale than when it worked for the Ba'athists. But it set a precedent for military units building local security forces that would be useful later.

Another promising concept came from the sheikhs, who took our incessant message that they needed to be involved in providing security, and turned it back on us, offering to do so if we would fund and equip tribal security forces. The Provincial Council offered to deploy five hundred new highway patrolmen supervised by local leaders, and Sheikh Bizi'e had a fully developed plan for pipeline, highway, and power line security that involved tribal leaders enlisting and supervising their young men. He reminded us this was what the British did in their various occupations, effectively paying local leaders to keep the peace in their sector. It struck me as a very cost-effective way to avoid continually rebuilding the electric towers that were being felled for scrap.

As with the police, there was an aspirational national program for electric line and pipeline security on the horizon through the Ministry of Electricity, but it fell into the tribal spoils of government, with a Kurdish company winning the contract. Outsiders, Bizi'e told us, would under no circumstances be able to deploy to the province, while we were missing an opportunity to employ local youth. In the end we didn't get Bizi'e's tribal system, and we didn't get the Ministry's program either. We did get a lot more felled power lines.

One unit took the entrepreneurship spirit a step further, simply forming up and going to work. They called themselves the Al Anbar Civil Defense Force, and their leader came to see me in late September. Yassin had written a letter to the governor asking for his "squad" of five hundred volunteer explosives experts to be regularized. He claimed that since April they had disarmed 102 explosives, 137 rockets, 1,600 cluster bombs and war remnants, as well as fighting 233 fires and conducting six rescue operations. To date they had had one fatality and one serious injury dismantling IEDs. They wanted training and a salary. Their record was quite impressive, really, and I connected them with Division Artillery, who oversaw the task of reducing the ordnance in the province. They were given some temporary funding, but we failed to get them regularized; this was unfortunate given that they were offering to do the most dangerous work we faced.

In retrospect what thousands of Anbar men were offering in the spring of 2003 was exactly what we ended up doing through the Anbar Awakening three years later, after the province was nearly captured by Al-Qaida. It was to be a costly three years. One wonders where we would have been if we had taken up the offer earlier.

The Bureau of Veterans Affairs into the Breech

Another entrepreneurial effort to improve security came from within the CMOC. For five days each month we were given a sobering picture of the ex-military as they queued up by the thousands two blocks down from the governorate building at a converted pay station. Alongside the aggressive de-Ba'athification program the wholesale demobilization of the ex-army was the action that most alienated the Sunnis. The CPA had been convinced that it needed to at least pay the former soldiers a small stipend to assuage their anger and by the summer of 2003 had developed a system to do so. Most of the ex-military seemed to accept it as an honest gesture, but it was humiliating to line up for a handout from the occupiers, especially for former officers. They were looking for a more structured way forward.

Based on earlier experience with demobilization programs in the Balkans and southern Iraq, Major Menegon formed a Bureau of Veterans Affairs to give the ex-military a means of networking and finding work. He invited a dozen Sunni Anbar officers to the CMOC and we heard them out. We asked them about work; there was none. How did they see the closure of Saddam's government? Glad to see it go but skeptical of what was emerging in its place for the Sunnis. How did they view the coalition? That depends largely on how things turn out in the future.

Menegon's Veterans Bureau was a hive of activity. Word spread among the ex-army, and soon former soldiers and officers in the hundreds were making their way to the Bureau on a weekly basis. Menegon's infectious enthusiasm and his understanding of business and finance added an element of gravitas to the notion that this program would start to yield real economic gains in the lives of this key constituency. The Bureau moved to a renovated Ba'ath Party building, with classrooms, training facilities, and conference rooms. Menegon pushed the veterans to organize themselves into interest groups and get involved civically. It was a largely successful enterprise that helped to give the ex-soldiers a stake in the future and a voice, and they would participate politically in the upcoming election.

An American Gulag

A somewhat darker function of the CMOC, handled by a major and two specialists, was the search for detainees. By the fall of 2003 there were thousands of Iraqis held in Abu Ghraib prison, a quarter to a third of them from Al Anbar. The major spent most of his day talking to Iraqis whose husband, brother, or son had been taken into captivity in a raid or sweep or failed attack. He worked feverishly to help Iraqis locate family members but soon began to express to me deep misgivings about our detainee system, a perspective my own experience reinforced.

In addition to the walk-ins, I was approached by prominent Iraqis at Provincial Council meetings or the governor's office. The most important was Falluja Sheik Mishan of the Al-Jamila tribe. He saw me weekly about his son Nabhan, who he admitted was wounded in an anticoalition attack that took the life of his other son and a cousin. "Keep him," he told me. "I understand that. I just want to know that he is alive." He had not heard from him since his capture, and all his efforts to get information at Abu Ghraib were futile.

We pressed the case incessantly. Brig. Gen. Janis Karpinski, commander of Abu Ghraib before the scandal made her famous, told me that, to the best of her knowledge, Nabhan was not in custody at Abu Ghraib, but that he could well be a high-value detainee at Camp Bucca. If so, she did not have access to him. I followed up with the Combined Joint Task Force J2, who demurred on the request. Every meeting with Sheikh Mishan was the same; we had no new information and simply did not know where his son was, or if he was still alive.

In the end we were successful in locating detainees in perhaps half the cases—stymied by the variety of places they could have been held, absence of a central database, problems with transliteration and ordering of Arabic names, and the black hole of high-value detainees who simply disappeared. We learned later of the broken and abusive system when it all blew up in the spring of 2004. But the importance of that cell of three soldiers who very carefully met with families and pushed hard to find their relatives, in an act of obvious goodwill, worked miracles in tamping down the rage that some of these families felt.

In counterinsurgency the peripheral tasks, like managing prisoners, are often as important as capturing the prisoners in the first place.

There was a more immediate side to all this that we also bumped up against, although we would not know the whole story until long after my departure. Sheikh Fawzi Fatikham Abd Alhameed of the Albu Risha, a minor but influential sheikh in his late forties, was one of our closest contacts. He had a compound just outside Ramadi and hosted us frequently for lunches and dinners. I assumed he saw the coalition coattails as something worth attaching himself to in the hopes of getting ahead in the tribal structure, and possibly getting some contracts along the way. But when I met his son, a well-educated and gentle individual with aspirations of studying in the West, I realized he was attaching himself to more than just the fortunes of the coalition. Fawzi wanted Iraq to join the family of nations and for his children to be connected to a wider world of justice and opportunity. He believed in our project for a new Iraq.

In November members of the 3rd ACR, unbeknownst to me, had asked Fawzi to help facilitate the questioning of Maj. Gen. Abed Hamed Mowhoush, a former Iraqi Air Force commander with suspected ties to the insurgency. With Fawzi's promise that it was a matter of questioning, not detention, Mowhoush agreed to turn himself in.

Two months later an officer came to the governorate building and said he needed to deliver the news of Mowhoush's death in captivity to Fawzi. I insisted on joining him, and we broke the news to Fawzi in the governor's office. He was saddened but not incredulous, indicating that Mowhoush was a very large man, and with the heat, well, heart failure was understandable. We told him we were very sorry, and he thanked us for our concern. Was there anything we could do for the family? No, Fawzi said, I will tell his wife and sons.

It wasn't until much later that the story of what happened in those interrogation sessions in November 2003 was made public.[7] The *Los Angeles Times*, reporting from the murder trial for Warrant Officer Lewis Welshofer at Fort Carson, Colorado, wrote that in the fall of 2003 the insurgency "was gaining strength and interrogators were under intense pressure to obtain leads from Saddam Hussein loyalists." Welshofer admitted he increased the physicality and humiliation of the interrogations, and at one point turned Mowhoush over to "a group of Iraqis who, according to published reports, were in the pay of the CIA." Two days later, Welshofer said, he had gone through all his techniques but one. By then the general had difficulty moving and was breathing heavily. The interrogators placed a sleeping bag over the general's head and torso and wrapped an electric cord around his three-hundred-pound frame. "Welshofer straddled his chest and continued to ask questions, occasionally putting his hand over the general's mouth ... stopping the detainee from calling to Allah." After several minutes Welshofer realized the general was dead.[8]

I had no contact with Fawzi after the truth became known. I assume he found out the details. I saw press reports later of several of Mowhoush's sons speaking out about the case. They were hostile to the coalition when I was there, and I imagine that, unlike so many of their peers in Anbar, who later came around, their hostility hardened and they will be our enemies for a very long time.

Every war has its atrocities. Patton's Third Army had several confirmed instances of shooting prisoners to avoid the drag of collecting and processing them; Vietnam gave us My Lai; Korea, No Gun Ri. But these cases lay fully outside the law of war, and were recognized as such; there was no effort to legitimize them. In the post-9/11 world, however, a moral fog engulfed us. The legal ambiguity about the status of captured individuals slipped into a moral ambiguity over whether they could be tortured. It was one of the most shameful things to happen in this period. And the ambiguity has still not receded, as the 2016 U.S. presidential campaign demonstrated.

Vladimir Bukovsky, who spent twelve years in Soviet prisons and endured a full range of torture, suggests that if some "cruel, inhumane or degrading (CID) treatment of captives is a necessary tool for winning the war on terrorism, then the war is lost already." He writes that torture's impact extends to those who perpetrate it, not just their victims: "If America's leaders want to hunt terrorists while transforming dictatorships into democracies, they must recognize that torture, which includes CID, has historically been an instrument of oppression—not an instrument of investigation or of intelligence gathering. No country needs to invent how to 'legalize' torture; the problem is rather how to stop it from happening.... And if you cynically outsource torture to contractors and foreign agents, how can you possibly be surprised if an 18-year-old in the Middle East casts a jaundiced eye toward your reform efforts there?"[9] A jaundiced eye at this point is probably on the low end of our worries.

Turning Around and Speeding the Withdrawal

By December, even without significant numbers of new Iraqi forces, we seemed to be turning a corner in security. Falluja remained the exception, with continued hostility and persistent attacks that never subsided, but everywhere else the division's maps that tracked anticoalition attacks and inflow of foreign fighters had turned from red to green. There was even the occasional humor associated with the security drive. Third ACR forces in Al Qaim were conducting house searches for weapons or evidence of insurgent activity. If no one was home they would break the lock on the door and leave a note asking the family to come to the local CMOC to be reimbursed $50 for the cost of replacing it. They got through one side of town the first day, then were diverted to another operation before they could finish. Residents from the unfinished half of the city came to the CMOC asking when the searches in their part of the city would be conducted. Apparently the average lock on a simple house cost far less than $50 to replace.

There were various theories about why the number of attacks was down, which I summarized for HQ. One was that the force had succeeded in "rounding up the bums," as Swannack put it, with high-yield raids in late November that took resistance leaders, financiers, and technical experts off the streets. Another theory was that apathetic Iraqis were helping more. Violence in Iraq is a form of political discourse and is culturally acceptable for score settling, so many turned a blind eye to it. But with the spate of attacks in mid-November culminating with the downing of the Chinook, there may have been a sense that the insurgents had crossed a line.

Lesser factors were that our engagement was helping and project money was flowing, giving more people a stake in stability. I raised the disheartening possibility that the insurgents were simply in an operational pause.

But the most likely factor I suggested was that there was a growing sense that the occupation was ending. The political calendar announced in Baghdad indicated there would soon be a new Iraqi government with full sovereignty. Swannack reinforced this by publicly stating that he would start to transition coalition forces out of major population centers as early as January or February, a date the governor had recommended from the beginning. Barjas conceded that providing security for Iraq would require an international force for many years, but he believed that we should follow the British model and quickly train a constabulary and then withdraw from the cities into bases in the desert, where we could oversee the development of an Iraqi government and security without day-to-day intrusion. In fairness, the British did not face Al-Qaida, but then when Barjas suggested this, neither did we.

It appeared that soft support for the insurgency could have been eroding at least temporarily with the simple calculus of individuals not wanting to risk their lives to achieve something that was going to happen anyway. The problem was this conclusion was based on a misunderstanding on the Iraqis' part, and when they realized the occupation was not going away, the number of attacks went back up.

I ended my report by expressing tentativeness:

There is no telling what the future holds.... There is also a sense among many Sunnis that we are clearly a temporary presence and other Iraqis [Shias and possibly Kurds] are the real enemy so in the long term it might be better to begin to gear up and position themselves for the fight to come. This would not in the end make the reduction in attacks a good news story. In short there is plenty of fight left in the Sunnis here and plenty of weaponry to carry on that fight. But the sharp and now continuing drop in attacks does give the coalition a much-needed respite whose continuation will be critical to successfully carrying out the very challenging political calendar before us.

And as always, I made another appeal for help: "Reinforcing this trend with resources and added attention will be critical to ultimate success."

Political Process: How Democracy Almost
Took Hold in Al Anbar

Elections Come to Al Anbar, August 2003

My arrival in Ramadi on August 4, 2003, coincided with the leadership election of the new Provincial Council. Military officers had been dealing one on one with sheikhs and community leaders for months and were eager to get more local political buy-in. The development of the Provincial Council was destined to be a very uneven process and a fascinating window on the natural democratic instincts in Arab culture. While Arabs may be partial to strong-man politics, they were also the originators of the *shura*, or council. There is a good deal of give and take, brokering, wealth distribution, and careful balancing of power among tribes and regions, amid the assassinations, coups, executions, marsh draining, and all the rest.

The thirty-seven sheikhs, two community leaders, and one female Christian civil servant on the existing Provincial Council represented all the towns of Al Anbar, roughly proportional to their population centers, although disproportional to the tribal breakdown. They had been selected after loose consultation with local leaders by the civil affairs unit. Third ACR commander Colonel Teeples laid out the parameters for the selection of the Provincial Council chairman, vice chairman, and general secretary. Each of the assembled individuals would cast one vote on a slip of paper. The one with the most votes would be the chairman, the one with the second highest vote count, vice chairman. It took a minute for this to sink in, but when it did, the room unwound like a giant spring that had just been released. There was shouting and scrambling and reclamas to the colonel and rapid sidebars with his people.

The gathering, it seems, was divided between the pretenders to the throne of the Dulaym tribe, the overall federation that included most of the smaller tribes in the region, and one of the subordinate tribes, the Albu Nimr, who were attempting to carve out as much power as they could. Sheikh Majid presented himself as the "Sheikh of Sheikhs" and Sheikh Ammer as the Dulaym group's preferred candidate for Provincial Council chair, while Sheikh Bizi'e was the Albu Nimr candidate. Most of the sheikhs present were aligned with Majid and Ammer, with just a handful with Bizi'e. They quickly figured out that the voting system was going to lead to Bizi'e's becoming the vice chair, as the vast majority of votes would go for Ammer and whatever was left would take a distant second, but second nonetheless. The Majid-Ammer camp was assuming two votes for each, one for the chair and one for the vice chair, assuring them both slots. "Two minutes," shouted Teeples. "I need your votes in two minutes." They pleaded for more time, as the leaders collected in small groups and tried to figure out a way around the voting process.

The clock ran out, and Sheikh Ammer Abdul Jabaar Ali Sulayman was elected provincial council president with thirty-seven votes, while his cousin and rival Sheikh Bizi'e Njriss al Gaoud, got three, and hence became the deputy. The Ammer bloc complained bitterly that this was not the will of the majority. To them, power was still very much a winner-takes-all affair. We gave them a brief lesson on the small state–big state divide in the Continental Congress, and there was begrudging acceptance as they planned their next move. The Council also affirmed Abdulkareem Barjas Al-Rawi as governor and Imam Khalid Sulaiman as general secretary.

So began the long road to democratic governance in Al Anbar province.

The Provincial Council

The Provincial Council met immediately and kept up a consistent schedule, guided by the firm hand of Imam Sulaiman, who ensured some structure to the body's work. At one point he added subcommittees to broaden the scope from assorted grievances to well-thought-out proposals. There was a good bit of drama in each meeting, with Governor Barjas chastising the leaders for not doing a better job of containing attacks, while tribal leaders responded with complaints about lack of security forces, electric power, and jobs.

I wrote to my family, "Underlying it all, there is an Arab sense of democracy. They are used to making decisions within their tribes in a way that we would probably consider representative in the outcome if not the process. What we have to do is take this traditional way of doing things and give it a modern structure that will allow them to actually get things done this week rather than next. It is progress, and is one of the things that is going well."

The body had an innocuous charter that made clear the limits of its powers in relation to the coalition, always a source of frustration, and it lacked a budget. A small stipend came with membership, which many found just large enough to be insulting. Several vehicles were supposed to be forthcoming, but that only insulted them further when they found it was to be a few shared minivans, not a vehicle for each member, as they thought their status deserved.

We tinkered with the composition, adding members from civil society and unrepresented towns. In a September 17 memo I credited the council with being "anxious to learn how to manage a democratic forum and willing to accept whatever training we could offer." But I also lamented that "to them the meeting itself

[was] the deliverable." Indeed it was a meeting-heavy and petition-heavy culture.

Our concept was for the council to be the link between the community and the provincial government, the province and the central governing council, and the coalition and the people. Their understanding of the council was a bit slower paced and more restrictive. They would meet weekly in the council building (*diwan*), make speeches, channel complaints from citizens, and offer broad directives to the provincial government and us. It was not perfect, but for a province whose size took up a third of Iraq and contained 1.2 million citizens, it was a credible place-holder on the road to representative democracy.

A Stirring of Civil Society and Political Parties

One of Saddam's most thorough achievements was the total crushing of civil society in Iraq. There were no clubs, mosques, churches, civic organizations, or professional associations that were not controlled by the Ba'ath Party. We believed a strong civil society would be essential to a stable and functional political and social order, and our open-door policy at the CMOC very early channeled citizens who were eager to get involved in building the new Iraq.

In early October Deputy Council Chair Bizi'e and Secretary Sulaiman gathered three hundred individuals from across the social and political spectrum to channel their involvement through the Provincial Council. The Young Businessmen's Association was interested in political involvement, and groups of students were forming under the leadership of the university president. Some imams began to collaborate, using their religious clout to foment societal change, which cut in both directions but could often be a source of something positive.

Falluja in this regard was always full of surprises. In early December 2003 a prominent Falluja sheikh and grand imam, Hisham Abdulkarim al-Allousi, formed a 160-person "advisory council for Fallujah" to represent the various components of society in a kind of expanded town council. Soon after a group of six twenty-something university graduates calling themselves the Scientific

Council for Development described in their introductory brochure how they sought a "union of educated persons in Falluja to help solve the city's problems" and foment a "renaissance in society." They were extremely well-dressed and articulate and presented eight compelling proposals on the environment, sewage treatment, water, the internet, and health. And the ex-army officers of Falluja formed a civic organization and managed several projects to fix their city and the province.

It was encouraging to see civil society reemerge after the zero-sum game of Iraqi politics and the total control of Iraqi society by the Ba'athists. But we also knew they had severe limitations and it was a tough space to work. All democratic forces were associated on a certain level with the coalition; because of this Hisham was shot three times in January 2004 in a debilitating attack that left him wheelchair-bound, and Khalid was shot and nearly killed in an attack in March 2004, only to recover and be killed in a bombing at the Umm al-Qura Mosque in Baghdad in August 2011, along with twenty-seven others. One of the first victims of war or dictatorship is civil society, and it is not always quick to recover. But it is an underpinning for everything else, and hence worth the effort to promote and protect.

Tribal Democracy

A persistent fiction from this early period is that the CPA did not engage the tribes and that they were somehow "discovered" only later, in the run-up to the surge. Joe Klein, for example, wrote in June 2007 that an alliance with the tribes was proposed by intelligence officers and rejected by the CPA on the grounds that tribes are part of the past and have no place in the new democratic Iraq.[10] Dave Kilcullen wrote in August 2007 that the CPA "deliberately side-lined the tribes in 2003 in order to focus on building a 'modern' democratic state in Iraq, which we equated with a non-tribal state."[11]

These were inaccurate shadings of reality. Everyone on the ground and most in Baghdad recognized the tribes as one of the only organizing entities when we arrived, and we all engaged the sheikhs incessantly. But we also found a broader context that I first encountered when I asked a local staff member which sheikh he fell under. He answered, with as much indignation as he could muster in a language not his own, "I am my own sheikh, Mr. Keith, my own sheikh." The challenge—and we could have found better ways to carry it out—was to engage the tribes while moving to a broader and more inclusive society. But we did not ignore the tribes.

We learned several things in our tribal engagement early on. First, we were getting only a small sample of the tribes through our outreach, and the ones that stepped forward were not in any way inclusive. Second, some of the tribes that were not in the mix were large, quite powerful, and would be needed to fully stabilize the province. Third, there was not full agreement among the tribal leaders of who was in and who was out, as Saddam had seriously manipulated the tribal structure. Fourth, the sheikhs we were dealing with were very interested (arguably most interested) in the material benefits of working with the coalition. And fifth, for the most part the sheikhs did not have a good deal of interest in directly managing things but rather wanted to be the titular heads who could mobilize a small cast of technocrats to do the real work of administration. That was how they ran their business interests as well.

The first issue I encountered I wrote up in a September 2003 cable whose title says it all: "Anbar Sheikhs Want More Respect." They complained about searches, lack of information, the paltry resources that came their way, and a basic lack of empowerment. "In a complaint-driven and entitlement-oriented culture," I reported, "some of these grievances can be dismissed as mere posturing. . . . But in an area where we have few friends and many enemies, it would be foolish not to try harder to show deference to the sheikhs to garner stronger support."

Eventually tribal engagement became part of the larger Sunni Engagement Strategy that recognized most anticoalition activities were coming from Sunni areas and took account of the litany of Sunni grievances, which CPA was also hearing. This strategy included some work on de-Ba'athification, support for Sunni political parties, empowerment of local councils, economic measures, and small security programs. But it didn't reach the crescendo we sought in Anbar of directly hiring tribes and tribal leaders for security and providing the walking-around money the sheikhs needed to deliver their areas and stop attacks. It was simply not convincing for leaders who were looking at their bottom line.

South Central Director Gfoeller, meanwhile, developed a vision for broadening the participation of key groups in a setting they were comfortable with by creating "tribal democracy centers," with a tribal council that would channel the participation of the sheikhs in support of the political process and stability. Our first challenge in establishing a tribal council was that there was simply no agreed list of who was a legitimate sheikh.[12] One source told us there were 720, another 92. We were hoping for 150 to 200 who could meet and select a tribal council of forty, which would then go back to meet with its local tribal leaders and serve as the conduit for their people. We were aware this was suboptimal, that in Iraq you are either in or you are out, and the idea of being represented by someone else meant being stripped of status. But it was one of many compromises, and the tribal leaders we met with were fully supportive (as long as they were one of the insiders).

After intense consultations that included multiple name checks to weed out the "fake sheikhs" and "wannabe sheikhs," tribal leaders arrived at a list of about a hundred and we did an inauguration in mid-December. By early January, however, some of those not chosen formed a second sheikhs council. We were concerned this would lead to a freeze in decision making, but they were able to reach consensus. In Iraq, we learned, success was about having a big enough tent.

The final piece of the tribal picture we needed to work was the inclusion of the Kharbit clan. According to most interlocutors, the Kharbits had a valid claim to the position of paramount sheikh of the Dulaym confederation and were the key to stability in the region. But acting on a tip from what many now believe was his rival sheikh Ammer that Saddam was hiding in their compound, on April 11, 2003, the United States bombed the patriarch Malik

Kharbit's home in Al Anbar, killing him and twenty-one family members, including his mother and several children. This left his brother Mudher to manage the aftermath, but he was either in exile at the time or went there after the bombing, leaving the tribe in the hands of a lesser tribal leader, Abdul Hamid. Our two agency field officers came to me one day and said they had an opening to bring the Kharbits around but they would need a seat on the Provincial Council, which I arranged. The military also steered some contracts their way. It was some of the most effective intelligence-military-diplomatic cooperation I have seen. We were able to bring the Kharbits at least partially into the emerging political structure and gain their tentative support.

Civil Administration and Governance

Our role in day-to-day provincial governance revolved primarily around paying salaries and advising the various local department heads. The budget was complicated, and civil affairs officer Marty Bishoff, a senior pharmaceutical executive who very skillfully managed public administration, generally had to drive to Baghdad and personally extract the money for our operating budget from the Ministry of Finance. In December he grew exasperated with the refusal of the Treasury to release $12 million in operations and maintenance funds and personally parked himself at the Ministry until they paid up. It led me to wonder how the periphery would fare when we were no longer present, another one of those not so subtle signals to the Sunnis that the central government did not have their best interests in mind going forward.

The civil affairs officers were matched with department heads, most of whom were holdovers from the previous regime and often quite knowledgeable and capable, although they were not used to having authority or autonomy. Their meetings with us were generally asks for things they wanted us to do for them, to which the governor would remind them that they now had the authority to act and needed to do so.

The most inspiring piece of civil administration in this period was the currency exchange. Like Afghanistan, Iraq had two currencies in circulation: the older Swiss dinar used by the Kurds in the North, and the Saddam dinar, with every denomination bearing Saddam's picture, in the rest of the country. The Saddam notes had plummeted in value due to sanctions and included a 10,000 dinar note in addition to smaller currencies. The exchange rate was around 1,200 to 1, down from a high of 3 to 1 before the Gulf War, and treasury officials were concerned it could collapse altogether. We had been paying salaries in dollars, but now the CPA printed some 250 dinar notes as an interim measure.

In October a small but security-heavy team from the contractor KPMG quietly arrived, and I accompanied them to local banks to exchange their currency for the new bills. We entered the bank vault where the old bills would be dipped in red ink to show they were being taken out of circulation before they were disposed of. The new bills were then laid out: the 50 dinar note with a Basrah grain silo and date palm tree; the 250 with an astrolabe and spiral minaret from Samarra; the 500 with the Dukan Dam in Sulaymaniyah and a winged bull from Nineveh; the 1,000 with a gold dinar coin and Baghdad's historic Al Mustansiriya University; the 5,000 with a waterfall and desert fortress; and the 10,000 with a portrait of the tenth-century mathematician and astrologer Ibn al-Haytham and the Al Habda minaret from Mosul. They were a balanced celebration of Iraqi history, achievements, and culture.

The woman at the bank was beaming as she helped dip the Saddam notes, telling us that for decades she had felt sullied by carrying these around with her and passing them out as a teller. She was ecstatic that the day had finally arrived when this daily reminder of the dictator would be gone. She was also clearly moved by the attractiveness of the notes and looked on with near reverence as they were unwrapped. It was a very good day. As in Afghanistan, the new currency was not only well received aesthetically but was also good for the economy, stabilizing the exchange rate and showing a commitment to the economic future of the country.

Building a provincial government was not an easy task, and we barely scratched the surface. In something as critical as government services, a longer-term mentoring relationship may have been worth the effort. The skills of managing the business of government on a daily basis were significant to shoring up the emergent regime and were often more important in the daily lives of citizens than the more abstract decisions coming out of the capital.

Reconciliation: Getting the Cornered Tiger beyond De-Ba'athification

Of all the issues we dealt with, getting the Sunnis to feel they had a seat at the table of the new nation was the most important. In a winner-take-all arrangement, which is what the Sunnis understood democracy meant, they were outnumbered by the Shias. And the most transparent evidence of what they perceived to be a loaded new system was de-Ba'athification. The policy excluded from active employment and political participation tens of thousands of individuals in the prime of their work and civic life because of previous membership in the Ba'ath Party, the majority of whom were Sunnis.[13]

De-Ba'athification came up in nearly every meeting I held. It had either affected individuals directly or, in the case of the sheikhs, one of their people. In October Sheikh Bizi'e brought fourteen former Ba'athist professors and police officers to explain their plight. They complained about the hardship of being thrown out of work when their only crime was membership in the one political party Iraq had for thirty-five years. They all disavowed any current allegiance to the Ba'ath Party, and most said they had no loyalty to the party even during Saddam's time but joined to advance their career. Most of the security professionals said they had verifiable proof that they had helped the coalition, and several said they were actively working with coalition forces when they were dismissed. They all expressed the shame of not being able to provide for their families. "What do we get out of democracy if our children don't eat?" one asked. Another asked rhetorically if we like having friends, then answered his own question: "This is not the way to make them."

I suggested to Baghdad, "These are the losers in the new Iraq and turning these losers into winners is the challenge we face if we are to prevail here. If a compromise on the de-Ba'athification order is possible, it would be the most expedient way to bring these men around."

The process was eventually put in the hands of the Higher National De-Ba'athification Commission, led by Ahmed Chalabi and several other members of the Governing Council. One of the commission's first directives expanded the problem by demanding the immediate dismissal of anyone who held the previously exempt lowest rung of Ba'ath Party membership, the *firqa*, and nullifying all previous exemptions. CPA brought in Chalabi to defend the policy in our December CPA meeting, before a room full of commanders and coordinators who were united in opposing the blanket nature of the policy. I challenged the measure on practical as well as historical grounds, pointing out that this deep an exclusion from public life for former regime members was not common in transitions in Eastern Europe, Latin America, or Africa, and was possible here only because the U.S. military was enforcing it. In negotiated transitions, I suggested, the old regime was generally given a way forward. Chalabi was unmoved and remained firm in executing the policy. In the end he was simply the wrong person to manage so vital an issue. James Glanz, a *New York Times* correspondent in Iraq who spent considerable time with Chalabi, said upon his death in 2015, "Strip away all the sophistication, and all the history, and he was an Iraqi with a grudge—and he was never going to be anything else, and he never really pretended to be anything else."[14]

In addition there was a larger national divide against which these issues were playing out. The new Sunni-Shia math and the threat it presented to the Sunnis were constantly on the minds of Anbar's leaders. On September 1, in a quiet but public demonstration, twenty local sheikhs gathered at the governorate building to stage a combination photo op and demonstration. They were nervous over a rumor circulating in the Baghdad press that the perpetrators of the recent Najaf shrine bombing were from Ramadi. They held signs that publicly denied any involvement by Ramadi citizens in the bombing and read a prepared statement by Governor Barjas. Things were quickly deteriorating into a tit-for-tat bombing campaign, and they wanted no part of it.

The Shia provinces at times also flexed their new muscles, add-ing fuel to the fire. In mid-November several of the desert sheikhs, led by Sheikh Owrance Mute'eb Mahroot, whose flowing white robe and immaculately placed headdress belied his centuries-old lineage, came to see the governor and me. They were exercised over the appearance of officials and police from the Shia province of Karbala at the town of Al-Nukaib on the Saudi border. The Shia officials had written backing from the Ministry of Interior to take over the border crossing at Ar Ar to better facilitate the primar-ily Shia pilgrims on hajj as they entered Saudi Arabia. It was the first time the long-standing discord between Sunni and Shia had played out territorially, and the first time a ministry in Baghdad directly backed sheer factionalism. I worked with the Ministry of Interior via the CPA to have them rescind the order and ensure Karbala knew the jig was up.

Then in mid-December the desert sheikhs came again to say that this time it was the governor and the police chief of Najaf, backed not by a piece of paper from the Ministry but by forty truckloads of men. Najafi officials wanted to shift the provincial border to the west to allow them to control a vital crossing into Saudi Ara-bia. Again we pushed it back through CPA and our fellow gover-nance coordinator in Karbala, but again we were worried about what would happen when we were not in place to calm tensions and maintain the status quo.

This was all on rich display in the aftermath of the capture of Saddam Hussein on December 13, 2004. The event was met with mixed reactions in Ramadi. The celebratory gunfire we heard the day after, which we assumed was delayed joy at his capture, we later learned was instead because of a rapidly spreading rumor that the news was inaccurate and he was still free. While much of the rest of the country erupted in celebration, Anbar stewed. Most Anbaris in the end were ready to bring the chapter to finality, but it left pending the much larger question of what would come next.

I saw an opportunity with the end of the Saddam era to make our case to the CPA and Washington for a sort of "new deal" with the Sunnis, hoping to capture all the various aspects of our policies that were going to make Iraq ungovernable. With an aggressive new start, I thought we could regain the initiative.

In a mid-December cable entitled "The Cornered Tiger: Iraq's Sunnis after Saddam," I summarized that the capture of Saddam closed one chapter but opened another. "The real issue here is less the future of Saddam than the future of the Sunnis, and people here continue to play the part of a cornered tiger, one that is being prodded and is lashing out." I suggested that most Anbaris were resigned to the coalition presence until the new security forces could be built. But inadvertently the coalition had chosen sides and was not just an occupying power but a power that was disempowering the Sunnis through the formation of the Interim Governing Council, the structure of the new Iraqi Army, and de-Ba'athification. I argued that in addition to rapidly building out the security forces, strengthening the economy, and softening de-Ba'athification, we should consider a series of local gatherings that fed into a conference of national reconciliation. I had been struck by the theatrical power of the Afghan Loya Jirga to present the nation to itself in all its variation and believed that single event bought years of stability for the Afghan project (albeit stability that was incomplete and not capitalized on by Afghan leaders or their international partners). Iraq did not have the same traditional mechanism, but the concept could easily have fit into standard big-tent tribal gatherings for decision making and reconciliation. I conceded it was a big ask, and in the end there was no way to modify the political calendar that had been developed to squeeze in my jirgas.

Over time we lost the battle on reconciliation. It was all part of a host of national-level issues that would follow, from the political structure of the country to the formation and leadership of the security forces and the distribution of oil revenues. It led, as Fareed Zakaria wrote on January 8, 2007, to a trajectory that was less "nation building" and more "nation busting" in their effects: "We summarily deposed not just Saddam Hussein but a century's old ruling elite and then were stunned that they reacted poorly. In contrast, in coming into power in South Africa, Nelson Mandela did not fire a single white bureaucrat or soldier—and not because he thought they had been kind to his people. He correctly saw the strategy as the way to prevent an Afrikaner rebellion. . . . We did not give [Iraq] a republic. We gave them a civil war."[15]

Paul Bremer, responding to this and other critiques at a time when the insurgency was on the verge of unhinging the whole project, defended his decision in an op-ed to the *Washington Post* on May 13, 2007. He said he was "weary of being a punching bag over these decisions (of disbanding the army and de-Ba'athification)—particularly from critics who've never spent any time in Iraq, don't understand its complexities, and can't explain what we should have done differently. These two sensible and moral calls did not create today's insurgency. . . . No doubt some members of the Ba'ath Party and the old army have joined the insurgency. But they are not fighting because they weren't given a chance to earn a living. They're fighting because they want to topple a democratically elected government and reestablish a Ba'athist dictatorship."[16]

Ambassador Bremer and I had two very different experiences. And there was much that was lost in translation.

Anbaris by this point were divided into those who would give democracy a chance and those who were convinced they would have to fight their way back into power. For those willing to work through a political process to get to the pluralistic Iraq they had been promised, our next event was the election of the Provincial Council. It was the last real bright spot in Al Anbar for many years.

Final Election

The growth of civil society, jostling of tribal leaders, Governor Barjas's leadership, the sullenness of Falluja, disruptive violence, the emergence of political parties, women's participation in society, all came together, if only briefly, in the Provincial Council elections of January 2004.

We went to work to explain the stages of sovereignty to groups of civic leaders and enlisted their ideas and support for how best to ensure Anbar was represented nationally. The Governing Council, I explained, was currently debating an administrative law that would ensure individual rights for all Iraqi citizens and define the procedure by which the new government would be formed. A new Provincial Council would then select delegates for the transitional government by June 2004, after which the Coalition Provisional Authority would dissolve and the new Iraqi government would be given full sovereignty. A national assembly would select a leader or leaders to represent the country and ministers to run the government. By the end of 2004 the transitional government would select a body to write a constitution and full elections would be held at the end of 2005 based on the new constitution.

It was an aggressive but not unreasonable timetable. And it was consistent with what we found locally, which was an interest in seeing the visible foreign military presence diminish and as much power as possible transferred to Iraqis. But Anbar's leaders were content to take things one step at a time.

We met with hundreds of Iraqis to discuss the plan—sheikhs, business leaders, members of political parties and civil society— but the real strategy meetings were held with Governor Barjas and a handful of his advisors. He had good instincts for what would work in the province and for how various groups would react to their place in the new schematic. He knew we wouldn't please everyone but wanted a process that was transparent and at least defensible.

The political parties had emerged earlier as viable players, albeit late to the game, compared to the Kurdish, Shia, and Baghdad-based parties. They were an interesting mix of six factions: the Iraqi Islamic Party, Arab National Democratic Party, Royal Coalition Union, Iraqi National Union, National Conference Party, and National Kurdish Union. The Islamic Party was by far the most popular. It had gone through ups and down under Saddam, who extended power when he was weak and withdrew it when he was strong, but had allowed it considerable freedom in the last years of the regime. They had a building, an organization, and a women's group. Governor Barjas explained that with no party having a track record, as a default many people would simply choose the Islamic option. "Who can argue with voting for Islam?" he mused.

Hikmat Jassim Zidan, a thirty-something Anbar native representing the Coalition for Iraqi National Unity, was the most hopeful of the new party leaders. He was educated and clear thinking and wired to participate in the political process, believing in and not fearful of a multiparty system. On January 15 Zidan's Coalition for Iraqi Unity held a peaceful demonstration in front of the governorate that drew 1,500. The crowds shouted, "Unity, Unity for Iraq!" and carried banners reading, "No to Terrorism and No to Those Who Harm the Helpless" and "We Demand the Return of Employees to Their Jobs." Press from Reuters, Abu Dhabi, and INM covered the event.

One of the more interesting parties was the Iraqi Constitutional Monarchy Party, whose representatives showed me several loosely bound books of paper with signatures of their supporters. They stressed that the monarchy had been progressive, at peace with the region and the world, and allowed for a multicultural society. I asked who they had in mind to take on the kingship and they offered Sharif Ali bin Hussein, whose mother was Faisal II's aunt and who was both available and interested in the throne. They envisioned a country with a government like Jordan's, which I conceded sounded pretty good at that point. The party never really took off in Anbar, but they stayed with it to the end and made their presence felt. They went on to compete nationally in 2005 but did not make the threshold for Parliament, still deemed outsiders by most Iraqis.

We wanted the caucuses to be as Iraqi-led as possible and did not impose ourselves on them but insisted on disqualification of top-level Ba'athists and those lacking educational credentials. The method of democracy may have been new, but the concept was quite intuitive, even for those living under the boot of a dictator for most of their adult lives. Whether it was perceived as an opportunity for individual and group expression or a way to get in on some of the spoils of governance, thousands of citizens embraced it.

The first caucus, made up of 250 lawyers and human rights activists, took place on January 17. After five-minute speeches by candidates and an opening for challenges, a vote was taken in an orderly

and transparent process that involved showing a judge one's cre-
dential to draw a three-by-five-inch ballot stamped with the Anbar
seal. Participants wrote the candidate's name on the card, depos-
ited it in a Saddam-era voting box, and filed out of the hall. After
the ballots were collected and organized, the assembly returned,
and the judge read out each ballot in front of the delegates as they
were tallied. He then announced the winner, and the results were
publicized the next day. I described it later as a "deeply moving
process, considering it may have been the first time a democratic
election was held in Al Anbar." But I also acknowledged that it
gave us a false sense of security, since lawyers "tend to know how
to do these sorts of things."

The Ramadi judiciary was now a key partner, and one of the
senior provincial judges was chosen as the authority for all the
caucuses. We were pleasantly surprised to find that the one place
left over from the Saddamist government that retained the overwhelming respect of the people was the judiciary. The deference
paid to a sitting judge would make the process go much smoother.

Religious leaders also passed without any drama. Forty-five
imams gathered in the afternoon of January 17; after their single candidate, the provincial council's general secretary Imam Sulaiman,
gave a brief outline of his credentials they nodded their agreement,
declining the indignity of a paper vote. When reminded that they
needed an alternate, they pinned that on with a voice vote as well.

We moved on to more challenging groups—teachers, business
leaders, engineers, doctors, labor, and common citizens—working
with the judge and Governor Barjas through walkouts, credential-
ing disputes, and procedural contests. We then got to the wom-
en's caucus. In an initial session only twenty women showed up,
frightened off by the TV cameras and early start time (not enough
time to square the husband and kids away before venturing out).
We rescheduled for January 22, after which they had seen several
other caucuses on TV and were more comfortable with the concept, although they still insisted on closed press. Over 250 women
were in attendance that day, making me realize I had not seen
more than ten women in my five months in Ramadi.

At the beginning of the caucus, three women announced their candidacy and gave well-prepared speeches. Their passion was in marked contrast to their male counterparts, most of whom simply listed their qualifications and in some cases went no further than their names. The first candidate was Nazek Daham Awad, an unmarried lawyer who had lost three brothers in one of Saddam's purges. She lobbied fearlessly for independence from husbands and for equality of women in public life. She also argued for Iraqi unity: "Iraq is one nation: Sunni, Shia, Christian, and Kurd. Our country has suffered enough, and now is the time for the women of Iraq to step forward and show what they are made of."

The second candidate, Afaf Abid al Razik, was associated with the Islamic Party and the Islamic Aid Association. She was the polar opposite of Daham, running on the conservative platform and emphasizing the key role of Iraqi women in the home. She mentioned the mothers of Jesus and Moses as being central to what their sons achieved in history, and stated that the most important role for the women of Iraq was as mothers. The third candidate, Amal Fadel, expressed optimism that the right to vote would play a role in ameliorating the suffering of Iraqi women. All three speeches received enthusiastic applause.

After the ballots were cast and the votes tallied, the conservative candidate emerged as the clear winner with 181 votes, while Daham ran a respectable second with 67. The third candidate curiously did not even vote for herself and received no votes. In a speech after the vote Daham said, "It is not about who won first or second place. The women of Iraq won today." The candidates embraced and promised to work together to improve the lives of the women of Al Anbar. In speaking with participants afterward it was clear that the leading candidates had mobilized their constituents—many women came fully veiled, while others expressed a desire for change. The image of these women thoughtfully voting, one by one, is seared into my memory.

In my report to Baghdad I wrote, "This was the most inspiring of the caucuses we have held to date. The women of Ramadi, like all women of Iraq, have borne the burden of Saddam's madness for the better part of a generation, and to see them actively gathering for the first time to express themselves politically made for a very good day after weeks of beating heads with sheikhs, educators, labor leaders and others."

The sheikhs held their caucus independently of us and it went better than we expected. The final ten delegates included just four from the previous council, our one transnational sheikh (Owrance from Nukaib), two members of the excluded sheikhs, and one member of the Kharbit tribe in a manipulated process that I devised to ensure they had a place. This was my only truly undemocratic maneuver, contrary to popular belief.

Caucuses for the smaller towns were also challenging but adequate. According to the newly arrived political officer, Steve Bitner, "each had its own character and temperament, ranging from the exuberantly friendly Anah to the sullenly hostile Rawah, just across the river." They each developed their own system for selecting their representatives, given the impossibility of carrying out a full vote.

Steve reported that interest in the caucuses grew at each stop as voters were informed about the event held in neighboring towns. Most of the mayors wanted to shift the balance of power from tribal leaders to educated technocrats, and failed for the most part. He concluded, "Relying on mayors and city councils to select electors is far from perfect. This was lost on no one. That said, the electors that were chosen did not shrink from challenging municipal officials or CPA representatives on the shortcomings of the process. Assured that more democratic elections were ahead, most agreed that the caucuses were better than anything they had before."

Falluja was by far the most difficult of the caucuses. I went there on January 21 to meet with sheikhs and town notables and realized how far behind they were, dealing with "very basic issues of paranoia about the national process and the place of the Sunnis in it" and having done little preparation for the caucus. In the end the caucus just happened. I was prepared to go back and observe it, but the day before it was scheduled the military unit sent word that the participants had gathered on their own and had selected their list. Given the real possibility of violence we were frankly relieved. Falluja had far greater problems than provincial caucus elections (although we didn't know just how much greater). All we needed was the final list.

By the end of January we had held over thirty caucuses that involved over five thousand people and had forty-one council members. We had a Provincial Council that was "as good as it gets," as I titled my final cable. I concluded:

> Both the process and the product of the new council were very imperfect. The end product includes a high proportion of Islamic Party members, several reps who have not completed secondary school, a Communist, and a few who are reportedly anti-coalition. The process was also messy, with every caucus a hard-fought battle, and many caucuses challenged during and after they were held. But in the end most citizens feel that whatever imperfections there are among the representatives who were selected, they are *their* representatives not *ours*. Significantly, in the process of conducting these caucuses there was a large advance forward in the development of civil society and confirmation that the citizens of Al Anbar want to be directly involved in choosing their leaders. The people of Al Anbar are far better prepared to participate in the upcoming phase of the political process than they were two months ago.

These final events were thoroughly and fairly covered by Anne Barnard of the *Boston Globe* and Dexter Filkins of the *New York Times*, who, like us, experienced a mix of awe, hope, and skepticism that it would all turn out. In the end it did not; these local gains were swept away by a much larger national picture that we were powerless to control. But for a brief moment there was optimism in Al Anbar.

Afterward

I had a few days to complete the turnover of the section to Stuart Jones, another Foreign Service officer on loan from Washington who would stay through the transition to the marines and into the violent summer and fall. I did some TV interviews to try to get the message out about the political transition with the help of a personally friendly but very anticoalition Iraqi Media Network producer. He asked the hard questions but allowed me to make the case for where the province was going, and I introduced my successor. The interview aired a number of times on the local channel (where there was never enough material to fill the programs) and nationally.

In late January a Blackwater security team showed up with our first armored Suburban, which conveniently was the same color as our previous unarmored vehicle. I assured the team we had gone downtown every day for seven months and never had an incident and had no reason to believe that was going to change, but we were open to their suggestions. They fell into our battle rhythm and saw how we did things while they developed their own assessment.

A few days later I stayed on base to pack while Stu and the team went downtown in the new Suburban and a convoy of unarmored Humvees and other vehicles. About a mile short of the governorate building they were hit by an IED that had been emplaced in a drainage pipe. It was a small device but really did a number on the car, blowing out the tires and shattering the bullet-proof glass while spraying shrapnel across the side of the vehicle. Amazingly nothing penetrated the vehicle itself, and the convoy limped on to the governorate building and the team got to work.

Apparently the insurgents were targeting only the main vehicle, which for the first time was armored, while none of the unarmored vehicles were hit. Stu said either they wanted me to stay and were trying to kill him, or they wanted to kill me and thought this was their last chance. We had a farewell lunch planned with tribal leaders and local government officials, and I asked Stu if we should proceed. He said he thought the odds were wildly in our favor as it was unlikely we would be hit twice in one day, so we went.

I finished my time and left in mid-February, taking an eight-hour taxi ride to Damascus with the brother of the governor's assistant and from there catching a commercial two-hour flight to Budapest, the same routine I had used to get home for Christmas.

It was good to be home. I hadn't been in Iraq long enough to have too many adjustment issues, other than still being seized with the challenges ahead. We were trying to keep our Central European allies supportive, most of whom had taken some casualties by then and all of whom were anti-interventionist by nature because of their own experience on the receiving end of foreign occupation. I did a speaking tour in Prague and lots of engagements around Hungary, which became infinitely more difficult when the first images of the torture and abuse at Abu Ghraib came out in April. I was the only one who could put the abuses in any kind of context, so I did the heavy lifting with the Hungarian press and think tanks about what had happened and what we were doing about it. But it was a hard sell.

Barjas continued as governor for several months after I left, eventually being forced out of office by insurgents. He later moved to Baghdad and then Jordan, and his sons now live in the United States and Canada. He was an Iraqi patriot, thrust into an impossible situation. But he did his duty and for that year was an incredibly strong leader.

During the first battle for Falluja in the spring of 2004 Sulaiman and several other moderate imams issued fatwahs for a peaceful solution to the conflict. Soon after leaving a meeting with coalition officers, he and three other moderate imams were attacked by Al-Qaida. Sulaiman took a bullet to the head and survived only through the intervention of coalition doctors and medical treatment in the United States. He later died in a bombing at the Grand Mosque in Baghdad.

When the battle for Falluja broke out in April after the brutal and very visual killing of American contractors, the narrative of a handover to the Iraqis was by then a much more complicated one and the future less clear. A wholesale unraveling of the progress we had made in the previous year was under way. But then we always knew we were leaving some pockets of simmering resistance that would have to be either brought on board politically or dealt with militarily by us or by the Iraqi security forces.

The selection of the interim government went through in May and the CPA closed up shop at the end of June, after fourteen months and one week of governing Iraq. The handover would play out poorly, however, as Shia Grand Ayatollah Sayyid Ali al-Sistani insisted on national elections as opposed to the more controlled national caucus system proposed by the CPA and threatened to have the Shias boycott the entire process. UN Special Envoy Brahimi worked through the crisis and an election was ultimately held, although by then the Sunnis were disenchanted and voting turnout in Al Anbar was as low as 2 percent. The national political process would take another decade to settle into a pattern with more or less full representation.

The CPA was a very flawed enterprise from the start, and enough analysis has been done on the organization that I don't feel I need to add much. It is worth considering, though, in the context of what has happened in Libya and Syria, that the CPA at least provided Iraq a way forward. And with all the missteps that came with that opportunity, it did include governance and some basis for reconciliation of the disparate factions. That may seem like a small consolation, but having now seen what total collapse and civil war looks like elsewhere, the cost could have been several million casualties rather than the several hundred thousand casualties Iraq has endured. And absent the CPA it is entirely possible there would not even be an Iraq today, certainly not one that is clawing its way forward militarily to defeat ISIS and struggling to find that political formula that will allow it to govern effectively. In this part of the world, it can always be worse. And Iraq is still fully in play.

In late June I was given the Dissent Award from the American Foreign Service Association. It has a direct link to some of the heroes of the Foreign Service, such as Tex Harris, who worked on the edges of legality to expose the excesses of the Argentine military junta and help its victims in the 1970s, at a time when our Cold War policy was okay with the first and indifferent to the latter. It was a good ceremony, and included Ron Schlicher, senior CPA advisor on the Sunni strategy, who was being feted for his work with the Palestinians. Both Ron and I were being honored for our new thinking rather than our criticism of policy, but criticism was in the air. As the *Washington Post* reported, "John W. Limbert, president of the American Foreign Service Association [noted] that he was a hostage in Iran with L. Bruce Laingen, who chaired the committee that selected the award winners. Limbert said to laughter, 'While Ambassador Laingen and I are ex-cons, neither of us are neo-cons!'" In my remarks I described the situation in Iraq as "too important to allow ideology to trump experience or imagination to trump reality." It is the award I am most proud of; when my deputy chief of mission wrote up the recommendation, she credited me with dissenting over a policy and then going on to try to help execute it when my recommendation was ignored. As any good Hobbit would, I suppose.

Lessons Learned: A New Look at Federalism

We transferred to Ottawa in the summer, where I was guilt-ridden for sitting out the wars after only brief stints, and in Canada of all places. But it was clear by then we were in for a long hard road in both Afghanistan and Iraq and I was not convinced we had the right blueprint. And our family dynamic was such that it would not have been a good time for a long separation. I wrote a piece for *Orbis* on force size and my observation that with what we needed to do in Afghanistan and Iraq our ground forces were simply too small. I suggested that our middle path between a post–World War II occupation of overwhelming force and the small advisor footprint of El Salvador was a recipe for instability.

I also knew that the key to Iraq's future would never center on security but on the country's political structure, which hinged on the position of the now politically displaced Sunnis. Canada turned out to be a rich place for fresh thinking on the problem of center-periphery relations and managing minority rights. Because of its recent history having to entice Quebec to stay in the federation, Canada harbors a large number of federalism experts and the premier think tank on the topic, the Forum of Federations.

The question of federalism in Iraq was a challenging one. Like Afghanistan, there was an effort to get the right mix between decentralization that would allow for a modicum of essential local control, and centralization that would keep together a country whose constituent parts produced natural centrifugal force. Those considering partition generally came back to the sheer difficulty of splitting up a country whose populace was so intertwined and whose resources did not fall into strict ethnic pockets. But the natural solution of tristate federalism would likely lead to a breakup into three countries. U.S. thinkers and policymakers, with a thin understanding of the complexities and options in federalism, tended to miss many of the opportunities that might have been available in getting the country to the right political end-state.

In May 2006 the Canadian government convened a conference on Iraq's political future, whose overall theme was the "chronic inability of the Iraqi polity to channel competition in peaceful, legitimate ways."[17] Federalism experts shared papers on the issues Iraq faced in getting to a system that produced political stability through what one expert called "balanced federalism," in which conflict is dispersed and institutionalized by governing arrangements. It was going to be incredibly difficult to meet the challenges of redesigning the Iraqi government in such a way that this could work.

I wrote one final piece on Iraq for the Foreign Policy Research Institute and the *Foreign Service Journal*, "After the Surge: The Only Iraq Worth Fighting For," in which I argued that the center of gravity in the conflict was "how Iraqis related politically to one another, as facilitated by the Iraqi government." I could see the surge ending with a victory over Al-Qaida and restoration of the Iraqi state, only to fall apart again over lack of a viable governing structure. I posited the need for a government that forced the provinces to collect their views locally and bring them to Baghdad, thus facilitating the breakdown of ethnic tension at a local level, where it could be collated and managed, rather than reorganizing in Baghdad along ethnic lines. I was not sure if there was a political structure that would facilitate that, but what I did know was that the current political arrangement would forever lead to Sunni disempowerment and rage.

In 2012, on my way to a later tour of duty in Afghanistan, I had lunch with Maj. Gen. Steve Townsend, with whom I had started my army career thirty years earlier in the 82nd Airborne. Townsend was a soldier's soldier, a truly gifted leader, and we had been in many of the same places, he in uniform and me in wingtips, as our country shifted from the low-intensity conflicts of the waning days of the Cold War, through the humanitarian interventions after the Cold War, and into the post-9/11 conflicts. We lamented the current train of thought, that Iraq had been a big mistake and that we had been duped by the issue of weapons of mass destruction. We agreed that with or without viable weapons of mass destruction, Saddam Hussein had been seeking the worst weapons for a very long time, and given the internal structural conflicts indigenous to Iraq, we believed the foundation would eventually have cracked. We thought there were better ways to have managed our involvement but agreed that in time we would eventually have gotten to the same place. We were never going to be able to ignore Iraq, and stabilizing Iraq was never going to be easy. Now it was a matter of staying with it until Iraq could stand on its own, however long that would take.

The next year ISIS would emerge on the scene, and three years later Townsend would be appointed commander of Joint Task Force Inherent Resolve, taking on the task of reducing ISIS while the Iraqi government continued with the task of political consolidation, whose absence led to the opening ISIS had exploited.

At the U.S. Institute of Peace in March of 2017, I listened to Prime Minister Haider al-Abadi make the case for continued U.S. support for Iraq's future, while the campaign against ISIS was still raging. He made it clear that Iraqis were inching closer to political consolidation, having learned so many painful lessons over the previous fourteen years. A viable political structure that facilitates power sharing among the various groups and regions is still the only answer if Iraq is to have a future. But they were not there yet.

Could the creation of a functional, multiethnic, democratic Iraq have been easier? Undoubtedly. But it may be equally true that Iraqis had to live through the near loss of their country to value it. The generation-long struggle for Iraq to find its footing will continue. And it would be reckless at this point for the United States not to continue to support the new country. It is far better placed to do so now, having learned the many hard lessons of that earlier period.

TEN

Afghanistan, 2012

Progress and Challenge in the North

A Diplomatic Surge

While not as clean as the Sunni-Shia divide in Iraq, there was a similar struggle for control in Afghanistan between the Pashtuns, who had been the main supporters of the Taliban, and the Tajiks, Uzbeks, and Hazaras of the Northern Alliance. As the Loya Jirga concluded in the spring of 2002 it was clear that the place of the Pashtuns in the new Afghanistan was the key to stability, and it was going in the wrong direction. Pamela Constable of the *Washington Post* wrote in July that the Pashtuns were "becoming rapidly disillusioned by a series of developments that have reinforced the power of rival ethnic Tajiks and militia leaders, left the former king politically sidelined and a Pashtun vice president assassinated, and subjected Pashtun villages to lethal U.S. air strikes."[1] The country was exhausted and the Taliban largely defeated, but by the end of 2002 insurgent attacks were starting up again. They accelerated through 2003–4 as the Taliban and others exploited the vacuum created when the international security force neglected to extend its presence throughout the country.

In 2006, when the strength of the Taliban resurgence led to concerns that whole segments of the country could be lost to government control, NATO upped its commitment. The international force grew to a coalition of forty-six nations blanketing the country with Provincial Reconstruction Teams that brought development and governance support, anchored by military units to confront insurgents and train and mentor local security forces. Inspired by the perceived success of the troop surge in Iraq, the United States added 33,000 troops to its Afghan force in late 2009, reaching a total of 100,000 by August 2010.

The military surge was matched by a "diplomatic surge," as the State Department sought to implant diplomats and aid officers in these field missions. It was the heyday of "expeditionary diplomacy," and by 2012 the State Department system for service in unaccompanied posts had become somewhat regularized. There were carrots and sticks as inducements to serve, lengthy training, and an improved architecture for life on embassy and regional platforms. But it was also clear that the missions were cresting. I had for four years been fully employed leading the Mérida Initiative in Mexico, the largest security cooperation mission we had ever attempted there, but sensing the end of an era of open and active engagement in the field, I secured the assignment as senior civilian representative (or consul general) to Mazar-e Sharif. I would lead a team of 30 Americans, 40 Afghans, and 130 security contractors that covered the nine provinces of northern Afghanistan.

I arrived in Kabul in May and checked in with Ambassador Ryan Crocker, who had had a few years' break after grueling service in Iraq. He looked tired and admitted as much but had no time to dwell on it. Crocker's focus was on keeping the broadest amount of engagement with the widest array of actors possible. He did not want to have to guess what was going on in the provinces and sought constant reporting based on direct observation by a trusted source. He was concerned but not obsessed with security and said he would not stop me from assuming a reasonable level of risk. He gave me his take on the warlords in the north and asked that I maintain a close and productive relationship with them, watching especially for indications of rearming and distancing from the central government.

The Northern Alliance and the Land of the Blue Mosque

The nine provinces of the north and their approximately nine million inhabitants comprise nearly a third of Afghanistan, bordering Turkmenistan, Uzbekistan, Tajikistan, China, and Pakistan. Once over the Hindu Kush the road descends through the Salang Pass, dropping four thousand meters in elevation to almost sea level in two hundred kilometers. A huge psychological barrier has been crossed, and one effectively enters Central Asia, with its rich history and a certain separateness, although not to the extent of wanting to split from the rest of the country. Northern Afghans, as one governor put it to me, are simply "too divided to divide."

The Amu Darya River is Afghanistan's northern border and a major source of water in the rich northern plains. Because mountains traverse two-thirds of the center of the country, the northern watershed is full of canyons and rivers that slice it into a thousand valleys, channeling commerce and conquest. It also creates small havens of agricultural potential—the mainstay of the region. And as one of the quirks of political geography, the British created a territorial finger in the east, giving Badakhshan province a border with China that serves to split Russia from Pakistan.

With its key border crossings the region is Afghanistan's window on Europe and Asia and the outlet for the so-called Northern Distribution Network for our military, which winds its way into Europe. Northern Afghanistan is also home to large-scale oil and gas deposits, including the Amu Darya fields, and some mining scattered across several provinces, primarily Baghlan with extensive coal deposits and gold. In addition, there was a somewhat small but progressive business sector based in Mazar-e Sharif. The region was relatively secure when I arrived and had less support for insurgent activity, sort of a giant ink spot of stability in traditional counterinsurgency theory.

While Kabul is one giant melting pot, the north continues to be the heartland of the Tajiks, Uzbeks, and Turkmen.[2] The ethnic mix would always be a factor in war and politics, but it was complicated. Fearful of revolt, at the turn of the twentieth century the Iron Emir sent Pashtun colonists north, where they settled in Faryab province in the west, Kunduz in the center, and Baghlan just over the Khyber Pass. These "Pashtun belts" were a constant source of instability because of their support for local Taliban movements. It was never simple, though; the Norwegians in Faryab pointed to the "Pashtun line" on the map, with electricity on the Uzbek side and darkness on the Pashtun side, a source of legitimate grievances. And they pointed out there was an Uzbek Taliban and a Pashtun Taliban that sometimes fought the government, sometimes fought each other, and sometimes fought among themselves.

Many northern Afghans, especially the younger generation, wanted to get away from ethnicity as a defining concept. But at the end of the day the Uzbeks would vote overwhelmingly for the Uzbek candidate in any election, and the Tajiks wanted a Tajik in the palace before they signed off on any governing agreement.

Because of a constellation of cultural, military, and geographic factors, northern Afghanistan has traditionally had a natural alignment with the United States. Its geographic barrier provided the defensible space for the Northern Alliance's last redoubt against the Taliban as they traversed from Panjshir up to Badakhshan before 9/11. The CIA, having supported the Northern Alliance during the war with the Soviets and maintained contact after the war, sought out these commanders after 9/11. Doug Stanton captures the period well in *The Horse Soldiers*, the tale of small teams of CIA and Special Forces operatives who helicoptered in from Central Asia and rode on horseback with their new allies through narrow mountain passes to the northern plains. There the Special Forces teams provided air support as the Northern fighters first broke the Taliban lines, and then systematically destroyed their forces.

After reducing the last northern Taliban holdout in Kunduz, the Northern Alliance moved over the Hindu Kush and into Kabul. They were natural allies, these Northern commanders, the Uzbek Dostum reportedly asking a senior U.S. official when it was all over where in the global war on terror his guys could attack next. Stanton tells an endearing story of General Atta Muhammed Nur, a more junior but also more controlled and politically astute commander, surrounding a Taliban contingent holed up inside a school in Mazar. In the fog of battle a U.S. Special Forces commander called in an air strike, not realizing Atta's men were inside; nine were killed along with the Taliban, and the American captain was crestfallen. Seeing his remorse Atta took him aside and said, "Captain, in war these things happen. It is very sad. But we understand." These were hardened commanders, but they were not without heart. They were focused on the bottom line, however, and were always planning their next move.

These battles produced the first post-9/11 U.S. casualty, CIA Special Activities officer Mike Spann, who was killed during a Taliban uprising inside the massive nineteenth-century Qala-i-Jangi fort just outside Mazar. During an uprising the prisoners took over a small building as their last stronghold, with hundreds packed inside a large cellar. As was common, Dostum and Taliban commanders talked by cell phone throughout the siege. They ultimately did not reach an agreement, and the Northern Alliance flooded the building, drowning several hundred Taliban in a torrent of water and mud.

We visited the fort on Memorial Day 2012 and paid tribute to Spann around a well-kept monument Dostum had erected in his honor. The basement was still under several feet of mud; it evoked an eerie feeling, knowing how the story ended. Drunk on the unconditional surrender we secured in the Second World War, we now tend to look at these conflicts as win-or-lose affairs, with the winner setting all conditions for the way forward. To the Afghans, however, as Atta and Dostum showed during these opening battles, there is a long back and forth of talking, fighting, surrendering, changing sides, fighting again, talking some more. It is an uncategorical form of warfare that we have yet to adapt to.

Along with both risk and opportunity in the north was the attachment and connections of some ethnic groups to their cousins across the border in Turkmenistan, Uzbekistan, and Tajikistan. Each of these countries had a consulate in Mazar, primarily for intelligence and commercial interests, but also basic representation. The presence of these Central Asian and other diplomats, in addition to some traders, made for a very active international community, with whom we enjoyed a monthly dinner or reception. I sought ways to leverage their potential goodwill in seeking a more stable Afghanistan, and we were constantly on the lookout for export opportunities in the Central Asian markets.

The Russians similarly had a three-man consulate, a mix of intelligence officers and diplomats. They were based at Hairaton port abutting the border crossing into Uzbekistan so that, in the wry words of their consul general, they could "make a speedy getaway." They were not unwelcome, for many of the Northern Alliance leaders were still partial to the Russians, with whom they sided during the initial struggle. The Russians too were watching more than doing, and as much as anything were watching us.

The Iranians were also present, and, hopeful of reconciling the United States and Iran, our Afghan hosts liked to seat the five-foot-two-inch Persian consul general next to me, six-five, at public events. He was normally stone-faced and constantly casting a backward glance at his intelligence minders, but I could get a laugh out of him by pointing to the imported Iranian juice we were drinking and telling him I needed to keep it on the sly as I was breaking the trade embargo.

Although there was nothing constitutional about it, Mazar was the de facto capital of the north. It was a few kilometers from the ancient city of Balkh, the capital of the Central Asian Bactrian Empire that thrived two millennia before the Common Era. Travel writers Bijan Omrani and Matthew Leeming write in the overly poetic way they describe much of Afghanistan that of all the great cities of Central Asia, "few can compete with Balkh for importance in history or prominence in legend. To the Islamic geographers Balkh was 'the Mother of Cities,' birthplace of Zoroastrianism, and a major trading route between the West, China, and India. It was a cradle of religion, a meeting point of cultures, and a capital of empire."[3] The remnants of the Bactrian Empire, by then a collection of warring but fierce tribes, was never controlled by Alexander, even after taking the local princess Roxana to wife.

Mazar is also home to the impressive Blue Mosque, believed by some Afghans to be the burial site of Hazrat Ali, cousin and son-in-law of Mohammed and the fourth caliph for Sunnis, the

First Imam for Shia Muslims. According to Afghan legend, Ali's companions took his body out of its burial place in Najaf (where a competing shrine exists), placed it on the back of a white she-camel, and allowed the beast to wander until it finally collapsed in what would become Mazar-e Sharif. It is now a shrine of great beauty and color, the cultural anchor of Mazar and in some ways the entire north. All doves are said to turn white when they land near the shrine. I can't say I ever saw a dove change colors, but I didn't see any brown doves.

Balkh was destroyed several times and eventually fell into disrepair, although the city walls are still extant, as is the outline of the city, which emanates outward like spokes from a central park. In the thirteenth century the poet Mawlana, or Rumi, was born in Balkh, although because he died in Turkey and because Turkey has more cash for cultural preservation, the Turks have done a better job of claiming him. But there is a mud house, largely in ruins, that is accepted as Rumi's birthplace, and the airport has been named in his honor.

This rich heritage did not inform day-to-day interactions, but one came to understand a certain pride of both place and ethnicity among the northern Afghans. We treated them as part of a proud religious and historic culture that had of late fallen on hard times but deserved our respect. It was on a smaller scale what the former diplomat Andrew Steinfeld believes is happening with China, Russia, and Iran, all former great powers feeling entitled to a prominent place in the modern world based on their glorious past. Respect in such places is its own currency.

In addition to pride, the Afghans, we found, have long memories. As part of its first mission as a NATO partner Mongolia sent contingents to Badakhshan and Camp Marmal, where the townspeople referred to them as "devils from the north." Genghis Khan and his Mongolian horde, it seems, had sacked Balkh in 1220 CE, killing most of the city's inhabitants. The Afghans never quite warmed up to the Mongols, even after the Mongols hosted several generous cultural events with local notables. Memories die slowly here.

On a personal level I found several characteristics about the northern Afghans that stood out. First, they were firmly committed to Islam. It reminded me of the journalist Sandy Gall's description of a band of mujahideen in the mid-1980s preparing for prayer: "Most of these young men were simple peasants . . . and yet there was about them a sort of nobility as they submitted themselves to a faith that has given them the strength to fight for seven years against a superpower quite prepared to destroy them and their families, their homes and even their country; a faith that could move mountains."[4] That sort of romanticizing of Afghan religiosity is less comfortable now that it is being turned on us, not the Soviets, but I found the core value of concentrated religiosity to be no less intense now than it was then.

Second, they maintain the core value of hospitality, of which so much has been written that it hardly needs repeating. It did seem to play out in the currency of Afghans offering their hospitality, generally food, and expecting our hospitality, projects for the most part, in return. There was always a bit of communism in those transactions—from each according to his means, to each according to his needs. They had naan bread and lola kabab; we had a hundred million dollars in assistance. It seemed like a fair trade to them.

Third, fighting and manhood were difficult to disentangle. Theirs was a martial culture, and there was no easy way to channel those instincts in a positive direction. Like Central America, this was a place where power was very primitively expressed and applied, in contrast to Iraq, where force had been controlled for so long that it played out more surreptitiously than directly. In Afghanistan there would always be a long queue of young men looking for a way to prove themselves.

The Platform

The Camp Marmal base was a sprawling facility abutting the Mazar airport five miles to the east of Mazar-e Sharif. Germany was the lead nation in the north and ran the base with three thousand soldiers. Germany had been slowly creeping into more assertive peacekeeping and postconflict missions in the post-9/11 period. By the time I left they had lost fifty-four soldiers and three policemen.

The Germans were joined by a thousand soldiers from fourteen other NATO nations or partners and four thousand U.S. soldiers.[5] It was an enriching environment, a rare place where half of Europe came together in a single location and each country put its national mark on its corner of the base. The Americans were there to provide "enablers" for NATO, primarily intelligence support and aviation, and to prepare for the out-shipment of U.S. equipment. The Germans have strict national rules about housing and hygiene, so I lived reasonably well in a dormitory-style building with eighty soldiers and European diplomats.

My own interagency team consisted of officers from State, USAID, and Agriculture. We covered political and economic reporting and engagement, public outreach, agricultural assistance, and rule of law, and we managed assistance programs for education, health, infrastructure, and governance. The Task Force for Business Stability Operations (TFBSO), a Pentagon-run freelance operation of business consultants with a healthy budget, were active from a downtown villa. The TFBSO concept started in Iraq, when a frustrated U.S. Department of Defense decided that the conventional development process was simply too restrictive to quickly reduce unemployment, stabilize the economy, and attract foreign investment, all viewed as security issues by the military. It was duplicative but justified in my view.

I directed six U.S. civilian teams that joined the European Provincial Reconstruction Teams (PRTs) across the north: Norway in Faryab, Sweden and Turkey in Jawzjhan, Sweden in Mazar, Germany in Kunduz, Hungary in Baghlan, and Germany again in Badakhshan. The U.S. teams were well-received by their European and Afghan hosts, who welcomed all the help they could get, especially if it came with project or budgetary support. Local officials also liked to know there was direct U.S. interest in their area.

At the national level, however, President Karzai had become critical of the PRT concept, telling a NATO audience in February 2011 that they "prevent the growth of the Afghan government" and that "their role confuses people—they ask who is in charge." He suggested, "As the Afghan government takes more responsibility and relieves you of the burdens and responsibilities, the parallel structures should be ended."[6]

The notion of parallel structures undoubtedly had its genesis in something Karzai had experienced, a PRT that overstepped its bounds or an honest feeling that, after ten years of assistance, local governments should have been functional. But his sentiment was not shared by governors, one of whom described the imminent pullout of the PRT as his "Y2K." He recognized the value of the PRT in backing up the provincial government when it stumbled, mentoring and training its government officials, especially in technical fields such as budgeting, and working with local security forces to ensure stability. He was in no hurry to see it leave.

As I took stock, it was clear we had come a very long way since 2002. But I also expressed some hesitation in an early letter home in May 2012: "One does pick up that for the Afghans it has been a very long ten years, as they realize they are even now just getting started in taking things on without international assistance. One gets a sense of frustration and foreboding, of powerlessness and a total lack of confidence." I also noted "an incredible sense of entitlement that wasn't here before"—gone was the near universal purposefulness I had seen in 2002. And there was now considerable blame that they didn't have time for a decade earlier—Pakistani meddling, Russia's disastrous war, a U.S. desire to weaken Afghanistan. "I do not sense the quiet nobility that drew me to Afghanistan the last time I was here," I concluded.

A Decade of Progress

In early meetings with Afghan officials the "What have you done for us lately?" narrative was so persistent that I asked my staff to develop a fact sheet to tell the story of Afghanistan's progress and our part in it. We showed that the number of children in school had grown from 1 million boys to 5.4 million boys and 3 million girls; access to health care increased from 9 to 60 percent; gross domestic product had increased from $4 billion to $17 billion and

GDP growth averaged 10 percent a year; access to electricity had tripled, from 6 to 18 percent of the country; the number of telephones had gone from one million to over twelve million; and life expectancy had advanced by nearly a third.

And there were other creative ways to mark the country's progress. Afghanistan had had four democratic elections since 2001; it missed the six Olympic Games between 1980 and 2000, but since 2004 it had attended every Olympics and won the first two medals in Afghan history; diplomatic relations had grown from three embassies under the Taliban to forty.

My favorite statistic was the wheat harvest, which had increased from an average of 2,000 million metric tons a year from 1995 to 2005, to 3,000 between 2005 and 2010. This was partially due to good rains, but significantly had much to do with our systematically replacing the wheat seed across the country with a more resilient and higher yielding strain.

Taken together the progress was arguably the most impressive by any nation in modern times. Admittedly the gains were the result of starting from a very low bar, all were tentative, and some, like GDP growth, were a product of large foreign donations. Still, even the most skeptical Afghan official found them difficult to argue with. Governor Atta Muhammed Nur's chief of staff, much to my amusement, conceded that they still got the same complaints from their people. He answered them by saying, "Where you once had donkeys you now have cars, where you once had 'natural remedies' you now have a pharmacy, where you once had a rutted road you now have asphalt." To which they answered, "Good point. Now we would like more cars, more pharmacies, and more roads."

A very extensive study by the U.S. Department of Defense captured the same sentiment, giving the country a "mixed progress" grade. It found that the Afghan government continued to develop its capacity to provide stable, effective, and responsive governance, "but long-term sustainability was challenged by corruption, revenue-generation shortfalls, and limitations in public sector management." All sectors told the same story: "progress in the justice sector is being made but remains slow"; the National

Assembly demonstrated "slow but growing capacity and political maturity"; in the health sector "Afghanistan ha[d] made significant achievements" over the previous nine years but remained dependent on international aid; the education sector had improved dramatically since 2002, but "significant challenges remain[ed]"; economic growth was high, but only sustained by international aid.[7]

There was plenty of room for debate on how much more effective aid delivery should have been, but the fact remained it was a very productive ten years, albeit with another few decades of sustained progress required.

An Economic Puzzle Where a Piece (or Two) Is Always Missing

As we took up our three lines of effort—the economy, security and the rule of law, and governance—we saw the economic piece as the most urgent, given the upcoming departure of the coalition and the impact this would have on Afghan public confidence. Despite talk of a golden age in the 1950s and 1960s, the Afghan economy has never been good. Per capita GNP in 1974 was $70, ranking seventy-third among eighty-three underdeveloped countries, and even then two-thirds of the country's revenue was foreign aid, as East and West vied for the country's favor.[8]

The Soviets after 1979 built furiously, leaving significant gains in the critical natural gas sector, but also roads, dams, schools, and government buildings. But from the Soviet pullout in 1988 to 2001 there was a steady deterioration of everything.

While Afghanistan has never had a robust export economy, contenting itself with trade and subsistence agriculture, it did once have niche products that brought in hard currency, such as Karakul hides, raisins and dried fruits, and carpets. It also had directed markets: pomegranates to Russia and the resin spice asafetida to India. But in the isolation created by thirty years of occupation and civil war, these markets disappeared. Much of the trading class went into exile and the abilities of those who remained atrophied, as did the land itself. In a visit to a newly planted Samangan pistachio field (a tree that takes seven years to yield fruit), for example, growers told me that many traditional plantations were burned for firewood during the civil war. Loss of export capacity in Afghanistan was exacerbated by external factors: shifts in markets, animosity with neighbors, the deterioration of the country's border infrastructure, and lack of access to capital markets. We knew that even as we defended the progress made to date we needed to help the north reestablish a self-sustaining export-oriented economy, organized in the short term around agricultural derivatives and transportation while the more lucrative mineral wealth that could underwrite higher-level progress was developed.

All members of the international team in the north, civilian and military, saw the urgency of building a sustainable economy that could outlast us. There were to be no silver bullets, just a long slog in each functional area. As S. Frederick Starr and Adib Farhadi, from the Institute for Security and Development Policy, put it, most Afghans "judge the country's contending powers in terms of their ability, or inability, to improve the economic lot of ordinary people.... An awareness of economic progress will do more than anything else to advance political stability."[9] One parliamentarian told me he feared the country would fall off a "fiscal and employment cliff" when the internationals departed.

Given the centrality of agriculture to the economy and society, our strategy was to take a halting revival in agricultural production to the next level: finding markets for new crops, preferably in Europe or the United States, adding value to current production, and developing products that could replace simple imports. Nuts, fruits, skins, carpets, and juices were the most promising, as they would employ the most people on the longest employment chain and there were notable successes in each.

There were several serious hurdles to getting products into international markets where they would draw the biggest yield—transit problems, phytosanitary issues, quality control, lack of investment capital, continuing poor infrastructure, and no real marketing culture. But our ag advisors took them on, training farmers, spreading new techniques, assessing agricultural potential, steering infrastructure projects dealing with irrigation, and helping connect farmers with markets and their own government. They persisted despite the obstacles, driven by the realization that there were no other good options and hoping we might just catch a break.

We explored the possibility of getting almond oils into the hands of U.S. suppliers, increasing the amount of Karakul skins and pushing them to the United States in addition to the European market, and working with a women's co-op that produced silk and wool scarves, a great project as it allowed the women to work from home. None of the projects were successful at the level we hoped, although there was some activity in the carpet sector with USAID and the U.S. Department of Agriculture's Sheep to Shop program, in which they trained and capitalized carpet weavers and dyers to return to the vivacious natural dyes that Afghan carpets were famous for, and some products began to move into South Asian markets. At a minimum hundreds of fields were now irrigated and productive, links with markets were established, and a vision of export promotion instilled in many officials and merchants.

The other sectors of the economy were in a similar situation, having visible potential but something missing to realize their full promise. Mazar had always been a hub for transit across Afghanistan and had a basic infrastructure to support a robust trucking sector, making Balkh Afghanistan's gateway to Central Asia and Europe. We hoped that as part of the "New Silk Road," an ambitious project to make Afghanistan a central trade and transit hub, it would develop into something profitable. The concept relied in part on piggybacking on the military redeployment scheme, which required the development of a world-class port and rail line on the Uzbek border at Hairaton, thirty minutes from Mazar on the Amu Darya River.

This retrograde mission brought a company of U.S. Army logisticians and a small team of border experts in the Border Management Task Force at Hairaton. These experts, mostly retired customs officers, were there to mentor, train, and advise the Afghan team in effective border management. Many on the Afghan side were eager to improve operations but soon bumped up against local strongmen for whom the border post was a cash cow. They too persisted, and the crossing looked more and more functional each month.

Another piece of the economic puzzle in the north was what was under the ground, which was conservatively estimated at $1.5 trillion but which TFBSO said could go as high as $3 trillion.[10] The estimate included fifty-nine trillion cubic feet of natural gas reserves; 1.9 billion barrels of "undiscovered technically recoverable crude," about the same as in Equatorial Guinea; and a smattering of gold, aluminum, iron, and other precious minerals, mostly in Baghlan and Badakhshan.[11]

Minerals, gas, and oil offered the promise of tax revenues, jobs, and the general development of a region that comes with that level of international interest and connectivity. USAID and TFBSO worked in parallel to first develop the natural gas fields, which had thrived under the Soviets. A hulking Soviet-era gas-processing plant was on life support in Sheberghan; a few wells were still generating some gas, but the field's full potential was waiting to be developed. The Overseas Private Investment Corporation got involved in financing, and TFBSO tried a project to encourage the transition of vehicles to liquid natural gas with the hope that it would provide a more lucrative alternative market. The overall project is ongoing, now with Turkish investment and some progress, though it is still several years away from reaching even part of its potential.

Extracting the crude oil was somewhat more complex. The Chinese Petroleum Corporation bid on the Angot field in one of the first national tenders, and by November 2012 had two hundred nervous Chinese workers drilling south of Jawzjhan. Local officials were wildly optimistic, the governor even suggesting the Angot well could "make Sar-e-Pul province the next Dubai." But the project was fraught with challenges, including the requirements for special refining given the nature of the crude, difficult transportation nodes, and, as always, security. Like most projects it is still a work in progress, now hostage to national politics and local security conditions.

There were a handful of highly functional factories in the north, primarily around Mazar. The Sadat bottling factory had over a hundred employees and was pushing out thousands of bottles of water a day under an extremely talented CEO who had spent years abroad and worked at the level of any Western executive. Another local success was the Ghazanfar brothers, who rose from a family that sold bottled water behind schoolhouses in their native Faryab to build an international corporation with offices in Dubai focused on fuel delivery, refining, and real estate. In the spring of 2013 I attended the opening of the Burj Ghazanfar, their opulent and well-furnished twelve-story answer to the Burj Dubai, at the side of the Blue Mosque in downtown Mazar. Waiting for dinner one evening at their lavish guest house I devoured shelled pistachios by the handful and pomegranate seeds by the spoonful. I asked them how they would transition when the internationals departed. They had a robust plan, including pivoting to the real estate boom they believed was coming, the high-end service sector, refining the oil the Chinese would be pumping (for which they needed several hundred million dollars in capital), and getting into media and banking. But they also conceded enough hesitation that they remained anchored in Dubai for security reasons and their children's education. They confessed to not being interested in conventional production and factories and would stay on the more high-end opportunities like oil and transport.

There were other small start-ups in the service and production industry with young CEOs and limited capital. At the Nowruz celebration in the spring of 2013 the Afghan Chamber of Commerce put together a business fair in which merchants could showcase their wares to an international and Kabul audience. Some fifty companies set up for the event, many in the agricultural derivatives area and NGO-supported handicraft sellers, as well as PVC and plastics firms and several construction companies. However, most firms were highly dependent on the presence of the internationals and it was not clear how they would be sustained after transition. Still, they did evince a certain scrappiness and demonstrated that under the right conditions they could achieve autonomous success.

Elsewhere across the north we found at least one critical component missing from the puzzle of a self-sustaining Afghanistan.

Several days in Baghlan demonstrated that their agricultural sales were constrained because of lack of cold storage. Cold storage was not available because there was no electricity. Electricity was not available because the dam in Pul-e-Kumri was functioning at a quarter of its capacity since the Ukrainian-built turbines broke down years earlier and the company that produced them went out of business.

The director of mines said he had run the cement factory for years, including through the Taliban period, and kept it at capacity until 2001, when it stopped functioning during the war. It was later privatized, and Kabul-based corruption forced the sale of some of the assets. The remaining parts of the plant needed coal, but to fully exploit the coal mine they needed a road, and the road was not on anyone's list of priority projects. So cement continued to be imported from Pakistan.

There was no culprit, really, just a very broken infrastructure and a mishmash of actors and interests that rarely aligned with a clear track of production and marketing. Our teams did what they could to piece it all together.

The government was a partner in some places and indifferent in others. Governor Atta of Balkh was the most visionary of the northern leaders; after our first meeting I commented that he was "all about business," seeing new markets in India, Iran, Uzbekistan, and the Gulf. He traveled widely, just as any U.S. governor would, to develop business ties.

In the spring of 2013 Minister of Finance and future president Ashraf Ghani spoke at a conference in Kunduz about the region's development. He said the fundamental challenge facing the north was not security but jobs, and asserted that it was time to move beyond production to a full competition strategy that would connect producers to exporters. He reminded the audience that there was much the country could do without the international community.

In the end we left Afghanistan with an unfinished economic project. In my final message to Washington I wrote, "Most local officials agree that stability over the coming years will hinge more on the provision of jobs than the development of the security forces—employment remains their obsession." All the gains were tentative, and there was still much to be done to evolve industries to the point of international competitiveness. "But there was also enough to encourage continued engagement."

Our failure was not for lack of effort, nor of capital or sacrifice. Most of our contribution could have gone better. But it could all still come together. Perhaps it is a generational issue and will just take a full transition to make it work. And perhaps there is simply a limit to what a rural, mountainous, disjointed economy with a largely rapacious leadership can bring about. But given the progress of the past fifteen years, if we can get even half that in the next fifteen, and then half again, and a few breaks, who knows? What we can be sure of is that Afghanistan won't be able to build a new economy on its own.

Security and the Rule of Law Where Everyone Is the Sheriff

The development of a lasting and viable security system had been through the same ups and downs as the economy, but like the economy was marked by steady progress. The north in 2012 had only 3 percent of the nation's security incidents and was largely permissive but included certain dicey sectors and the potential for things to fray rapidly. In ten years the United States and NATO had put almost $450 million into the security force basing infrastructure in Balkh alone, and there were training facilities and a robust logistical system in place across the north. It was all still very dependent on the International Security Assistance Force (ISAF), but for a ten-year project was impressive.

In addition to a Kabul-directed recruiting and training system, each PRT did what it could to train and mentor the forces in its sector and conducted what direct action missions and patrolling it could within the limits of its national caveats. U.S. Special Forces worked across the entire sector and carried out missions at will to take out bad actors and contain threats at their source. These raids were much appreciated by local governors, but when they went wrong they were a political problem for the Afghan government. I asked several governors which they would pick if they had a choice between a one-year extension of the PRT, a million dollars for their security forces, or an indefinite extension of night raids. They invariably opted for the night raids. They knew the Afghan national forces were simply unable to confront and control the terrorist threat alone.

The national force was making progress, however, and it often showed. To ensure a safe Nowruz festival for hundreds of thousands of pilgrims coming into Balkh in March 2013, Governor Atta took control of all security forces in the city under a single command, even the national commanders deferring to his leadership. He assembled 6,200 officers from the police, border guards, and army and developed four cordons of successively tighter security. It ran like clockwork and with no visible coalition presence.[12] It was a good example of how the full security system could come together when properly led.

Such leadership was not initially available several weeks later, when a band of insurgents in the tight Wakkan corridor in Badakhshan ambushed an Afghan Army column, killing a dozen soldiers. The perpetrators were a curious mix of criminal enterprise and religious extremism. The attack set off a month-long scrum by the army and police to reestablish their presence in some of the country's toughest terrain and laid bare the security forces' lack of cohesion, planning skills, morale, air power, and leadership. Above all it questioned the division of labor, with the army wanting to be the "clear" force to the police's "hold" force, but the police arguing they had little to hold with. To their credit the security forces collectively clawed their way back into Wakkan and reestablished a government presence there.

Across the north the security forces adjusted to changing conditions, the army came in when called, and they largely muddled through. The local PRTs took more and more of a hands-off approach but tried to support the force with mentoring and training, staying out of the perpetual appeals for logistical support, something the Afghans never quite mastered.

However, the national security system never fully overcame the local forces that had been active for so long. The strongmen maintained their private security forces through either informal or formal networks, and there was continued space for insurgent groups to operate. The governor of Faryab province in the west told us he was in a "bidding war" with insurgent leaders for the loyalty of the province's young men. The governor of Taliban-heavy Baghlan conversely believed that the police worked for money while the Taliban worked for faith; he claimed, "One hundred Talibs could overcome one thousand police." It is a continuing struggle to establish the primacy of the national government throughout the country, not unlike what Colombia has finally prevailed in during its nearly fifty-year fight with the FARC. It is simply a resource-intensive, lengthy, and often bloody scrum.

One of the programs the United States and the United Kingdom implemented to overcome this lack of security in the countryside was the Afghan Local Police, or ALP. It was a somewhat controversial program because, as the International Crisis Group concluded, the ALP often preyed on the people they were supposed to protect.[13] But after observing a training session and interacting with an ALP unit outside Kunduz, I found it difficult to argue with the logic of doing something to fill the vast gap of security in the countryside, even while seeing how, if unsupervised, they could become just another armed group. President Ghani was sold on the program and wanted to increase their number from twenty-nine thousand to forty-five thousand.

In addition to security forces, several nations, notably the Netherlands, had modest programs for rule of law and judicial support. In most of the provinces we found that there was some judicial activity in the provincial capital and little in the districts. The supporting U.S. effort funded a network of advisors and defense attorneys and attempted to improve both the quality of the judicial system and the ability of the many moving pieces to coordinate their actions. The system occasionally worked, including in June 2012, when four ALP were sentenced to sixteen years in prison for the rape of a young girl. But this was the exception; the more common assessment came from an Afghan colleague who said he found that people were again turning to the Taliban for justice against the predations of local strongmen. Sustaining the new system was going to be difficult, and we knew we were working only on the margins.

One of many negative outcomes of the lack of a viable judicial system was corruption—the one constant across most sectors and provinces. In the north the levels of corruption were not on the order of what one found in the capital; one of my European colleagues described it as "modest, consistent, and predictable," allowing businessmen to simply build a reasonable take into the cost of doing business. But that turned out to be too facile.

Sarah Chayes, who spent years in Afghanistan and became one of the leading voices on fighting corruption, said in a 2015 interview after a trip to Kunduz, "In an arid place like Afghanistan, almost entirely dependent on high-end agriculture . . . stealing someone's land is worse than murdering them." The ability of local strongmen to take land, she went on, meant that "years of built-up grievances and no avenue of recourse drive people to extremes," with a "thoroughly corrupt" government implicated on the wrong side of the issue.[14]

We did what we could to press the matter with local authorities and support anticorruption programs, one of which was run by Shamshullah Jawid, head of the local High Office of Oversight and Corruption. Jawid was one of the new class of bureaucrats in the government, not connected through birth or tribe to power but hopeful of having influence through professionalism, technical competence, and fairness. He was working on a corruption awareness campaign and had reached 2,700 people in seminars and conferences; he had sixty-five cases ongoing and an additional ninety pending. It was, like so many things, as good as it got at that point. Jawid is still in his position, continuing the fight.

The security forces and the judiciary continue to have a very long way to go. But a rudimentary infrastructure is in place, a new generation of leaders has been trained, and with political will and consistent outside resources continued progress is conceivable. Of the two the judiciary will be the more difficult and will likely end up with a much more localized flavor.

Politics and Governance: The Center of Gravity
for Northern Afghanistan

One key piece of a successful transition was getting local warlords to lay down their weapons and participate in politics in order to avert yet another historic meltdown. It could be a hard sell for men who had lived by the gun for so long. But the primacy of politics was starting to sink in for local strongmen who were less focused on building militias and more focused on the massing of wealth, media influence, and coalition building as preparation for legitimate play in the political process. We were cautiously hopeful it was the sign of a post-warlord society, where the former strongmen would retain the means of force as a last resort but were more interested in politics and business.

We visited General Dostum in his compound in Sheberghan in the spring of 2013 to take stock of the theory. Over a lavish lunch he unfolded a large map with his electoral strategy. He summed it up by saying "The election is the new AK for the Afghan family." In the future, Dostum said, he would fight with politics, not guns.

This played out as the north prepared for the 2014 election. Among the Uzbeks the younger generation was anxious to move to multiple parties, but they knew that their collective voice would matter only if they voted as an ethnic bloc for a single candidate. And the only real choice was Dostum, who had delivered more power than the Uzbeks ever had. As one analyst told me, "Before Dostum the Uzbeks had colonels and office directors. Now they have generals and ministers." Dostum started with the idea of using his bloc of Uzbek votes to barter for a more decentralized state but in the end played a more direct role and became Ghani's running mate.

The other major political player in the north, Governor Atta of Balkh, floated various concepts for coalitions and toyed with the idea of declaring himself a candidate. But he ultimately decided the president had to be Pashtun and contented himself with working from the sidelines.

It became clear that both the *process* and the *product* of the election needed to be valid for the center in the north to hold. And it was clear that the election would do more to burnish stability there than any other single development. In the end it was just barely good enough.

Against this national backdrop governance capacity at the provincial level was progressing slowly and unevenly. Many of the centrally chosen and placed governors were quite capable and connected to their province, especially if they were not sent from Kabul to quell any moves toward autonomy. Many of the districts (or counties), however, were largely without effective governance of any kind.

There were several small programs administered by USAID, the Aga Khan Foundation, and European donors to improve the functioning of government at the provincial and district levels, and they were helping to develop a rudimentary capacity to budget, plan, and deliver services. Military civil affairs units also stepped into the breach, often bringing critical skill sets that were not otherwise available for mentoring and training a local civil service. Local officials were generally accepting of the assistance so long as it was respectfully delivered and consistent.

We realized early on that we ourselves were a political player and needed to devote some resources and effort to building our own influence. But with nine thousand villages and very little TV and internet penetration in the north it was to be a challenge. Radio, we decided, would be our best bet, and we found several local stations that were tired of Afghanistan being portrayed as a basket case and were anxious for a positive message. We fed them a steady stream of interviews and events, focusing heavily on being visible, present, and proactive. Another side to our public diplomacy programs that produced a positive view of our presence was historic preservation. It occurred to me that a connection to history was missing in many postconflict states, a distracting footnote in the daily grind to survive. But a connection to a once great culture, something to anchor the hard work required for progress, could be of value. We supported the restoration of Noh Gunbad (Nine Domes), Central Asia's oldest Islamic building, and work on the Balkh city walls, restoring its centrality as a major cultural center.

As we conducted local engagement, religious leaders were also high on our list. In early November 2012 a negative video on the prophet Mohammed was about to hit online and we wanted to stave off the violent reaction that in April 2011 had led to the killing of seven UN employees in Mazar after one of the Quran-burning incidents in Florida. I met with the governor and the Sunni and Shia imams to warn them of the imminent release, and the imams promised to do their part to calm their congregants. The Sunni imam, having spent time in Kentucky on a State Department International Visitors Leadership Program, promised to take a firm message to the mosque that this single incident did not represent the American people. He had experienced, much to his surprise, the generosity and respectful pluralism of the United States firsthand. Governor Atta was similarly determined not to allow another round of violence over the incident and directed the security forces not to allow demonstrations outside of compounds.

Their responses reminded us of the criticality of local leadership, but also of taking the time to develop the relationships that would ensure the leaders were on our side. And it reminded us that there was no substitute for face-to-face encounters and for experiencing U.S. culture firsthand.

Another key constituency was youth. While they might not have had an easy opening to participate politically, the youth of the north had a hunger for education that was insatiable. There were 650,000 students in Balkh province alone, 42 percent of them female, and 10,000 students from across the country at Balkh University, including southern Pashtuns.

The girls were in fact the real story in education. The director of education explained how he had to continually fix the results in best student competitions or the girls would walk away with the bulk of the prizes. We had a variety of programs to support education, but it was hard to keep up. It was a sector that would take all the help we could give it.

I met with students in every trip to the provinces and consistently found them energetic, focused, and curious, with a schizophrenic mix of hope and despair. I tried to place these students in the larger political context and the country's future. They had no real outlet for their political energy; the parties were not organized to engage youth and they had no direct access to the media. But their sheer numbers could not be ignored, and they appeared to be taken more and more seriously by power brokers. While 2014 would not be their election, by 2019 they could be a force to be reckoned with. I was convinced they would not be cannon fodder for conflict, for they had seen a future that was better than what their parents accepted and they seemed set on seizing it.

Paying the Price

We never forgot that whatever progress Afghanistan was making was underwritten by lives lost. Each week we observed a moment of silence as Ambassador Crocker read the list of the American fallen in our country team. There were weeks when the list was long—on August 12, 2012, it included fourteen U.S. service members. The ambassador pointed out that he attended a ceremony at the ISAF base each week for the fallen of partner nations. Afghan leaders at these ceremonies, he said, honored their fallen not by name, for which there would not be time, but by a simple numeric count: Afghan Army sixteen, police fourteen, border guards eight, and so on. No one, Crocker said, should think that Afghans are not paying a price to build their country.

We had nothing like the casualties in the south but did have our share of memorial ceremonies. In June a U.S. Army major was killed in a tragic accident, and some months later two U.S. pilots were killed on a special operations mission. We gathered several other times before the year was up for allied deaths. A wall was built on the east side of the camp with a place for the memorial plaques and for gathering. Two German soldiers flanked the newest plaque with medals and flags, and commanders and a few others spoke of the fallen before the plaque was mounted on the wall. It was a reminder of the price some paid for the mission. The Afghans we worked with were not indifferent to this, nor were the northern leaders. They expressed condolences and shared in our grief.

In a journal entry dated May 21, 2012, I wrote of a "memorial

ceremony for two apache pilots who were killed when their helicopter went down south of our sector," "Nicely done ceremony
with the German commander and chaplain saying a few words.
These never get any easier, I oddly felt a sense of relief that the
captain did not have any children and the warrant officer just a
daughter. I guess I am hoping to limit the circle of grief. Undoubtedly not right." The wall had dozens of other names on it, raising
the question "Was it worth the price?" Only a family can answer
that, I suggested.

> What I know is that a small group of committed fanatics attacked
> a great city out of the chaos that was Afghanistan, and we are
> determined to make of that chaos something less threatening.
> That will require bloodshed—ours and theirs—until the chaos
> yields. Less theoretical, these two men died in the service of a
> great nation, seen off before their flight by friends and comrades,
> all of whom would have gladly taken their place. They were doing
> a job they loved, and that only a small number of people on the
> planet could do. They have helped roll back the power of men
> who reek of darkness. Not one man in 10,000 has this privilege.

The "green on blue" attack, in which Afghan soldiers or police
turned their weapons on their trainers or mentors, was a particularly insidious kind of attack that was at an all-time high that year.
In one incident six U.S. Marines were killed in one sector, and in
one incident in the north before I arrived an Afghan tower guard
shot a female officer who was jogging in a compound, apparently
distraught by her physical training uniform.

It was a tough year for diplomats as well. In August 2012 a sui-
cide bomber killed USAID Officer Ragaei Abdelfattah and three
soldiers on a mission in eastern Konar province. Then on September 11 Ambassador Chris Stevens was killed in Benghazi. Chris and
I were in the same entry class into the Foreign Service; he was the
best of our generation and his assassination affected us deeply. It
was tragic to see the politicization of his death and the truly misguided understanding of Benghazi that swept the heartland. He
was a courageous ambassador doing his duty as he saw fit in a

dangerous place, knowing full well the risks. I still think of him often and he inspires me.

It hit even closer to home when I received word on April 4, 2013, that Anne Smedinghoff, who had been my intern several years earlier, was killed by an IED along with three soldiers, an Afghan doctor, and an Afghan American interpreter. Anne's, Chris's, and Ragaei's families were strong in their acceptance of their loss, proud of what their family members had achieved, and cognizant of what they were a part of.

A crass comment appeared on a website soon after Anne was killed, asking if it was worth her life to deliver some "crappy books" to an Afghan school. It hit me personally, having directed people on similar missions. I wrote on Facebook:

> I admire all those who are working to improve the lives of Afghans through education; it is a noble and worthwhile cause. But I am also reminded of the quote by German philosopher Heinrich Heine—"Where one burns books, there one will also burn people." This is not just about providing reading material to young students in a poor country, it is a struggle between two competing models for civilization—one violent, ignorant, depraved, the other enlightened, hopeful, just. Where one kills educators and those who support them, there one will also kill the future; where one destroys millennia-old cultural monuments, there one will also destroy cities. In an age of open borders and weapons of atomized destructive power, this is about more than just books.

Both local and national Afghan politics were progressing, but unsteady. The real test of their progress, as with the economy and security forces, would be with the pullout of the international force across the sector during 2013–14.

Transition: Taking the Wheels Off and Finding the Bicycle Wasn't There

From the day I arrived transition—the handover to Afghan forces and government—was job one. The German Force commander Maj. Gen. Jörg Vollmer likened it to conducting a "relief in place," turning over bases and operating space to Afghans while in many cases under fire. He reminded his staff this was one of the most difficult missions a unit can conduct, directing them, "We will go out with our heads held high, not rushing to the door, but not lingering."

In October 2012 several NATO ambassadors held a discussion in Mazar with local governors and security commanders. The message from the Afghans was of a vast unfinished project that was on track but needed continued attention and resources to conclude successfully. They stressed the importance of ongoing support to the security forces, but placed even greater importance on a steady flow of development assistance that would lead to jobs and poverty reduction.

The most visible part of transition was the closure of PRTs. Over the course of eight months in late 2012–13 the Norwegians, Swedes, Germans, and Hungarians decamped from six PRTs, until by the summer of 2013 only Mazar was left. Even with months of preparation it was a very inconsistent process. One senior allied military advisor told me in November 2012, when transition was in full swing, "When we take the training wheels off, we sometimes find there wasn't a bicycle there to begin with."

In some provinces we weren't sure what would happen with the withdrawal of the PRT because we simply couldn't fully gauge what impact the PRT was having on stability to begin with. In many places international forces had stopped doing active patrolling months ahead of the withdrawal, and in some cases national caveats had kept them away from assertiveness. But it soon became apparent that the mere presence of an international force had been keeping negative actors at bay.

Most allies did try to reinforce stability by leaving behind as much as possible. The Norwegians, Germans, and Swedes developed a creative program for ongoing development assistance and had a relationship with the security forces that would continue to a limited extent, largely by bringing them to Norway, Germany, or Sweden for training and mentoring. Some international development personnel were able to stay, and in one province entire American families remained. It was helpful, but the change was still palpable.

The early withdrawals went well enough and were predictable. Faryab suffered a bombing at a mosque, and in some districts in Baghlan the Taliban shadow government squeezed out the poorly financed legitimate government and overtook the security forces. All of this was made worse by the corruption and the predatory nature of some local officials, which resurfaced as the Taliban came to be seen by many citizens as the lesser of two evils. The *New York Times* reported that outside Kunduz City "residents complained that the local militias were worse than the Taliban in part because while the Taliban would only demand payment once for a harvest, there was often more than one militia, each demanding its own share. Over time, as villages threw their lot in with the Taliban, the insurgents' cordon around Kunduz grew tighter."[15] The Taliban strategy involved more than just being marginally less corrupt; they had been working to build a multiethnic coalition including Hazaras and Tajiks and presented a softer touch than the previous Taliban regime.

Kunduz fell to the Taliban in August 2015, and it took weeks, with a stiff application of ISAF air power and ground advisors, to take it back. The Taliban assaulted Kunduz again in October 2016, was again beaten back, and left the populace more shaken than ever.

The challenge we faced was to keep our presence visible enough to support the Afghans in the transition after the withdrawal of military forces. In January 2013 I wrote, "The Afghans are slowly gaining confidence in their own abilities, but always with a backward glance to see that we are still with them. . . . The United States can play a decisive supporting role in maintaining the generally positive trajectory of the north, but only if we are here. . . . We need to be visible, present, and engaged."

We explored several ways to remain engaged, at least with some peripheral tasks of key leader engagement, support for the rule of law, anticorruption efforts, and economic development, even if carried out through local partners with only occasional face-to-face encounters. But after the politicization of the Benghazi incident there was no space left for the risk that would have been required for even such indirect engagement. In the end, the Afghans were starting to realize that in most places withdrawal meant withdrawal.

Building the Stuff That Can Outlast a War

My one-year war ended in May 2013, "a very long 13½ months," I wrote at the time. It was a "completely unfinished project," on which I wished I could do more. It took a grueling forty-eight hours to get back to Mexico City, where Cecile had stayed with our son Dan to get him through high school. He has always resented the fact that my going to Afghanistan meant his siblings "got one more country" than he did, a Foreign Service kid to the end.

Before I left Mazar I wrote a final cable with the basic theme that the ball was still very much in play in the north:

> While gravitating more to Central than South Asia, northern Afghans still see themselves as Afghans first and seek only a better bargain from the center, not its failure. In urban areas there is a post-warlord political culture developing that is being buttressed by a postwar generation to create exciting new possibilities for the future. Rural areas, especially those that are cut off geographically from cities, however, are not part of this progressive picture, and even some more connected areas such as Kunduz are still at the mercy of the guy with the most shooters. The [Afghan National Security Force] has its work cut out for it and will need to pick up the pace if it is not to be outrun by the devolving security environment. Economically we are seeing the fruits of ten years of rebuilding the agricultural sector, but production must now be matched with internal and external markets to create jobs, something that will require extensive international assistance.

I saw a region where nothing was set, struggling to find its footing economically, its place politically, and whose security was still tenuous. But I also believed everything was moving in the right direction and that some projects may have passed the point of no return. I said I would be surprised to return in five years and find anything other than another block of hard-won progress. I concluded that the international community would continue to play a vital role in all this both through continued direct assistance and by beating back the chilling narrative of abandonment.

"Going forward, showing up will be at least half the job here." It was a bit on the optimistic side. But I sensed that pessimism was in such rich supply that there was simply no point in piling on.

Five years on the setbacks have been worse than I would have thought, and the progress less obvious. The Asia Foundation Survey of the Afghan People for 2016, polling a record number of Afghans, saw the national mood switch over a one-year period from 58 percent believing the country was moving in the right direction, to 29 percent. Key factors in this pessimism were insecurity (49 percent of respondents), unemployment (38 percent), and corruption (15 percent).[16]

Yet it is impossible to write the project off just yet. The Afghan National Security Force continues to make progress, and hundreds of Afghans feel strongly enough about their country to give their lives in its defense. Elections, imperfect as they are, continue to yield democratically elected leaders. Education edges along, and health care access and implementation remain strong.

I closed my final cable saying:

A recent commentator said of the advances in education in Afghanistan: "There's stuff born in those classrooms that can outlast a war. If there is anything that the people of Afghanistan need right now, it's the durability of an education that students can never thereafter be deprived of." From a year spent across northern Afghanistan I too believe that there's stuff born in the fields that can outlast a war; there's stuff born in the media that can outlast a war; there's stuff born in the courtrooms that can outlast a war; and there's stuff born in the security forces that can prosecute that war to a successful conclusion. From the north, it appears this one is still very much ours to lose.

It is debatable whether Afghanistan will ever be a fully functional, inclusive country; it is simply hard work to pull a medieval country into the modern age. But it is nearly guaranteed to fail without our continued focus and resources.

Epilogue

Retooling the American Way of War

On my Facebook page one morning a curious post appeared about how three U.S. Marines staved off a Viet Cong battalion during the Vietnam War. It had gotten twenty-seven thousand likes and thousands of reposts, including from no fewer than three of my friends (none of whom, curiously, were marines). Americans do love to fight well, and in battle America is rarely defeated. The resources and technology and training that have been poured into winning battles have left the United States without a military peer. The U.S. military can fight and win on virtually any terrain, on any continent, and fully dominates the air, sea, and, increasingly, space.

Much of the inherent support for military power goes back to the place of the Second World War in the American psyche, an unthinkably difficult success that required the total mobilization of America's citizens and resources. The exhilaration of this victory, however, left the United States unprepared for most of what would follow. From 1945 on, the country would try desperately to plug all its wars into a World War II framework of total victory and total defeat. Few of them fit. In the future it is possible this model will have little relevance at all.

Several aspects of the World War II experience have been the most limiting. First is a reliance on military means alone. No civilian agencies were materially involved in World War II abroad other than those building alliances and mobilizing resources and manpower. Since World War II we have added intelligence and development agencies and have dabbled with a field role for diplomats.

But we remain ambivalent to the development of a full nonkinetic capability to manage the essential political, economic, and societal factors required to consolidate military victory and build long-term stability and alliances in fragile states.

Second, in addition to clear victories Americans want fast victories. As the U.S. diplomat Lawrence Pezzullo put it, "We're a developed nation that is accustomed to quick answers because we produce quick answers in almost every other area. But when you throw yourselves into a revolution, there are no quick answers."[1] Americans want conflicts to end when the fighting stops and are hesitant about committing forces and resources for the long term. One of the less helpful points of the so-called Powell Doctrine was that there should be a "plausible end-state to avoid endless entanglements." This has led to artificially designed and preemptively deployed conclusions that have served primarily to encourage spoilers and to artificially rush complex processes. As one of my colleagues said, America doesn't lose wars; it loses interest.

A third limiting factor is a desire for easy, uncomplicated partners. The alliance that fought World War II was largely composed of four countries from the Anglosphere plus the Soviets, who were desperate for our assistance. After the war, the rebuilding of the defeated powers was complex but still within the realm of advanced societies whose cultural issues needed only to be respected for them to reconstruct their countries. (And it helped to galvanize acceptance of our economic and political model that the alternative for these societies was Soviet domination.) Today's partners are often starting from a very basic, often primitive level and are fraught with political, religious, and cultural idiosyncrasies. They are going through multiple transitions at once and are traumatized and strained to the breaking point. They require a long-term partner, not a weekend fling.

Never again can we expect to face threats in countries with such a clear and complete center of gravity and transformative capacity. So we are left with the hard work of nation-building. As Clare Lockhart and Michael Miklaucic explain, the only antidote to the degenerative threats of today is the "establishment of states capable of effective governance throughout the world."[2] Only by addressing this challenge head on will the United States transition from winning battles to achieving strategic success. And the issue takes on added urgency as we appear set to enter another decade of sustained combat, reinforcing the already battle-winning military while stripping all other components of our national power of resources and people. It also has broad application to nonmilitary situations. Few experts believe we will ever control migration to the United States without building viable institutions and ultimately societies in the countries that produce the desperate migrants in the first place.

Is There a Doctrine for Nation-Building?

When soldiers conduct an ambush, they are operating according to a doctrine. That doctrine involves principles of security, surprise, and application of firepower. Terrain might modify its application, but the overall principles remain intact.

When conducting nation-building there is no such doctrine, only a body of experience. To date it has been a very ad hoc process. A doctrine should include at a minimum the following principles:

First, *the absolute priority in stabilizing and bringing back to health failed and fragile nations is to get right the political compact that defines those nations*. Absent a political arrangement that provides a place for all citizens, it will be extremely difficult to build a functional nation-state. In Iraq this is now a fifteen-year-old problem that is relatively unchanged. As Hassan Hassan, an analyst at the Center for Global Policy, said in the fall of 2016, "The war against the Islamic State is unwinnable without filling the political and security vacuum that now exists in too much of Iraq. The Islamic State's eventual retreat from Mosul will be a much-needed victory for the country. But unless the government in Baghdad enables Iraqi Sunnis to fill that void, it will once again emerge from the desert."[3]

In her essential work on the issue of consolidating battlefield success into political victory, Nadia Schadlow, former deputy national security advisor, writes, "To wage war effectively, civilian and military leaders must operate as successfully on political battlefields as they do on the physical."[4] The journalist and commentator Fareed Zakaria avers, "In almost every situation that U.S. forces are involved in, the solutions are more political than military.... Military force without a strategy or deeply engaged political and diplomatic process is destined to fail, perhaps even to produce unintended consequences—witness the past decade and a half."[5] The international community did this relatively well in El Salvador, Colombia, and the Balkans, less well in Iraq and Afghanistan. Without a satisfactory political settlement, no amount of fighting will forge a nation.

Second, *a rapid buildup of capable, diversely skilled, and wide-ranging security forces is essential.* For all our experience at it, this is not something we do well. Security forces are supportive of stability, not the main driver of it, but small numbers of spoilers can crash an otherwise good arrangement if the security forces are not fully on task. They must have broad geographic coverage and a full range of capabilities to deal with the inevitable threats to stability during the fragile postconflict period. They must also be backed up by a strong and capable judiciary and penal system. These have a short window to forestall negative reactions to a new regime and must be trained, equipped, and deployed fairly quickly. In El Salvador and Colombia we generally got this right, with rapid build-ups and full-spectrum programs; in Iraq and Afghanistan we left glaring gaps. In Haiti we had generally adequate programs but without the raw materials to make them work.

Third, *economic reform should not be pressed until the political compact is secure.* Too fast a push for a neoliberal economic framework can strain the political process and derail the consolidation of political institutions that are the centerpiece of stability. In Hungary's transition from communism the political elites insisted on giving the country four full years of political stability before the Bokros Plan put a proper neoliberal capitalist framework in place. Respectable jobs that keep spoilers gainfully out of the equation and demonstrate that the new political arrangement comes with dignity, respect, and hope are the key indicator of this. The framework must be sustained over the long term, and hopes for private sector "relief" should not be premature. "Institutionalization before liberalization," as Roland Paris, the Canadian academic who wrote the definitive work on the subject, puts it. We have not gotten this right anywhere.

Fourth, *potential spoilers need a clear alternative path forward.* During the height of the insurgency El Salvador had nine thousand insurgents. It now has sixty thousand gang members. In postconflict space we are competing for the loyalty of young men against warlords, criminals, and terrorists. One of my mentors saw this as one of the easiest areas to attend to but also one of the easiest to ignore. He was convinced we could outbid these potential spoilers by giving youth something to do that satisfies the urge for status and excitement. It will always be cheaper and easier to engage them than to fight them. We have provided that engagement in most cases in the short term but have not sustained it.

Fifth, *all peace is local.* However national and regional conflicts play out, and whatever government comes to power, citizens will support peace and governance only if their local issues are a part of the equation. National peace must be reinforced village by village, satisfying the local populace along the way. Governments need the resources and people to be present. Left unchecked, local issues and vacuums of authority will unravel any national plan. The analyst Oliver Kaplan's systematic field research shows how Colombia is currently applying a body of experience in this regard that is yielding real results, after ignoring it for decades.[6]

Sixth, *the supported government must own the nationalist card.* In their impatience Americans are prone to take over conflicts, believing only they can do things right. In doing so we end up robbing the regime we are supporting of the nationalist card that is worth far more than arms and financing. Rufus Phillips, a provincial affairs officer during the Vietnam War, sums it up this way: "The official American view of the war missed the single most influential component—a South Vietnamese political cause worth fighting for—while the enemy, the Vietcong, framed every action as furthering its political cause against colonialism and feudalism, and for unification."[7] We seem to learn and unlearn this principle fairly quickly.

From Vietnam we went on to get it largely right in Colombia and El Salvador, then lost sight of it by Afghanistan and Iraq.

Seventh, *nation-building is a very long game and we should pace ourselves.* In areas of vital interest to the United States, we need to be able to work across the full spectrum of preconflict, conflict, postconflict, and post-postconflict for as long as necessary to yield success, albeit at a sustainable level of effort. This starts in the preconflict realm, where many cases have shown that skillful diplomacy and statecraft can ward off conflict in the first place, a lesson our machismo-prone policy apparatus tends to gloss over. This is the phase when we also need to either commit to the long term or decide to leave well enough alone, as our involvement can often do more harm than good if it will not be sustained. As Lockhart and Miklaucic argue, "Any international actor . . . that wants to help build a state, must be in it for the long haul, with modest expectations for short-term benchmarks and no delusions about succeeding on the cheap."[8]

When conflict is joined there are many processes that simply cannot be rushed. It is arguable that Haiti had to live through several bouts with Aristide to realize he was not the right leader to build a progressive country. The Iraqi Shia have similarly learned through painful experience that they cannot dominate the Sunni the way they themselves were dominated for centuries. There may have been no shortcuts to those lessons.

On the tactical front, Kael Weston, who spent seven tough years in Afghanistan and Iraq on provincial reconstruction teams, through the ups and down of surges and withdrawals, believes that "a smaller but enduring force would be smarter on all fronts: It would appeal to the Afghans, who chafed at the presence of so many foreign soldiers on their soil; it would compel the Afghan army to more quickly assume responsibility for fighting the Taliban and securing the population; it would encourage the Taliban to come to the negotiating table; and it would force the Americans to focus on only the most essential missions. . . . Afghanistan . . . is a marathon, not a sprint. The surge was a sprint. And America got winded too quickly."[9]

Rather than setting unrealistic timetables, settling in for the long haul would yield a better outcome. Colombia is probably the best example of staying with a country through a long process at a sustainable level of effort.

Eighth, *eliminate the artificial and dangerous divide between hard and soft power*. Mick Mulvaney, then director of the office of management and budget, said of the administration's proposed budget in 2017, "There's no question this is a hard-power budget. It is not a soft-power budget.... [We want] to send a message to our allies and our potential adversaries that this is a strong-power administration. So you have seen money move from soft-power programs, from foreign aid, into more hard-power programs."

President Reagan would have been unimpressed. When he determined that U.S. interests required that the countries of Central America not fall to communist insurgencies, he did not debate the merits of soft, hard, and smart power, favoring some and dismissing others. Rather he gathered all the tools at his disposal—economic, military, diplomatic, and intelligence—and developed what could best be called *full-spectrum power*. In his key speech on the threats in Central America and the Caribbean of March 1983 he listed security assistance, economic aid, land reform, political reform, and human rights as critical to the achievement of the overriding U.S. objective of building functional states that could outbid the communist cause we were pitted against. As Senator Lindsay Graham said in June 2017, only a combination of soft power and hard power will be effective in stabilizing the backyard of key countries, which in turn will be the key to making our own backyard safer.[10]

Ninth, *leadership, theirs and ours, matters*. The kind of inclusive, open, and confident leadership needed in a transitional country is rare. I experienced numerous times when, for lack of good leadership, it was nearly impossible to see a way forward. We and our hosts simply had to wait for the right leadership to emerge. It is also critical to have good leadership throughout the chain of command, and especially in the field. I experienced a wide range of leaders, including several whose lack of experience and judgment probably led to failures in cases that could have succeeded. In the field it is a rare individual who can effectively lead in these cases, as the experience and temperament required are difficult to find in a single individual. We should look outside the mainstream for these leaders, in places without the natural ramparts in conventional assignments that shield most of our leaders from failure.

Tenth, *don't be afraid of the gray zone.* The opening battles in Afghanistan should have given us a clear vision of what was to come. Northern Alliance commanders had cell phone numbers for their Taliban colleagues and called them during the fighting. Thousands of Taliban surrendered, were imprisoned, revolted, negotiated, surrendered again, and many were then killed during transit to Kabul. The Afghans are accustomed to a long back and forth of talking, fighting, surrendering, changing sides, fighting again, talking some more. Other cases were similar. This is a form of warfare that we have yet to adapt to. Sometimes the gray area may be good enough, while the black and white of total victory and total defeat will only lead to unrealistic expectations and unnecessary fighting.

Do We Have the Right Architecture?

There is a huge mismatch between the resources and preparation on the military and civilian sides of these operations. Because of this we often achieve our initial security objectives but have little to throw in to finish the often longer-term and more complex political follow-on. Tracking the three main areas of politics, economics, and security, we can enhance our toolkit in several areas.

Political Action Officers and an International Public Administration Academy

Former defense undersecretary for policy Michèle Flournoy recalled a meeting in the embassy in Baghdad during "one of the most difficult moments of the Iraqi government formation." She asked the senior political officer what the U.S. strategy was to help the Iraqis cohere, aware that the United States was not going to dictate the outcome but would be the key player in helping the new government move forward. His response was telling. "Well," he replied, "that's not my job. My job, as the political officer, is to observe and report." To which Flournoy responded, "I'm sorry. We invaded a country. We are occupying this country. Your job *is* thinking about the political strategy that's going to help put it back together again on sustainable terms." But, she lamented, that's not what we train or resource people to do.[11]

In a similar vein Rufus Phillips in 2014 reflected on the years he spent as a political field officer in Vietnam and the lessons for current U.S. efforts to induce stability in various parts of the globe: "At present, the U.S. is involved in a protracted competition on multiple fronts and with a diversity of adversaries who are opposed to the U.S. and hostile to the core democratic principles that we share along with many of our allies and other actors worldwide. . . . One of the most glaring gaps in the U.S. capacity to meet these challenges is the lack of an adequate . . . 'political action' capability. Such a capability would be designated to support stabilization and democratic transitions in vulnerable states as an alternative to exploitable and short-lived authoritarianism."[12] Phillips envisions a small cadre of diplomats being specially selected, trained, and deployed for a variety of tasks. These would include analysis based on extensive field research of the competitive environment in the country, development of new strategies for being an effective player in that environment, fostering economic and social improvements with a positive political impact, and developing relationships of mutual trust and confidence with local leaders.

The United States is hardly the only player in this space. The United Nations, because of its larger pool of seasoned senior international diplomats with cultural and language skills, can often bring in better talent, for longer periods, than the United States. A close and supporting relationship with UN field missions is critical, and seconding U.S. officers to UN missions would go a long way to providing them with vital training that is simply not available in our own system. It would also be an opportunity to put into play much of what Flournoy and Phillips suggest.

We also need better capacity in the realm of institution-building. President Ashraf Ghani captures this well in an interview in northern Afghanistan in 2009. Upon hearing that $4.2 billion would be available for the reconstruction of Afghanistan, a woman asked that the money not be spent on short-term distribution of food, pointing out, "We've been hungry for twenty years." Rather, she said, she wanted her "children and their children to have a better life. And the only way for that to happen is for the money to be . . . spent on building an accountable civil service that would be able to provide for their life chances."[13]

There is a need for trained, experienced international civil servants to be able to deploy rapidly to back up and mentor the newly appointed civil service of a reconstituting state until it can stand on its own. To date this has been handled in a very ad hoc way, best exemplified by the reliance on military officers to fill mentoring positions for ministries in Afghanistan, even in areas far from their expertise. A standing deployable cadre could fill this gap. It should be rounded out by an international public administration academy, where newly selected civil servants could go for training, coupled with a standing capacity to quickly implant such academies within postconflict states.

Economic Development Teams with Flexible Funding

On the economic side of transitions, the technocrats and institutions could be enhanced. Development officers are in short supply and will be even sparser in the future. They are less technically capable than previously, as they are largely in the contracting business and are not hired for their skills. More technically capable officers would be more effective.

More important is having sufficient funds to do what needs to be done in the first place and having the money in funding streams that allow it to be rapidly deployed. Stabilization doesn't come cheap. But if there is an either-or choice, it is a whole lot cheaper than fighting. As Schadlow writes, "Oxford University's Paul Collier has estimated that the cost of a failing state over the entire history of its failure, for itself and its neighbors, is $100 billion, not counting civil wars or the horrors generated by disorder."[14] Between 2000 and 2019 the United States invested approximately $12 billion in Plan Colombia.[15]

Those attempting to induce stability on the ground will also need flexibility in the funding they are given. For all its flaws, the Commanders Emergency Response Program, which provided flexible funding for military units in the field in Afghanistan and Iraq, was one of the most important tools in the inventory for diplomats and soldiers. It should probably be normalized for future conflicts.

Advance planning and preset funding streams should also be developed for job creation during a transition, something that rarely goes well. This will usually cross political, economic, and security lines, as it will involve large numbers of security-sector jobs that must be politically and ethnically balanced. Funding tools to induce local ownership of programs and allow for local oversight that is often stronger than our own should also be sought in our funding process. And it would be helpful to move away from the current distaste for infrastructure and infatuation with capacity building. There are times when infrastructure is simply what is needed, and capacity building less so. Finally, we should think hard about any Buy America policies that require us to shop at higher-priced and less capable U.S. firms when local options are available and would better serve the greater U.S. interest.

A Bureau of Civilian Security Assistance

Nowhere in the U.S. government is there a standing capacity to build civilian security institutions, backed up by solid doctrine and organizational responsibility. After the missed opportunity for training and equipping security forces in Iraq and Afghanistan, the United States shifted large numbers of personnel to this mission, where progress has been steady if uneven. But all the training institutions the United States has built to deliver this assistance are one-time organizations that are disbanded when their mission finishes. The United States simply lacks the institutional means to rapidly train, equip, and mentor the full gamut of military, law enforcement, judicial, intelligence, and security institutions.

Shifting some of our combat and law enforcement power (and the resources that are attached to them) to developing a *standing capacity* to build combat power and establish security forces for new allies would pay incredible dividends going forward. We also need a civilian security assistance agency with standing personnel, resources, and facilities to quickly and decisively build law enforcement, judicial, and intelligence institutions in struggling states. This could work alongside a newly empowered defense security assistance agency that commands a division's worth of trainers and stores of equipment ready to be deployed to build capacity in proxies, allies, and friendly institutions. We should get over the current aversion to paying the salaries for security personnel in postconflict societies, one of many misguided ideological planks of recent operations that have left thousands of individuals for us to fight against rather than with.

Hard power alone will not be adequate as the United States faces the challenges of the coming decades. Only adherence to full-spectrum power that pulls together all the implements and implementers of national power will be adequate to the task. And that full-spectrum power needs to be deployed across the entire range of the contest, from preconflict, through conflict, fully into postconflict, and with a strong, capable component for the lengthy post-postconflict. With this commitment the United States can go beyond winning battles to winning wars.

ACKNOWLEDGMENTS

This book was many years in the making and many people were involved in its completion. My good friend Mike Sheehan first had the idea to build out my experiences and try to capture the historical themes on either side of them that would give them meaning. It seemed like a heavy lift at first, but his encouragement kept me going; I wish I had finished it before his passing. Margery Thompson, publishing director for the Association of Diplomatic Studies and Training, which has adopted the book for its Diplomats and Diplomacy Series, was my de facto agent, promoter, and patient coach throughout the process. I doubt it would ever have come together without her. Thanks also to Roy Godson and Rufus Phillips for reviewing earlier drafts and offering useful context and suggestions, and for championing the project from start to finish.

Special thanks goes to my wife, Cecile, for her encouragement, and especially for covering for me when I was gone. We were in the thing together, along with Jonathan, Joshua, Rachel, and Daniel, who were kind but tough editors and critics.

There would not have been a story to tell without the many colleagues and comrades who sacrificed to do their part to bring our country's often lofty aspirations to a successful conclusion. They were tough and resourceful and we helped one another stay sane. These include my many companions in Colombia, especially Stan Crawforth and Oscar Buitrago; the men of 3rd Platoon, B/2-505 in Grenada; Maj. Bill Council in Honduras; Adrienne Marks and Tim Carney in Somalia; Carl Schonander and Del Junker in Haiti; Eythan Sontag and Hideo Ikebe in Darfur; Mike Metrinko in Afghanistan; the officers and men of the 304th Civil Affairs Brigade, and Harry Christian, Paul Mades, George Younes, and Vassil Yanco in Iraq; and Matt Lowe, Janae Cooley, Steve Berk, and the Regional Command–North Team in Mazar-e Sharif.

I was both instructed and inspired by the many partners I had in these places, interpreters like Alex Laguerre in Haiti and Kanishka Bakhshi in Afghanistan, local officials like Governor Barjas in Ramadi and Governor Atta in Mazar, security officials like Major Pereira in Honduras and the officers of 5th Officer Candidate School Platoon in El Salvador, and community leaders like Imam Sulaiman in Anbar and Shamshullah Jawid in Mazar. They were imperfect individuals thrust into tough but historically critical situations and performed admirably, often heroically.

I was mentored throughout by some extraordinary individuals: Colonels Reynaldo Garcia, Charles Stulga, and John Waghelstein; Ambassadors Jim Dobbins, Bill Swing, and Ryan Crocker; and Special Representative to the Secretary General Lansana Kouyaté. Special thanks to Bing West, who taught me that we never have to be satisfied with not getting things right.

Finally, I am grateful to Nancy Lindborg and the team she has built at the U.S. Institute of Peace, where I completed much of the core writing. The values and vision I captured there, that peace is possible and the institutions that will secure peace buildable, provided a good deal of the inspiration for the larger themes of the book.

NOTES

Preface

1. Fukuyama, *State-Building*, 119.
2. Ignatieff, *The Lesser Evil*, 151.
3. Ignatieff, *Lesser Evil*, 151.
4. Elisabeth Malkin, "A Remarkable Day in El Salvador: A Day without a Murder," *New York Times*, January 13, 2017.
5. Schadlow, *War and the Art of Governance*, 1.

Introduction

1. Michael Ignatieff, *Blood and Belonging: Journeys into the New Nationalism* (New York: Farrar, Straus and Giroux, 1995).
2. Kyle Weston, "Experiencing War through a Twin," *New York Times*, December 23, 2013, War Blog, https://atwar.blogs.nytimes.com/2013/12/23/experiencing -war-through-a-twin/.
3. Clare Lockhart and Michael Miklaucic, "Leviathan Redux: Toward a Community of Effective States," in *Beyond Convergence: World without Order*, edited by Hilary Matfess and Michael Miklaucic (Washington DC: Center for Complex Operations, 2016), 297.
4. The process was, however, limited by the exclusion of the Taliban and thus many of the Pashtuns.
5. James F. Dobbins, *After the Taliban: Nation-Building in Afghanistan* (Washington DC: Potomac Books, 2008), 130.

1. Colombia, 1978

1. June Beittel, "Colombia: Background and U.S. Relations," *Congressional Research Service*, November 14, 2017, 10.
2. "IHS Jane's Fuerzas Armadas Revolucionarios de Colombia (FARC): Key Facts," *Jane's World Insurgency and Terrorism*, January 3, 2013.
3. Eugenia Sanchez and Rene Uruena, "Human Rights, Forced Displacement and Economic Development in Colombia: Considerations on the Impact of International Law on Domestic Policy," *Groningen Journal of International Law* 5, no. 1 (2017): 76.

4. See executive summary in Peter DeShazo, Johanna Mendelson Forman, and Phillip McLean, *Countering Threats to Security and Stability in a Failing State: Lessons from Colombia* (Washington DC: Center for Strategic and International Studies, September 2009).

5. Stuart Lippe, "There Is No Silver Bullet and Other Lessons from Colombia," *Interagency Journal* 5, no. 3 (Fall 2014): 5.

6. Marcus Sales, "Plan Colombia. A Success?," Colombia Politics, May 14, 2013, http://www.colombia-politics.com/plan-colombia/.

7. Lippe, "There Is No Silver Bullet," 27.

8. DeShazo, Forman, and McLean, *Countering Threats to Security and Stability*.

9. Lippe, "There Is No Silver Bullet," 26, 34.

10. Lippe, "There Is No Silver Bullet," 24.

11. Juan Forero, "In Colombia Jungle Ruse, U.S. Played a Quiet Role; Ambassador Spotlights Years of Aid, Training," *Washington Post*, July 9, 2018.

12. Beittel, "Colombia," 28.

13. Beittel, "Colombia," 7.

14. Beittel, "Colombia," 6.

15. Beittel, "Colombia," 7.

16. Beittel, "Colombia," 10.

17. "History Will Judge Colombia's Outgoing President Kindly," *Economist*, July 28, 2018, https://www.economist.com/the-americas/2018/07/28/history-will -judge-colombias-outgoing-president-kindly.

18. Kris Kraul, "Colombia Has a Peace Deal, but Can It Be Implemented," *LA Times*, March 13, 2017.

19. "Colombia to Aid U.S. in Taliban Fight," CBS News, 27 July 2009.

2. Grenada, 1983

1. Adkin, *Urgent Fury*, 3.

2. See Adkin, *Urgent Fury*, 12.

3. "Soviet Comment on Leftist Inroads in Americas found in Grenada," *New York Times*, November 15, 1983.

4. "D-Day in Grenada." *Time*, November 7, 1983, 26.

5. "D-Day in Grenada," 26.

6. Adkin, *Urgent Fury*, 105.

7. Adkin, *Urgent Fury*, 103.

8. Adkin, *Urgent Fury*, 336.

9. Keith Nightingale, "An Airborne Thanksgiving," *Small Wars Journal*, November 22, 2014.

10. Adkins, *Urgent Fury*, 106.

3. El Salvador, 1984

1. LaFeber, *Inevitable Revolutions*, 313.

2. LaFeber, *Inevitable Revolutions*, 313.

3. William Durham, *Scarcity and Survival in Central America: The Ecological Origins of the Soccer War* (Palo Alto CA: Stanford University Press, 1979), 48.

4. P. J. O'Rourke, *All the Trouble in the World* (New York: Atlantic Monthly Press, 1994), 132.

5. LaFeber, *Inevitable Revolutions*, 74.

6. Schoultz, *National Security*, 71.

7. Moodie, *El Salvador*, 30.

8. Robert Armstrong and Janet Shenk, *El Salvador: The Face of Revolution* (Boston: South End Press, 1982), 184.

9. Armstrong and Shenk, *El Salvador: The Face of Revolution*, 197.

10. Ronald Reagan, "U.S. Interests in Central America," U.S. Department of State, Current Policy 576, May 9, 1984.

11. Reagan, "U.S. Interests in Central America."

12. John F. Kennedy, U.S. Military Academy Commencement Address, West Point, New York, June 6, 1962, https://www.americanrhetoric.com/speeches /jfkwestpointcommencementspeech.htm.

13. Jim Graves, "Garcia on Guerrillas: RMTC Colonel Tells How to Beat Gs," *Soldier of Fortune*, June 1984, 47.

14. Graves, "Garcia on Guerrillas," 49.

15. John Waghelstein, "Ruminations of a Pachyderm, or What I Learned in the Counter-Insurgency Business," *Small Wars and Insurgencies* 5, no. 3 (Winter 1994): 360–74.

16. Waghelstein, "Ruminations of a Pachyderm."

17. F. J. West Jr., *The Village* (New York: Harper and Row, 1972).

18. Stanley Karnow, *Vietnam: A History* (New York: Viking Press, 1983), 382.

19. Phillips, *Why Vietnam Matters*, xiv, 305.

20. George Packer, "Why Rufus Phillips Matters," *New Yorker*, October 9, 2009.

21. De Soto, *The Other Path*, xvi.

22. De Soto, *The Other Path*, 257.

23. All personal quotations are from diaries I kept from 1978 to 2013.

24. George Shultz, "Low Intensity Warfare: The Challenge of Ambiguity," speech before the Low-Intensity Warfare Conference, US Department of State, Current Policy No. 783, January 15, 1986.

25. Shafik Handal, Secretary General of the Partido Comunista de Salvador, "El Poder, el Carácter y Via de la Revolución y la Unidad de la Izquierda," *Fundamentos y Perspectivas*, vol. 1, 1982, https://www.marxists.org/espanol/handal/1981 /001.htm; Villiers Negroponte, *Seeking Peace*, 40.

26. Villiers Negroponte, *Seeking Peace*, 40.

27. Villiers Negroponte, *Seeking Peace*, 103.

28. Victor M. Rosello, "Lessons from El Salvador," *Parameters*, Winter 1993–94, 103.

29. "El Salvador: The FMLN after the November 1989 Offensive," CIA declassified report, January 26, 1990.

30. "Open Forum Speakers Program: Alvaro de Soto, Special Advisor to the UN Secretary General, on the El Salvador Peace Agreements—Two Years Later," *State Department Cable*, March 8, 1994.

31. Villiers Negroponte, *Seeking Peace*, 116.

32. LaFeber, *Inevitable Revolutions*, 15; minutes of cabinet meeting of November 1, 1959, microfilm, 2, Dwight D. Eisenhower Library, Abilene KS.

33. LaFeber, *Inevitable Revolutions*, 362.

34. Moodie, *El Salvador*, 1.

35. David Holiday, "El Salvador's 'Model' Democracy," *Current History*, February 2005, 77.

36. Holiday, "El Salvador's 'Model' Democracy," 82.

37. Robert Pear, "Congress Is as Skeptical as Ever on Salvador Aid," *New York Times*, January 14, 1990.

38. Villiers Negroponte, *Seeking Peace*, 163.

39. Villiers Negroponte, *Seeking Peace*, 129.

40. His mother, curiously, was Rosa Lopez, O. J. Simpson's maid, who figured prominently in the O.J. trial.

41. David H. Ucko, "Counterinsurgency in El Salvador: The Lessons and Limits of the Indirect Approach," *Small Wars and Insurgencies* 24, no. 4 (2013): 689.

42. Roland Paris, *At War's End: Building Peace after Civil Conflict* (New York: Cambridge University Press, 2004), 113, 125.

43. Graciana del Castillo, *Rebuilding War Torn States: The Challenge of Post-Conflict Economic Reconstruction* (Oxford: Oxford University Press, 2008), 113.

44. Holiday, "El Salvador's 'Model' Democracy," 81; Ucko, "Counterinsurgency in El Salvador," 686.

45. Cesar Villalona interview with Elaine Freeman, "El Salvador: Has the FMLN Government Been an Economic Failure?," *Revista Envio*, September 2013, http://www.envio.org.ni/articulo/4749.

46. Jorge Kawal, "El Salvador: Funes Starts Fifth Year with Mixed Review," *Pulsamerica*, June 2013.

47. U.S. Agency for International Development, "Assistance to the Transition from War to Peace: Evaluation of the USAID/El Salvador and Special Strategic Objective" (Washington DC: USAID, 1996).

48. Charles T. Call, "Assessing El Salvador's Transition from Civil War to Peace," in *Ending Civil Wars: The Implementation of Peace Agreements*, edited by Stephen John Stedman, Donald Rothschild, and Elizabeth Cousens (Boulder CO: Lynne Rienner, 2002), 399.

49. Jonathan Watts, "One Murder Every Hour: How El Salvador Became the Homicide Capital of the World," *Guardian*, August 22, 2015.

50. Angel Rabasa, John Gordon IV, Peter Chalk, Audra K. Grant, K. Scott McMahon, Stephanie Pezard, Caroline Reilly, David Ucko, and S. Rebecca Zimmerman, *From Insurgency to Stability* (Santa Monica CA: RAND, 2011), 2:100.

51. Alex Renderos, "El Salvador President Under Fire," *Los Angeles Times*, June 24, 2010.

52. Quoted in Charles T. Call, "Democratisation, War and State-Building: Constructing the Rule of Law in El Salvador," *Journal of Latin American Studies* 35 (2003): 828.

53. Oscar Martinez, Efren Lemus, Carlos Martinez, and Deborah Sontag, "Killers on a Shoestring: Inside the Gangs of El Salvador," *New York Times*, November 20, 2016.

54. Watts, "One Murder Every Hour."

55. Martinez et al., "Killers on a Shoestring."

56. Martinez et al., "Killers on a Shoestring."

57. Jose Miguel Cruz, "The Root Causes of the Central American Crisis," *Current History*, February 2015, 48.

58. Elisabeth Malkin, "A Remarkable Day in El Salvador: A Day without a Murder," *New York Times*, January 13, 2017.

59. "Open Forum Speakers Program: Alvaro de Soto."

60. Ucko, Counterinsurgency in El Salvador, 689.

61. Rabasa et al., *From Insurgency to Stability*, 2:111.

62. Kimbra Fishel, "From Peace Making to Peace Building in Central America: The Illusion versus the Reality of Peace," *Small Wars and Insurgencies* 9, no. 1 (Spring 1998): 33, quoted in Paris, *At War's End, 125*.

63. Paris, *At War's End*, 179.

64. Sonja Wolf, "Chronicles of Everyday Lawlessness," *Current History*, February 2017, 78.

65. Villiers Negroponte, *Seeking Peace*, 171.

4. Somalia, 1994

1. Said Samatar, "Unhappy Masses and the Challenge of Political Islam in the Horn of Africa," June 28, 2006, paper adapted from a May 2002 address in Italy.

2. Charles L. Geshekter, "The Death of Somalia in Historical Perspective," unpublished paper, 1993.

3. Douglas Collins, *A Tear for Somalia* (London: Adventure Books, 1960).

4. Lewis, *A Pastoral Democracy*.

5. UNOSOM II Division of Political Affairs, "Director of Political Affairs Talks about His Days in Somalia and Looks towards the Future," internal memo, February, 19, 1994. I worked closely with Kapunga when he was head of Political Affairs, a very skilled political operative who executed what he was given to do with the meager resources at his disposal.

6. Geshekter, "The Death of Somalia in Historic Perspective."

7. UNOSOM II Division of Political Affairs, "Director of Political Affairs Talks about His Days in Somalia and Looks towards the Future," internal memo, February, 19, 1994.

8. UNOSOM Kouyaté to Howe, interoffice memo, April 29, 1993.

9. Bowden, *Black Hawk Down*, 327–28.

10. John Drysdale, "Somalis through the Looking Glass: A Glimpse of Somali Society and Culture," UNDP, unpublished paper, 1993.

11. Copy of Adrienne Marks's journal in the author's possession. Quoted with permission.

12. "Ban Welcomes Inauguration of Somali Parliament as 'Watershed Moment,'" *UN News*, August 20, 2012, news.un.org/en/story/2012/08/417872-ban-welcomes-inauguration-somali-parliament-watershed-moment.

5. Haiti, 1996

1. Donald E. Schulz, *Whither Haiti?* (Carlisle PA: U.S. Army War College Strategic Studies Institute, April 1, 1996), 3.

2. Bob Shacochis, "There Must Be a God in Haiti," *Outside*, November 1996, 120.

3. Gold, *Best Nightmare*, 11.

4. William Lacy Swing, "Haiti: In Physical Contact with History," Yale Divinity School, February 8, 1995.

5. Shacochis, "There Must Be a God in Haiti," 164.

6. Shacochis, "There Must Be a God in Haiti," 114.

7. "Wards of the United States," *National Geographic*, August 1916, 177.

8. "Wards of the United States," 170, 177.

9. C. L. R. James, *The Black Jacobins: Toussaint L'Ouverture and the San Domingo Revolution* (New York: Vintage Books, 1989), 86.

10. James, *The Black Jacobins*, 88.

11. Chetan Kumar and Elizabeth Cousens, *Peacebuilding in Haiti* (New York: International Peace Academy, April 1996), 1.

12. Robert Fatton, "From Predatory Rule to Accountable Governance," paper presented at the Conference on Dialogue for Development, September 23, 1995, 2.

13. Shacochis, "There Must Be a God in Haiti," 122.

14. Swing, *Haiti: In Physical Contact with History*, 2.

15. Schulz, *Whither Haiti*, 1.

16. Rachel Neild, "Policing Haiti: Preliminary Assessment of the New Civilian Security Force" (Washington DC: Office on Latin America, September 1995), 7.

17. George J. Church, "Taking over Haiti," *Time*, September 26, 1994, 21–27.

18. "Destination Haiti," *Time*, September 26, 1994, 25.

19. Douglas Farah, "Aristide Returns to Acclaim in Haiti," *Washington Post*, October 16, 1994, https://www.washingtonpost.com/archive/politics/1994/10/16/aristide-returns-to-acclaim-in-haiti/685e4e3e-918d-4bfb-9d65-6be3db9ead7f/.

20. United Nations Security Council, "Report of the Secretary General on the Question concerning Haiti," s/1994/1143, September 28, 1994.

21. Tracy Kidder, "The Siege of Mirebalais," *New Yorker*, April 17, 1995, 75.

22. Kidder, "The Siege of Mirebalais," 73.

23. Quoted in Shacochis, *Immaculate Invasion*, 334.

24. United Nations Mission in Haiti, "Background," https://peacekeeping.un .org/sites/default/files/past/unmihbackgr2.html.

25. Larry Rohter, "Haitian Leader's Angry Words Set Off New Wave of Violence," *New York Times*, November, 19, 1995.

26. Girard, *Haiti*, 178.

27. Elizabeth Rubin, "Haiti Takes Policing 101," *New York Times Magazine*, May 25, 1997, 44.

28. William G. O'Neill, "No Longer a Pipe-Dream? Justice in Haiti," in *Haiti Renewed: Political and Economic Prospects*, edited by Robert I. Rotberg (Washington DC: Brookings, 1997), 200.

29. Jean-Joseph Exumé, quoted in "Battle for Haiti," PBS *Frontline*, January 11, 2011.

30. Sara Lechtenberg, *An Overview of the Haitian Justice System* (Lawrence: University of Kansas, Institute of Haitian Studies, 1996), 2.

31. "Strategy of Aristide Government for Social and Economic Reconstruction," Occasional Paper 4, University of Kansas Institute of Haitian Studies, 1994, 3.

32. The former security forces received $85 per soldier and $115 per sergeant, while per capita income was somewhere around $300 a year.

33. Schulz, *Whither Haiti*, 27.

34. Robert Perito, "Haiti's Drug Problem," U.S. Institute of Peace, June 1, 2007, http://www.usip.org/publications/haitis-drug-problem.

35. "Haitian First Lady Mildred Aristide Speaks from the National Palace in Port Au Prince," *Democracy Now! Independent Global News*, February 27, 2004, https:// www.democracynow.org/2004/2/27/special_broadcast_haitian_first_lady_mildred.

36. Quoted in "Helping Haiti Heal," *Newsweek*, August 19, 1996, 52.

37. Girard, *Haiti*, 148.

38. Robert Oakley and Michael Dziedzic, "Sustaining Success in Haiti," National Defense University Strategic Forum, Number 77, June 1996, 3.

39. Schulz, *Whither Haiti?*, 9.

40. Larry Rohter, "Growing Gap between Old Allies Creates New Obstacles for Haiti," *New York Times*, March 29, 1997.

41. Donald E. Schulz, "Haiti Update," U.S. Army War College Strategic Studies Institute, special report, January 1997, 4.

42. Girard, *Haiti*, 178.

43. Girard, *Haiti*, 183.

44. Girard, *Haiti*, 202–3.

45. Republic of Haiti, Submission to the United Nations Universal Periodic Review, 12th Session of the Working Group on the UPR Human Rights Council, October 3–14, 2011.

46. UN Security Council Resolution 2313, October 13, 2016, http://www.un.org /en/ga/search/view_doc.asp?symbol=S/RES/2313(2016).

47. "Human Development Report 2015: Work for Human Development," UNDP, http://hdr.undp.org/sites/all/themes/hdr_theme/country-notes/HTI.pdf.

Misery remains more the norm than the exception today; in 2008, for instance, *National Geographic* reported that in places such as Cité Soleil, "cookies made of dirt, salt, and vegetable shortening have become a regular meal." Jonathan M. Katz, "Poor Haitians Resort to Eating Dirt," *National Geographic*, January 30, 2008.

48. Donald Kagan, *Pericles of Athens and the Birth of Democracy* (New York: Free Press, 1998), 273.

49. Kagan, *Pericles of Athens*, 3.

50. Kagan, *Pericles of Athens*, 274.

6. Darfur, 2007

1. My time in Darfur occurred after the later chapters on Iraq and Afghanistan, but for thematic consistency I include it here, since it was another purely humanitarian operation.

2. Flint and de Waal, *Darfur*, 3. They also point out that "Darfurians—like most Africans—were comfortable with multiple identities."

3. Flint and de Waal, *Darfur*, 2.

4. Flint and de Waal, *Darfur*, 9.

5. Flint and de Waal, *Darfur*, 15–16.

6. Flint and de Waal, *Darfur*, 76.

7. Flint and de Waal, *Darfur*, 84.

8. Alex de Waal, "I Will Not Sign: Alex de Waal Writes about the Darfur Peace Negotiations," *London Review of Books* 28, no. 23 (November 30, 2006): 17–20. While true it was ultimately about the politics, the peacekeepers did stop the humanitarian crisis. And as it turned out, the peace was going to take a very, very long time to get right.

9. The agreement covered power and wealth sharing, demilitarization, integration of the rebel groups into the armed forces and police, humanitarian assistance, and plans for a referendum on the future of Darfur.

10. When Minni Minawi made peace he started using the SLA/MM moniker to distinguish from the SLA/M (Movement) they had used earlier. But some blending of the two occurred over the years that followed. I have left SLA/M in some places where a group retained the original, that is, without Minawi, but not with Abdul Wahid either. When a group is directly aligned with Minawi I use SLA/MM.

11. The name sounds limp in English, but in Sudan it effectively comes across as Che Guevara; at least he was not Salad Bob, another of the rebel leaders.

12. Rod Nordland, "Onscene in Ravaged Darfur," *Newsweek*, January 19, 2007, no longer available.

13. Sector 4, Kabkabiya, Weekly Report, January 23–29, 2007, in author's possession.

14. Nordland, "Onscene in Ravaged Darfur."

15. Nordland, "Onscene in Ravaged Darfur."

16. The U.S. Institute of Peace, whose mission is to reduce violent conflict worldwide, gives extensive emphasis to the training of facilitators for conflict resolution. On the road to a full solution to a conflict, partial successes can prepare the parties and ensure things do not get worse, saving lives in the process. While such mediators are often found within a society, training and support networks of mediators are a crucial component of conflict resolution.

17. His figure was wildly exaggerated; our estimate was that he had 5,250.

18. Nicholas Kristof, "How Do You Solve a Crisis Like Darfur?," *New York Times*, March 12, 2007.

19. "Unifying Darfur's Rebels: A Prerequisite for Peace," *International Crisis Group Policy Brief*, October 6, 2005, 17.

20. "War in Darfur Is Over," *BBC News*, August 27, 2009.

21. UN Security Council, "Report of the Secretary-General on the African Union–United Nations Hybrid Operation in Darfur," December 23, 2016, 1.

22. Marianne Nolte, "Time Overdue for a New International Strategy for Darfur," *Sudan Tribune*, July 15, 2008.

23. "The Chaos in Darfur," *International Crisis Group Policy Brief*, April 22, 2015, 1, 7, 15.

24. Nolte, "Time Overdue."

7. United States, 2001

1. The many programs and policies related to the Soviet Nuclear Threat Reduction Act of 1991 (Nunn Lugar Act), for example.

2. Richard Butler, *The Greatest Threat: Iraq, Weapons of Mass Destruction, and the Growing Crisis of Global Security*, (New York: Public Affairs, 2000).

3. Amin Maalouf, *The Crusades through Arab Eyes* (New York: Schocken Books, 1984).

4. Ignatieff, *Lesser Evil*; Bobbitt, *Shield of Achilles*.

5. Bobbitt, *Shield of Achilles*, 811–13.

6. Ignatieff, *Lesser Evil*, 152–53.

7. Ignatieff, *Lesser Evil*, 153–54.

8. Ignatieff, *Lesser Evil*, 156.

8. Afghanistan, 2002

1. The commission initially planned for 1,051 delegates from districts, 100 refugees, 25 Kuchi nomads, 53 from the interim administration, and 160 women. Another 280 were added for politically or regionally underrepresented segments of society (including former mujahideen parties that had decided not to run but changed their minds), and 25 for poets and intellectuals, for a total of just under 1,700.

2. Anders Fange, *The Emergency Loya Jirga* (Afghanistan Analysts Network eBook, July 2012), 2.

3. Fange, *The Emergency Loya Jirga*, 1.

9. Iraq, 2003

1. Lin Todd, *Iraq Tribal Study: The Tribes of Al Anbar Governorate*, Quantum Research International and Global Risk, http://www.comw.org/warreport/fulltext /0709todd.pdf.

2. Todd, *Iraq Tribal Study*.

3. Khalid Sulaiman, "Towards a World without Terror: A Proposed Workshop," unpublished paper provided to the author in October 2003.

4. Steve Hedges, "Shortages of Power, Parts, Jobs Drain Iraqi's Patience: Beleaguered Province Reflects Scope of Nation's Woes," *Chicago Tribune*, November 9, 2003.

5. Informal Weekly Situation Report, 304th Civil Affairs Brigade, May 23, 2013, in author's possession.

6. "Producing Stability through Job Creation," internal memo from Coalition Provisional Authority Al Anbar Team to Coalition Provisional Authority Headquarters, November 4, 2003.

7. Miles Moffeit, "Army Officers to Be Charged," *Denver Post*, June 24, 2004, 1.

8. "Trial Illuminates Dark Tactics of Interrogation," *LA Times*, January 20, 2006, 1.

9. Vladimir Bukovsky, "Torture's Long Shadow," *Washington Post*, December 18, 2005, B1.

10. Joe Klein, "Is Al Qaida on the Run in Iraq?," *Time*, June 4, 2007.

11. David Kilcullen, *Small Wars Journal Blog*, August 2007.

12. In a letter home within weeks of my arrival I said, "Being Sheikh strikes me a little like being a Vice President in a bank, there seems to be an awful lot of them per capita."

13. CPA Order Number 1 on May 16, 2003, disestablished the Ba'ath Party of Iraq, authorizing the "elimination of the Party's structures and the removal of its leadership from positions of authority." It evolved over the months, generally in the direction of reaching down to exclude even more individuals from participation in civic life or employment.

14. Alex Gerdau and Emma Cott, "Ahmad Chalabi, 1944–2015," *New York Times*, November 3, 2015, video, https://www.nytimes.com/video/world/middleeast /100000004016579/ahmed-chalabi-1944-2015.html.

15. Fareed Zakaria, "Vengeance of the Victors," *Newsweek*, January 8, 2007, 25.

16. L. Paul Bremer, "What We Got Right," *Washington Post*, May 13, 2007, B1.

17. Markus E. Bouillon, David M. Malone, and Ben Rowswell, eds., *Preventing a New Generation of Conflict* (Boulder CO: Lynne Rienner, 2007).

10. Afghanistan, 2012

1. Pamela Constable, "Pashtuns Losing Faith in Karzai, U.S.," *Washington Post*, July 13, 2002.

2. The country as a whole is approximately 42 percent Pashtun (including Kuchis), 27 percent Tajik, 9 percent Uzbek, 9 percent Hazara, 4 percent Aimaq, 3 percent Turkman, and 2 percent Baluch.

3. Bijan Omrani and Matthew Leeming, *Afghanistan: A Companion and Guide* (Hong Kong: Odyssey Books and Guides, 2011), 234.

4. Sandy Gall, *Afghanistan: Travels with the Mujahideen* (Kent, UK: New English Library, 1989), 135.

5. Among the other sending nations were Norway, Hungary, Sweden, Croatia, Turkey, Armenia, Bosnia, Denmark, the Baltics, and Finland.

6. Judy Dempsey, "Karzai Seeks End to NATO Reconstruction Teams," *New York Times*, February 6, 2011.

7. U.S. Department of Defense, *Report on Progress toward Security and Stability in Afghanistan of December 2012*, report to Congress, December 2012, https://dod .defense.gov/Portals/1/Documents/pubs/1230_Report_final.pdf.

8. Maxwell J. Fry, *The Afghan Economy: Money, Finance, and the Critical Constraints to Economic Development*, (Leiden: E. J. Brill, 1974), 4, 158–60.

9. S. Frederick Starr with Adib Farhadi, "Finish the Job: Jump-Start Afghanistan's Economy. A Handbook of Projects," *Silk Road Paper*, Central Asia–Caucasus Institute, Silk Road Studies Program, November 2012, 11, https://www .silkroadstudies.org/resources/pdf/SilkRoadPapers/2012_11_SRP_StarrFarhadi _Afghanistan-Economy.pdf.

10. Eltaf Najafizada, "Study Finds Mineral Deposits Worth $3 Trillion in Afghanistan," *Bloomberg*, January 29, 2011.

11. Amie Ferris-Rotman and Ramya Venugopal, "Exxon Explores 'Very Promising' Oil and Gas Fields in Afghanistan," Reuters, September 7, 2012.

12. By comparison the U.S. presidential inauguration of that year had twelve thousand.

13. "The Future of the Afghan Local Police," International Crisis Group Report 268, Asia, June 4, 2015.

14. Theresa Riley, "Sarah Chayes on Why Afghanistan Is Going to Fall to the Taliban Again," *Moyers and Company: Perspectives*, October 5, 2015.

15. Joseph Goldstein, "A Taliban Prize, Won in a Few Hours after Years of Strategy," *New York Times*, September 30, 2015.

16. Asia Foundation, "Afghanistan in 2016: A Survey of the Afghan People," 2016, https://asiafoundation.org/publication/afghanistan-2016-survey-afghan -people/.

Epilogue

1. "Lawrence Pezzullo, 91, Dealt with Crisis in Nicaragua and Haiti in a Long Career in Foreign Service," *Washington Post*, August 4, 2017.

2. Lockhart and Miklaucic, "Leviathan Redux," 300.

3. Hassan Hassan, "The Islamic State after Mosul," *New York Times*, October 25, 2016.

4. Schadlow, *War and the Art of Governance*, 2.

5. Fareed Zakaria, "The U.S. Is Stumbling into Another Decade of War," *Washington Post*, June 22, 2017.

6. See the very comprehensive book by Oliver Kaplan, *Resisting War: How Communities Protect Themselves* (Cambridge, UK: Cambridge University Press, 2017).

7. Phillips, *Why Vietnam Matters*, xiv, 305.

8. Lockhart and Miklaucic, "Leviathan Redux," 314.

9. Rajiv Chandrasekaran, "The Afghan Surge Is Over, Did It Work?" *Foreign Policy*, September 25, 2012.

10. Comments at the U.S. Institute of Peace, June 28, 2017.

11. Alicia P. Q. Witmeyer, "Battle-Tested: Insiders Debate America's Misfires in Iraq and Afghanistan," *Foreign Policy*, March 4, 2013.

12. Rufus Phillips, "Breathing Life into Expeditionary Political Action," National Strategy Information Center Working Paper, Fall 2014, http://docplayer.net/124113 -Breathing-life-into-expeditionary-diplomacy-a-missing-dimension-of-us-security -capabilities.html.

13. Ghani and Lockhart, *Fixing Failed States*, 178.

14. Schadlow, *War and the Art of Governance*, 281.

15. June Beittel, "Colombia: Background and U.S. Relations," *Congressional Research Service*, November 29, 2019.

SELECTED BIBLIOGRAPHY

In each of the countries I served there were a few essential works that helped us to understand the historical and cultural context of what we were stepping into. And in many cases a later work has now given us a better grasp of the context of the operation. I offer here a few of these essential works.

Colombia, 1978

Bouvier, Virginia. *Colombia: Building Peace in Time of War*. Washington DC: U.S. Institute of Peace Press, 2009.

Bushnell, David. *The Making of Modern Colombia: A Nation in Spite of Itself*. Berkeley: University of California Press, 1993.

Kaplan, Oliver. *Resisting War: How Communities Protect Themselves*. Cambridge, UK: Cambridge University Press, 2017.

Karl, Robert A. *Forgotten Peace: Reform, Violence, and the Making of Contemporary Colombia*. Berkeley: University of California Press, 2017.

Palacios, Marco. *Between Legitimacy and Violence: A History of Colombia, 1875–2002*. Durham NC: Duke University Press, 2006.

Grenada, 1983

Adkin, Mark. *Urgent Fury: The Battle for Grenada*. New York: Lexington Books, 1989.

Dujmovic, Nicholas. *The Grenada Documents: Window on Totalitarianism*. Washington DC: Pergamon-Brassey's, 1988.

Grenade, Wendy C., ed. *The Grenada Revolution: Reflections and Lessons*. Jackson: University Press of Mississippi, 2015.

Sandford, Gregory. *The New Jewel Movement: Grenada's Revolution, 1979–1983*. Washington DC: Foreign Service Institute, 1985.

El Salvador, 1984

Clement, Charles. *Witness to War: An American Doctor in El Salvador*. London: Bantam Press, 1984.

de Soto, Hernando. *The Other Path: The Invisible Revolution in the Third World*. New York: Harper and Row, 1989.

LaFeber, Walter. *Inevitable Revolutions: The United States in Central America*. New York: Norton, 1993.

Montgomery, Tommie Sue. *Revolution in El Salvador: Origin and Evolution*. Boulder CO: Westview Press, 1994.

Moodie, Ellen. *El Salvador in the Aftermath of Peace: Crime, Uncertainty, and the Transition to Democracy*. Philadelphia: University of Pennsylvania Press, 2012.

Schoultz, Lars. *National Security and United States Policy towards Latin America*. Princeton NJ: Princeton University Press, 1987.

Villiers Negroponte, Diana. *Seeking Peace in El Salvador: The Struggle to Reconstruct a Nation at the End of the Cold War*. New York: Palgrave Macmillan, 2011.

Somalia, 1994

Bowden, Mark. *Blackhawk Down: A Story of Modern War*. New York: Atlantic Monthly Press, 1999.

Drysdale, John. *Stoics without Pillows: The Way Forward for the Somalilands*. London: Haan, 2000.

Laitin, David, and Said Samatar. *Somalia: Nation in Search of a State*. Boulder CO: Westview Press, 1987.

Lewis, I. M. *A Modern History of the Somali: Nation and State in the Horn of Africa*. Athens: Ohio University Press, 2003.

———. *A Pastoral Democracy: A Study of Pastoralism and Politics among the Northern Somali of the Horn of Africa*. Suffolk, UK: James Currey, 1999.

Menkaus, Ken. *Somalia: State Collapse and the Threat of Terrorism*. London: Routledge, 2017.

Haiti, 1996

Girard, Philippe. *Haiti, the Tumultuous History: From Pearl of the Caribbean to Broken Nation*. New York: St. Martin's Press, 2011.

Gold, Herbert. *Best Nightmare on Earth: A Life in Haiti*. New York: Touchstone, 1991.

Heinl, Robert Debs, and Nancy Gordon Heinl. *Written in Blood: The Story of the Haitian People, 1492–1995*. Lanham MD: University Press of America, 1996.

Shacochis, Bob. *The Immaculate Invasion*. New York: Viking, 1995.

Darfur, 2007

Flint, Julie, and Alex de Waal. *Darfur: A New History of a Long War*. London: Zed Books, 2008.

Prunier, Gerard. *Darfur: A 21st Century Genocide*. Ithaca NY: Cornell University Press, 2008.

Cockett, Richard. *Sudan: The Failure and Division of an African State*. New Haven CT: Yale University Press, 2016.

United States, 2001

Bobbitt, Philip. *The Shield of Achilles: War, Peace, and the Course of History*. New York: Knopf, 2002.

Clunan, Anne L., and Harold Trinkunas. *Ungoverned Spaces: Alternatives to State Authority in an Era of Softened Sovereignty*. Stanford CA: Stanford University Press, 2010.

Fukuyama, Francis. *State-Building: Governance and World Order in the 21st Century*. Ithaca NY: Cornell University Press, 2004.

Ignatieff, Michael. *The Lesser Evil: Political Ethics in an Age of Terror*. Princeton NJ: Princeton University Press, 2004.

Afghanistan, 2002, 2012

Addleton, Jonathan. *The Dust of Kandahar: A Diplomat among Warriors in Afghanistan*. Annapolis MD: Naval Institute Press, 2016.

Chandrasekaran, Rajiv. *Little America: The War within the War for Afghanistan*. New York: Knopf, 2012.

Eliot, Jason. *An Unexpected Light: Travels in Afghanistan*. London: Picador, 2011.

Gall, Carlotta. *The Wrong Enemy: America in Afghanistan, 2001–2014*. Boston: Houghton Mifflin Harcourt, 2014.

Malkasian, Carter. *War Comes to Garmser: Thirty Years of Conflict on the Afghan Frontier*. New York: Oxford University Press, 2013.

Neumann, Ronald E. *The Other War: Winning and Losing in Afghanistan*. Washington DC: Potomac Books, 2009.

Rubin, Barnett. *The Fragmentation of Afghanistan: State Formation and Collapse in the International System*. New Haven CT: Yale University Press, 2002.

Stanton, Doug. *The Horse Soldiers: The Extraordinary Story of a Band of U.S. Soldiers Who Rode to Victory in Afghanistan*. New York: Scribner's, 2009.

West, Bing. *The Wrong War: Grit, Strategy, and the Way out of Afghanistan*. New York: Random House, 2011.

Iraq, 2003

Bremer, L. Paul, III. *My Year in Iraq: The Struggle to Build a Future of Hope*. New York: Simon and Schuster, 2006.

Butler, Richard. *The Greatest Threat: Iraq, Weapons of Mass Destruction, and the Crisis of Global Security*. New York: Public Affairs, 2000.

Dobbins, James, Seth Jones, Benjamin Runkle, and Siddharth Mohanda. *Occupying Iraq: A History of the Coalition Provisional Authority*. Washington DC: RAND Corporation, 2009.

Hard Lessons: The Iraq Reconstruction Experience. Washington DC: U.S. Government Printing Office, 2009.

Makiya, Kanan. *Republic of Fear: The Politics of Modern Iraq*. Berkeley: University of California Press, 1989.

Marr, Phoebe, and Ibrahim al-Marashi. *The Modern History of Iraq*. Boulder CO: Westview Press, 1987.

Ricks, Thomas E. *Fiasco: The American Military Adventure in Iraq*. New York: Penguin, 2006.

Sky, Emma. *The Unraveling: High Hopes and Missed Opportunities in Iraq*. New York: Public Affairs, 2015.

West, Bing. *No True Glory: A Frontline Account of the Battle for Fallujah*. New York: Bantam, 2005.

———. *The Strongest Tribe*. New York: Random House, 2008.

Wright, Donald, and Timothy R. Reese. *On Point II: Transition to the New Campaign. The United States Army in Operation Iraqi Freedom, May 2003–January 2005*. Ft. Leavenworth KS: Combat Studies Institute Press, 2008.

The Art of Nation-Building

Chesterman, Simon, Michael Ignatieff, and Ramesh Thakur. *Making States Work: State Failure and the Crisis of Governance*. New York: United Nations University Press, 2005.

Dobbins, James, Seth Jones, Keith Crane, and Beth Cole DeGrasse. *The Beginner's Guide to Nation-Building*. Washington DC: RAND, 2007.

Fukuyama, Francis. *The Origins of Political Order: From Prehuman Times to the French Revolution*. New York: Farrar, Straus, and Giroux, 2011.

Ghani, Ashraf, and Clare Lockhart. *Fixing Failed States: A Framework for Rebuilding a Fractured World*. New York: Oxford University Press, 2008.

Hodge, Nathan. *Armed Humanitarians: The Rise of the Nation Builders*. New York: Bloomsbury, 2011.

Kaplan, Fred. *The Insurgents: David Petraeus and the Plot to Change the American Way of War*. New York: Simon and Schuster, 2013.

Matfess, Hilary, and Michael Miklaucic. *Beyond Convergence: World without Order*. Washington DC: NDU Press, 2016.

Phillips, Rufus. *Why Vietnam Matters: An Eyewitness Account of Lessons Not Learned*. Annapolis MD: Naval Institute Press, 2008.

Schadlow, Nadia. *War and the Art of Governance: Consolidating Combat Success into Political Victory*. Washington DC: Georgetown University Press, 2017.

INDEX

Abadi, Haider al-, 283–84

Abbala people (Darfur), 144

Abd Alhameed, Fawzi Fatikhman, 254–55

Abdelfattah, Ragaei, 310

Abdullahi, Farah, 97

Abdul Wahid (SLA/A), 148

Abizaid, John, 242

Abu Ghraib prison (Iraq), 246, 253, 254–55

Abu Shakeen (Darfur), 156

Abu Shouk refugee camp (Darfur), 152, 153

Abu Sikkin (Sudan), 160–61

Addis Agreement, 82, 88

Afghanistan: agriculture within, 187, 295, 296–97; banking within, 196–98; casualties within, 196, 201, 289, 303, 308, 309–11, 324; challenges of, 294, 301–2, 315; Chamber of Commerce, 300; civil service within, 326; corruption within, 305; counterattacks to, 185–91; currency within, 196–98; demographics of, 187–88, 340n2; diplomatic surge within, 286; donor assistance within, 195–96; drought within, 189; economy within, 191–98, 196, 294–95, 296–302; education within, 294, 308–9, 311, 315; elections within, 206–7, 295, 306–7, 315, 339n1; electrical power within, 295, 301; foreign investment within, 193–95; France and, 199; geography of, 286–87; Germany and, 199, 292–93, 312; government structure of, xviii, 212–13, 306–9, 339n1; health care within, 187, 294; Hungary and, 199; industry within, 191–93, 294, 297–98, 299–300; infrastructure within, 210; Islam within, 292; markets within, 296–98; Mongolia and, 291; mortality rate within, xix; nat-ural gas within, 299; Netherlands and, 304; Norway and, 312; Nowruz festival within, 303; oil within, 299; politics of, 306–9; power plants within, 193; prog-ress within, 294–96; reconstruction of, 326; refugees from, 190–91; religion and state within, 208–9; security within, 198–202, 302–5; Soviet Union and, 26, 296; Sweden and, 312; Taliban and, 288–89, 313; terrorist network within, xviii; tran-sition of, 311–13; United States and, xv, xxiv, 198, 199, 213, 293, 295–96, 302; war-lords within, 306; war on terror and, 202; withdrawal from, 313; women within, 210–11; youth within, 308–9. *See also* Loya Jirga; *specific cities/provinces; specific tribes*

Afghan Local Police (ALP), 304

Afghan National Security Force, 314, 315

Africa, xiii, xx. *See also* Darfur; Sudan

African Union (AU), 148–49, 150–51, 173

Aga Khan Foundation, 307

Agawi, Martin, 171

agriculture, 39, 46, 74, 89, 107, 133, 187, 295, 296–97

Ahadi, Anwar ul-Haq, 196

Aidid, Mohamed Farrah, 75, 76, 83, 84, 86–87, 93–101

Air-Land Battle Doctrine, 56

Al Anbar (Iraq): attacks within, 225–26; business seminar within, 240–41; cam-paign plan for, 228–29; Civil Defense Force, 251; economy within, 230; elec-tions within, 258–60, 277, 280; mean-ing of, 223; Public Security Academy, 249–50; United States and, 221–27; view-points within, 269–70, 271

Related ADST Book Series Titles

Intervening in Africa:
Superpower Peacemaking
in a Troubled Continent
Herman J. Cohen

Reconstruction and Peace
Building in the Balkans:
The Brčko Experience
Robert William Farrand

High-Value Target:
Countering Al Qaeda in Yemen
Edmund J. Hull

Mission to Algiers:
Diplomacy by Engagement
Cameron R. Hume

From Hope to Horror:
Diplomacy and the Making of
the Rwanda Genocide
Joyce E. Leader

Vietnam and Beyond:
A Diplomat's Cold War Education
Robert H. Miller

The Other War: Winning
and Losing in Afghanistan
Ronald Neumann

Witness to a Changing World
David D. Newsom

Plunging into Haiti:
Clinton, Aristide, and the
Defeat of Diplomacy
Ralph Pezzullo

Prelude to Genocide:
Arusha, Rwanda, and the
Failure of Diplomacy
David Rawson

The Craft of Political
Analysis for Diplomats
Raymond F. Smith

Losing the Golden Hour:
An Insider's View of Iraq's
Reconstruction
James Stephenson

For a complete list of series titles, visit adst.org/publications.

CPSIA information can be obtained
at www.ICGtesting.com
Printed in the USA
LVHW101320240723
753295LV00007B/105